INDEPENDENCE AND INVOLVEMENT

INDEPENDENCE
AND
INVOLVEMENT

A Christian Reorientation
in Political Science

RENÉ DE VISME WILLIAMSON

LOUISIANA STATE UNIVERSITY PRESS : 1964

To my wife
VIRGINIA
and my sons
PARKER, WARREN, *and* ROGER

PREFACE

IT has often been said that many professors who are Christians lead a dual existence—one in the university and another in church. No one who sees them in the university would guess that they are Christians or find that they differ in any manner from their colleagues who are not Christians. On the other hand, no one who sees them in church would guess that they possess the intellectual curiosity and scholarly knowledge which are supposed to be characteristic of academic life. This is an unhealthy situation which does no credit to either the university or the church.

Since World War II there has been a reaction against this unscholarly and un-Christian dual existence, a reaction that has taken the form of the still rather amorphous Faculty Christian Movement. This movement has been partly spontaneous and partly sponsored by denominational boards. It has expressed itself mostly in a multitude of small reading and discussion groups springing up on various campuses and in state and regional conferences sponsored and financed by denominational boards. The nearest thing to a national expression of this movement has been the Faculty Christian Fellowship of the National Council of Churches and its publication, *The Christian Scholar*.

I have attended and taken an active part in many of these conferences and served for several years on the Executive Committee of the Faculty Christian Fellowship. I fully share the belief of my colleagues that we professors who are Christians should re-think our professional knowledge in the light of our faith. There are risks involved, but we must take the plunge. Believing that groups, committees, and teams are ill-suited to the work of intellectual pioneering, I have taken the plunge and written this book.

I doubt that there is any field in which this kind of intellectual pioneering is more needed than in political science. We who are interested in political life either as students or as practitioners are not even asking the right questions, much less suggesting helpful answers. Those of us who are Democrats are fond of criticizing the Republicans for not having caught up with the twentieth century, and there is much truth in the criticism. But the Democrats are in no position to boast and take a holier-than-thou attitude, for they too live in the past. The days of Franklin D. Roosevelt are over, and the world is facing a whole array of new problems, among which are communist imperialism, racial tensions on several continents, world peace in an atomic age, intercultural contacts of baffling complexity, social revolutions, new scientific vistas from automation to outer space, politically explosive religious situations. We are confronting these problems at the very time when the political ideologies have lost their glamour and stand exposed as barren. Even liberalism and conservatism have pretty well outlived their usefulness, like mineral veins which have been mined out. Where shall we turn for spiritual strength and intellectual guidance, for an adequate frame of reference or approach within which we can work out solutions to our problems? I propose that we turn to the Christian faith.

I have therefore attempted to re-think such basic concepts of political science as state, constitution, civil rights, law, liberty, citizenship, and representation in the light of the Christian faith and to develop a more Christian conception of the proper relations between church and state. In attempting this task of intellectual reconstruction, I am addressing myself primarily to the believer. I want to point out to fellow Christians what I believe to be some of the political consequences of the religious convictions we share. The extent of my concern with non-Christians is not so much to argue against their positions as it is to give a positive and constructive answer to their frequently voiced question: What have you Christians got to offer besides criticism? This book is an expository, not an apologetic, work.

I am keenly aware of the fact that no two fields are more sensitive than religion and politics. There are many kinds of people who call themselves Christians and who passionately disagree with each other. For anyone who believes, as I do, that the Christian faith is involved in, but also independent of, every particular political movement and ideology, there is no way to avoid treading on many toes. I regret the necessity of giving offense and hope that my friends will forgive me. In view of the controversial nature of practically everything I discuss and of the difficulty of escaping the limitations growing out of one's preferences and affiliations, it would be wise to say a few words about my own commitments. I think that what I have to say in this book can stand by itself independently of the way I arrived at it; hence I have adopted the traditional impersonal mode of discourse. However, the reader might not agree and is entitled to know what my personal commitments are so that he can, if he thinks necessary, discount my conclusions accordingly.

In politics I am a lifelong Democrat, who has generally supported liberal candidates for office and the liberal side of most public issues, but I do not share the liberal philosophy. I find myself more in sympathy with the conservative philosophy but am generally opposed to conservative candidates and most of the specific measures they advocate. I think both liberalism and conservatism need to be transcended. They have contributed much that is invaluable to civilization, but their day is over.

In religion I am a Presbyterian Christian and an elder in the Presbyterian Church in the United States. I stand squarely on the Bible and the Westminster Confession of Faith, but I believe that there is a basic core of Christian doctrine and Christian life reaching back to the apostles and permeating the various Christian communions. I can therefore find myself at home in these other communions, including the Roman Catholic, even though I am convinced that this basic Christian core is purest in the evangelical Calvinist Reformed tradition.

I hope that some of my readers will be stimulated to contribute to the great task of re-thinking their professional fields and occupational problems in terms of the Christian faith.

CONTENTS

Preface, *vii*

I PERIL AND PARALYSIS 3
Science and survival, *4*
The threat of bipolarity, *8*
Growing chaos in the family of nations, *13*
The threat of meaninglessness, *18*
The impotence of social science, *28*

II PROMISE AND PERFORMANCE 31
Promises of the Christian faith, *31*
Performance and the Christian faith, *44*
Toward a new Reformation, *58*

III INDEPENDENCE AND INVOLVEMENT 65
The Christian concept of the state, *66*
The classical liberal concept of the state, *67*
The conservative concept of the state, *70*
The totalitarian concept of the state, *82*
The modern liberal concept of the state, *89*

IV CHARTER AND CHOICE 98
Importance of the Constitution in American thinking, *98*
Constitutions and national values, *100*
National values and Christian appraisal, *103*
Constitutional law and national morality, *105*
The Constitution and objective norms, *108*
The supremacy clause of the Constitution, *116*
The Constitution and the scriptural concept of law, *123*

V LAW AND LIBERTY 129
The nature of civil rights, *129*
Individualism, human nature, and civil rights, *134*

Collectivism, human nature, and civil rights, *142*
The Christian doctrine of man and civil rights, *147*

VI   PARTICIPATION AND POLITICS   169
Secular concepts of citizenship, *169*
The church as a political society, *172*
Church membership as citizenship, *182*
Christian citizenship and secular citizenship, *188*
Representation: secular and Christian concepts, *192*

VII   SEPARATION AND STABILITY   207
Christianity and the First Amendment, *209*
Religious views of the framers of the Constitution, *213*
The logic of radical separationism, *225*
Christian stability, *239*

VIII FAITH AND FUTURE   246
Definition of faith, *247*
Political power of faith, *252*

Notes, *257*

INDEPENDENCE AND INVOLVEMENT

Chapter I

PERIL AND PARALYSIS

E VERYONE who thinks about the present situation at all knows that we are living in a most critical time. The survival of civilization, perhaps of the human race itself, is at stake. The thermonuclear weapons we possess and those which will be developed in the years to come, not to mention the potentialities of bacteriological warfare, threaten us with unimaginable suffering and destruction to the point of annihilation. The lethal uses to which modern scientific knowledge can be put is a subject which not many people think about.

For one thing, we do not like to think about unpleasant situations, especially when they are so unpleasant as to be terrifying. Like the proverbial ostrich, we prefer to hide our heads in the sand. This type of reaction should not be too quickly and carelessly condemned as immature and irresponsible, even though it may prevent us from taking whatever civil defense measures might alleviate the effects of a thermonuclear attack—if one can speak of mitigating the incommensurable. Such a reaction is probably reprehensible, as long as something can be done, but it is understandable. There are realities so stark, so appallingly evil, so personality-shattering that psychological escape is the only way to keep our sanity. Paradoxically, escape can itself constitute insanity when carried beyond a certain point. There are realities so terrible that no human being can face them. It would take God himself to face them. The Christian faith, of course, affirms that God can and did do precisely this with the death and resurrection of Jesus Christ. But we are not Christ, and contemporary man, not being Christian or being such in a merely nominal sense, lacks the spiritual resources which would give him the strength to face the terrifying realities that engulf him.

A second reason why we do not like to think about the threat of thermonuclear warfare is that so much of it escapes our comprehension. The ordinary person could see, understand, and manipulate bows and arrows, swords and shields, and guns. And he was familiar with what happened when they were used. It is otherwise with the newest weapons. To understand these requires a very rare scientific and technological competence. To determine what their use can visit upon us is difficult because the effects transcend our experience and, to a considerable extent, our imagination. The difficulty here is analogous to that of the average person when he tries to think about the national budget or grasp the financial operations of very large corporations or understand the meaning of astronomical space and geological time. Sheer magnitude overwhelms him. Contemporary armaments are thus part of the infinitely complex scientific culture which has created them. This complexity baffles us and forces upon us a painful realization of the finiteness of the human mind, the creatureliness of man so ably analyzed by Reinhold Niebuhr.[1] Under these circumstances, our tendency is to give up the attempt to understand the danger which confronts us.

A third reason for our psychological flight from reality is a pervasive feeling of helplessness. What can we do about the situation anyway? We do not feel that we can control the gigantic forces which we have unleashed. The feeling may reflect a defeatist attitude, but it is certainly not without pretty solid foundations. The military people used to think that for every offense there is a corresponding defense. Many of them doubtless still think there is—at least in the abstract. The point is debatable in view of the enormous power and destructiveness of the forces at our disposal. In any case, the advocates of the theory that there is a defense for every offense have always recognized that a time element is involved. The time element, however, has become crucial. What comfort is there in knowing that an adequate defense can be developed if there is no one left to develop it? William F. Ogburn's cultural lag has become a lethal lag. The chances of correcting this lag are not enhanced by the accelerated pace of what one sometimes hesitates to call scientific progress. Obsolescence hovers over us. Huge amounts of money, both public and private, are being spent on research, and we know that new and deadlier weapons will be the result. The prospects for coping with the problem of obsolescence, therefore, are bleak. Several factors tend to make them so.

SCIENCE AND SURVIVAL

There is the accumulation of scientific knowledge, which is so vast that no sensible person, however gifted and well educated, can hope to master it. Gone are the days when, with Francis Bacon, we could take all knowledge to be our province. Scientific knowledge has to be distributed among many persons and groups, and a breakdown in communications ensues. The breakdown is caused by the number and variety of the findings of science, by the inevitable growth of specialized technical terms (virtually languages), which fewer and fewer people understand, and by the increasing complexity of the thinking process, some of which now extends beyond the capacities of the human mind and requires the use of very costly and therefore not universally available computers and other "thinking machines."

The situation was illustrated in one of our large state universities recently when the Department of Mathematics petitioned the Graduate Council to grant an exception to the rule that every Ph.D. candidate should have an external minor (work in an allied department) and authorize an internal minor (work wholly in one department). The argument presented by the mathematicians was that the different branches in their field had become so specialized and advanced that the faculty members could no longer keep up with or understand one another and that, consequently, graduate work in one branch should be considered external to work in another branch even though all the work was offered within a single department. The petition was granted. The relation of this kind of development to the problem of obsolescence is obvious: you cannot tell what is obsolete and what is not obsolete unless you know what is going on and understand it.

Another contemporary development operates in the same direction. World War II and its aftermath have injected security considerations into the realm of science. New problems of security clearance and classified information arise. We have not even begun to realize how incompatible this kind of concern is with the traditions of modern science, whose essence is freedom. Up to now, the nature and spirit of modern science were symbolized by the motto of the International College of Surgeons: "La Science n'a pas de Patrie" (science has no fatherland). Through professional meetings and publications on a world-wide basis, the findings and methods of scientists were disseminated, criticized, and checked. This process reduced duplication of effort and resources, enabling one scientist to begin where another left off. It promoted a more rapid elimination of errors and the correction of mistakes. It also created a kind of international brotherhood among scientists, which was intellectually stimulating and conducive to the conception of new hypotheses and other forms of creative imagination. It promoted a moral climate favorable to freedom of research and inquiry. In consequence, scientific knowledge has been the one realm which exemplified the ideas of thinkers like John Stuart Mill and Justice Oliver Wendell Holmes concerning the discovery and nature of truth. It was in the natural sciences, far more than in the social sciences or the humanities, that the body of knowledge could be said to have resulted from rational argument, critical weighing of evidence, rigorous testing for consistency and applicability, and constant appraisal and reappraisal, without regard to emotions, political pressures, economic interests, cultural backgrounds, and ideological considerations. Mill and Holmes were wrong in believing that this process is the only one through which truth could be established, but there can be no question as to the great value and fruitfulness of this process.

To interfere with the freedom of search for scientific truth, even for security reasons, is to dry up the wellsprings of scientific creativity. This is a serious matter at a time when this very creativity may well provide the decisive edge in the balance of political power. Much scientific activity remains free, to be sure, and there is a desire to confine security considerations to militarily "sensitive" projects. But there is little basis for hope in attempts to salvage the freedom of science: the dependence of applied science on pure science is becoming more evident and the concept of total war tends to make all research "sensitive."

The injection of security considerations has a direct bearing on the problem of communications and on the accompanying danger of obsolescence. Security clearance separates scientists from one another by the compartmentalization characteristic of the CIA and intelligence work in general, and it further cuts down communications by creating an atmosphere of suspicion. To classify the findings of research means that these findings cannot be subjected to the widespread testing and checking which had been characteristic of scientific work and that the scientists in one country can no longer know how their work compares with similar work in other countries. As more and more countries join the "Atomic Club," each with its own growing body of security regulations, the breakdown in communications will become more complete, the uncertainties more acute, the threat of obsolescence more pressing, and the chances of control more remote.

In the light of these developments, the current feeling of helplessness concerning the threat of thermonuclear warfare is understandable. Psychological flight from reality even begins to look rational! We know, for instance, that cities like New York and Chicago are perfect targets for nuclear bombs. Can modern science come to the aid of civil defense in dealing with this situation? Perhaps it could if scientific development were stationary, but we know that such is not the case. What good would it do from a civil defense point of view to disperse the population over a wide area if new bombs with an ever growing range are developed? What gain would there be in building underground cities if the whole project degenerated into a race between the depth of cities and the depth of bomb craters? It is very doubtful that people could be persuaded to undertake the incalculable expense and accept the enormous readjustments in their daily lives which solutions like population dispersion or going underground would entail, even if they could be assured that they would thereby be saved from destruction. Without such assurance, which cannot be given, solutions of this kind lie beyond the realm of possibility.

Popular apathy in matters of civil defense thus finds some justification in the fact that there is no defense against big-scale thermonuclear warfare. National defense in such an eventuality is a misnomer and an illusion. Retaliation, not defense or conquest, is the only reality here, and retaliation means total destruction without regard to friend or foe. Big-scale thermonuclear war (though not the threat of it) is incompatible with many traditional ideas, such as levying war as an instrument of national policy or as a means of vindicating national rights. On the other hand, popular apathy is not justified if it is carried to the point of pacifism or of neglecting preparations for lesser forms of war, e.g., "conventional" wars, limited wars, localized wars, and "brushfire" wars. There are values like freedom and justice which can be preserved and promoted by the use of force in the international realm as they are in the domestic realm. To be sure, the so-called "lesser forms of war" are a barbarous way of achieving a worthy end, and there is a point beyond which these forms are self-defeating. This point is highly relative, of course, but statesmen have the heavy responsibility of determining where it lies. It is precisely because it is relative that neither pacifism nor its opposite can be legitimately entertained. Unfortunately for those who like to think in terms of black and white, peace is not synonymous with either pacifism or appeasement.

After all qualifications have been made, however, there emerges from the foregoing discussion the hard and irreducible fact that there is no solution to the threat of thermonuclear warfare in terms of science. To say this by no means implies a rejection or depreciation of science. Because of science we stand on the threshold of awesome new knowledge, the most spectacular of which concerns outer space and the worlds that lie beyond. Much of our new knowledge will unquestionably be beneficial to man, e.g., in the field of medicine. Scientific achievement is not merely discovery but construction and creation, and it requires the ability to imagine and to conceive as well as to calculate, test, and apply. It is wrong, therefore, to contend that scientific activity is morally neutral. Its creativity in both pure and applied knowledge is evidence for the biblical truth that man was made in the image of God and in some respects, therefore, partakes of the divine nature.

The fact remains, however, that science cannot control the means of annihilation which it has produced. There is no scientific solution for total disaster. To many people this will be a distressing thought. It is true that the age of scientism is gone, when the prevailing belief was that science had the answer to *all* problems. We have learned that truth is much more comprehensive and many-sided than scientific truth and that the scientific method can never grapple with more than a part of reality. Nevertheless, our respect for science and technology is enormous, as curricular changes in our schools and universities and the financial support of governments and private foundations amply demonstrate. From that old false religion called "scientism" there remains the more modest idea that, if science cannot solve all problems, it should be able to solve those problems which science itself has created. That idea, too, must now be discarded.

Some people arrived at that conclusion long ago. They realized that the crux of our problem is the use to which the achievements of science are put, that whether this use is beneficial or harmful to mankind depends not on scientists but on public officials, industrial leaders, educators, clergymen, and the general public. In other words, we must leave the realm of nature and turn to the realm of the human. We must stop making demands on the natural scientist which he cannot meet and address ourselves to the social scientist and see if he can do any better. At first glance, the step seems logical and proper since the social scientist is supposed to be a specialist in human behavior. Whether appearances are justified, whether the social scientist can really show us how to control those who control the uncontrollable, remains to be seen.

Insofar as the problem is the immediate one of survival, i.e., preventing World War III, we are in the realm of foreign policy. At this point, however, our concern cannot be with particular foreign policies because what is possible or impossible in foreign policy depends on larger factors which are the province of political science. An analysis of these factors will show that the prognosis for world peace and the survival of mankind is not good.

THE THREAT OF BIPOLARITY

One very obvious factor is the threat of bipolarity. Two world wars have reduced the number of great powers to two, the United States and the Soviet Union. These two powers are like magnets in that the other states tend to be aligned with one or the other as satellites or allies. Some states try to resist the gravitational pull of the great powers and are variously known as "unaligned," "neutralist," or "uncommitted" nations. Some states like India and especially Red China may be on their way to becoming great powers in their own right. New centers of power could someday be formed by the combination of existing states, e.g., the United States of Europe. None of these possibilities is likely to materialize soon, and none can alter appreciably the enormous preponderance of power now clustered in the Eastern and Western blocs and the bipolar tensions which emanate from them. In any case, the issue of survival is likely to be decided before these possible developments have had time to take place.

Now the study of power falls in the subject matter of political science. Some political scientists think that power is the sum total of their subject, while others assert that the ends which power serves and ought to serve should also be included. Whatever the outcome of this debate may be, political scientists are in a position to make certain valid generalizations about the distribution of power which are relevant to our problem. The generalizations are these: (1) power in one center means tyranny; (2) power in two centers means war; (3) power in many centers means anarchy.

All three generalizations are distasteful, but the third one has to be qualified because it can mean stability and peace if the distribution among many centers occurs within a framework of law and morality. This qualification is the justification for the common saying that there is safety in numbers. Lasting and truly civilized existence, therefore, requires a proper distribution of power by constitutionalism on the domestic level and by the balance of power on the international level. A classic exposition of what this requirement means on the domestic level can be found in Federalist No. 10 by James Madison. The distribution of power does not of itself guarantee civilized existence, however, because there are other values involved, but these other values cannot flourish unless they are rooted in a proper distribution of power.

The first generalization has been adequately disposed of in Lord Acton's famous dictum: relative power corrupts relatively, absolute power corrupts absolutely. It is understood, of course, that the dictum applies only to human beings. There is a theological way of expressing the same thought, i.e., that omnipotence is an attribute of God and constitutes no threat to mankind, because God is also omniscient and infinitely good. These attributes are inseparable parts of the Divine Being, but they assuredly are not the possession of that finite and sinful being which is man. The trouble with totalitarian dictators is that they strive for the omnipotence of God without God's omniscience and goodness, and they demand a degree of allegiance which properly belongs to God alone. The Hitlers, Mussolinis, Khrushchevs, *et al.,* do not see the matter in this light. The Roman Caesars were more logical!

Attempts to qualify the first generalization have been much less successful than in the case of the third. These attempts have followed two lines: one by limiting power to a point where it is not too much of a threat, the other by raising the intellectual and moral level of the wielder or wielders of power to a point where they can be trusted with power. In one case power can be limited only by countervailing power and this means distribution again; in the other case power cannot be "tamed" to the necessary extent, because too great demands are made on human nature. Even philosopher-kings would have to be human.

We now find ourselves left with the second generalization, i.e., that power in two centers means war. Of the three generalizations, this one is the most unstable because it has a tendency to turn into either the first or the third. As with all tendencies, there is a time lag involved. This time lag has of late come to be known as coexistence. Although the term is recent and refers primarily to the relations between the Eastern and Western blocs, the situation which it denotes is as old as man. It is not eternally present, but it is eternally recurring in different forms, and it has been resolved by either the victory of one or by the fragmentation of both.

In order to last, coexistence requires that both sides be willing and able to keep the peace and that they know how to do so. Each side must believe in the good will and the competence of the other. The good will is generally lacking because the two camps usually embody opposing value systems which make mutual trust and understanding difficult. This is notably the case in the relations between the U.S.A. and the U.S.S.R. The concentration of power in each country is awesome enough by itself to create apprehension, but the ideological element of communism makes mutual trust vastly more improbable. There are many reasons why this is true, e.g., communism is hostile to the church, to private enterprise, to free competition in economic life, to civil rights, to freedom of association in political parties. Even if we could ignore all these things, in which Americans deeply believe, there would remain the fact that Communists are committed to the irreconcilability of the class struggle and the inevitability of world revolution. This commitment makes it impossible for Communists to trust us and also for us to trust them. The communist philosophy makes communications, without which there can be no mutual trust, a difficult enterprise. Key words like value, state, social class, and democracy have different meanings on each side of the Iron Curtain.

Even if good will and mutual trust existed on both sides, there would still have to be a belief in each other's competence, which includes good judgment, self-restraint, and a rational understanding of which policies are conducive to peace and which are conducive to war. Essentially, what is at stake is the ability to manipulate power successfully. Power is a constantly changing thing responding to the ups and downs of morale at home and prestige abroad, to changes in the size and distribution of population, to alterations in economic potential, to growth in scientific advance, and to the different personalities of those who occupy positions of leadership. We find it hard to ascribe to our own leaders the kind of ability to manipulate power that we need. It is asking a great deal more of a people to ascribe that kind of ability to the leaders of a foreign and hostile people.

History is full of examples which point to the fragility of bipolar situations and indicates that war is the termination we can expect. As far back as the bipolar situations between Athens and Sparta or Rome and Carthage, this was true. Ancient history has even bequeathed us a term for the outcome: a Carthaginian peace. But the most convincing example is the rivalry which once existed between Austria and Prussia and the way it ended.

Before any unification had taken place, the situation in what was then sometimes called "the Germanies" resembled that of the world today. Austria and Prussia were the two great powers; there were several middle-sized powers like Bavaria and Saxony and a large number of little powers like the free city of Hamburg. The first attempt at unification failed because Austria and Prussia could not get along with each other. Their inability to do so is significant and should not be dismissed with the comment that it was natural for that to happen. Most things look natural in retrospect because we do not realize that what we think of as a foregone conclusion is often nothing more than familiarity with that conclusion. After all, Austria and Prussia had much in common, far more than the great powers of today. Both were dynastic states headed by absolute monarchs ruling by divine right; both had legitimism as their political philosophy; both had a traditionalist and aristocratic social structure; and both were German in language and culture. Moreover, they had very strong incentives to cooperate. The Germanies had been the storm center of diplomatic intrigues and the battleground of European armies from the wars of religion to the Napoleonic Wars, and all the German states had a vital interest in putting a stop to that situation. The German princes, including the Hapsburgs and the Hohenzollerns, were also deeply concerned with stamping out the ferment left among their peoples by the French Revolution. In spite of all these favorable factors, Austria and Prussia jostled for position. The end came with the Seven Weeks' War in 1866 when Prussia forced Austria to withdraw from German affairs, and German unification was achieved, in the words of Bismarck, by blood and iron. If Austria and Prussia could not make a go of coexistence, is it reasonable to expect that the U.S.A. and the U.S.S.R. can do better?

The trouble is that the usual outcome of bipolar tensions is no longer open to us. A Carthaginian peace today would not be for Carthaginians only but for everybody. Our second generalization must be revised to read: power in two centers means annihilation—eventually. Power in one center, therefore, is not a probable conclusion, because it is self-destructive by way of force and unthinkable by way of agreement. In spite of Bertrand Russell, there are many people who would rather be dead than Red and many more who would refuse to concede that this is the only choice before them.

The only rational and desirable solution to bipolar tensions lies in the fragmentation and redistribution of power. We have recognized this solution in the economic field, and economists are now working with the concept of countervailing power. When concentration of power in the form of monopoly took place and threatened independent businessmen and consumers, we turned to fragmentation through antitrust policies and to limitation through government regulation. When the power of businessmen threatened labor with exploitation, the answer was the growth of countervailing power in the form of labor unions. Recognizing the correctness of Justice Holmes's observation that liberty of contract begins where equality of bargaining power begins, the government adopted a policy of supporting unions in order that liberty might flourish. Now that many labor unions have grown big and become important centers of power, the problem is to democratize and supervise them without damaging their usefulness. In all this economic field we have had only moderate success, but it has been enough to preserve a substantial amount of freedom and to prevent the enslavement of the many by the few. It is to be noted, however, that economic liberty was the result of government policy and not of the so-called "free play of forces." Free private enterprise is not something one drifts into but a goal to be worked for and achieved.

Is it possible to work out a satisfactory distribution of power without the assistance of a directing force from above? Can it be achieved by reflection, deliberation, and choice? Early American history indicates the affirmative. The groundwork for a reasonable distribution of power under which a constitutional order and political liberty could thrive was laid when the states ceded their western claims to the United States collectively. Some states had huge claims in the West, and some had none. If those claims had not been surrendered, the unequal distribution of power would have been so great that the weaker states would have been insecure, and the national government would have been too easily challenged. The future of the United States was made possible by what amounted to a great renunciation. How great a renunciation it was can be imagined if one asks what would have happened if membership in the old League of Nations or in the United Nations had been made conditional on the previous surrender of all colonies. A similar renunciation, this time by the United States collectively, was implicit in the Northwest Ordinance of 1787 because it meant that the original thirteen states decided not to treat the West as a colonial empire and that the distribution of power would be maintained by the admission of new western states. The framers of the Constitution at the Philadelphia Convention of 1787 wisely accepted the foundation which had thus been laid for them, although the equality of the new states with the old was made implicit rather than explicit, and the admission of the new states was left to future congressional action.

The framers of the Constitution set about the double task of equipping the new federal government with important enumerated and implied powers and of curbing the states with a list of specific prohibitions. A system of separation of powers and checks and balances within the federal government completed the work of distributing governmental power in such a way as to make it safe. The first ten amendments were then added to set further restrictions and standards designed to make the new federal government even safer. The constitutional order which was thus created proved adequate as the instrument through which the religious, moral, social, economic, and political values of the American people could be expressed and fulfilled.

It should be noted, however, that the founding fathers did not break up an intrenched and centralized power, nor did they work from a bipolar situation. Reflection, deliberation, and choice they did use, but it was against a background of the very decentralized situation under the Articles of Confederation. The American experience, therefore, proves nothing insofar as solving a bipolar situation is concerned. Furthermore, while the founding fathers distributed power in a manner well calculated to meet the needs of the American people internally, they could not do the same externally. Indeed, their intention was to create a central government fully as strong as that of any foreign state. They could and did create a government safe for Americans, but they could not make it safe for foreigners. It is true that, to some extent, such features as the election of the President, the consent of the Senate for appointments to major offices and for the ratification of treaties, and the necessity for congressional action for enabling legislation and for financial expenditures have had the effect of protecting foreign peoples from the kind of irresponsible and arbitrary actions characteristic of totalitarian dictators. But these are side effects of the internal democratic structure of the country, and they do not prevent the United States from being one of the two giant centers of power in the modern state system.

An analysis of the nature of power and a survey of the lessons of history thus point to a pessimistic conclusion. Bipolarity leads to eventual destruction and can be prevented only by a general redistribution of power. But who is going to balkanize the U.S.A. and the U.S.S.R.? No one has the power to do it, and there is no prospect of these powers balkanizing themselves. Even if balkanization were somehow feasible, who would fashion the fragments into a viable constitutional order? The more modest task of restoring the old balance of power is not to be thought of without a balancer. But we do not have a balancer any more, only participants. Even the minimal task of preserving what is left of the family of nations or modern state system is unpromising.

GROWING CHAOS
IN THE FAMILY OF NATIONS

One of the troublesome facts we have to deal with is growing chaos in the family of nations. The concept of the family of nations has been the basis of international relations and the framework of foreign policy for a long time, and we do not realize how much we have taken it for granted and depended upon it. It was the concept which replaced that of the unity of Christendom spiritually in the Roman Catholic Church and temporally in the Holy Roman Empire. The rise of national monarchies and the eruption of the Protestant Reformation broke up the unity of Christendom in the sense that there remained no single organization, ecclesiastical or temporal, to express it. Some new form of order had to replace the old. That form was the modern state system. It was first known as the family of nations because the prevalence of monarchy made the term seem natural. Nations were governed by royal families, and these families constituted a kind of international brotherhood through inter-marriage, frequent contacts, a common geographic base on the continent of Europe, and a common Christian allegiance.

In the long struggle which attended the emergence of the new state system, the legal doctrine of sovereignty was developed, and served as a principle of order. Sovereignty in its internal aspect meant national uni-fication against the competing claims of feudal lords, regions, and locali-ties. It determined where people should look for the making, interpreting, and enforcing of law. It thus clarified a complicated situation and brought order out of confusion and disorder. Sovereignty in its external aspect fulfilled the same function by determining who was a person at interna-tional law. It answered the question: With whom do we have to deal and what can he do? In an age of grand duchies, free cities, principalities, kingdoms, and empires, there had to be some way of determining status and authority. Sovereignty as legal authority not answerable to any other earthly authority became the solution to the problem. Around sovereignty there developed basic concepts like people, territory, jurisdiction, and government, which are the component parts of the state system. Grad-ually the system was extended to fit new developments like the transition from monarchies to republics and the admission of non-Christian and non-European states such as Turkey and Japan. These developments made the family of nations look less and less like a family, but they did not fundamentally alter the state system itself.

We may not admire the modern state system very much. We may charge it with doing a bad job of maintaining the peace. We may argue that it leans more toward anarchy than order. We may feel that the Roman Empire was more adequate. We may hope that new and better forms of order more suited to the maintenance of a peace that is stable and just will someday be created. The fact is, however, that the modern state system is all we have. There are no presently available alternatives. The Roman Empire cannot be resurrected. New forms of order are not now at hand or even discernible. Whatever undermines the existing state system, therefore, must be recognized as a threat, at least for the present.

In this connection it is important to note that the state system needs a strong centripetal force commanding the loyalty of the people and giving direction and purpose to the government. The fashionable term to identify this force is myth. The myth does not have to be the same everywhere, but there needs to be one of some kind. The most successful one in mod-ern times has been nationalism. Where nationalism has conflicted with another myth, the results have sometimes been explosive. The old Turkish and Austrian Empires were broken to pieces by it and recon-stituted into a number of national states. Nationalism detached Ireland from the British Empire and fused the separate parts of Italy into a national state. Nationalism has also enabled existing states to retain their unity through revolution and to survive drastic changes in their forms of government. Thus, the French have consistently reserved the word France to identify their nation and have used different words to designate their state. The nation has been the source of unity and the forms of the state, a source of division. Only the old Bourbon kings were presumptuous enough to call themselves "kings of France." The two Napoleons were emperors of the French; Louis Philippe was King of the French; the heads of the several republics since 1875 were presidents of the French Republic, and even Marshal Pétain styled himself "Chief of the French State."

There are signs, however, that nationalism is a waning force and that we are entering a post-nationalist age. The aftermath of World War I saw the emergence of rival myths, the ideologies or isms. One of these was fascism, especially the German brand. Although camouflaged in the form of strident nationalism, German fascism was a denationalizing force, an aggressive and imperialistic racialism. Its corrosive power was great enough to undermine the unity of even so old a nation as France. Before World War II there were Frenchmen whose slogan was: "I would rather have Hitler than Blum"; and the war itself divided the French people into Free French and Vichy French, patriots and collaborationists.

The most challenging rival myth today is communism. In spite of the Russian domination within the Soviet Union and the opportunistic communist support of nationalist movements in Asia and Africa, communism is intrinsically international and antinational. The Communist Manifesto appealed to the workers of the world regardless of nationality; communist parties everywhere formed an international group (e.g., The Third International); and the letters U.S.S.R. emphasize the class character of the Soviet Union and disclaim a national base. The real nature of communism is apparent in the hostile reaction of the Soviet world to the nationalist communism of Yugoslavia and in the admission by French communist leaders some years ago that they would fight on the side of the Soviet Union against their own country in case of war. Like all the ideologies, communism undermines the modern state system by corroding the national myth upon which that system rests. For this reason communism is widely and properly regarded as a fundamental menace, its satellite states as puppets, its parties as conspiracies, and its adherents as disloyal citizens.

Nationalism is also disintegrating from within, even without the help of fascist or communist infiltration. This tendency is usually discussed in terms of national purpose. Some ten years ago I had the occasion to talk with Pierre de Gaulle, brother of the French president, on this subject. I had made the point that the Gaullist emphasis on the revamping of the French executive power rested on a superficial diagnosis of the French predicament and that the basic trouble was the loss of a sense of national mission. M. de Gaulle immediately agreed and wistfully compared the immobility of France with the vigorous recovery of the Germans. "The Germans have it easy," he said, "for their national mission is obvious. It is the reunification of Germany." When I suggested that the French might recover a sense of national mission by pursuing some great ideal like liberty or justice, he made the following significant comment: "Ah, but these are the things which *divide* us." It is evident that his brother the president has not solved the problem, in spite of having given his country a new constitution tailor-made to fit his ideas. President Charles de Gaulle seems to think that national grandeur is a matter of fervor and not of content. Unless he can give his country something to work for and live for on which the French people can unite, he will be unable to shake the indifference and the *incivisme* which paralyze it.

Unfortunately, the loss of a sense of national purpose or mission is a phenomenon which is not limited to the French. It afflicts us too. The seriousness of the problem received official recognition when President Eisenhower appointed a commission to answer the question: What do we believe in? It reminds one of the story about a newly founded college whose first student body held a meeting and made the decision: Let's get some traditions! The current emphasis on Americanism and the American way of life is a similarly bad sign because it assumes that fervent breast-beating and loud protestations of loyalty are an adequate substitute for solid meaningful content. Washington and Jefferson experienced no doubts or ambiguities about national destiny; neither did Monroe when he declared that further colonization of the Western Hemisphere by the Holy Alliance or an extension of "their system" was contrary to the national interest of the United States; and neither did Lincoln when he delivered the Gettysburg Address. Today, however, we are full of doubts, uncertainties, and confusion.

There are observers who say that even in Russia, where communism is supposed to supply all the answers, the question of national purpose is being raised by the younger generation. According to Edward Crankshaw, who visited Russia in 1959 as correspondent on Soviet affairs for the London *Observer,* the younger people are not satisfied by the rising standard of living, because they take it for granted and are searching for other values which communist propaganda does not supply. "It is an interesting situation," he observes, "and a difficult one for Khrushchev, who does not in the least take the recent improvement in living conditions for granted, and who perhaps finds it impossible to think himself into the minds of countless youngsters, whole generations, who are crying out in effect not 'See how far we have come!' but rather, 'Where do we go from here? And quickly.' " [2] Crankshaw offers the following diagnosis: "What is lacking, in the Soviet Union, as in the 'capitalist' West, is a sense of direction, of place, of belonging." [3] The diagnosis is only too familiar, but the astonishing thing is that it should apply to Russia, which is not supposed to have problems of that kind.

In addition to the disruptive effect of ideologies from without and signs of disintegration from within, nationalism as the basis of the modern state system is also being challenged by the rise of new states in Africa and Asia. These new states are all supposedly based on nationalism, but the word is highly fictional as applied to them. How can you have nationalism without a nation? What, for instance, is the Congo Republic? It does not have any of the attributes of a nation. It is an arbitrary assortment of primitive and mutually hostile tribes, who lack a common culture and speak not one but many languages. The only common past it possesses is that produced by a limited number of years of Belgian administration which did not take root. The French language could be a common bond and would be an adequate means of communication and culture, but it is understood only by a small and widely dispersed number of Europeanized Congolese (*évolués*). The dynamism which brought the Congo Republic into existence was anticolonialism and racial resentment, not nationalism. A similar situation obtains in the other new African states such as Ghana, Guinea, and Nigeria.

Confusion likewise prevails in the Arab world. There is undoubtedly something which may properly be called Arab nationalism, but states like Jordan and Iraq are not nations. It could be that Arab nationalism will become strong and vital enough to create a true and comprehensive Arab federal republic. However, the vested interests of existing dynasties, the personal ambitions of Arab politicians, and interference by non-Arab powers stand in the way of such a development. For the present, therefore, Arab nationalism must be regarded as a disruptive rather than constructive force because it threatens states whose myths are shadowy or nonexistent, whose constitutional order is fragile, whose boundaries are probably temporary, and whose continued existence is problematical. The Arab world is obviously in a state of flux and likely to remain so for many years to come, and its states are undependable members of the family of nations.

Conditions in East Asia are also unstable. India may survive and grow in strength and stability because it has an authentic and rich culture and because a long period of British administration left it with a viable governmental structure and a trained Indian leadership. The identity of states like Cambodia, Laos, and Vietnam as nations is nebulous, and the future of federations like Indonesia and Malaysia is uncertain.

In the new states of Asia and Africa, the principle of the self-determination of peoples was applied before the prior question of *selfhood* had been resolved. Curiously enough, these new states are in much the same position that so many individuals find themselves in today. They have to ask themselves such questions as: Who are we? What are we? What do we live for? Until these questions are answered, there cannot be any real "image," so dear to the public relations experts, because identity precedes image. Anticolonialism, distrust of the West, and racial resentments provided the dynamic forces which created these states. But it should be noted that these forces are all negative, and political units which are built solely or mainly on negation are not likely to be successful or permanent. In spite of all these facts, the new Afro-Asian states are technically members of the family of nations and voting members of the U.N. To refer to them as a "family" is ludicrous; to say that they are "nations" is unrealistic; and to admit them to the U.N. is dangerous (though probably inevitable). The general effect is to introduce an element of chaos into the modern state system.

Yet another source of dissonance in the modern state system is the presence and recognition of the Soviet satellite states. These states, including East Germany, Poland, Czechoslovakia, Hungary, and Rumania, are national entities, but they lack the necessary requisite of sovereignty. The legal fiction is that they are sovereign national states, but in fact they are Soviet puppets. It is expedient for us to have diplomatic and commercial relations with them, and it is not feasible to eject them from the U.N., but they do not really belong to the modern state system. They are, instead, part of the new and rival conception of the world order which is propounded by communist ideology.

THE THREAT OF MEANINGLESSNESS

During the 1961 meeting of the Advisory Council on Higher Education of the Presbyterian Church in the United States, the question was raised as to what is the greatest threat confronting the West with which Christian higher education should be concerned. Someone suggested the fashionable answer that communism is the culprit. One of the most distinguished Presbyterian ministers present, Dr. Warner Hall, dissented. He said: "I think that the greatest threat confronting us today is the threat of meaninglessness." What he meant is that meaninglessness is a more subtle and pervasive sickness of the mind and spirit, a person-destroying and nation-destroying condition which leaves one defenseless against communism or any other enemy, a kind of spiritual leukemia, whose only end is certain death. To paraphrase the Supreme Court's clear-and-present-danger rule and apply it in a different field, meaninglessness constitutes the clearest and most present danger of a substantive evil, which Congress has a right to prevent but which, unfortunately, Congress has no power to prevent.

Meaninglessness is the consequence of a number of trends which, in the aggregate, shed light on its nature. One of these is the trend away from rationality. It is too much to say that the nonrational and the irrational have no meaning. Psychology has indeed taught us that they can be full of meaning. Nevertheless, the fact remains that nonrational and irrational behavior must be understood by the use of reason and can be controlled by reason even when nonrational techniques are employed.

Reason is effective only when the terms it uses are intelligible, when their meaning is definable and ascertainable. There must be clarity of contours and fixity of content, or else they are useless. This prerequisite exists where common usage is stable because the community is stable and characterized by consensus on values or where an authoritative body like the United States Supreme Court in law or the French Academy in letters defines the terms. In a society which is rapidly changing and in which there is less and less consensus on values, usage reflects confusion and does not afford a safe guide for clear reasoning. On the other hand, no argument is needed to prove that bodies, official or unofficial, with the authority to define terms are not to be found anywhere except in a few limited fields like law, and even here excessive and increasing elasticity of meaning is giving trouble.

The result is that man is erecting a new Tower of Babel, aided by the growth of technical terms (e.g., in the natural sciences), which are legitimate but unintelligible to the ordinary person; by a flood of jargon (e.g., in the social sciences), much of which is illegitimate and designed not to identify facts or ideas but to show off the supposed erudition of its inventors; and by the distortions of propagandists who deliberately twist and pluralize the meaning of old established words. We are caught in a verbal quagmire from which it is extremely difficult to extricate ourselves. The more we struggle with terms, the deeper we sink by contributing new variants to old terms and by disseminating the variants of other people. And yet define terms we must. The academic discipline which deals with the problem of terminology is semantics, and the most fashionable concern of contemporary philosophy is, significantly, language.

The situation is easily illustrated by the word socialism. Many people use it as though its meaning were clear and unambiguous. But is it? There are many kinds of socialism, e.g., utopian socialism, Marxian or "scientific" socialism, national socialism, democratic socialism, and guild socialism. The utopian kind, which generally refers to pre-Marxian thinkers like Robert Owen, does not apply to any movement or organization and has anarchistic overtones. The Marxian kind used by the Communists means state ownership of all the means of production and describes a stage in historical evolution which is supposed to lie between capitalism and communism. Democratic socialism is evolutionary and constitutional rather than revolutionary, opposes all dictatorship, and aims at the nationalization of key industries only, such as public utilities.

National socialism means fascism and is therefore authoritarian and totalitarian. Guild socialism means the decentralization of industry and a weak supervising state.

In addition to these several varieties of socialism, some attention must be paid to the uncertainties and ambiguities which have invaded socialist circles. Nationalization of industry, which was once treated as a panacea and the hallmark of socialism, has become a very doubtful criterion. It used to mean that an industry would be taken over by the state and administered by a government department or ministry on the model of the post office, but that was before the advent of the public corporation. There are Socialists, especially in France, who distinguish between nationalization and socialization and argue that the latter is preferable. British Socialists have used the public corporation to nationalize several industries, but they are not so sure as they once were that nationalization is the cure for the ills of capitalism, and it is doubtful that they will push it much further if or when they return to power. The German Socialists have evolved to a position which seems close to a kind of regulated capitalism.

We must also take into account the efforts of propagandists who use the word socialism to suit their own purposes. The Communists, for example, insist that there is only one correct usage, i.e., state ownership of all the means of production such as is found in the Soviet Union, where every component state is officially designated as a Socialist Republic. They simply refuse to acknowledge the claims of socialist parties anywhere else in the world. On the other hand, the extreme right in the United States also do their bit to muddy the terminological waters. Sometimes they use the word socialism in the same sense as the Communists and insist that no other concept is legitimate. At other times they use it in a broad and loose fashion to include liberalism and any other position to the left of Senator Goldwater. In both cases, their use of the word callously ignores the claims of millions of Socialists in the West and the denials of millions of liberals in the United States and elsewhere.

By the time changing historical facts, the uncertainties of the adherents of socialism, and the misrepresentations of the extreme right and left have been examined and weighed, who can tell what socialism means? Does it mean anything at all or, to put it another way, does it not mean too many things? There is always the option, of course, of taking the time and trouble to make it known in a reasonably clear fashion in which of these several senses one uses the word socialism. What makes such a procedure truly laborious and excessively demanding is that other words like liberalism and conservatism are likely to be involved in the discussion, and these words are equally ambiguous and would require equally lengthy disquisitions. By the time explanations, qualifications, and differentiations have been completed, the writer and the reader are apt to feel like a small boy who has taken apart a complex and delicate piece of machinery and is unable to reassemble the pieces.

At this point someone might argue that the linguistic confusion is not as bad as it seems. The argument would be that words like socialism, liberalism, and conservatism are normative words which refer to ideal and therefore somewhat vague types and which are colored by emotions and distorted by partisan controversy. If this argument were valid, we would expect that empirical words would be clearer and more definite, for such words describe "facts" and are relatively freer of emotional coloring and partisan distortions. Unfortunately the difference, if any, is not great enough to help us. The reason is that the facts themselves are in a growing state of flux, and so must the words be which describe them.

The concept of war exemplifies what has been happening to empirical words. There was a time when it was generally understood that war was a legal relation between states with reasonably marked beginnings, reasonably clear and well-understood legal consequences, and a reasonably definite and recognizable termination. But now where are we? We have total wars, hot wars, cold wars, "phony" wars, "brushfire" wars, local wars, thermonuclear warfare, economic warfare, psychological warfare, and "police" action. We have neutrals, nonbelligerent neutrals, cobelligerent neutrals, friendly neutrals. No man can tell contraband from noncontraband, combatant from noncombatant, the front from the rear. Soon after World War II (whenever that was) we found ourselves the legal allies of our political enemies the Russians, and we were giving economic aid to our legal enemies the Germans and the Japanese. In short, the distinction between war and peace has been seriously blurred.

The beginnings of war were once reasonably clear. International law classified wars as declared or undeclared, the former being "perfect" and the latter "imperfect." The former, at least, was quite clear and the latter reasonably so. The Hague conventions around the turn of the century attempted to clarify the matter further by ruling that all wars must be declared, and went on to codify the so-called "laws of war." But these were relatively stable times, and the whole evolution of the world through two major wars has been in the direction of instability. The beginnings of war are no longer safely predictable or clearly ascertainable.

The termination of war has become even more uncertain and murky. A war used to be terminated by a peace settlement. A peace settlement was a fundamental and comprehensive disposition (usually recorded in a treaty of peace) of the factors exercising a controlling influence on the relations between states. It included important decisions on such matters as boundaries, territorial changes, colonies, reparations, and forms of government. These decisions were expected to be permanent or at least to last for a very long time. People knew when the war was over and could look forward to a future on which they could count for a generation or longer. Peace was normal, war was abnormal, and both were clear. World War I was terminated by a normal peace settlement. Even in this case, however, the status of the new Soviet Union was something of an exception to normality and foreshadowed things to come. No clear termination marked World War II, and the postwar period has certainly not been one of peace in the traditional sense. World War II did produce a number of peace treaties, but there was no true peace settlement. Much was left *un*settled, e.g., the future of Germany and the status of Berlin. By the time the Korean War came along, we dispensed with peace treaties altogether and had to accept an unsatisfying armistice of indefinite duration.

The softening process of deterioration to which a key concept like war has been subjected is contagious and necessarily affects other concepts related to it. Civil rights, for instance, are directly involved. The framers of the Constitution took the trouble to define treason in the Constitution itself. This was a very unusual step since the framers almost invariably assumed that the words they used were either unmistakably clear or could be safely left for future interpretation. In this case, however, they produced a very precise and strict definition of treason for the purpose of protecting people from being loosely branded as traitors by political opponents because of unpopular views or affiliations. But the definition speaks of enemies and waging war against the United States, i.e., it hinges on the legal concept of war as it had been traditionally understood. The deterioration of the concept of war was thus bound to undermine the concept of treason. The constitutional definition of treason is so tightly drawn, however, that a frontal attack was difficult. The way in which the difficulty was met took the form of bypassing the definition and resorting to related concepts, such as subversion and sedition, which are not defined in the Constitution, whose substance is more conveniently elastic, and for which the type of evidence required is less exacting. The framers' definition of treason therefore stands unsullied and unbreached, but their purpose in formulating it is largely thwarted. A great many other elements in our Constitution are similarly affected by the blurring of the concept of war, e.g., the separation of powers between the President and Congress, the distribution of powers between the federal government and the states, the nature and operation of our economic system.

It should be evident by now that the terminological confusion in which we are enmeshed is the consequence of both ideologies and conditions. The confusion, in turn, engenders cynicism wherein people abandon the struggle to be clear. What, for instance, is a direct tax? The question has to be asked because the Constitution requires that direct federal taxes be apportioned among the states. It has generally been held that in the case of a direct tax the incidence of the tax lies where its impact is, i.e., the one who pays the tax is also the one who bears its burden. In the case of an indirect tax, the impact and the incidence are not the same, i.e., the tax can be "passed on." At this point two considerations arise: one is that the determination of when the incidence of a tax is or can be separated from its impact is a difficult problem which is much disputed among economists, and the other is that apportionment of taxes among the states is cumbersome and impractical. What is the way out for a cynically minded thinker? simply to define a direct tax as one which has to be apportioned and an indirect tax as one which does not. In this manner the whole debate about impact and incidence is bypassed; the problem of apportionment is eliminated; and the constitutional requirement is rendered meaningless.

It should not be supposed, however, that the threat of meaninglessness is solely a matter of vocabulary. After all, vocabulary is an effect as well as a cause. Meaninglessness is a much deeper phenomenon and has been the subject of a variety of analyses following different lines of inquiry. Some of these look to sociological conditions which induce meaninglessness. One of the most perceptive writers along this line is Glenn Tinder.[4] Among the conditions which he discusses are the separation of man from nature in urban communities where people live in an almost exclusively man-made environment, the mobility of modern man whose residence changes frequently from birth to the grave and thus prevents him from taking root, the increasingly abstract and impersonal nature of property, the disintegration of the family as a unit including several generations living together in one locality, the superficial and tangential nature of human relationships in an age of commuting and occupational specialization. These conditions, says Tinder, produce "cosmic homelessness." [5] Other analyses look to the realm of beliefs, the breakdown of objective values, and the rising tide of subjectivism.[6] Still other analyses concentrate on cultural disintegration and the loss of potency of symbols. Paul Tillich argues that the "most basic symptom of the cultural disintegration is the feeling of *meaninglessness* and the resulting cynicism. Not only the religious symbols of earlier centuries had lost their power of giving meaning to life, but also the philosophical and political symbols which were supposed to replace them." [7]

Not all the writers concerned make use of the concept of meaninglessness, but the concept is relevant to their work and would certainly not be rejected by them. What they are analyzing is the interrelationships between individual and group, and the idea which keeps coming up most frequently is that of conformity. Among the best known are David Riesman in social psychology, William H. Whyte in business, Philip E. Jacob in education, Will Herberg in the sociology of religion, and Sheldon S. Wolin in political theory. These writers are having a great impact on the thinking of our day. Riesman's conceptual apparatus—the terms "tradition-directed," "inner-directed," and "other-directed"—have passed into common usage. Whyte's *The Organization Man* is also on everybody's lips, so much so that it is now treated more often as a category of thought than as the title of a book. Jacob's *Changing Values in College* stirred widespread comment and controversy in the educational world even before it came out in print and has penetrated the churches through their campus Christian life activities. Herberg's book *Protestant-Catholic-Jew: An Essay in American Religious Sociology,* by tracing the development of religious life in the United States in this century and subjecting the current revival in religion to a searching analysis, has aroused the interest of the churches and forced upon secular-minded people the realization that religion is part of our culture and not a mere side show beside the main show. Wolin's book *Politics and Vision* is too recent to have had much influence as yet, but it is one of the most important contributions to political theory in many years, and one does not have to be a prophet to predict that it will have a vast and lasting impact on scholars.

What is it that these writers are saying with so much effect? In their several ways, they are saying that contemporary man is losing his individuality—his very selfhood—and is unsuccessfully trying to recapture it. This is also substantially what the existentialist philosophers have been contending for a longer period of time but in an inexcusably abstruse language and with answers that are highly dubious.

Whyte discusses the passing of the strong-willed, technically competent, risk-loving business executive, who was very much of an individualist and ran his establishment in a distinctly personal way. The new type of business executive is a specialist in human relations rather than in the technical aspects of his business, a careful sophisticated man, who was shaped by the internal pressures of the organization through which he rose and who survived psychological personality tests designed to eliminate any nonconformity of character, a public relations conscious man skilled in the techniques of reaching decisions through committee discussions and action.

Jacob finds that modern college students are conformists who nevertheless tolerate diversity, obey the law "without complaint but without enthusiasm," believe in religion without being controlled or even seriously influenced by it, and have more homogeneous values as seniors than they had as freshmen. He finds that neither teacher, nor teaching techniques, nor curricula, nor textbooks make any appreciable difference in the values of students. The only exception he can find is that some colleges have a "peculiar potency," but that potency is only the sheer weight and pressure of an organization which makes somewhat different demands on the students than most colleges. He puts the matter succinctly: *"What* is expected is *not* the same." [8]

Herberg finds that contemporary religion has lost its content and become a means of identification, a mere tag. "Unless one is either a Protestant, or a Catholic, or a Jew," he observes, "one is a 'nothing'; to be a 'something,' to have a name, one must identify oneself to oneself, and be identified by others, as belonging to one or another of the three great religious communities in which the American people are divided." [9] In other words, the contemporary answer to the problem of identity or selfhood is no longer "I believe" but "I belong."

In his critical survey of the evolution of political thought from Plato to the present, Wolin finds that we have arrived at a breakdown of the general political order and have sought to evade the intellectual problem of understanding and the political problem of reconstruction by taking refuge in organizations. The problem of properly relating organizations to one another is left untouched and unsolved, and so is that of the autonomy of the individual within the organization. The social scientist is looking for something "manageable." Says Wolin: "He is inclined to analyze men in terms of class-orientations, group-orientations, or occupational-orientations. But man as member of a general political society is scarcely considered a proper subject for theoretical inquiry, because it is assumed that 'local citizenship'—man as trade-unionist, bureaucrat, Rotarian, occupant of a certain income-tax bracket—is the primary or determinant influence on how man will behave as a political citizen." [10] Wolin believes that the major task of political theory is to revive "that form of knowledge which deals with what is general and integrative to men, a life of common involvements." [11] If we fail to do this work of reconstruction of a general order capable of restoring meaning to the life of individuals and groups, the totalitarians will undertake it. Indeed, they are doing precisely this, but in a manner which we do not relish and which is doomed to eventual failure—if, in the meantime, mankind has not committed atomic suicide.

It is notable that these writers do not like their own findings. Will Herberg, for instance, attacks contemporary religion from the standpoint of the Judeo-Christian tradition to which he adheres:

The burden of this criticism of American religion from the point of view of Jewish-Christian faith is that contemporary religion is so naively, so innocently *man-centered*. Not God, but man—man in his individual and corporate being—is the beginning and end of the spiritual system of much of present-day American religiosity. In this kind of religion there is no sense of transcendence, no sense of the nothingness of man and his works before a holy God; in this kind of religion the values of life, and life itself, are not submitted to Almighty God to judge, to shatter, and to re-construct; on the contrary, life, and the values of life, are given an ultimate sanction by being identified with the divine. In this kind of religion it is not man who serves God, but God who is mobilized and made to serve man and his purposes—whether these purposes be economic prosperity, social reform, democracy, happiness, security, or "peace of mind." [12]

An equally vigorous indictment of his own findings is made by William H. Whyte:

He must *fight* The Organization. Not stupidly, or selfishly, for the defects of individual self-regard are no more to be venerated than the defects of co-operation. But fight he must, for the demands for his surrender are constant and powerful, and the more he has come to like the life of organization the more difficult does he find it to resist these demands, or even to recognize them. It is wretched, dispiriting advice to hold before him the dream that ideally there need be no conflict between him and society. There always is; there always must be. Ideology cannot wish it away; the peace of mind offered by organization remains a surrender, and no less so for being offered in benevolence. That is the problem.[13]

An explanation of these several findings on modern trends toward organization and conformity lies in Riesman's concept of "other-direction." His own formulation of it is as follows:

What is common to all the other-directed people is that their contemporaries are the source of direction for the individual—either those known to him or those with whom he is indirectly acquainted, through friends and through the mass media. This source is of course "internalized" in the sense that dependence on it for guidance in life is implanted early. The goals toward which the other-directed person strives shift with that guidance: it is only the process of striving itself and the process of paying close attention to the signals from others that remain unaltered throughout life.[14]

It is easy to see, when you stop to think about it, why other-direction would progressively lead to meaninglessness. As long as there are enough people in positions of leadership who pursue some definite direction, it does not matter that the rest are other-directed. But when other-direction reaches the top, when *everybody* is other-directed, the result is either chaos or immobility. In either case the culture is directionless. In a completely traditionalistic culture, a part of this result is obviated since immemorial custom supplies the goals *for individuals*. There is, therefore, no chaos, and individual life has meaning. But there is cultural immobility. The tradition-directed culture is stationary and directionless, which is why it is generally said not to have a history even though it might last a thousand years. In any case, tradition-direction is not a live option for us because our culture is dynamic in practically all respects. Direction for both society and individuals has to come from leadership.

Leadership and other-direction are contradictory terms. Other-direction generates the kind of leader who tries to defend his conduct by saying: "I was their leader; therefore I had to follow them." Such a justification abolishes the distinction between leader and follower. There are no leaders any more, only followers—with nobody to follow. Riesman says that the other-directed individual lives as though equipped with

radar. In one way the observation is very apt since it applies to people
who take their cue from other people. In another way, however, the observation is not so apt because radar is useful only to a person who already knows where he is going. Where he is going is precisely what the
other-directed person does not know.

What other-direction as a standard of human behavior means is evident in a multitude of ways, which it would be tedious to dwell upon.
One all too common illustration will suffice. Let us imagine a committee
meeting charged with an important decision and composed of other-
directed members. In such a committee there will be no agenda, no working papers supplying background information, no reports presenting alternatives to choose from. There will be a chairman, but no leader. There
will be much talk, but the talk will be empty, futile, and frustrating because no one is *saying* anything. Each one is marking time and waiting
for someone else to propose something. Some may have ideas but are not
expressing them lest these ideas fail to meet with approval. The meeting
is paralyzed by vacuity or timidity or both. There is a general desire to
conform, but the problem is that there is nothing to conform to. How
can you con*form* to that which has no form? The trouble with a meeting
of this kind is that it is *meaningless*. If there is a decision which simply
must be made and cannot be postponed, the committee will eventually
drift into one, but only after hours of pointless talk, which some people
mistakenly regard as the quintessence of the democratic process.

Nietzsche foresaw the nature and consequences of other-direction and
denounced them in colorful, scathing, and prophetic language. It is significant that he concentrated his wrath on the intellectual leaders. Nietzsche was very wrong in many ways, but he was also very right in other
ways, and it was often for being right that he was attacked. His term for
the other-directed individual was "the objective man," whom he described thus:

He is only an instrument; we may say, he is a *mirror*—he is no "purpose in
himself." The objective man is in truth a mirror: accustomed to prostration
before everything that wants to be known, with such desires only as knowing
or "reflecting" imply—he waits until something comes, and then expands
himself sensitively, so that even the light footsteps and gliding past of spiritual
beings may not be lost on his surface and film. Whatever "personality" he still
possesses seems to him accidental, arbitrary, or still oftener, disturbing; so
much has he come to regard himself as the passage and reflection of outside
forms and events. He calls up the recollection of "himself" with an effort, and
not infrequently wrongly; he readily confounds himself with other persons,
he makes mistakes with regard to his own needs, and here only is he unrefined
and negligent.[15]

The description is too accurate for comfort, and Nietzsche drew the
conclusion that the multiplication and prevalence of this kind of man

could mean only one thing: *paralysis of the will.*[16] It is our misfortune that this paralysis, which Nietzsche called the "European disease," has grown to ominous dimensions and that its growth coincides with the greatest peril which ever confronted mankind in all its history—thermonuclear suicide. It is the confluence of peril and paralysis, perhaps, which imparts some credence to the definition of an optimist as one who thinks the future is uncertain.

THE IMPOTENCE OF SOCIAL SCIENCE

Bipolar tensions and growing chaos in the family of nations point to an inexorably pessimistic conclusion regarding the prospects for peace. On the other hand, meaninglessness destroys our ability to reverse the process upon which these conclusions are based. The evidence is, therefore, that the social scientist finds himself in the same position as the natural scientist: both of them point to an approaching catastrophe, and both are helpless to prevent it.

Social science, as that term is generally understood in the United States, is positive, descriptive, and empirical. It is concerned with the discovery, comparison, and classification of the facts of human behavior. It seeks to measure and weigh those facts, to identify and describe patterns of behavior, to analyze the interrelationships of facts and patterns, and to make valid generalizations regarding changes and trends. It is constantly accumulating, scrutinizing, sifting, and checking data. The result is called knowledge; the process by which it is obtained is known as research; and progress in social science is regarded as the increase in the amount and reliability of knowledge.

Progress understood in this limited sense has been very great. New refined techniques of research, better instruments for discovering and recording facts, the work of universities, private foundations, and government agencies are all adding constantly to the mass of information dealing with human behavior. Voting behavior, for example, is being analyzed from a great many angles including age, sex, ethnic origin, income, education, religion, geography, and party affiliation. Indeed, the amount of information we are collecting is so vast as to be bewildering.

Social science is also operating with a more adequate conception of facts. Gone are the days when a social scientist like the psychologist John Broadus Watson could say that whatever could not be found in his test tube or would not register on his instruments does not exist. The social scientist now acknowledges that values are part of the facts he is studying. He is quite willing to admit that a religiously sanctioned caste system like the one in ancient India profoundly affects the economic system or that whether a labor union is based on a communist, syndicalist, or capitalist ideology makes a great deal of difference. He recognizes that what men believe is related to what they do. Even a so-called "behavioral scientist" operates with a much broader conception of what behavior entails. He is willing to study the beliefs themselves (although he usually prefers to call them "value systems") and to accept the findings of psychology and psychiatry as relevant to his work.

Progress in social science is important to us because many of the decisions we have to make—though by no means all—hinge on questions of fact. Economists can tell governments which measures are inflationary and which are not. Specialists in public opinion and social psychology can tell candidates for public office which issues are worrying the voter and which leave him indifferent. Political scientists can tell state governments which factors attract new industries and which keep them away and cause them to locate elsewhere. There are many generalizations which are currently accepted but which scientific investigation might prove to be false, and some of these can be important from the standpoint of public policy. Moreover, social scientists are sometimes able to tell a policy-maker how to effectuate his policy or what the probable consequences will be. Social science is obviously related to the problems of predictability and control. While its contributions in these matters are imperfect and tentative, they are significant and likely to become more so.

Nevertheless, social science operates under severe limitations, which time will not lessen and which should moderate our expectations. All science assumes definite concepts, stable materials, and reproducible conditions. None of these assumptions applies to social science to an extent sufficient to make it comparable to natural science. We have already seen how social science is sinking in a terminological morass; hence conceptual precision is unattainable. The material with which social science must work is unstable. One man is never exactly like another, nor is he himself exactly the same from one time to the next. Social conditions cannot be exactly reproduced. A truly controlled situation such as is available to the chemist or the physicist is not at the disposal of the social scientist. Experience, not experiment, is characteristic of social science. The social scientist, therefore, must do the best he can within these severe limitations.

This best is further modified by the involvement of the social scientist himself. Unlike the natural scientist, the social scientist is part of the data with which he works. His own values influence his judgment, determine the hypotheses he conceives and prevent other hypotheses from occurring to him, influence his decision as to which hypotheses he will go to the trouble and expense of testing, and affect the way he classifies his findings and the importance he ascribes to them. More disturbing still is the fact that his own findings become part of the conditions he is studying so that he is a fact-*maker* as well as a fact-finder. For example, if he makes a study of the sexual life of a people and finds that there is widespread promiscuity, this finding may become the cause of still greater

promiscuity, and a subsequent study will show this to be so. In this case
the social scientist could be said to make his facts come true! On the other
hand, his original finding might have the opposite effect and provoke a
reaction against promiscuity so that the next time he makes a survey he
will "prove" himself to have been "wrong." In either case he has become
part of the situation he is studying. Under such circumstances, how
can one speak of complete objectivity and disinvolvement?

Even if complete objectivity and disinvolvement were possible, there
would continue to be an essential difference between social science and
natural science which no amount of objectivity could alter. The natural
scientist works with something that is given, i.e., pure facts. The social
scientist, however, works with something created by man, i.e., artifacts.
Social, economic, and political facts are those that people made in the
past and are making in the present. Those facts can be accepted, but they
do not have to be—at least not entirely. They will change and, what is
even more important, they can be changed.

Now we come to another world, the normative world. We are dealing
with *what ought to be,* and when we do, we reach a level of reality which
lies beyond the competence of social science. It is true that social science
has to be concerned with this level of reality because the normative penetrates and alters human behavior. But while it cannot ignore normative
questions and may shed light on them, it cannot answer them. Social science is just as available for evil ends as it is for good ones. You can
study economics to cheat your fellow man; political science, to oppress
and enslave people; psychology, to hoodwink the public; and law, to produce shysters who will "beat" the law. Social science does not tell anyone what is good or bad, what is beautiful or ugly, what is meaningful or
meaningless. It does not answer the basic questions concerning life and
destiny. We sometimes believe otherwise because some of the findings of
social science strike us as obviously good or obviously bad, but we forget
that we are judging them in the light of standards of good and evil which
we take for granted because they are generally accepted and seldom challenged. Nevertheless, these standards are not categories of social science,
and so we must come to the conclusion that social science is impotent in
solving the crisis of our time. As a social scientist who has the intellectual
integrity to stand by his findings even when they are repugnant, one has
no choice but to reiterate that we are heading for disaster and that social
science is powerless to prevent it. If there is an answer to our predicament, that answer must lie elsewhere.

Chapter II

PROMISE AND PERFORMANCE

I T is a curious fact that a civilization which calls itself Christian should not look to the Christian faith for the answer to its most critical and pressing problems. If natural science and social science cannot save us, what about the Christian faith? Of course, there is no dearth of people who pay lip service to Christianity. "If everybody was a Christian," they are fond of saying in a sacramental tone of voice, "everything would be all right." Statements of this kind are often uttered by emotionally cold, spiritually inert, vacant-minded people and receive the frosty approval of similarly petrified brethren. Sometimes the speaker is genuinely pious and really means what he says, but unfortunately he has no idea what he means. He is steeped in vagueness and ambiguity. He has never struggled to think through the intellectual problems involved or to translate faith into action. There may be warmth in his heart but no light in his mind or steel in his will. His pious statement is a form of escape, and non-Christians are quick to sense it. In spite of the unreceptive and occasionally derisive attitude of secular-minded people and the inadequacy of so many professed Christians, a serious effort should be made to determine whether or not the Christian faith can succeed where the sciences have failed.

PROMISES OF THE CHRISTIAN FAITH

A very obvious reason for making the effort is that Christianity holds out impressive promises. The world lives by promises to an extent that is truly remarkable. Marriage rests on promises. The entire economy depends on promises to pay. The Constitution of the United States is anchored in the promises of its preamble. The platforms of our political parties and the speeches of candidates for public office are mostly promises. Educational institutions live by the promises they make to liberate the mind, to push further the frontiers of knowledge, and to equip young people for their careers. Unpromising plans are rejected and unpromising people are given a low priority. The appeal of the great ideologies comes in great part from their promises to usher in a new and better world. Thus, communism promises a classless society, in which there will be no more exploitation of man by man and in which the ruling principle will be "from each according to his ability, to each according

31

to his need." The peoples of the new Afro-Asian states are attracted by Russian promises that they too can develop in fifty years from poverty and illiteracy to economic power and an educated citizenry, without mortgaging their political independence.

Now we all know that promises are one thing and performance is another. Some promises are not kept because they were never intended to be kept. Others are not kept because they are impossible of performance. Still others are ignored because the people to whom they are addressed are not interested in them. Promises can be too distant in time or they may have distasteful conditions attached to them. These are all factors which have to be considered, but they do not come first. The first thing to do is to see *what the promises are.*

What does the Christian faith promise to those who are committed to it? It comes as a surprise to discover that no one begins the discussion with this question. We might expect that non-Christian thinkers would ignore it because they are apt to look upon the promises of Christianity as improbable, if not downright incredible. Even so, this judgment is usually pronounced in general terms without previous examination. The promises are evidently not deemed worth stating and exploring. Such a disposition of the matter is hardly consistent with the traditional liberal adherence to the truth regardless of association or source, but it is not strange since there is no commitment to Christianity involved. From dedicated Christian thinkers, however, this is really strange. Perhaps they do not take those promises seriously and fail to realize the fact, or perhaps they assume that everybody already knows what they are, or perhaps they do not appreciate to what extent people demand and depend on promises.

Whatever the reason may be, the omission is significant and damaging. It is not until the promises of the Christian faith are actually stated and explained that one perceives how stupendous they are and how amazingly well they fit and satisfy the needs of our time. In a world full of promises Christianity should be pre-eminent because it outpromises every ideology, religion, and philosophy. Certainly the promises of communism are pale, shabby, and ungenerous in comparison.

In order to make the relevance of the promises of the Christian faith to the crisis of our time as clear as possible, it is necessary to concentrate on a few of the essential ones rather than to attempt a comprehensive inventory. It is also necessary to avoid theological terms like justification, atonement, salvation, and sanctification. These terms are important and full of meaning, but our secular culture is unfamiliar with them. While we must eventually learn these again, it is possible to interpret them in ways that are meaningful to modern man. Among the promises of the Christian faith, the following are certain to get a hearing as soon as they are presented: life, liberty, happiness, community, and forgiveness.

Life

In a world worried about survival, Christianity promises life. How high a value Christ set on human life is manifest in a multitude of instances, e.g., the parable of the lost sheep wherein the life of a single sheep is worth saving and the shepherd "rejoiceth more of that sheep, than of the ninety and nine which went not astray." [1] The parables of the good Samaritan and of the prodigal son make the same point. In the Sermon on the Mount Jesus reiterates that human life is sacred in the eyes of God, who looks after the fowls of the air and the grass in the field. Jesus broadened and deepened the commandment "Thou shalt not kill" by extending it to include anger against one's brother, reformulating it in effect: Thou shalt not kill, even in thought. Wherever he went, Jesus saved lives and instructed his disciples to do the same. No one was too young, too old, too humble, too sick, too immoral, or too insignificant for Jesus. No human being is expendable, for life comes from God. "In him," says the apostle John, "was life; and the life was the light of men." [2] For the life of man—*all* men—Jesus laid down his life.

The Christian faith does not view life in negative terms. Life is not to be equated with mere existence. Vegetating is not living: men have a much more positive and dynamic destiny. "I am come," said Jesus, "that they might have life, and that they might have it more abundantly." [3] The Christian conception is that life is to be lived to the full and not on a minimal plane strewn with unused potentialities. The man with the one talent was not censured because he destroyed his talent, for he saved it and returned it intact, but because he buried it and thereby prevented it from increasing. Life is something that grows and blooms and multiplies. It is not to be cramped by narrow Pharisaic regulations, eaten up by routine, circumscribed by unalterable plans and programs, and stunted by limited conceptions of truth. It is not intended to be lived in economic poverty, intellectual superstition, and political terror. The Christian faith promises an *abundant* life, which means growth rather than deadening safety and predictability, and total fulfillment rather than mere self-preservation. It is creativity, not mere adjustment and conformity.

The boldest promise of the Christian faith is *everlasting* life. "For God so loved the world," says the Bible, "that he gave his only begotten Son, that whosoever believeth in him should not perish, but have everlasting life." [4] It is noteworthy that no impersonal merger of a soul with an oversoul or all-soul is involved here. Personal identity is retained. Nor is a ghostly existence contemplated, since the resurrection of the body is affirmed. Unlike Hinduism which holds that the body is evil and matter is an illusion, Christianity affirms that the body is glorified and matter is transfigured. Earthly life is first made acceptable in the sight of God, fit for eternity, by regeneration and atonement. Anything less than this would be incompatible with the nature of God, and to continue the physical and mental misery and the moral ugliness of so much of earthly life would be everlasting torture. Finally, everlasting life is not the dead perfection of Platonic immortality, for the Christian is a living person who continues to have fellowship with other living persons and with a living God who is a person too.

This tremendous promise of the Christian faith is not presented as speculation or conjecture but as a fact based on the historical evidence of the resurrection of Jesus Christ. That evidence is offered in the Scriptures with a wealth of detail which has the ring of truth. Many people, from Paul's Athenian audience on Mars Hill to the present day, have rejected it. The very people who were closest to the event had trouble believing it. People with such varied viewpoints and personalities as Peter, Thomas, and Paul were far from expecting it. No merely spiritual apparition could have convinced them. Only an actual historical fact imposing itself on doubters, mourners, and enemies could have carried enough conviction to transform a defeated and discouraged little band of disciples into a victorious church which conquered the Roman Empire.

Non-Christians continue to question everlasting life, but they cannot deny that the church has affirmed it throughout the centuries. Neither can they deny that none of the ideologies dares to make any such promise. Liberalism, for instance, ignores it, and communism flatly rejects it. Some non-Christian religions make promises of immortality, but none of these promises are comparable to those of the Christian faith. Christianity is the greatest, fullest, and most audacious affirmation of life that is possible or conceivable.

Liberty

In a world filled with demands for liberty, where even despots profess to believe in it, Christianity emphatically promises liberty. After Jesus had been tempted in the desert, he returned to his home town of Nazareth and announced his ministry in the synagogue. He chose as his text a passage from Isaiah in which liberty is mentioned twice. He said he had been anointed "to preach deliverance to the captives" and "to set at liberty them that are bruised." [5] To his disciples Jesus said: "If ye continue in my word, then are ye my disciples indeed; And ye shall know the truth, and the truth shall make you free." [6] Christian liberty was one of the themes most heavily emphasized by the apostle Paul.

The Christian conception of liberty is first and foremost a matter of the spirit, an inner condition of human personality. It affirms the liberation of man from the thralldom of sin. It obtains by the inner conversion of the heart and the renewal of the mind what could not be achieved by the regulations of the law, whether temporal or ecclesiastical. Man becomes free in the measure to which he can be trusted with freedom. This spiritual freedom becomes the source and foundation of the more external freedoms such as civil liberty, economic liberty, and academic freedom; but it is not dependent on these external freedoms. Even in a concentration camp a Christian can be free in the sense that matters most, and sometimes it is the only sense that exists. On the other hand, the most complete external freedoms are meaningless to one who is not free within himself. As Augustine pointed out, "the good man, although he is a slave, is free; but the bad man, even if he reigns, is a slave. . . ." [7] Because this freedom comes from God, it is inalienable, as the American Declaration of Independence explicitly recognizes. Other liberties, the external ones, are alienable—temporarily. As long as Christian liberty lives, other liberties will grow back and bloom just as perennial plants do after a long winter, provided that their roots remain intact.

Happiness

One of the most outstanding and daring promises of the Christian faith is blessedness. The word blessedness means happiness, but it is a special kind of happiness, i.e., one which bears the stamp of divine approval. It has nothing to do with the hedonistic conception of the utilitarians, which equates happiness with pleasure. Blessedness is not a temporary inebriation, which injures the one who experiences it. Unlike alcoholism, it is not followed by a hangover the day after and *delirium tremens* some years later. Neither does it thrive at the expense of other people, as with prostitution and gambling. It is not dependent on the possession of things "where moth and rust doth corrupt, and where thieves break through and steal." [8] Commenting on this point, the apostle Paul said that neither prosperity nor poverty could unsettle him, "for I have learned, in whatsoever state I am, therewith to be content." [9]

Blessedness or Christian happiness is also radically different from the Aristotelian conception. Christianity makes happiness a by-product, one of those things which will be added unto us if we seek first the kingdom of God. Aristotle called happiness the chief good of man, the end which includes all other ends. He thought of this end in strictly rationalistic terms, in accordance with his idea that reason alone makes man uniquely and distinctively human. He who thinks his way through to the mean between the excess and the defect knows how to be good and has the secret of happiness. The effect of this is to make happiness an intellectual problem, and Aristotle did not shrink from the logic of his conception: "And so it is hard to be good: for surely hard it is in each instance to find the mean, just as to find the mean point or centre of a circle is not what any man can do, but only he who knows how: just so to be angry, to give money, and be expensive, is what any man can do, and easy: but to do these to the right person, in due proportion, at the right time, with a right object, and in the right manner, this is not as before what any man can do, nor is it easy; and for this cause goodness is rare, and praiseworthy, and noble." [10]

Aristotle's mathematical comparison is most appropriate because it illustrates the nature of his conception of ethics and happiness. It offers an interesting, useful, and often enlightening technique for handling the problems of life, but it does mean that only intellectuals can be happy. It also means that mediocrity becomes the rule of life, for the heights as well as the depths of human behavior are excluded. Aristotle was ready to give up the ideal and settle for the manageable.

By contrast, the Christian conception of happiness, is a democratic one in that it is available to all men, intellectual and nonintellectual. Christianity does not deny the limitations of human reason any more than did Aristotle. It admits that the majority of men are incapable of the kind of reasoning which Aristotle prescribes as the necessary condition of happiness. Indeed, it goes beyond him by insisting that the reason of the most intellectual men is warped by original sin so that even those few cannot, without the aid of divine grace, successfully make the kind of calculation demanded by Aristotle. The fundamental difference is that Aristotle knew nothing of divine grace. The Christian does. The Christian has access to a wisdom infinitely greater than his own, that mind in us "which was also in Christ Jesus," [11] the guidance of the Holy Spirit, which can make him wise beyond his intellectual power, beyond his knowledge, and beyond his experience.

It is important to observe that Christianity definitely promises happiness, whereas Jeffersonian liberalism as expressed in the Declaration of Independence makes only the *pursuit* of happiness inalienable. Jefferson, a Deist, would not commit himself as to the outcome of the pursuit. Christianity clearly outpromises liberalism. Furthermore, the thing promised is much more valuable, for it is free of the defects of hedonism and Aristotelianism. Happiness, in Christian terms, is serenity of spirit, the strength of a being fulfilling the destiny which God intended for him, a quality of life which is warmly responsive and yet invulnerable to attack, a zest for life which knows no dullness, staleness, or bordeom. Nazi concentration camps cannot stifle it; communist brainwashing cannot erase it; utilitarianism cannot debase it; and positivism cannot dehydrate it. Even death itself cannot extinguish it: "Verily I say unto thee," said Jesus to the thief on the cross, "Today shalt thou be with me in paradise." [12]

Community

Among the promises of Christianity there are few which concern modern man more vitally than community. In community, "belonging," he seeks refuge against the uncertainties of life whether these be military, political, economic, or psychological. In community he hopes to find deliverance from the threat of meaninglessness, and the Organization Man is only the latest personification of this hope. Every movement which has been an effective force in the world has recognized this concern of man for community. Communism recognizes it with its use of the term comrade. Liberalism recognized it in the motto of the French Revolution whose third element was fraternity. Does Christianity outpromise its rivals in this case also?

There is no doubt that Christianity has from the very beginning affirmed and reaffirmed the reality and importance of community. That reality is the church, the Holy Catholic Church in the sense of the Apostles' Creed, and its importance was stressed in vivid and vigorous terms as when the apostle Peter said: "But ye are a chosen generation, a royal priesthood, an holy nation, a peculiar people; that ye should shew forth the praises of him who hath called you out of darkness into his marvelous light: Which had not obtained mercy, but now have obtained mercy." [13] Note that Peter is presenting the Christian community as an accomplished fact, a promise already fulfilled.

The Christian community includes nature. A Christian feels at home in nature because it is his Father's world. Genesis teaches that God created the heavens and the earth, beheld his creation and saw that it was good. It was his handiwork, and as with all handiwork, he put a great deal of himself into it and rested on the seventh day. The Psalms pick up this theme and describe the universe in beautiful language familiar and dear to every Christian. There are no Godforsaken places, no matter what we sometimes say, whether they be the jungles of Africa and South America, the wastelands of the Arctic regions, or the deserts of Asia and Africa. Jesus himself referred to the beauty of the lilies of the field, compared the Spirit to the wind which "bloweth where it listeth" and spoke of the lightning which "cometh out of the east and shineth even unto the west," talked of fields which are "white unto the harvest," and in so many ways showed that he saw nature as full of divine meaning and glory. The Book of Genesis says that the Garden of Eden was man's first home. Now a garden is the projection and reflection of a personality. It is something which someone designs, makes, loves, and cares for. This garden was "pleasant to the sight and good for food," and man's instructions were "to dress it and to keep it."

When man became alienated from God, the world ceased to look like a garden in man's eyes and became a hostile and foreign environment. It became something to be desecrated by shacks, slums, and junkyards. It was something to be exploited for selfish advantage without regard for the future. It was ravaged by the wanton destruction of forests, the wasting of soil, the indiscriminate killing of game resources, the pollution of rivers and lakes, and now the pollution of the atmosphere with radioactive "ashes of death." It ceased being a bond between men and was treated as a bone of contention between them. It split the natural sciences from the social sciences by removing the common ground for the reality of both and began the disintegration of the university into a pluriversity.

None of the ideologies has as powerful and consequential a theological undergirding for its concept of community as Christianity. Moreover, the same transcendental basis which suffuses the physical universe with life and meaning also governs the human relations side of the Christian community. This community is catholic—not Roman Catholic, Anglo-Catholic, or Greek Catholic, but catholic in the original sense of the word— universal. It is available to all men regardless of geographic, racial, national, ideological, political, or class limitations. It is being rediscovered in the ecumenical movement, which is piercing the barriers and "curtains" which separate men from one another. Personal encounters across these barriers are making Christians realize that their common faith in Christ is a stronger centripetal force than any of the centrifugal forces which pull them apart.

In this respect Christianity differs from Stoicism, which also affirmed the brotherhood of man. Stoicism rightly deduced the brotherhood of man from the fatherhood of God and is therein compatible with the Christian teaching that man was made in God's image. But Stoicism was too rationalistic, and its God was not a person. Like Plato's philosopher-king, he never became flesh nor dwelt among us full of grace and truth. The God of Stoicism might receive intellectual assent, but not loyalty, faith, and love. The tragedy of men is that though they are brothers, they do not feel and act like brothers. Men will not do so for the sake of a concept or because it is an obligation of natural law. They will do so for Christ's sake if they have faith in him.

The Christian community is one of love, not of dislikes. Therein it differs from all communities which have a negative basis. Men are all too often united by opposition to other men. Thus, a Frenchman and a German will feel their national ties strongly by way of contrast. Take them to America and leave them there awhile, and they will feel like Europeans. Move them to Asia, and it will not be long before they refer to themselves as Westerners and admit Americans to community with them. This phenomenon is recognized in politics in the familiar saying that politics makes strange bedfellows. Not so familiar is the converse, i.e., that strange bedfellows make strange politics! Entire ideologies have constructed their concept of community on a negative basis, and the greatest one at the present time is communism, which is based on the supposed irreconcilability of the class struggle. It is characteristic of communities based on hate, dislikes, or conflict that they are neither solid nor permanent. What modicum of community existed between the U.S.A. and the

U.S.S.R. during World War II was supported only by the common enemy and disappeared with him.

The Christian community has nothing to do with negativism. It dares to proclaim that community can be based on positive grounds alone without an admixture of conflict. As a community of faith, it is limited to those who share the faith. Nevertheless, it is not exclusive, because it is also a community of love. The Christian does not isolate himself from the world but is commingled with it, and his love includes non-Christians. It becomes possible, therefore, for him to work with those who do not share his faith. He does not try to *impose* his faith upon others, because even if he succeeded, he would fail. A conversion which is not the result of a full and free assent of the intelligence and the heart of men is no conversion at all but a travesty of the real thing, a wretched abuse of power, a fraud perpetrated on the human mind. Just as the Christian community does not seek to impose its faith on non-Christians, it does not seek to condemn them. Its purpose is redemptive, and redemption comes from love through identification. "For God sent not his Son into the world to condemn the world," says John, "but that the world through him might be saved." [14]

Because of its inclusiveness, positive character, and transcendental moorings in the Holy Spirit, the Christian community solves the problem of meaninglessness. It is simultaneously inner-directed and other-directed. It is inner-directed because Christ dwells in us, transforming our hearts, minds, and wills from within. It is other-directed because Christ, an objective reality and a person in his own right, is the head of the church and as such is outside, around, and among us. The contemporary Organization Man is unaware of this inclusiveness of the Christian community and tries to settle for something less. He joins organizations, such as civic clubs, whose purposes are legitimate enough but too narrow to satisfy his quest for meaning. He tries to lose himself in his work, i.e., his business or professional group, only to find that man does not live by bread alone and that his group is not spiritually and culturally spacious enough to lose himself in. He seeks release and fulfillment in his country and does better because a country is culturally richer and more inclusive, but he finds that the national community entails enmities in a broken world and lacks ultimate transcendence.

In the midst of all these sociologically fragmented, intellectually limited, culturally cramped, and spiritually unripe communities, the Christian faith promises man a community that is full, creative, vital, and transcendent. Finally, the Christian faith again reaches the ultimate in boldness: it promises eternity. This promise came in connection with Peter's great confession. Peter had just demonstrated the insight that Jesus was not a mere prophet, teacher, or great leader but the Christ, the son of the living God. Referring to this insight as one which came from God the Father, Jesus made the promise in these words: "And I say also unto thee, That thou art Peter, and upon this rock I will build my church; and the gates of hell shall not prevail against it." [15] Families will live and die, fortunes will be made and unmade, empires will rise and fall, cultures will run their cycles and disappear, but the Christian community will endure through all eternity. No ideology dares to make so startling and ambitious a promise.

Forgiveness

Thus far we have dealt only with values which the world recognizes and wants. Life, liberty, happiness, and community are universally sought and often officially endorsed in public documents like the American Declaration of Independence and the Constitution of the United States. Whoever promises them receives immediate attention. There may be arguments about priorities but none about desirability. It is now necessary to add another promise of the Christian faith, namely, forgiveness.

A peculiar thing about forgiveness is that though the world needs it, the world does not want it. At least, the world does not ask for it. About the only recognition of forgiveness is to be found in the pardoning power. Full or conditional pardons, commutations of sentence, and general amnesties do imply that there exists a need for forgiveness of some people in some circumstances. But the pardoning power is thought of as exceptional, as something which most people do not need. Forgiveness is not mentioned in constitutional preambles, national bills of rights, public resolutions, and party manifestoes. On very rare occasions a great public figure may recognize and endorse it as did Abraham Lincoln in his second inaugural address, but the popular response is usually extremely disappointing. Vengeance, not forgiveness, is what popular clamor demands. It is not surprising, therefore, that the Christian promise of forgiveness goes unnoticed.

Forgiveness is central to the Christian faith. When Peter asked how often he should forgive his brother, Jesus replied: seventy times seven (which was the Hebrew symbol for infinity). A petition for forgiveness is included in the Lord's Prayer. Many of his parables dealt with the theme of forgiveness, and he constantly instructed his disciples to be forgiving. In the Sermon on the Mount Jesus told his disciples to love all men without regard to friendship or enmity, "That ye may be the children of your Father which is in heaven: for he maketh his sun to rise on the evil and on the good, and sendeth rain on the just and on the unjust." [16] Even when he was crucified, Jesus said: "Father, forgive them; for they know not what they do." [17]

Why did Jesus lay such stress on forgiveness? because he knew its therapeutic value, its power to heal and to restore. The case of the apostle Paul is a striking example of its efficacy. Paul had been a narrow-minded and fanatical Jew, who had persecuted the church and who was on just such a mission of persecution when he was converted. Jesus appeared to him on the road to Damascus, thus proving to Paul that the Christians had been right in saying that Christ was not dead but alive. And if Christ were alive, then he, Paul, had been terribly wrong: Christ was everything the Christians said he was. Worse still, Paul was terribly guilty, the man responsible for the martyrdom of noble people like Stephen. The past was irrevocable. His guilt was there, glaring and deadly. Paul deserved death and expected it. But instead of punishment and death Paul received forgiveness. He also received a new assignment in life: carrying the gospel to the Gentiles. The reconciliation thus effected by forgiveness brought gratitude, and gratitude begat love and faith. Paul was a new man. He moved from narrow nationalism to broad cosmopolitanism, from legalism to faith, from hate to love. Saul of Tarsus became the apostle Paul.

It was the same story with Peter, who had denied his Lord and been forgiven and thus transformed from the impulsive and unstable Simon to the rocklike Peter. It was the same with the quick-tempered John, who was changed into the great apostle of love and light. "We love him," he said out of his own experience, "because he first loved us." [18] It was not the same with Judas. Judas was good enough to realize the enormity of what he had done. He believed in the righteousness of God and contemplated his own unrighteousness: he could not bear the sight. Because no amount of repentance on his part could remove the guilt, he assumed that no one else could or would. And so he committed suicide. Forgiveness was available to him, but he did not believe it and could not accept it.

It is apparent from the experience of the apostles that the healing power of forgiveness is dependent on there being someone who is able and willing to carry the guilt of other people and to communicate his strength to others. Christian theology teaches that Christ is that person and that he demonstrated it by his death and resurrection. "All power is given unto me," said Jesus, "in heaven and in earth." [19] On another occasion he said: "In the world ye shall have tribulation: but be of good cheer; I have overcome the world." [20]

Far more than it realizes, the world lives by the truth that the unsound depend on the sound. It takes someone who is financially solvent to pay the debts of the insolvent and to save the reckless and the negligent from bankruptcy. It takes adults to make good for the misdeeds of children. It takes teachers who know, to correct the mistakes of pupils who do not. The ability to accept abuse without flinching or retaliating, to understand those who do not understand themselves, to accept blame which properly belongs to others, and to do work for which others receive credit is what keeps families, organizations, and nations together and makes life livable. Retaliation merely keeps evil moving in an endless chain reaction of woe, destruction, and death. Evil does not stop its fatal march until someone accepts it and keeps it, thus taking it out of circulation once and for all. Only one who is himself strong enough to do this and not be destroyed by it can render this indispensable service. Whoever renders this service is marching in the footsteps of the Master.

The world also lives by the positive side of forgiveness. We are all in debt to other people, so deeply in debt that there is no possibility of re-payment. The young student who goes to one of the leading graduate schools of his country cannot possibly pay for the learning of his profes-sors, which is the product of lifetimes of scholarly work; for the reputation of his graduate school, which was built over many years; or even for the economic cost of his education, much of which is paid for by private endowment or government subsidy or both. He cannot begin to pay for these blessings, and it would be a sign of immaturity to think that he could. Nevertheless, he will get a position on the strength of the reputation of his professors and of the institution which granted him his degree, and he will ride along to better positions with the same support. His per-formance in the field of research is dependent in considerable measure on the quality of the instruction he received. He may well be gifted with a brilliant mind and have worked long and hard, but his personal merit can never equal his indebtedness. He may and should be grateful, but he cannot repay.

What, then, can he do? He can give to others what he himself re-ceived. As he grows older, younger people will owe their intellectual awakening to his influence, and they will get positions on the strength of his recommendations. He will add luster to the institution which granted him his degree and to the one in which he works. If he does all this, he will be fulfilling a fundamental rule of Christian living: *to pass on the blessings he has not earned to others who do not deserve them either.* He will be initiating a new chain reaction whereby the grace of God moves and spreads in all directions to heal, reconcile, restore, and vivify. "Be ye therefore perfect," Jesus admonished his disciples, "even as your Father which is in heaven is perfect." [21] Blessings cannot be paid for by the one who receives them, but they can be *transmitted.*

Great as the promise of forgiveness is, secular-minded people have dif-ficulty accepting it. Secularists are usually cultural determinists. It so happens that there is much in American culture which is incompatible with forgiveness. We do not admire people who fail to demand their rights, and we call them "sissies." We look down on people who take the blame for someone else, and we call them "suckers." We think of the drama of human evil as a battle between heroes and villains in which the heroes always win out—and in the nick of time! Victory, not recon-ciliation, is the proper objective of the red-blooded American. It was this attitude which threw the American public into the terrific emotional binge which accompanied the dismissal and return of General MacArthur and which today gives so much impetus to the angry bitterness of the extreme right in matters of foreign policy.* The truth is that it is the Lone Ranger, not Jesus Christ, who symbolizes our concept of righteousness. One day a Sunday school teacher was narrating the story of the Crucifixion and trying to explain its meaning, but he was not getting any class participation whatsoever. Finally, in desperation, he exclaimed: "Won't somebody please say something?" It was then that one little boy volunteered the following comment: "Well, all I've got to say is that it wouldn't have happened if the Lone Ranger had been there." Could anything express more accurately a total failure to understand the meaning of the Cross?

Another element in American culture which blocks an understanding of forgiveness is the ideal of the self-made man. Innumerable success stories, especially of businessmen, have nurtured the idea that we are doing all right on our own and do not need divine grace. As some wit has put it: "No one worships his Maker more sincerely than the self-made man." Another wit put it this way: "This thing of divine grace has been greatly overrated." The insistence on being one's own savior distorts reality, causing businessmen to forget that they are indebted to the universities for the technology they use, to the United States government for the monetary system and for a nationwide market, to the school system for the quality of their labor force, to the law for their property rights, and to the police and the armed forces for the protection of their business. The effect is to interrupt the chain reaction of grace. "Freely ye have received," said Jesus to his disciples, "freely give." [22] Our trouble is that people are convinced they have not received freely but have earned all that they have, so why should they give freely? And so it comes about that another competitor, Horatio Alger this time, gets in our way. The Lone Ranger prevents one chain reaction from being stopped; Horatio Alger prevents the other chain reaction from being started; and we are deprived of the blessings of forgiveness.

It is obvious that the world stands in desperate need of forgiveness, but forgiveness implies that there is guilt, and many people refuse to acknowledge guilt. Psychiatrists have popularized the idea of guilt feelings to the point where we speak of such feelings quite freely and without embarrassment. We do not worry, however, about the kind of logic which supposes that there can be guilt feelings without guilt, because to do so would compel us to recognize that not all values are relative. Nevertheless, deep in our hearts we are dimly aware that not all is well within us. We are more willing to admit the existence and virulence of guilt when we

---

* It was the same attitude which caused the ancient Jews to prefer Barabbas to Jesus, for the Christ they expected and wanted was a national hero riding on a white charger (not a humble donkey) to chase the Romans out.

look beyond our own borders and consider the chain reaction exemplified in the tensions between black and white in Africa, Moslem and French *colon* in Algeria, Arab and Jew in the Near East. We saw it clearly in the brutal repression of Hungary by the Russians. In these distant and extreme situations we can see the logic of evil, the inexorable sequence of hate and fear and violence which in turn generates another and yet another sequence of hate and fear and violence, until the specter of annihilation stares us in the face. An evil spirit takes possession of people and distorts reason, prostitutes scientific integrity, falsifies history, besmirches reputations, corrupts morals, and debases religion. One is led to wonder if Jacques Maritain might not be right when he speaks of a Satanocracy. What is manifest in acute cases is latent in all cases. The apostle James diagnosed the situation thus: "From whence come wars and fightings among you? come they not hence, even of your lusts that war in your members? Ye lust, and have not: ye kill and desire to have, and cannot obtain: ye fight and war, yet ye have not, because ye ask not. Ye ask, and receive not, because ye ask amiss, that ye may consume it upon your lusts." [23]

With the acceptance of forgiveness comes one of the things which the world needs and wants most—peace. This peace is not appeasement or an armed truce or the mere absence of war. Its essence is reconciliation. "Peace I leave unto you," Jesus promised, "my peace I give unto you: not as the world giveth, I give unto you." [24] It is the "peace of God, which passeth all understanding," [25] of which Paul speaks. In the light of the present world crisis, could any promise be more attractive and important than forgiveness, which is the prerequisite to peace?

PERFORMANCE
AND THE CHRISTIAN FAITH

When confronted with the evidence, the secularist may concede that the Christian faith outpromises all the isms, philosophies, and religions. The concession, however, does not settle the matter. The problem of performance remains. He argues that the promises of Christianity are preposterous. Why get excited and waste time over something which cannot be fulfilled? He compares the promises of Christianity with the record of the Christian church stretching across twenty centuries, and he is not impressed. He finds that Christianity can promise but cannot deliver. He has a case to make.

The case against the church

The Christian church has not always shown a high regard for human life. The most glaring instance, of course, is war. In every country the church has usually blessed the armed forces of the nation and prayed for victory almost as a matter of course. The church has actually instigated some wars, e.g., the Crusades. It has supported wars which were obviously indefensible, even if one grants the validity of the distinction between just and unjust wars. Even Martin Niemoeller was willing to fight for Germany in World War II, in spite of the fact that a German victory would have meant the triumph of one of the most barbarous forms of racialism and despotism known to man. Martin Luther did not hesitate to urge the brutal and bloody repression of the peasants by the German princes. The Inquisition is a blot on the record of the Roman Catholics and has become a symbol of ecclesiastically sponsored murder. Calvinists have the burning of Servetus on their conscience.

The record in the matter of liberty is likewise spotty. At one time or another the church has fought and tried to suppress the findings of biology, geology, and astronomy. The Roman Catholic Church today maintains a list of books which its adherents are forbidden to read except by dispensation from a priest. The Puritans in colonial New England were certainly not tolerant and are still remembered for their witch-hunts. The fundamentalists of today still operate with a narrow orthodoxy and condemn in the harshest terms anyone who deviates from it. Religious, philosophical, and political dissent has been fought by the church again and again. In general there has been in every age a noteworthy timidity within the church concerning new ideas, a timidity which has more to do with fear of truth than dedication to it. History also records that the methods used or supported by the church in stifling liberty have included libel and slander, misrepresentation, censorship, boycott, banishment, imprisonment, torture, and capital punishment. On the other hand, a great deal of the intellectual progress of mankind has come from people who were not Christians or who, when they were Christians, did not derive their inspiration and encouragement from Christianity. The Renaissance, for example, was not a Christian movement, and neither was the Enlightenment. In the same way, the movement for political liberty was often led and won by secularists (*libre pensadores,* as the Latin Americans call them) against the opposition of the church.

It would be disingenuous to contend that the church has always brought happiness to the people inside and outside of it. In too many cases it has brought anxiety, insecurity, and misery. The church has quite rightly fought hedonism but has unfortunately failed to substitute for it the higher Christian conception. Because happiness is a by-product and not "the chief end of man" as Aristotle thought, the church often allowed itself to espouse the notion that it does not matter whether people are happy or not—especially since so much of Christian living was somber and joyless. This meant that people turned to other institutions in their search for happiness, often to their own great loss. In some circles it almost seems sinful to be happy.

On the score of community, too, the church has at many points failed to deliver. The church is embodied in institutions. It is a legal entity with the right to sue and be sued in the civil courts. It owns lands, buildings, schools, and hospitals. It is an employer with a paid professional staff. It publishes magazines, newspapers, and bulletins. It is *organized,* with all that this implies by way of constitutions, officers, official records, membership requirements, rules of discipline, budgets, and programs. Some institutionalization is inevitable if the church is to carry out its functions of public worship, instruction, preaching, counseling, and evangelism.

One result of institutionalization is that the church is deeply enmeshed in the world and strongly influenced by it. The Christian community or church is one, but its institutions are many. The church is fragmented along national lines, so that national diversity interferes with Christian unity. It is also fragmented along denominational lines in response to differences in matters of doctrine, liturgy, and polity. It tends to be culture-bound, so that when missionaries go out to Asia and Africa they are looked upon with suspicion or hostility as propagating Western culture, imperialism, and colonialism rather than the Gospel. It acquires a class orientation, as did Roman Catholicism with feudalism and Protestantism with capitalism. The result of class orientation has been to alienate the working class from Christianity. The church has also become identified with political regimes, e.g., the identification of the Russian Orthodox Church with the czarist regime and the long alienation of the Roman Catholic Church from the French Republic. There are American Christians who want to make of the church a front organization for free private enterprise and European Christians who want to make it a front for socialist movements. The entanglement of the church is so deep as to appear ineradicable and constitutes the basis of the charge that the church conforms rather than transforms and that the Christian promise of community is lost in a welter of man-made divisions.

The historical record in the matter of forgiveness is also spotty, as is true of the other promises of Christianity. The church has engaged in feuds (e.g., Roman Catholics and Protestants, fundamentalists and liberals, Christians and Jews), which have left wounds that were slow to heal and scars that remain visible and ugly. It has not stopped the chain reaction of evil, because it refused to accept blame for anything, no matter whose it was. It has also failed to initiate the chain reaction of grace, because hardness of heart and narrowness of sympathies have choked off the power of love and because pride has prevented the church from identifying itself with sinners, thereby making its message unacceptable because its bearers were themselves unacceptable. The church has given the impression that indignation rather than compassion characterized its attitude toward sinners. This is probably one of the reasons, though assuredly not the only reason, why so many people who are in trouble prefer to go to a psychiatrist. They feel that a minister would condemn them or, at least, would be shocked. On the other hand, they feel that the psychiatrist is shockproof and will not be indignant but understanding and helpful.

When we consider the Christian church as the agency through which modern man can find the solution to the desperate crisis in which he is caught, there are two disagreeable facts which must be taken into account. The first of these is that the church has lost ground in the Christian West. The situation in Europe is symbolized by the empty church. Church attendance is at a very low point and indicates that people are looking to other institutions for guidance and meaning. It is not so much that the Christian message is rejected but rather that it cannot even get a hearing. People will not come to worship, to read, to study, to listen, or even to argue. They just do not come. In the United States the situation looks more favorable—on the surface. Church membership and attendance are at an all-time high. Religious books are among the best sellers. To study and discuss the Christian faith is once more intellectually respectable in the universities. Cultured people are expected to know something about theologians like Barth, Brunner, Tillich, Bultmann, and the Niebuhrs. Church buildings are multiplying and church budgets are swelling. Unfortunately, much of this revival is not healthy from a Christian point of view. A good deal of church membership, as Will Herberg and Vance Packard remind us, is a form of status-seeking. Many Christians are only nominally such. They know little about the Christian faith, and their commitment to it is superficial. Interest in religious books often is an indication of searching, not an expression of a faith seeking deeper content and fuller meaning. Facts such as these have led some observers to characterize our contemporary world as a post-Christian world.

The second fact that must be reckoned with is the emergence of the non-Christian and non-Western peoples as organized, self-conscious, and growing forces. This emergence is accompanied by a revival of non-Christian religions like Islam and Buddhism, except where communism has taken over as in China. The result is that the Christian faith is once more in a minority position now that the world is no longer synonymous with the West. The most common way to express this is to say that we live in a pluralist world. The conclusion is drawn that the church should give up the Great Commission to preach the gospel to all nations unto the uttermost parts of the earth and be satisfied with coexistence. Missionary activity is described as futile because it cannot shake Red China loose from communism or the Near East from Islam, and as wrong because it violates religious liberty whereby all peoples have the right to worship as they please or not to worship at all. That so many church-affiliated people should take this position is a sad commentary on the low ebb to which the church has fallen, for it means an outright rejection of Christ's command to evangelize the world, a disbelief in the power of the Gospel, and a libertarian attitude toward truth which is either atheistic or polytheistic. The position is one of sheer defeatism. Can the world be saved by defeatists?

The case for the church

The case against Christianity is true as far as it goes, but it is not the whole truth. There is another side to the record of the church. The Christian concept of the sacredness of human life has had a growing impact on the world. It has become externalized in the many protections which constitutional law bestows on persons accused of crimes, in attempts by international law to spare noncombatants and civilians from the ravages of war, in public health programs, in legislation to prevent accidents and to promote safety, in public and private standards regulating the practice of medicine. Christian motivation has been very strong and often decisive in all these cases.

The Christian concept of liberty has also become externalized over the ages. The Christian church was born in a world in which human slavery was an accepted thing and in which immediate emancipation was impossible. But the Christian church abolished it first as a spiritual fact within the confines of its own community. The apostle Paul asserted that the church knows only freemen in Christ and demonstrated in the case of Onesimus how Christian brotherhood makes legal emancipation flow from inner liberation. Augustine and Aquinas both denied that slavery was natural or part of God's purpose in creating man. Christian ferment eventually led to the legal abolition of slavery throughout the civilized world. It also led to the emancipation of women from the many restrictions and disabilities once imposed by law and custom to the present full recognition of their civil and political rights as persons. The Christian church also preserved the liberty of the mind of man, in spite of the exceptions and deviations already noted. The Roman Catholic Church preserved the Greco-Roman culture as well the heritage of Christian thought in its monasteries and founded all the older universities of Europe. Protestantism promoted education everywhere and founded all the oldest institutions of higher learning in the United States. Civil liberty and the bills of rights and constitutional procedures which sustain it all grew out of the Reformation. Freedom of worship was the source from which political, economic, social, and intellectual freedoms sprang and spread. Freedom under God historically preceded freedom under law.

The record of the Christian church with regard to happiness is more difficult to appraise because happiness is primarily an inward phenomenon. Much of happiness remains unexpressed because it is so intensely personal in nature, and for the same reason, what little is expressed follows no set pattern. You cannot institutionalize happiness. Nevertheless, it is common knowledge that the Christian faith has in all ages brought consolation to the bereaved, courage to the disheartened and the disillusioned, and strength to the weak and the sick. It has dispelled fear and rekindled hope. Physical affliction, which can sentence a man to bitterness and cause him to take that bitterness out on other people, has been transformed into a source of strength and growth. A typical instance of this power is the reaction of John Milton to his blindness:

There is, as the apostle has remarked, a way to strength through weakness. Let me then be the most feeble creature alive, as long as that feebleness serves to invigorate the energies of my rational and immortal spirit; as long as in that obscurity, in which I am enveloped, the light of the divine presence more clearly shines; then, in proportion as I am weak, I shall be invincibly strong; and in proportion as I am blind, I shall more clearly see. O! that I may thus be perfected by feebleness, and irradiated by obscurity! [26]

As Augustine says: "So material a difference does it make, not what ills are suffered, but what kind of man suffers them." [27] In the nature of the case, statistical evidence for happiness is unobtainable and always will be, but the stream of witnesses who can testify out of their own personal experience as to the power of the Christian faith to bring happiness is as wide as the world and as long as Christian history.

As has been pointed out, the fragmentation of the Christian community cannot be denied. Sectarian spirit, religious prejudices, and institutional interests have marred the Christian community. However, they have not destroyed it. The unity of the church has never ceased to shine through the diversity of the churches. We often fail to recognize it because we too easily identify community with organization, and unity with uniformity. The multiplicity of denominations may well be part of God's purpose to prevent the subordination of community to institution, the substitution of organizational interests for community purposes, and the identification of the church universal and invisible with a particular and visible church. The multiplicity of denominations forms a defense against the human tendency to try to imprison the Holy Spirit in fixed man-made structures, and it facilitates the full and free expression of worship in ways that are appropriate and meaningful to different types of people.

Those who think of the ecumenical movement as a succession of church mergers overlook the dangers of organization and try to do the very thing which Christ refrained from doing. Christ did not leave us an organization with officers, job descriptions, and organization charts. He left these matters flexible so that one group's manner of witnessing should not become an impediment to another group's. He knew the temptations of hierarchy and warned his disciples against it: "Ye know that they which are accounted to rule over the Gentiles exercise lordship over them; and their great ones exercise authority upon them. But so shall it not be among you: but whosoever will be great among you, shall be your minister: And whosoever of you will be the chiefest, shall be servant of all." [28] The Reformation was, among other things, a protest against the ecclesiasticism of the Roman Catholic Church. Surely, a Protestant Church of America would be a very un-Protestant thing, and bureaucratic imperialism being what it is, might well become increasingly non-Christian. This is not to say that existing denominations are sacrosanct and should under no circumstances be discontinued or combined. Small organizations are not necessarily better or more Christian than big ones. The error comes in the assumption that mergers are good per se and in the presumptuous claim that the Holy Spirit is always on the side of bigness.

Another frequently encountered misconception is found among those who think of the ecumenical movement in nondenominational, undenominational, or even antidenominational terms. They make the mistake of denying the richness of the Christian content of denominational heritage. They brush aside this heritage as unimportant and dismiss those who cherish it as vestigial remnants of a dead past completely irrelevant to modern life. They erroneously suppose that we have to be the same in order to be one. If we were all the same, what would we have to contribute to someone else that he does not have already? Political unity is frequently obtained by the elimination or the concealment of differences, and the result is likely to be an insipid, amorphous, and ambiguous amalgam of platitudes. Christian unity is attained by identification, and to identify is to particularize. Was Jesus less of a man because he was a Jew or less divine because of the Incarnation? It is not differences per se which divide men but the way in which one looks at them and the uses to which they are put. Only he who has a heritage and is loyal to it can understand how someone else feels about his heritage, and that understanding is a bond between them. Christian community is built on mutual respect.

It follows from this discussion that the fragmentation of the church is a denial of community only to the extent to which the fragments are animated by hatred, prejudice, and narrowness of sympathy and understanding. To some extent, therefore, fragmentation is also the foundation of community. Furthermore, at no time has the concept of the Christian community as the fellowship of all believers in Christ been completely obscured. There has always been a common core of Christian doctrine based on the Scriptures and expressed in the great creeds of the church like the Nicene Creed. In all churches there have been a deep love of Christ and an enduring belief in his divinity. All churches celebrate Holy Communion and baptize their members, however different some interpretations of these sacraments may be. All churches know the meaning of prayer, worship, and forgiveness.

These common elements have always been present, and Christians have been aware of them, albeit sometimes dimly and reluctantly. Even John Calvin, who was certainly not partial to Roman Catholics, did not deny that there are fellow Christians among them.[29] On the other hand, Roman Catholics have interpreted their claim of being the one and only true church in such a way as to admit that Protestants can be Christians too. The admission is grudging, hedged in, and a bit ungracious since it is based on the supposition that Protestants do not know any better, but the admission is there nonetheless. Through all differences of belief, practice, mode of worship, and organization, there has always been a Christian community. When confronted with genuinely Christian convictions held in a Christ-like spirit and manifested in authentically Christian virtues, Christians experience a strong sense of kinship, which transcends their peculiarities as Presbyterians, Baptists, Methodists, Roman Catholics, Lutherans, and Episcopalians. This strong sense of kinship also pierces through the barriers of language, nationality, race, and culture.

It is one of the great merits of the ecumenical movement that it is fostering and emphasizing this strong sense of kinship and the common Christian elements which lie at the heart of that kinship. Moreover, the ecumenical movement is rendering this invaluable service not by denying or ignoring differences in the household of faith but by teaching Christians of all communions to take a new look at their differences in order to see what each can contribute to all. Finally, the ecumenical movement is creating new conciliar structures, such as the National Council and the World Council, which can express the Christian community without smothering or supplanting it.

The record of the church with regard to the promise of forgiveness is difficult to appraise because forgiveness, like happiness, is an inward spiritual reality. A reality of this kind, not being an empirical category, cannot be measured. However, it is translated into empirical realities which can be observed, if not always measured. The best way to understand the record of the church in this matter of forgiveness is to examine it in the context of a particular problem. For our particular problem, let us choose the agonizing issue of racial segregation in the South. The selection is especially appropriate because segregation is such an emotionally laden and politically explosive issue that any contribution of the church to its solution should command immediate respect, all the more so since so many people believe that the record of the church in this field is practically nil.

In the first place, let us note that the Christian doctrine of man is responsible for the movement against segregation. Man was created in the image of God, and as the Presbyterian Catechism puts it, his destiny is to glorify God and enjoy him forever. The brotherhood of man is rooted in this common origin and destiny. The limitations under which man lives, such as the finiteness of his mind and the propensity of his heart toward evil, are human, not racial, limitations. Whether or not there are racial differences with regard to capacity for cultural achievement, government, and social organization in no way affects the right of human personality to fulfill its destiny or to command the respect of the state. The parable of the talents applies to races quite as much as to individuals. Whatever their native gifts may be, it is God's purpose that they be not buried but multiplied. Centuries of Christian teaching have imbued American life with the sacredness of human personality regardless of race, color, class, sex, age, or culture. Widespread guilt feelings, uneasy consciences, and hypersensitiveness on racial matters all testify to the effectiveness of Christian teaching. The eighteenth-century Deists who spoke of the natural rights of man and the twentieth-century liberals who denounce discrimination have generally been unwilling to acknowledge the source of their concern, but they are nonetheless indebted to the Christian faith for that concern.

To a considerable extent, the Christian doctrine of man is embodied in the Constitution of the United States, particularly the Bill of Rights. The very phrasing of several of the key provisions in the Bill of Rights indicates clearly that no *person* shall be deprived of life, liberty, or property without due process of law; be denied the equal protection of the law; or be prosecuted on account of his faith, thoughts, or writings. It makes no difference whether he is a citizen or an alien, a resident or a transient. It makes no difference what his race, color, sex, creed, or political affiliations may be. It makes no difference whether that person believes in these rights insofar as his enjoyment of them is concerned or whether he would deny them to others if he were in a position of power. Like the Father Almighty who "maketh his sun to rise on the evil and on the good, and sendeth his rain on the just and on the unjust," so the Constitution of the United States bestows civil rights on all who happen to be under its jurisdiction and affirms the principle that the power of government, which belongs to all, shall be impartially exercised for the benefit of all, and shall not be used by one group to victimize any other group. What the Constitution really does in the realm of Christian ethics is to set up a legal standard which encourages the good, restrains the evil, and enlightens the ignorant and the doubtful. It throws the power of government and the prestige of the American way of life on the side of those who want to put into practice the Christian principles of conduct in race relations and other human relationships.

The logic of these Christian and constitutional principles clearly points to the correctness of recent Supreme Court decisions in the matter of racial segregation. State-imposed segregation on the basis of race is un-Christian, unconstitutional, and un-American. This is a good principle, but it does not of itself solve the crisis which engulfs us. No principle ever does. Like the law which the apostle Paul once tried so hard to live by, constitutional principles can do no more than convict us of guilt. They do not give us the insight to understand how God's will can be translated into living practice nor the power to overcome the inner and external fetters which hold us in subjection. Christians are saved and regenerated by faith in Christ, not by a Pharisaic adherence to even Christian principles. There is a sense in which it can be said that there are no Christian principles at all, i.e., if principles are treated as idols for which human life, happiness, and well-being are sacrificed. Paraphrasing what Christ said of the Sabbath, we may say that principles were made for people and not people for principles.

The rationalist conception of principle lies at the root of both extreme positions. The extreme segregationist and the extreme integrationist are alike in their willingness to pay a horrendous price in human lives, property, rights, and suffering. The preservation of the Union, the integrity of our constitutional rights, the continuation of public education, the reputation of the United States abroad, the peace and harmony of the church, the maintenance of law and order, and the continued existence of good relations among neighbors and friends are all at stake. Both sides are willing to sacrifice these things—one for the principle of segregation, the other for the principle of integration. The principles are different, but the result is the same. How far the extreme segregationists are willing to go is only too evident because they are more directly and immediately involved, but there is no moral difference between them and the extreme integrationists insofar as the consequences are concerned. It was only a few years ago that an eminent Northern Presbyterian clergyman publicly stated that he looked forward to the use of tanks and guns in our Southern states to enforce integration.

At this point someone is sure to observe: "Even if the results are the same, you will have to admit that one side is right, namely, the one which fights for Christian principles in race relations." This observation reminds one of the story of a victim of an automobile accident whose dying words were: "At least I had the right of way." In such situations, being right becomes irrelevant, and we have to decide whether we want to save people or to vindicate principles. That is not to say that Christians favor *un*principled behavior but rather that they insist that principles not be treated as ends in themselves, that principles not be pushed to such lengths that we suddenly find ourselves compelled by circumstances to argue that the end justifies the means.

It is true, of course, that the Cross is part of the Christian faith. There can be no denying that Jesus knew that preaching the gospel would bring persecution to his disciples, that his demands would disrupt families and friendships, that his followers would have to be ready to sacrifice property, position, and even life itself. Jesus foresaw these consequences and did not shrink from them either for himself or his disciples. Certainly the life and martyrdom of apostles like Peter and Paul clearly show that they had understood what their Lord meant and paid the expected price.

Let us not conclude from this that Christ was a thoughtless hero, who rushed into situations heedless of consequences. He was a full grown man before he announced his ministry and was slow in declaring publicly that he was the Messiah. He did eventually go to the Cross, but not until the time had come for him to do so. On one occasion when he was about to be thrown from the top of a hill by an angry mob, he did not let the situation turn into a showdown and "passing through the midst of them went his way." [30] At the same time that he sent his disciples out for the first time and warned them of persecution, he also instructed them to be "wise as serpents and harmless as doves." [31] He called the peacemakers blessed. When he assured John the Baptist of the authenticity of his own mission, Jesus did not do it in terms of principles but of consequences: "The blind receive their sight, and the lame walk, the lepers are cleansed, and the deaf hear, the dead are raised up, and the poor have the gospel preached to them." [32] Jesus also showed a very fine discriminating evaluation of people when he spoke to them, telling them what they could understand or needed to hear. To Herod he spoke not one word, but to Nicodemus he spoke fully and at length. He several times denounced the Pharisees to their face in very forceful language, but there is no record of his having criticized the Romans, who were certainly not beyond criticism. He had a keen sense of timing: "I have yet many things to say unto you," he said to his disciples, "but ye cannot bear them now." [33] All these and other examples conclusively prove that Christ had in the highest degree that quality which he commended to his disciples—wisdom.

Now wisdom is a very complex and delicate quality. It includes but transcends knowledge; it calls for that degree of identification with people and situations which leads to understanding; and it involves a careful weighing of consequences. Furthermore, it requires very skillful timing: when to push ahead, when to retreat, when to stand still. Under certain circumstances it means escape as when Paul was let out in a basket over the city wall, and under other circumstances it means climbing Mount Golgotha. Its essence is effectiveness. But this effectiveness has nothing to do with the pragmatism which consists in the piecemeal accomplishment of short-range and unrelated objectives devoid of any general frame of reference. It is judged in the light of principles which are no longer idols but points of reference, and it is guided by the Holy Spirit, who is resourceful and creative and whom we recognize because we know Jesus Christ.

When this kind of wisdom is applied to the problem of race relations, it becomes immediately apparent that segregation is not the simple matter that extremists assume. Segregation is not wrong per se. We segregate criminals from society. We sometimes segregate our children for the sake of domestic peace. Marriage itself is a kind of segregation. The constitutional freedom of association is tantamount to a governmental endorsement of voluntary segregation. Civil service segregates those who are qualified for government positions from those who are not. Segregation becomes morally wrong when it is injurious to a person or group and constitutionally wrong when the injury is inflicted or supported by state authority. Whether or not segregation is injurious depends on facts, and facts can change. Thus, it would not necessarily be wrong to segregate the schools on the basis of sex (as was once the general custom). However, if this means that women would receive an inferior education or that there was a stigma attached to such education, damage would be done. The same comment could be made about school segregation on the basis of intelligence. The Supreme Court was right in its decision in the school cases because it is a fact that racial segregation seriously injures Negro children. Racial segregation carries with it a stigma of inferiority, which runs deeper than any possible inequality of physical facilities and involves the refusal to accept the Negro as a brother and fellow citizen.

The Southern Christian cannot solve his problem by running away to places in the North where segregation is not an issue and thus leave the South to the extremists. Though we are not of the world, we are in it by Christ's own command. As Calvin would put it, our vocation is to remain in the South where God has placed us and to look upon our predicament as a post to which the Lord has assigned us. The purpose of the assignment is redemptive. We must be like the salt of the earth of which Christ spoke. As salt brings out the flavor of the foods in which it is dissolved and cannot itself be tasted, so we Southern Christians must be dissolved in Southern society and bring out the best, not the worst, that is in every element of that society. It is not our function to be briny, i.e., to be garish and noisy crusaders who defeat the purpose to which they are supposedly committed. We must let our light shine before men, not that we might bask in publicity and draw upon ourselves the cheers of uninvolved people in faraway places, but that we might shed light where it is most needed and quietly bring about solid and enduring results pleasing in the sight of God.

The objective of the Christian in situations like the one in which we are caught up is not victory but reconciliation. Many critics look upon reconciliation as an escape, but is it really? To think so is to deny one of the central themes of Christianity, which stresses the reconciliation of man to God through Jesus Christ and of man to other men; which insists that reconciliation to one's brother is prerequisite to acceptable worship of God; which equates service to the least of our brethren without regard to merit as service to Christ himself.

How is reconciliation achieved? certainly not by playing the part of

Jonah, who sat on the hillside and nearly died of sunstroke while waiting for Niniveh to be consumed by fire and brimstone. We must recognize
that both segregationists and integrationists can be good Christians. That
all of them have faults is obvious. It was never part of the Christian faith,
however, to assert that Christians are perfect people. If it were, it would
be unthinkable that Paul should speak of the saints who were at Corinth
or Ephesus. Many Southern segregationists are good Christians in the
sense that their faith in Christ is strong and deep, that their dedication to
the church is beyond question, that their private lives breathe the spirit
of Christ and is an inspiration to others. Sometimes they are better Christians than those who attack them. It is not irrelevant that they are wrong
on the race problem, but who among us is not wrong about something,
usually many and important things? Reconciliation is not to be had by
denying what is right and noble in Southern Christians who are segregationists. Neither are Southern moderates encouraged by criticisms which
minimize or ignore their achievements and take no account of the magnitude of their difficulties.

The problem of racial segregation, like all moral problems, is inherently spiritual. External measures may help, but their greatest weakness is that they are not definitive. Freedom riders may succeed in forcing
a white man to sit next to a Negro in a bus, but this does not mean that the
Negro is accepted. Federal court orders may compel white and Negro
children to attend the same school, but this does not mean that the Negro
children are wanted or welcome. Sit-in demonstrations conducted in an
orderly, dignified, and peaceful manner may result in opening restaurants
to Negroes, but they will not cause the whites to open their hearts to
these Negroes or even appreciate the restraint of Negro leadership.

External compliance is a shoddy substitute for real acceptance on the
level of the spirit, an unstable truce which is subject to the ever shifting
play of forces and pressures. At its best, it is a preparation and prelude
for a deeper compliance based on love and appreciation. At its worst, it
is a source of resentment and frustration, which can erupt into violence
and irreparable damage. Christ saw this clearly on the religious level when
he castigated the Pharisees for an external compliance which was the
basis of a monstrous hypocrisy among them and of bitter hate among their
critics. He said that man is not defiled by what happens to him but by
what proceeds from him. Rousseau saw this same truth on the political
level when he stressed that nothing worth-while is achieved unless strength
is transformed into right and obedience into duty.

It is this transformation on the level of the spirit which the Christian
seeks to effectuate. Once this is understood, it becomes possible to evalu-
ate the achievements of the church in the agonizing field of race relations.
The one great hope and common denominator in the situation is that
Christianity is so strong in the South. It pervades white segregationists,

moderates, and integrationists. Nor should we forget that it pervades the Southern Negroes too. Southern Negroes have shown a truly remarkable capacity for patience, self-restraint, and moderation whose source is obviously Christian in both their leadership and their rank and file. Even when challenging state law, they have been nonviolent and orderly, frequently singing hymns, and usually led by their ministers. We take this Christian behavior on their part quite for granted, and very wrongly. It is one of the truly remarkable aspects of the segregation crisis. Where would we be if these Negroes had been inspired by communist or fascist principles? The truth is that the Christian citizenry of the South, both white and colored, carries within itself the seeds of its own redemption.

In spite of many compromises and much lack of courage and ingenuity on the part of the church, the fact remains that practically all local support for racial justice in the South has been church-inspired. Ministerial associations in cities like Richmond, Atlanta, and Baton Rouge have issued public statements whose effectiveness can in part be gauged by the reactions of the extreme segregationists. When Southern legislatures pass segregation bills, the Christian ministers are almost wholly alone in appearing to testify against them. For every public statement on behalf of public schools, law and order, and racial justice, there are innumerable quiet endeavors within the church to restrain, to persuade, and to convince.

The Christian citizenry of the South is affirming Christian principles through its churches and thus patiently building that backlog of Christian convictions and attitudes which is indispensable to reconciliation. For example, the General Assembly of the Presbyterian Church in the United States (Southern Presbyterian Church) has solemnly declared on three different occasions that segregation should not be practiced in its churches, colleges, and seminaries. These declarations do not have the force of law, but they do have great moral force because they come from people whose Christian commitment, understanding, and spiritual stature have raised them to the highest court of their denomination. The weight of this moral force is all the greater because the Southern church is still separate from the national body (the United Presbyterian Church in the United States of America); hence no one can say that "the Yankees" imposed their convictions on us.

Desegregation is already a fact in the Southern Presbyterian Church at the assembly and synod levels, and in some presbyteries (e.g., the Presbytery of New Orleans). What this means is that real desegregation has been accomplished where the Christian faith was strongest. The same developments are taking place in other denominations in the South. Thus it has come to pass that at the very time when racial tensions are exacerbated, the Southern churches provide the only regular channels and influential points of contact, conversation, and communication between the races. It is only in these Christian communities that one finds white and black, segregationist and integrationist, extremist and moderate, Northerner and Southerner still on speaking terms, capable of accepting one another as brothers in spite of disagreements over principles and tactics. Upon the spread of this fellowship of reconciliation from the highest church levels to the lowest congregational level depends the eventual solution of the racial conflict.

It would be easy to dwell on the failures of the Southern churches, for these are obvious to everybody. Among these failures are church members who find scriptural bases for racial segregation, hate all "Yankees" and persecute Southern moderates, and denounce the federal government in terms that border on sedition. In the churches there are moderates who are silent on occasions when speaking out would be an effective witness, who harbor a deep resentment against the federal courts, who fail to defend their minister when he takes a stand for integration, open schools, or respect for federal law. The wonder is that there are successes, and the significant point is that success varies in direct proportion to the degree of Christian commitment in the churches. None of these successes means that support from the outside or from the federal government is not highly desirable. But support implies that there are local forces to be supported, and it is the church which is generating these local forces. What is important for us here is that *where the Christian faith thrives, the promises of Christianity are fulfilled.*

TOWARD A NEW REFORMATION

A survey of the case for and against Christianity in the matter of performance shows both fulfillment and nonfulfillment—or, if one prefers, partial fulfillment—of the promises of the Christian faith. There is enough in the record to give encouragement and to make outright dismissal of the Christian promises unwarranted. But is the record sufficiently encouraging to justify the hope that the Christian faith can succeed where the natural and social sciences have failed, and to do so in time to save us from disaster? The answer must be in the negative if it is based on the historical record alone. The depravity of human nature is too profound and the engines of destruction devised by human intelligence are too powerful to support any but pessimistic conclusions. But the answer must be in the affirmative if it is based on the goodness, omniscience, and omnipotence of God. On this basis a Christian can be optimistic about the outcome. The reason is not that the Christian is optimistic about man but rather that he is optimistic about what God can do through man. The historical record does show that Christianity has fulfilled its promises where the Christian faith was tried, and has failed where that faith was not tried or was too diluted with extraneous elements. What modern man needs, therefore, is a Christian faith that is deeper and purer in a "post-Christian" world and much more widely shared in a religiously pluralistic world. If we are to meet this challenge, we must eschew the lack of discernment which King Louis XVI is said to have revealed in his own troubled times. When the King heard a commotion outside the palace and asked: "What is this, a revolt?" one of his attendants answered: "No, your majesty. It is a revolution." This answer points to the kind of discernment which the magnitude of the crisis of our time calls for. Reform is no longer adequate—if it ever was. The proper word is Reformation. Nothing less will do.

What would a new Reformation entail? Can it come about spontaneously and automatically as a by-product of the preaching of evangelists like Billy Graham? It hardly seems likely. The reason is not that Billy Graham's preaching is false: on the contrary, it is true and also indispensable. Without a personal encounter with Christ and a personal commitment to Christ, nothing Christian can be accomplished except for occasional coincidences and congruences which cannot be relied upon. There can be no substitute for personal evangelism. Our problem is that personal evangelism is not enough, or better still, that it is too narrowly conceived. There must be a larger message which takes into consideration the social, economic, and political concerns of living men. We must recognize that people can be reached through their associations, that the Holy Spirit shines through institutions to men as well as from personal experience to institutions. To meet this challenge for a larger message, a huge intellectual effort is required so that the relevance of the promises of the Christian faith to the issues over which men are agonizing can be made apparent, instructive, and directive.

Can this challenge be met without hopelessly compromising the gospel? The issue raised here is often presented in the form of an antithesis: evangelization *versus* Christianization. In 1959 Philippe Maury, a French Protestant and the General Secretary of the World Christian Movement, wrestled with the issue in his book *Politics and Evangelism*.[34] In general, Maury's position is that evangelization is mandatory but that Christianization is impossible and should not be undertaken. "In trying to Christianize the world," he says, "the church only secularizes itself, dechristianizes itself, loses the sense of its mission, ceases to evangelize." [35] What he means by "Christianizing" is the attempt to reformulate political thought and reconstruct political institutions so as to bring them into line with the Christian faith and make them embodiments of the Holy Spirit. He condemns this attempt as "syncretism," i.e., importing concepts alien to Christianity and sanctifying them. "History has shown," he argues, "that whenever the church abandons itself to this Christianizing of human institutions and cultures, it becomes their prisoner." [36]

Maury's pessimism is widely shared by contemporary Protestant theologians. Paul Tillich, for example, carries it much further by questioning the particularization of the Christian faith itself: "And every faith has a concrete element in itself. It is concerned about something or somebody. But this something or this somebody may prove not to be ultimate at all. Then faith is a failure in its concrete expression, although it is not a failure in the experience of the unconditional itself. A god disappears; divinity remains. Faith risks the vanishing of the concrete god in whom it believes." [37] To be even more specific: "Many Christians, many among us, cannot find a way of joining honestly with those who pray to Jesus Christ. Something in us is reluctant, something which is genuine and valid, the fear of becoming idolatrous, the fear of being split in our ultimate loyalty, the fear of looking at two faces instead of at the one divine face." [38] If Tillich can be this pessimistic about theology, he can scarcely be less so about efforts to incorporate the mind and spirit of Christ into political institutions. "The judgment applies to the political creeds," he warns us, "whether they glorify a past tradition or a coming utopia, whether they believe in revolution or reaction or progress. The old traditions have disintegrated; created continuous mass disappointments. The judgment applies to the nationalistic ideologies whose demonic implications have become more and more visible, and it applies to the cosmopolitan superstructure which is envisaged either by pacifistic idealism or by imperialistic will to power." [39]

An analogous, though not quite so deep, pessimism concerning politics appears in the thought of Karl Barth. "The civil community as such," he warns, "is spiritually blind and ignorant. It has neither faith nor love nor hope. It has no creed and no gospel. Prayer is not part of its life, and its members are not brothers and sisters." [40] The spiritual impotence of the state is matched by the political impotence of the church: "It is not in a position to establish one particular doctrine as *the* Christian doctrine of the just State. It is also not in a position to refer to any past realization of the perfect State or to hold out any prospect of one in the future. There is but one Body of Christ, born of the Word of God, which is heard in faith. There is therefore no such thing as a Christian State corresponding to the Christian Church; there is no duplicate of the Church in the political sphere." [41] Barth somewhat modifies the severity of his position by conceding that "the State is not a product of sin but one of the constants of the divine Providence and government of the world in its action against human sin: it is therefore an instrument of divine grace." [42] This is still, of course, a negative way of looking at the state. The nearest he comes to a positive attitude is his statement "that the Christian line that follows from the gospel betrays a striking tendency to the side of what is generally called the 'democratic' State." [43] But the statement is immediately hedged in by the reservation that democracy "is certainly not necessarily the form of the State closest to the Christian view. Such a State may equally well assume the form of a monarchy or an aristocracy, and occasionally even that of a dictatorship." [44]

The Barthian position is, or comes very close to being, that the church must always say a loud emphatic "no" whenever the state is judged in the light of the Holy Spirit. Barth's refusal to take sides between the East and the West is based on the belief that both are so deeply and equally compromised with evil that it would be misleading to favor either side. He says "no" to both of them. He did take sides against the Nazis. Even in this case, let it be noted, the answer was still "no," and the very qualified endorsement of democracy which he made at that time was hardly more than a passing by-product of his anti-Nazism. Many fundamentalists, especially the dispensationalist faction, take the same position and hold that the world is completely bad, that politics is the devil's game, that all attempts at reform are foredoomed, and that all we can do is to await the Second Coming of Christ.

The pessimism of contemporary Protestant thought concerning Christianization is to some extent the result of the influence of existentialism. To an even greater extent it is the product of profound disillusionment over the fruits of the ideologies. So many movements which once seemed so promising have turned out to be shallow, short-lived, barren, or evil in spite of all the time, money, thought, energy, and even blood that were expended to support them. The reaction therefore is wholly natural, but we must remember that the natural is not the standard of Christian life and thought. Protestant thought errs grievously when it departs from the original standard which gave it birth—the authority of Holy Scripture.

In the light of that standard, Paul Tillich's position is defective. To recognize the tendency of the human mind to idolatry is salutary and needed, but to fear idolatry to the point of being unable to pray to Jesus Christ lest one see two faces instead of one is quite another matter. The apostles had a remedy for this ailment when John pointed out that "perfect love casteth out fear" [45] and when Paul warned us that "whatsoever is not of faith is sin." [46] Nor is Tillich to be confuted solely on the basis of a few isolated biblical passages, however trenchantly appropriate. The whole weight of the Christian message is against him. "The Unconditioned" did become "concrete and conditioned" (in Tillich language), i.e., God was incarnate in Jesus Christ (in Christian language). The Christian faith is not so transcendental and otherworldly that it cannot unscramble enough of the ambiguities of politics to guide us in our political thinking and decisions. To deny the ambiguities of politics would be to lack Christian realism, but to surrender to these ambiguities would be to lack faith in the intelligibility of Scripture and in the power of the Holy Spirit. What sense would it make for God to reveal himself to us if we cannot use that revelation? What good would it do for the Bible to be the word of God if that word cannot be heard and understood by man? Transcendence requires immanence not because of man's need, great as it is, but because of God's will, which is irresistible. Human eyesight is weak and faulty, but the divine light is strong and luminous.

The same fear of idolatry troubles Maury, though in his case it does not corrode the essentials of the Christian faith. It does, however, affect the applicability of the Christian faith to social conditions. When he says that the Christian church becomes the prisoner of institutions and cultures, he is right. But is that a valid reason why it should not? There is a sense in which it should. Paul describes himself as the prisoner of the Lord. Like his Lord, he became a prisoner that others might be free. So the church too must become a prisoner of culture in order to save and transform culture. Maury is impressed, of course, by the difficulties which missionaries encounter due to the fact that Christianity has been westernized and is thus objectionable to non-Western peoples. How can the church extricate itself from these difficulties? by becoming indigenous. This means that nations like India and Burma must do what England and America have done already, i.e., to naturalize the church and make the Christian faith their own. Jesus was not less universal and divine because he was a carpenter and a Jew. Why then should the Body of Christ, which is the church, not be simultaneously Indian, Burmese, Congolese, and Korean as well as British, American, and German? Some divinity is lost in the process of assimilation, but we are not to hold back on that account. We have Christ's promise: "I am with you alway, even unto the end of the world." [47] When Christ prayed for his disciples and said, "I pray not that thou shouldest take them out of the world," [48] he closed the door once and for all on disinvolvement as an alternative for the Christian. In effect, he said: You can be ecumenical only by becoming indigenous, and you will find that the ensuing result is both a divine mystery and a human fact.

In spite of the pessimism of contemporary Protestant thought, there is considerable appreciation of the necessity for involvement and commitment. Reinhold Niebuhr recognizes it when he says: "There is, therefore, no way of understanding the ultimate problem of existence if we are not diligent in the pursuit of proximate answers and solutions." [49] Karl Barth recognized it when he opposed the Nazis. Paul Tillich, in his own unique way, recognizes it too when he speaks of the risks of faith which must be taken and when he expands the Protestant doctrine of justification by faith to cover human error as well as human sin. Philippe Maury recognized it when he joined the Resistance movement during the Nazi occupation of France. "From 1940 to 1941," he says, "I chose the underground Resistance, knowing, however, that I was assuming before God the terrible responsibility for disorder, violence, and hatred." [50]

These thinkers, however, do not go beyond affirming that the risks of decision must be taken. They either affirm involvement as a general principle or they defend particular instances of involvement. Among contemporary writers who deal specifically with politics from a Christian standpoint, there is a disposition to go somewhat further. Thus, William Muehl recommends that Christians enter politics and suggests several ways in which individuals may make their Christian witness felt, e.g., by running for public office on a party ticket, by joining pressure groups, and by taking a stand on particular local issues.[51] Alden D. Kelley is also quite clear that the Christian must take part in politics; he develops a concept which he calls "incarnational politics" and recommends the construction of a new image for the politician.[52] Even these writers, however, do no more than to sketch the terms in which they think the problem of Christianity and politics should be analyzed and to lay the groundwork for a later advance. In Kelley's words: "There remains, nevertheless, the problem of developing Christian guides to political thought and action. This is an undertaking of immense difficulty, which requires specialized training and skills." [53]

We have now gotten to a point where we must reach out beyond the pessimism which denies the possibility of Christianization, beyond purely general affirmations that the Christian faith requires involvement in politics, and beyond self-containment in particular instances of involvement divorced from any larger frame of reference. We need a systematic and sustained reinterpretation of political science in Christian terms; we need to provide a body of concepts as part of a guiding political philosophy which is Christian in spirit, conclusions, and techniques. The promises of the Christian faith cannot save the world unless the world is Christianized, and Christianization demands an intellectual effort to guide political effort. People have a right to ask how Christianization can be accomplished, and they will want to know in what specific ways it will make a difference.

Christianization is as necessary as evangelization. The two terms are not antithetical, as Maury seems to think, but are two facets of the same reality. The former is subjective and refers to the inner conversion of man, whereas the latter is objective and refers to the kingdom of God. The kingdom of God was central to Christ's teaching and the object of almost all his parables. His prayer includes the petition: "Thy kingdom come. Thy will be done *in earth,* as it is in heaven." [54] This is no mere invitation to wait for the Second Coming in the future but a call to action in the present. It does not ask us to wait for a miracle but to participate in one. He made his meaning unmistakable when he said that our *first* concern is to seek the kingdom of God and his righteousness.[55]

As theologians like Tillich and Niebuhr constantly remind us, the risks are unavoidable and many will not be met successfully. The most rigorous kind of thinking will not bring all the enlightenment we want, and there will be an admixture of darkness. Just as physical light contains infrared and ultraviolet rays which the eyes of man cannot see, so the divine light encompasses more truth than the mind of man can perceive. Furthermore, to follow our visual analogy, astigmatism and myopia will inevitably distort our vision and thus fail to do justice to what light is available to us. The subtle influence of personal temperament, cultural conditioning, and political preferences is ever present and affects thought and practice.

What the pessimists forget, however, is that Christians walk by faith and not by sight. This is why we can give a positive "yes" as well as a Barthian "no" to political life. We have Christ's explicit promise: "Ask, and it shall be given you; seek, and ye shall find; knock, and it shall be opened unto you." [56] The answer will not be complete, and it would be incomprehensible to us if it were. It will not always be the answer we expect or want, and neither will the timing necessarily be convenient. Nevertheless, we are not to worry about the incompleteness or the timing, because we shall receive enough for the need of the hour.[57] We are asked only to think and to act to the limit of our ability, and God will rectify the mistakes of our minds and forgive the sinfulness of our hearts. The greatest achievements of politics have been accomplished in just this way, as attested by the closing words of the American Declaration of Independence: "And for the support of this declaration, *with a firm reliance on the protection of Divine Providence,* we mutually pledge to each other our lives, our fortunes, and our sacred honor." (Emphasis supplied.)

Chapter III

INDEPENDENCE
AND INVOLVEMENT

O NE of the most basic concepts of political science is the state. Because it is so basic and so universal a datum of experience, you can scarcely find anybody who does not know what the state is. Moreover, political science has some fairly definite observations to make about the state, e.g., that its component elements are territory, people, and government. There is no argument about these elements, for all are deemed indispensable. It is also generally held that sovereignty is another necessary element, but there are differences of opinion about what sovereignty means and about whether there can be such a thing as a nonsovereign state. The term state has had a considerable number of equivalents or near equivalents such as polis, republic, commonwealth, realm, kingdom, empire, principality, union, dominion, federation, and confederation. This terminological variety has historical origins, but it is not particularly relevant to modern conditions and does not seriously affect the equivalence. Still in the general area of agreement is the idea that the state is concerned with power and purpose.

Beyond these general observations lies a very wide area of disagreement. This area is especially noticeable when one tries to classify states. We have or have had states classified as democratic, oligarchic, aristocratic, despotic, dynastic, theocratic, centralized, decentralized, liberal, constitutional, national, socialist, authoritarian, and totalitarian. The variety has several sources. One comes from the attempt to classify states according to empirical types whereby states exhibiting like characteristics are put in the same categories. The attempt runs into difficulties because the characteristics are never exactly alike and are always changing. Behavioral reality is too dynamic and too rich to permit the construction of neat and stable empirical types and imposes upon the political scientist decisions which, while necessary and useful, are in some measure arbitrary. Another source comes from the attempt to construct ideal types whereby states are classified according to several conceptions of what ought to be. These types are primarily ideological and may even be utopias. The difficulty with ideal types is that what men think ought to be varies quite as much as what men actually do; hence precise classification along this line is likewise impossible. Yet ideal types cannot be dismissed from consideration, because there are always idealists, reformers, and revolutionists who strive to translate ideal types into empirical realities and who meet with enough success to compel attention. The truth is that empirical and ideal types interact on one another. Finally, there is the influence of great personalities, which sometimes causes states to be classified with reference to them, e.g., Bismarckian, Hegelian, Marxist, Jeffersonian. Needless to say, these last classifications do not jibe perfectly with either empirical or ideal types.

THE CHRISTIAN CONCEPT OF THE STATE

Does the Christian faith shed any light on the large area of disagreement which is reflected in the classification of states? Some of the thinkers who have dealt with this question tried to develop a specifically Christian concept of the state. The origin of this attempt, however, is more Greek than Christian. It is especially associated with Plato, who constructed an ideal type (aristocracy) and treated all other states (timocracy, oligarchy, democracy, and tyranny) as progressive degenerations from the ideal. Some commentators have improperly characterized Plato's theory of state forms as a cycle. There is no cycle at all, but only a descent from which there is no return. Plato's ideal state was a specific application to politics of his general philosophy, according to which reality is expressed in intelligible patterns. These patterns are perceived only with the mind and are static. That which changes is unreal; only the eternal and unchanging is real. The consequence of Plato's conception for politics was concisely expressed by Wolin: "The art of ruling becomes the art of imposition." [1]

The soundness of Wolin's observation has been repeatedly demonstrated. The latest and most obvious instance is provided by communism. It is true that communism differs from Plato in that it is dynamic rather than static and has an eschatological element which is lacking in Plato. Nevertheless, communism shares an all important rationalism with Plato. The communists believe that they have discovered absolute truth, i.e., "scientific" socialism. The scientific study of history and society, they think, yields but one conclusion—their conclusion—and all other conclusions are wrong and must be regarded as deviations from the truth. Communism is therefore an ideology, a set of ideas and doctrines, and its adherents are engaged in the ambitious task of imposing their ideology on the whole world. The methods vary all the way from a doctrinaire type of education and government-sponsored propaganda to naked force, but the end is unchanging and unyielding. There must be a uniform and universal acceptance of the communist ideology.

The enormous influence of Plato on Christian thought has often led to an overemphasis on orthodoxy and has produced similar consequences.

Wherever Christianity has been reduced and frozen into an ideology, political tyranny has ensued. But there is no scriptural warrant for turning Christianity into an ideology. While the Christian faith is in no way skeptical about truth and ascribes great importance to sound doctrine, it asserts that ultimate truth is spiritual. Intellectual truth is derivative. The propositions formulated by the mind of man may be true, but they can never be the *whole* truth because such is not the nature of reality and because it would amount to a limit on the freedom of God, who is spirit. And if God is not free, man cannot be free either. This is probably what Paul meant when he said that "where the Spirit of the Lord is, there is liberty." [2] Furthermore, the finiteness of the human mind and the propensity of sinful man to rationalize would prevent propositional truth from being identical with ultimate truth even if that truth could be imprisoned by the intellect.

On the other hand, the Christian faith avoids the danger of the so-called "vitalistic" philosophies like fascism which overlook the fact that the realm of the spirit can be demonic as well as divine. Christian truth is personalized in Jesus Christ. Christ himself made it uncompromisingly clear in these words: "I am the way, the truth, and the life: no man cometh unto the Father, but by me." [3] In that one central affirmation, in the supreme revelation of God which took place in the Incarnation, man is delivered from enslavement to Nietzsche's will to power, Bergson's *élan vital,* and fascism's "wave of the future." In the person of Christ, he has the test of truth and the standard which enables him to discern the nature of the spiritual forces he encounters; he can identify and judge the spirit which inspires philosophies; he can determine the kind of spirit which animates political movements and which comes to life in the faces of people; and he is delivered from conjecture and speculation.

It follows from this analysis that we cannot speak of *the* Christian concept of the state as an absolute abstract formula, as an ideal pattern conceived in the Platonic manner. On the other hand, it does not follow that the Christian faith has nothing to say about the state. A fruitful approach would be to appraise a number of concepts of the state in Christian terms and see what emerges.

THE CLASSICAL LIBERAL CONCEPT
OF THE STATE

The classical liberal concept of the state is essentially negative, holding the state to be a necessary evil, and it found its most popular formulation in the Jeffersonian maxim that that government is best which governs least. It is born of a profound trust in the individual and an equally profound distrust of the state. This dual motivation was accurately reflected in Locke's contract theory of the origin of the state. According to Locke, individuals contract with one another to avoid what he calls the "inconveniences" of the state of nature and to create a limited instrument for the better protection of their prepolitical natural rights. To insure that the state thus created would remain confined to the tight bonds it was intended to have, the Jeffersonian philosophy stressed the Bill of Rights, separation of powers, states' rights, and the strict construction of the Constitution. The distrust of political power implicit in these institutional arrangements was not limited to the federal government but extended to the governments of the several states, which were to be limited by similar arrangements in favor of local governments and individual rights.

To these constitutional provisions of liberal political theory was added the weight of the theorists of the classical school of economics, who advocated a government policy of laissez faire and a theory of free competition which was supposed to make government intervention in the economic sphere practically unnecessary. The Physiocrats added their voices to the liberal chorus by propounding a narrow view of production whereby government and business are held to be parasitic and only mining and agriculture are productive. The transcendentalists like Emerson and Thoreau contributed the idea that only individuals are culturally creative and that the state is culturally barren. Any religious significance had already been stripped from the state by secularism. The effect of these converging lines of thought was to reduce the state to a weak organization, considered as a piece of machinery devoid of transcendental or ethical significance and instituted for the performance of minimal functions such as defense against external aggression, the repression of crime, and the settlement of disputes between individuals. This liberal concept of the state was appropriately dubbed by a German socialist as "the night watchman state."

It is one of the ironies of our time that the so-called "new conservatives" have taken up the classical liberal concept of the state as their own, while the modern liberals have given it up in favor of a much more positive concept. The new conservatives, especially the extreme or radical right, have adopted a highly restrictive view of governmental activity. They are opposed to public power, welfare legislation, civil rights legislation, and federal activity in the fields of education and health. They mean to abolish the income tax, curtail social security, and liquidate the TVA. They are willing for the government to take a strong lead only in the field of national defense. Their attitude amounts to a complete endorsement of the classical liberal concept of the state and found expression in the grudging admission by a member of the radical right in Louisiana that "it would be all right for the federal government to issue a few weather reports."

To spell out the classical liberal concept of the state is to bring out its incompatibility with the Christian faith. It was an error to strip the state of transcendental significance. Scripture teaches very plainly that the state is of divine origin, part of God's purpose for the good of man. That teaching received its clearest formulation in the frequently quoted thirteenth chapter of the Epistle to the Romans. In this chapter Paul insisted on the duty of the Christian to obey constituted authority, not merely as a matter of prudence or expediency, "but also for conscience sake." [4] He based this duty on the proposition that all power comes from God and that the magistrate "is the minister of God to thee for good." [5] Jesus himself made this same point when he told Pilate: "Thou couldest have no power at all against me, except it were given thee from above . . . ." [6] The same theme is reiterated throughout the history of the church by such great figures as Augustine, Aquinas, Luther, and Calvin. Perhaps none of them was more emphatic than Calvin when he asserted that the state "is equally necessary to mankind as bread and water, light and air, and far more excellent." [7] Anticipating the later contention of classical liberalism that the state is a necessary evil, Calvin was careful to point out "that the authority possessed by kings and other governors over all things upon earth is not a consequence of the perverseness of men, but of the providence and holy ordinance of God. . . ." [8] Anticipating again what was to be the Jeffersonian maxim that that government is best which governs least, Calvin assigned a broad scope to government functions which went far beyond such temporal concerns as the maintenance of order and the protection of property.*

The classical liberal concept of the state is incompatible with Christianity not only conceptually but spiritually. The apostle Paul gave us a useful standard on this point when he said that "whatsoever is not of faith is sin." [9] By this standard Paul did not mean to reject a wise recognition of danger, a realistic appraisal of difficulties, or a reasonable caution in making decisions. What he condemned was negativism, i.e., attitudes and philosophies which are oriented wholly or primarily *against* something or somebody. Pre-eminent among these is fear. In the light of this standard, the classical liberal concept shows up poorly. Historically this concept was rooted in the fear of power. It is true, of course, that power can be and has been abused and that its wielders need to be checked. What is needed is a proper balance, the kind of balance which Edmund Randolph displayed in repelling liberal attacks in the Virginia convention against the ratification of the Constitution of the United States. These attacks, characteristically, were centered on the contention that the Constitution vested too much power in the federal government. Randolph replied thus:

* I am aware of the probability that many readers will find the authority of Calvin unpersuasive. I nevertheless choose him because I believe that, among the great thinkers of Christendom, Calvin was the most accurate expositor of the teachings of Scripture and the most discerning and reliable interpreter of the great body of Christian doctrine and tradition which followed the apostolic age.

The gentleman expressed a necessity of being suspicious of those who govern. I will agree with him in the necessity of political jealousy, to a certain extent; but we ought to examine how far this political jealousy ought to be carried. I confess that a certain degree of it is highly necessary to the preservation of liberty; but it ought not to be extended to a degree which is degrading and humiliating to human nature; to a degree of restlessness, and active disquietude, sufficient to disturb a community, or to preclude the possibility of political happiness and contentment.[10]

This spiritual defect, so evident in the classical liberal concept of the state as the enemy of man, has become even more apparent in the hands of its newest champions, the radical right. It feeds on a fear of communism which sees subversion everywhere, on the fear of government regulation and higher taxes, on the fear that the Roman Catholics will invade our public schools, on the fear of labor unions, on the fear of international organizations like the U.N., on the fear that racial segregation will come to an end, on the fear of socialized medicine and public health programs. This fear generates hate, breeds distrust of democratic processes, leads to contempt for constitutional rights, sows suspicion among the people, and thus undermines that sense of community which is indispensable to constitutional government. It has gone so far as to denounce government, especially the federal government, as the one great enemy of the American way of life. The apostle Paul was indeed correct: "whatsoever is not of faith is sin." In a way we should be grateful to the radical right for bringing into the open the hidden but inexorable logic of the classical liberal concept of the state.

THE CONSERVATIVE CONCEPT
OF THE STATE

Conservatism, like liberalism, is a word which usage has made ambiguous. Clear thinking requires that its meaning be specified. Fortunately there is a rather general consensus, including both opponents and proponents of conservatism, which holds that Edmund Burke was its most authentic spokesman. We shall take the thought of Edmund Burke, therefore, as the most accurate and acceptable solution for what would otherwise be the usual troublesome ambiguity.

Burke was a great foe of the classical liberal idea that the state is a kind of machine, an instrument created by the deliberation and choice of a great legislator or a constitutional convention in the light of immutable and eternal abstract principles. He thought, instead, that the state is more like an organism, a living thing which is the product of a long evolution, something which grows and has a future. He thought that this organic analogy was more in keeping with the facts of history and political life than the mechanical analogy, and he defended it on the ground that it is more compatible with the limitations of human nature in both its individual and collective aspects. His most striking and famous formulation of the organic conception is to be found in his version of the social contract, which he defined as a contract between the living, the dead, and those yet to be born.

It is no accident that the living are outnumbered two to one. Burke was convinced that the living never possess the knowledge, skill, experience, self-control, and wisdom that would be necessary to remake the institutions under which they live. Man's abilities are too limited to permit the successful realization of grandiose schemes and reforms. Limited repairs and improvements lie within the competence of the living, but total reconstruction does not. Burke included the dead among the partners in the social contract because he wanted to stress the indebtedness of any generation to all preceding generations. The knowledge and skills we possess, the concepts we use, the institutions under which we live, the very language we speak are all things which are given to us, parts of an inheritance handed down to us, capital assets which we use and can increase or decrease but did not make. For that reason the institutions of man, including the state, are the product of the wisdom of the race or species which takes in but far transcends the wisdom of any single generation. By including the third parties to his contract—those yet to be born —Burke was saying that even the accumulated wisdom of the ages is insufficient. Allowance must be made for the discoveries and insights which future generations will contribute. There is now and always will be much to be learned, invented, experienced, mastered, and developed in all fields of human activity. Thus, true conservatism can never be a closed system of thought or a freezing of the status quo.

Wedged between the past and the future, the present becomes a three-dimensional reality endowed with perspective and depth. By itself, the present is one-dimensional and flat. This is something which Jefferson, the foremost prophet of classical liberalism in America, did not appreciate. Jefferson was inclined to look upon the past as a burden on the living; he thought that each generation should make or at least revise its institutions every twenty-five years, even if it took a revolution to do so. This insistence on the total and absolute self-determination of the living unhampered by the inheritance of the past led him to oppose any commitments, such as the national debt, which would limit the freedom of action of future generations. Jefferson's position was based on a highly optimistic view of human nature according to which men, provided they were educated and free, could be trusted to govern themselves without restrictions other than self-imposed restrictions.

Burke, on the other hand, was much less optimistic about human nature. He and Jefferson both believed in limited government. They were both constitutionalists, but Burke did not think that self-imposed limits would suffice. His organic conception of the state was well adapted to his purpose, for the claims of yesterday and tomorrow would circumscribe the freedom of action of today. Sovereign authority in the sense of rightfully and factually unrestricted power is thus ruled out. The French Revolution introduced a new distinction in political science: constituted authority (*pouvoir constitué*) and constituent authority (*pouvoir constituant*). The former is created by law and operates under law. The latter creates law (including the constitution) and is therefore above and beyond law. Burke rejects this distinction, as he does most of the works of the French Revolution. For him there are constituted authorities only, and constituent authorities are anathema. Amending clauses and limited constitutional conventions may be useful and are therefore allowable, but unlimited constitutional conventions are a delusion and a menace.

Burke approaches the problem of the state from another angle which leads him to the same conclusion and which has been one of the hallmarks of conservative thought everywhere. What is involved here is a sense of the infinite complexity of human affairs, the hidden connections, the vast network of contingencies and ramifications. As one might express it: everything is inextricably intertwixt. Burke himself put it more elegantly: "Our constitution stands on a nice equipoise, with steep precipices and deep waters upon all sides of it. In removing it from a dangerous leaning towards one side, there may be a risk of oversetting it on the other. Every project of a material change in a government so complicated as ours, combined at the same time with external circumstances still more complicated, is a matter full of difficulties: in which a considerate man will not be too ready to decide; a prudent man too ready to undertake; or an honest man too ready to promise." [11] There emerges from this attitude a characteristic tendency to analyze social and constitutional change in terms of balancing principles and consequences, with emphasis on consequences.

Suppose, for example, that it were proposed that our fifty states be abolished and replaced by a smaller number of rationally worked out regions. Such a proposal could be defended by many valid arguments. One could say that our state lines are irrational barriers erected by historical accident and the surveyor's caprice, that many states do not make any economic sense, that some states yoke together in one jurisdiction areas that are radically different and uncongenial culturally, such as East and West Tennessee and North and South Louisiana, that most state governments are inefficient and not a few are downright corrupt, that the existence of states encourages parochialism and a narrow local selfishness which destroy party discipline on the national level and interfere with the proper functioning of Congress. Surely all these arguments are largely sound, and a strong case could be made for a much more rational decentralization of the country into regions designed to make political, cultural, and economic sense. In spite of all this, such a proposal would be wholly academic and would get no support—not even from those who agreed with the arguments advanced for the proposal. The reason for this lack of support is not that the proposal would violate a deep sentimental attachment to the existing states. There is some attachment, but it is far weaker than the advocates of states' rights would have us believe.

The real reason appears from the moment we begin to consider the consequences which the abolition of our states would necessitate. Article I of the Constitution would have to be rewritten because the Senate is based on the equality of states, and the House has its seats apportioned on the basis of the population of the states. Bicameralism and reapportionment, both of which are thorny and explosive issues, would be thrust into the forefront. Article II would also have to be rewritten since the election of the President is now geared to the states through the Electoral College. Depending on how the problems involved here were solved, the presidential system of government which we have lived under since 1789 would be at stake. Article III would have to be revised on account of the references to the states which enter into the jurisdiction of the federal courts, and we would have to decide whether we want to retain senatorial confirmation of judicial appointments (assuming we still had a Senate). There would be some sentiment for making federal judges elective.

In any event, the door would be wide open for thoroughgoing attacks on the federal judiciary from Southerners who do not like federal court decisions on segregation, from Northern economic interests who would like to reinstate substantive due process in the field of property rights, from those groups who feel alarmed over court decisions on the subject of communism and subversion, and perhaps even from liberals who remember the conflict between Roosevelt and the Supreme Court. The whole structure and operation of our major political parties, which now rest on state machines, would be called into question and would upset the plans and calculations of professional politicians and officeholders. Existing vested rights under state constitutions, state statutes, and state court decisions affecting business, labor, the professions, and domestic relations would suddenly be put in jeopardy. It would be tedious to go on outlining in greater detail the necessary, probable, and possible consequences of the abolition of our states. The consequences would be immense, incalculable, and unmanageable. Everyone would recoil from them, and that is the real underlying reason why our states are inviolable and indestructible.

This kind of thinking which stresses the complexity of life and the results of action is characteristic of conservatism. Obviously conservatives vary in the degree of their conservatism, and few go as far as Hegel by saying that the actual is rational and the rational is actual, thus identifying what ought to be with what is. Nevertheless, the effect of conservative thinking is to inhibit, circumscribe, minimize, and even disguise change. Change ought to be confined to what is predictable and manageable.*

Another basic element in Burke's thinking is his reliance on institutions. He conceived of the civil order as a composite of foci of power rooted in habit, emotion, service, and belief. Among the political institutions he valued most highly were the monarchy, the House of Lords, and the House of Commons. Each of these had its history, prestige, power, rights, and privileges. In their interplay hinged the liberty and welfare of the English people. He further believed that the proper functioning of these political institutions depended on their being organically related to other institutions, among which property and the Church of England were pre-eminent. Both the limitations and the effective exercise of political power require that there be individuals and groups outside of the government with enough independence to challenge or to give effect to governmental decisions and policies. Conservatives are disinclined to make excessive demands upon human nature and do not rely on heroes. Landowners and businessmen have economic resources which enable them to oppose the government without endangering their livelihood or their future. Clergymen likewise enjoy considerable independence because of their spiritual authority and moral prestige, which are not derived from the state even where establishment obtains. It should not be inferred that these institutions are justified solely or even mainly on account of their political significance. The church cultivates the moral virtues and promotes the spiritual welfare of the people, and property develops the inventiveness and satisfies the need for productivity of those who own it and work with it. In a discussion of the conservative concept of the state, however, the political aspects are naturally emphasized. The political role which Burke assigned to institutions indicates that his conception of the social order is thoroughly antitotalitarian and exhibits tendencies toward pluralism.

It is clear from the preceding discussion of Burke's political philosophy that conservatism makes for a strong state. Since conservatives do not share the optimism of classical liberals about man, the conservative state must be one equipped with enough power to curb the antisocial behavior of individuals and actively promote the common good which individual selfishness would neglect. Furthermore, since conservatism does not hold the classical liberal view which postulates a self-regulating harmony of society, the conservative state must have the power to coordinate groups and institutions for the common good. It was one of the most conserva-

---

* Typical of the conservative attitude was the statement I heard the late Professor H. L. McBain of Columbia University make in a public lecture many years ago when people were talking about the need for constitutional change. Said he: "We must make haste—slowly, very slowly."

tive regimes in Europe, the Bismarckian empire, which was the first to adopt welfare legislation. The conservative rulers of imperial Germany were opposed to socialism, but their opposition was not due to any reticence about state intervention in economic life or any hesitancy concerning the propriety of state ventures in cultural and social matters. What they did not like about socialism was its internationalism and its working-class orientation. Conservatives in every European country were traditionally on the side of monarchy, which meant strong government, and their long association with mercantilism is ample evidence of their belief that international trade and the domestic economy are things to be controlled for the public good rather than left to the free play of "natural" forces. Similarly, the Hamiltonian economic program shows that the conservatives who made our Constitution and put it into operation under the administrations of George Washington and John Adams also believed in the strong guiding hand of government. Our Constitution itself was the work of conservatives who were hostile to states' rights and intent upon creating a really powerful national government capable of realizing the objectives of the Preamble.[12]

The conservative concept of the state harmonizes in many ways with Christianity. A common sense of history pervades them both. Christianity is an historic religion. In the Bible God is revealed as the God of Abraham, Isaac, and Jacob. He is the God who delivered the people of Israel from bondage, who led them through the wilderness, who gave them law, who taught them how to worship, who gave them the promised land, who spoke to them through the prophets. He is the God who became incarnate in the historic person of Jesus of Nazareth. He is the God who has guided and inspired the church through all ages. An almost Burkean conception of the bond which unites the living, the dead, and those yet to be born lies at the heart of the Christian understanding of the church universal and invisible to which all believers belong regardless of generation. As with the Burkean state, so it is with the Christian church: the living members are held together by their consciousness of a common past and a common destiny.

Another source of kinship with conservatism is the organic approach. Jesus often spoke in organic terms, urging us to look at the lilies of the field and see how they grow, comparing the kingdom of God to seed which yields an abundant harvest, explaining his relationship to his disciples as that of the vine and its branches, drawing a parallel between the religious faith that is manifest in ethical conduct and the tree that bears good fruit. He was constantly referring to sowing, grafting, germinating, growing, ripening, and other organic processes. Paul characterized the church as the Body of Christ and often used physiological analogies to illustrate the kind of relationships which should exist among church members. He saw the church as a living organism which grows in size through new members and new congregations over ever widening geographical areas. The church also grows in depth with the greater knowledge, the purer morals, the stronger spiritual life, and the closer sense of belonging of its members. In Paul's mind, no sharp line separated the religious from the political, since the church was also a kingdom whose members are citizens bound together by a common allegiance to Christ the King and a common discipline of life.

The conservative view of human nature has a certain affinity with the Christian doctrine of man. Christianity affirms both the limitations and the sinfulness of man. His most brilliant achievements in the realm of knowledge fall short of omniscience. The more he knows, the more clearly he sees what he does not know. Knowledge can be compared to a campfire at night: the brighter the flames and the higher they leap, the greater the span of the encircling darkness. Were it not for the sinfulness of man, the most learned would also be the most humble. The sinfulness of man, i.e., his innate and inherited propensity toward evil and the dark and bitter fruits which this propensity produces, is an inseparable part of the historic teaching of the Christian church. Conservatism accepts these truths concerning human nature quite readily. In periods like the eighteenth and nineteenth centuries when an extravagant optimism about the intellect and goodness of man was dominant, conservatism became the natural ally of the church.

Great as these resemblances, affinities, and sympathies between conservatism and Christianity are, it will not do to conclude that the Christian faith unequivocally enjoins the acceptance of the conservative state. There is dissonance as well as harmony. Just how great that dissonance can be, loudly forces itself upon us when we remember that it was the conservatives of his day who crucified Christ. Who were his enemies? Not the publicans, the harlots, the poor, the fishermen, the common people. His enemies were the scholars, the priests, and the superpatriots.

What did the scholars have against him? that he taught without having gone through the customary formal schooling of his day. In our time that would mean that he presumed to teach without having the usual prerequisites such as academic degrees, years of teaching experience in recognized and accredited educational institutions, letters of recommendation from established scholars, publication of books and articles, offices held in professional associations. Worse still, he taught as one having authority, not as one of the scribes!

What did the priests have against him? that he did not belong to the hierarchy and had not been commissioned by the ecclesiastical authorities to carry on religious work. He taught doctrines which were at variance with the official position. He performed priestly acts such as forgiving sins, although he had not been ordained—unless one regards that rabble-rousing tent preacher John the Baptist as a proper authority. He undermined the monopoly of the religious establishment by teaching people like the Samaritan woman at the well that someday everyone would know that one can worship God anywhere in spirit and in truth without having to go to the temple in Jerusalem.

What did the superpatriots have against him? that he was not as anti-Roman as every good 100 per cent Jew was supposed to be. Did he not approve of paying taxes to Caesar and consort with publicans who collected the taxes and were the collaborationists of their day? He did not align himself with the zealots who were dedicated to the overthrow of the Romans by force. He dared to see good in the despised Samaritans, to heal a Syrophoenician woman and compliment her on her faith, to praise a Roman centurion for his faith, and in general to insist that God loves all peoples and not only the Jews. He was a do-gooder and a one-worlder. He disregarded many of the rules which could be called "the Jewish way of life," calling them mere commandments of men, and taught his disciples to do the same. In short, the teachings of Jesus, if accepted and followed, would have had the effect of destroying the Jewish people as a separate segregated nation. Did not these questionable associations, these instances of "coddling" Romans and other Gentiles, these "un-Jewish" doctrines constitute a pattern of disloyalty and subversion? Caiaphas, the high priest, thought so and said "that it is expedient for us, that one man should die for the people, and that the whole nation perish not." [13]

It will not do, however, to pin the entire blame for Christ's crucifixion on the conservatives alone. The frustrations of the scholars, the priests, and the superpatriots were indeed the immediate cause of the event, but the underlying cause was the fundamental and universal fact of human sin, which blights all mankind, conservative and nonconservative. And behind this underlying cause was the love of God for all men, expressed in Christ's voluntary redemptive sacrifice. Caiaphas spoke more truly than he knew when he said that one man had to die for the people. It was to this baffling interaction of human motives and divine purpose that Jesus was referring when he said: "Father, forgive them; for they know not what they do." [14] If Christ could forgive these conservatives (and the rest of us for whom these conservatives were on that occasion the unwitting agents), neither should we condemn them.

Nevertheless, what happened to Jesus stands as a warning to all conservatives, for the people who wanted Jesus dead were the most respectable people of that time. Their morals were purer than those of the Gentiles and the publicans; their conception of God was on a higher plane than that of any other people; their knowledge of Jewish history and Jewish law was great and valuable. They were the preservers and transmitters of the revelation of God in the history of Israel. What was there about these consecrated worshipers of God that prevented them from recognizing the presence of God in their own midst? What was there about these dedicated patriots that caused them to misunderstand so completely the meaning and mission of their beloved nation?

Basically it was a tendency to idolatry, which consists in treating as absolute that which is relative, in confusing the wholeness of truth with one's own fragmentary grasp of that truth, in not making enough allowance for the freedom of God to reveal himself to men and to alter the achievements of men to suit his purposes, however disturbing and bewildering these alterations can sometimes be. Institutions tend to become prisons as their original purpose is dulled by familiarity and lost in time. Doctrines, however true, become distorted as the conditions which required their formulation change or disappear, or when they are held in a spirit different from the one which gave them birth. Noble achievements become dead weights as tired old men begin to doubt their ability to do better or even as well again. Nicodemus put it very aptly when he replied to Jesus: "How can a man be born when he is old? can he enter the second time into his mother's womb, and be born?" [15] Perhaps the learned Pharisee Nicodemus forgot that Abraham was even older when he dared to embark on a radical new venture on the strength of God's improbable promises. Nicodemus lacked the secret of perpetual renewal and growth. Nations, too, run into the same difficulty. Their culture and their institutions can become so calcified, so unresponsive to changing needs, so hostile to new insights, so complacent in their unquestioned greatness that the only possible divine judgment is to shatter, disperse, or annihilate the nation.

The applications of this scriptural record to conservative politics and the conservative concept of the state are easy to perceive. Nationalism, especially in its exaggerated form of chauvinism or jingoism, is an ever present danger for conservatism. The temptation to transform a legitimate devotion to one's country into an uncritical and exclusivist passion is insidious and persistent. It is implicit in the excessive concern for the needs and pecularities of one's own country and the consequent unconcern for other nations. It was the classical liberals who spoke of the rights of man. The conservatives spoke of the rights of the *English*man and the *French*man. The temptation becomes explicit when the claims of other nations are rejected, their culture is downgraded, their needs are ignored or denied, their rights are violated, and their wealth and strength are turned into objects of exploitation.

The political effects of yielding to the temptation are many. Foreign aid is decried as "operation rat-hole," and we are told that we have no business "giving milk to the Hottentots." We hear that we should discontinue helping other nations because they are not grateful to us and that the best way to make an enemy of people is to give them a "handout." The national interest is said to be the sole proper objective of foreign policy, for have we not got to "look out for number one," and is not self-preservation the first law of life? National sovereignty is erected into an idol so that the U.N. is looked upon with distrust, and the authority of any future international organization is excluded in advance. Fear of foreign commitments, especially if these require direct domestic readjustments, leads to demands for crippling the treaty-making power through proposals like the Bricker Amendment.

These political effects are demonstrably contrary to the Christian ethic. To give foreign aid on condition that the recipients be grateful would make us like those hypocrites Jesus spoke of in the Sermon on the Mount who do good that they might be praised of men. To assert that self-preservation is the first law of life is to deny the validity of Christ's warning that whoever would save his own life shall lose it but that he who would lose his life for Christ's sake shall find it again. To absolutize the national interest is to overlook the fundamental and constantly more evident fact that God made men and groups of men so interdependent that the interest of each can be achieved only through the interest of all. Clothing man with national sovereignty does not exempt him from the duty of being his brother's keeper, ministering unto these the least of Christ's brethren, observing the divine command to love his neighbor as himself, and heeding Paul's injunction that the strong should bear the burdens of the weak.

There can be no denying, of course, that *indiscriminate* giving is not part of the Christian faith and that some gifts may be harmful to the recipients. Self-reliance may be weakened and the moral fiber sapped by too much dependence on others. Intelligence and careful study are part of true generosity. It is necessary to know when the interests of others are best advanced by giving, withholding, or denying aid. It is also true that while there is a world community of interest, there is no world consciousness of it and no world commitment to it; hence the essential prerequisites of world government are lacking. Under present conditions it would be irresponsible to surrender our sovereignty to an international body like the U.N., but national sovereignty as it is now generally understood is nevertheless evil because it is rigid and implies the rejection of all obligations that are not self-imposed. We already have moral, political, and legal obligations which are not self-imposed and which are binding even though there is no earthly government to which we are answerable. What we need is a far more flexible conception of national sovereignty compatible with the establishment in the future of some kind of world order, a conception quite unlike that of Hobbes which brooked no limits whatsoever, and more like that of Bodin which subjected sovereignty to natural law and the fundamental law of the realm. What is dangerous about nationalism is that it inhibits people from doing the proper kind of thinking about these problems of international relations because selfishness is in control, a selfishness which is disguised by being collectivized. And nationalism is a danger to which conservatives are peculiarly susceptible.

Another danger to which the conservative is especially vulnerable is conformity. His natural reverence for old ways and for what is established, his dislike for change, and his discomfort in the face of the unpredictable incline him to be intolerant of criticism and dissent. Skepticism concerning the capacity of human beings to conceive abstract truth or understand any truth which is not already embodied in existing institutions makes him distrustful of intellectuals. Like his patron saint, Edmund Burke, he dislikes metaphysics, abstractions, and ideologies. Skepticism regarding the power of the Holy Spirit to inspire and to renew, to reshape old structures and create new ones, and to generate new truth fills him with apprehension. Spiritual people are unsafe, for they take seriously that disturbing statement: "Behold, I make all things new." [16] For that reason the conservative is often a better churchman than he is a Christian, and he is sorely tempted to transform the church into a front for the existing social order. Against the grain run the words of Paul: "And be not conformed to this world: but be ye transformed by the renewing of your mind, that ye may prove what is that good, and acceptable, and perfect will of God." [17]

The tendency toward conformity, like the one toward nationalism, has important political effects. The most striking of these effects concerns the Bill of Rights. The reason is that the Bill of Rights protects the nonconformists, i.e., the critics, dissenters, innovators. The fact that it does protect these people puts the conservative in a quandary. On the one hand, he respects the Bill of Rights as a part of the Constitution which he reveres, as a needed restraint on the power of government, as a basic element in our national heritage. He recognizes that it is woven into the very texture of our daily lives and that property, personal liberty, cultural autonomy, and social institutions are all anchored in it. In short, the Bill of Rights is an indispensable part of the social order which he, as a conservative, is bound to conserve. On the other hand, constitutional freedom of speech and press permit the dissemination of ideas some of which are troublesome, unpopular, unorthodox, and subversive. Freedom of association can lead to conspiracy or, at least, to the accession of nonconformists to political power. Religious liberty may lead to fragmentation and strife. These possibilities can be contemplated in quiet times with a minimum of anxiety. In times of rapid change and widespread conflict, however, the conservative's anxiety reaches the breaking point. His devotion to the Bill of Rights wanes; he is willing to cut corners and condone the disregard of "technicalities;" he tries to persecute where he cannot prosecute; and he subconsciously comes to feel that the end justifies the means. When that happens, he is well on the road to fascism, and all that is left of his conservatism is the name. He has been corrupted by fear and a gnawing sense of insecurity.

The conservative, like the classical liberal, falls short when judged by Paul's standard that "whatsoever is not of faith is sin." At first glance this might seem not to be the case because the conservative believes in institutions, including governmental institutions, whereas the classical liberal is afraid of them. However, when one looks more closely at the conservative's belief in institutions, it sometimes turns out that his belief is a form of defeatism. In such cases institutions are a refuge against the attempt of people to create better ones. The conservative then believes in the American way of life by default. In the absence of objective external standards, which he feels do not exist or cannot be known, he falls back on what he has. As a consequence his attitude toward the university, especially toward academic freedom, is uncertain. If a university were simply the custodian and transmitter of a nation's culture, it would receive his unqualified support. A university, however, is also a research institution in which new truth is discovered, new hypotheses are conceived, old ideas are questioned and tested, new techniques are developed, and new insights are discussed and disseminated. University professors do not confine themselves to the legendary ivory tower. They write books and articles, make speeches to civic clubs and church groups, read papers before professional societies, sign petitions, and advise government officials. These are the aspects of university life which arouse the conservative's fears and sometimes make him an unreliable supporter of higher education.

Pessimism regarding the creativity of man is paralleled by a similar pessimism regarding the likelihood of God's intervention in human affairs. He can recite the Apostles' Creed and say: "I believe in the holy catholic church." But he does not want the church to make any pronouncements that question the social order or suggest that there might be a better one. Revelation took place once and for all, and we need not look any further. He feels that new revelation could not be authenticated. There are no prophets any more, only crackpots.

This deep pessimism reaches a maximum insofar as the common people are concerned. The conservative believes in social classes and wants decisions to be made by the enlightened few. Burke spoke for him when he said:

The Chancellor of France at the opening of the states, said, in a tone of rhetorical flourish, that all occupations were honourable. If he meant only, that no honest employment was disgraceful, he would not have gone beyond the truth. But in asserting that anything is honourable, we imply some distinction in its favour. The occupation of a hair-dresser, or of a working tallow-chandler, cannot be a matter of honour to any person—to say nothing of a number of other more servile employments. Such descriptions of men ought not to suffer oppression from the state; but the state suffers oppression, if such as they, either individually or collectively are permitted to rule. In this you think you are combating prejudice, but you are at war with nature.[18]

The conservative is moderate enough to realize that the enlightened few, being human too, need to be checked, wherein he differs from the totalitarians who are quite sure that the elite can be trusted with absolute power. But he instinctively feels that the masses need to be checked a great deal more because they are fickle, gullible, and irrational. He forgets that the greater abilities and attainments of the enlightened are balanced by greater temptations and by the one-sidedness associated with overspecialization, that enlightenment is neither hereditary nor inseparable from social position, and that enlightenment must be not only real but recognized and accepted as such by the masses.

This bias against the common people and in favor of the few creates a tension for the conservative when the social order happens to be democratic, as is the case in the United States. A democratic social order is based on majority rule, even if one concedes that this rule is circumscribed by consensus and minority rights. When majority rule results in change, whether change originates in intellectual or spiritual vitality, the conservative tends to become distrustful of the democratic process and may turn authoritarian. Such a reorientation, of course, does not come easily or painlessly, because there is a deep contradiction involved. The conservative, as a conservative, is obligated to defend the existing social order. But this order, being democratic, is an open one because the channels of intellectual and spiritual progress are guaranteed by the Bill of Rights to the people as individuals and by majority rule to the people as a nation. An authoritarian social order, on the other hand, is a closed social order. The conservative's predicament is that he must be either an unhappy democrat or a remorseful authoritarian. There is no way out of this predicament except through faith. If his conservatism is based on the faith that God can stimulate, control, and direct the mind and destiny of man, conservatism and a democratic social order are compatible, and he will be found among the defenders of democracy. If his conservatism is based on skepticism, i.e., a disbelief in objective truth and a defeatist attitude toward the possibility of man's apprehending that truth and living by it, conservatism and a democratic social order are incompatible, and he will take his place among the enemies of democracy.

THE TOTALITARIAN CONCEPT
OF THE STATE

The totalitarian state is a recent phenomenon in history, a product of the twentieth century. Its novelty does not lie in its authoritarianism, though it is undeniably and blatantly authoritarian, but in its inclusiveness. Totalitarian means all-inclusive. Mussolini made this point clearly and concisely: "Everything in the State, nothing against the State, nothing outside the State." [19] The totalitarian state has ideological roots which reach far back into the past, notably in the philosophy of Thomas Hobbes. It is also true that the authoritarian monarchies of Europe and the military dictatorships of Latin America have had totalitarian tendencies. However, in the case of the authoritarian monarchies, totalitarian tendencies were checked by traditional social structures (nobility and clergy), notions of constitutional law (fundamental customary law of the realm), and a belief in natural law. In the case of the Latin American dictatorships, totalitarian tendencies were not accompanied by a corresponding ideology, so that there was no "system" capable of surviving the dictator. They were personal despotisms unassociated with a *Weltanschauung,* as the Germans would say.

It was not until the twentieth century that the theory and practice of totalitarianism were joined together, giving rise to established regimes with clearly identifiable characteristics. These regimes have taken two forms, the fascist and the communist. Some differences separate the two forms, but the similarities far outweigh the differences. Fascism and communism are variants of the same creed, produce the same institutional patterns, use the same political strategy and tactics, are animated by the same missionary zeal and imperialistic designs, and hurl the same challenge to Christianity and to all past and present political systems. Both fascism and communism are secular, authoritarian, militaristic, and totalitarian.

A short dictionary definition of secularism reads thus: "Regard for worldly as opposed to spiritual matters." [20] Secular is any antireligious or nonreligious view of life, any philosophy which interprets the world in terms which deny or ignore the existence and intervention of God. By this standard communism is obviously secular. Communism is officially and specifically atheistic. It denies the existence of God, except as the figment of a culturally conditioned imagination, and it contemptuously rejects all religion as the opiate of the people. It is officially materialistic and regards even science and philosophy as superstructure determined by the process of economic development. To the Communist, therefore, the state can have no divine or transcendental significance. It cannot be the embodiment of the common good because the doctrine of the inevitability and irreconcilability of the class struggle denies that there can be a common good. It cannot embody any eternal realities because it is only an instrument of class oppression, which is destined to disappear when the classless society has been achieved. Its hallmarks are two brutal facts: coercion and class interest. Could any concept of the state be more secular?

Fascism is just as secular as communism, but not as obviously so. There is a greater element of disguise and deceit in fascism. On the surface fascism is nationalistic and claims to embody spiritual values. It does not at first openly deny the existence of God, and in its early stages it poses as a defender of religion. Time and closer analysis, however, disclose the secular character of fascism. The nation conceived as an historical and sociological formation by Mussolini, and the *Volk* conceived as a racial community by Hitler are not one whit less secular than the communist proletariat. The Fascists, like the Communists, start with a secular concept (sociological in the Italian version and biological in the German version) and treat all other reality as superstructure, including religion. All three concepts (i.e., nation, *Volk,* and proletariat) are secular, and each resolves itself into a configuration of power. This position brought the Fascists into conflict with religion and led to the same kind of repression and persecution of religion which one finds in the Iron Curtain countries today. The religious policies and practices of the German Democratic Republic of East Germany are not different from those of the now defunct Third Reich.

The totalitarian state is also authoritarian. This means that it will not tolerate opposition or dissent and that power flows from the top down, not from the bottom up. The Nazis called this the leadership principle (*Fuehrersprinzip*). Governmentally this means that there can be no separation of powers, checks and balances, or local autonomy. Politically this means the one-party state where a single political party monopolizes political power. The Nazi slogan was: The party commands the state. The ruling party, in turn, is elitist in that it comprises only a small proportion of the people, and hierarchical in that its organization culminates in a single leader through a channel of command. Civil rights as legal restraints on the government for the protection of individuals are nonexistent. There may be certain individual liberties, but they are matters of expediency, not of right. The state is absolute, and no higher authority is acknowledged in heaven or in earth.

The differences between communism and fascism in the matter of authoritarianism are superficial, and in this case it is the Fascists who are forthright and the Communists who are deceptive. The Fascists frankly make the state into an absolute, whereas the Communists claim that the state is a transitory phase in the evolutionary process. But the Marxist state is absolute in practice, even if not in theory. The authoritarianism of the Soviet Union is justified by the Communists as necessary for the fulfillment of the logic of history, and whoever opposes it in any way is guilty of defying history. The Soviet Constitution would lead one to think that the regime has government controls and is territorially decentralized, but the absolute dominance of the Communist Party makes puppets out of the Soviet governmental organs and of the several Soviet republics. Obviously and admittedly, the communist regime is a one-party state. The party's authority is derived from the fact that it is supposed to be the class-conscious vanguard of the proletariat. The party itself is as authoritarian as the fascist parties. It is true that the Communists muddy the waters a bit by claiming that they believe in collective leadership and eschew the personality cult. But here again the practice belies the theory. It is plain to everyone on either side of the Iron Curtain that leaders like Lenin, Stalin, and Khrushchev have the same authority and prestige as Hitler and Mussolini. All the characteristics of authoritarianism are present in the Soviet Union: the legally unrestricted government, the absence of constitutional checks, the monopoly of power by a hierarchically organized and personally led party, the rejection of criticism and dissent.

The totalitarian state is militaristic. On this point also the Communists are more deceitful than the Fascists. The Fascists glorify war and consider aggression to be the very essence of life. Mussolini once said that only in the trenches can one tell who is a true friend, and Hitler characterized the citizen of the Third Reich as a political soldier. The Communists, on the other hand, claim to love peace, and use the word warmonger as a term of opprobrium. Yet it is common knowledge that they are anything but pacifists. Class war is held by communist theory to be inevitable and righteous. Is civil war or revolution any less warlike than international war? Even international wars are held by the Communists to be righteous if they are wars of "liberation" to free African or Asian peoples from colonial domination and Western peoples from capitalist exploitation, or if they are wars for the defense of the Soviet Union.

Last, but by no means least, the totalitarian state is totalitarian. This statement is an obvious tautology, but unfortunately it is a very meaningful tautology. In neither fascist nor communist states are institutions free, and their society is therefore the antithesis of a pluralist society. Unions, corporations, universities, and churches are all closely controlled by and integrated into the state. This process of absorption was called "co-ordination" (*Gleichschaltung*) by the German Fascists, while the Italian Fascists spoke of it as the "corporative" aspect of their state. The theory behind the institutional aspect of totalitarianism was spelled out long ago by Hobbes in his *Leviathan*.[21] Its central thesis is that institutional independence is tantamount to conspiracy. Any institution, be it union or corporation or church, which possesses power that is not derived from the sovereign must inevitably challenge the sovereign because it is the nature of power to grow indefinitely and shun all restraints. Logic therefore requires the totalitarians to take a definite position on the much disputed nature of corporate personality. They do. They affirm the fiction theory. According to the fiction theory, when a sovereign authority incorporates a city or grants a charter to a corporation, it is creating a reality of which the charter is the evidence. The alternative theory, that of the real personality of corporate bodies, says that in such cases the sovereign authority is not creating but merely recognizing something which is already a living fact. Clearly the fiction theory is compatible with the totalitarian concept of the state, whereas the real personality theory is not.

Totalitarianism, of course, absorbs the individual as well as institutions. Individuals derive their importance from the state and are therefore expendable. They are but insignificant little specks in a national entity headed toward world conquest or in a proletarian entity headed toward world revolution. By Aquinas' criterion they are slaves because they are treated not as ends but as means to ends. They have no civil rights and enjoy only such liberties as the government deems suited to its own purposes. But the totalitarian state is not content with absolute control of the behavior of individuals: it demands their minds and their souls as well. Government censorship, party propaganda, monopolistic control over education and all means of communication, the use of terrorism and brainwashing, the rewriting of history and the doctoring of the news, and all other manipulative techniques with which the Fascists and the Communists have familiarized us are designed to assure the complete possession of the individual by the state. This stupendous endeavor for the complete absorption of the individual by the totalitarian state means the rejection of one of the most basic tenets of liberalism which had received well-nigh universal acceptance in the West.

It had been the accepted liberal theory, which found classic expression in John Stuart Mill's *Essay on Liberty,* that whereas the external behavior of men is a fit subject for governmental control under certain carefully delineated circumstances, the inner life of men should be absolutely free not only of political but even of social control. The realm of the mind and the spirit is a private sphere in which each individual is sovereign and ought therefore to lie wholly outside of any external jurisdictions. Constitutional protection of freedom of thought, scientific inquiry, artistic expression, conscience, and worship came as legal implementation for this fundamental distinction between the internal and external aspects of human life. Separation of church and state, legal safeguards extended to universities, constitutional guarantees of freedom of the press and of association were further attempts to implement this distinction by assuring the inner realm of mind and spirit a minimum of institutional expression. Even the innermost life of man needs some outlet.

The totalitarians reject the basic distinction between the internal and external aspects of life. They contend that the two are inseparable. They say that a man's religious convictions and philosophical views are never politically irrelevant. Though there is always a gap between theory and practice, they do interact. As a man believes, so he will act. The totalitarians therefore quite logically conclude that the liberal distinction is politically unrealistic and philosophically false. There can be no control of behavior without thought control. This is why Hobbes made truth a matter not of discovery but of definition, rejected all revelation except through the channel of the sovereign, and specified that the control of opinion is an indispensable attribute of sovereignty. His general position on what today would be called "the engineering of consent" was expressed in a passage which might well be the platform of all totalitarian ministers of propaganda: "the Common peoples minds, unless they be tainted with dependance on the Potent, or scribbled over with the opinions of their Doctors, are like clean paper, fit to receive whatsoever by Publique Authority shall be imprinted in them.[22]

Christians in this country have had an easy time denouncing totalitarianism. To denounce it, especially in its communist form, is a very popular thing to do. Too often, however, the conflict is reduced to a low level whose drift runs more or less on this order: "They don't like us, so we don't like them." It is important that we raise the discussion to a higher level and ascertain at what points and in what respects the totalitarian state is incompatible with Christianity.

The secular aspect of the totalitarian state is, of course, unacceptable to a religion which affirms that God is the supreme reality, the ground of all being, the maker of heaven and earth, and the Lord of all history. There can be no neutrality on this point, for even to ignore God is to deny him. Christianity is theistic; secularism is not. The militaristic character of totalitarianism also conflicts with Christianity. Peace is one of the great values of the Christian faith. The love of peace, the blessedness of the peacemakers, and the peace of God which passeth all understanding do not enjoin pacifism or appeasement, but they are most assuredly inconsistent with the glorification of war and aggression. The guiding principle was stated by Paul thus: "If it be possible, as much as lieth in you, live peaceably with all men." [23]

The authoritarianism of the totalitarians cannot stand the test of Christian criticism either. To make the state an absolute value is to violate the first commandment: "Thou shalt have no other gods before me." [24] It also contradicts the Lord's Prayer: "For thine is the kingdom, and the power, and the glory, for ever." [25] In plain words: authoritarianism is idolatrous. This conclusion was easier to see in ancient times when political rulers openly claimed divinity. The early Christians faced it decisively when they refused to take part in emperor worship. It was still fairly visible during the sixteenth and seventeenth centuries when a perverted version of the divine right of kings theory was widespread and caused John Milton to say: "Absolute lordship and Christianity are inconsistent." [26] In our times it has been obscured by the fact that twentieth-century pretenders are too sophisticated to make open claims to divinity. That they do claim divinity by implication is manifest in the kind of allegiance they demand, the omnipotence to which they aspire, and the wisdom with which they wish to be credited. The claim, however obscured and unavowed, is preposterous as well as blasphemous. Martin Niemoeller challenged it publicly when he defied Hitler with the ringing words: "God is my Fuehrer." [27]

There seems to be an inclination on the part of present-day Christians to overlook the idolatrous nature of the totalitarian state. At least we do not hear it denounced very often, and other grounds of opposition are preferred. This is a serious mistake for which there is no warrant in Scripture. One of the most consistent and repeated theses of the Old Testament is that idolatry is fatal, bringing with it moral decay, political ineptitude and corruption, military weakness, economic exploitation, and national disintegration. It is the one sin which engenders all others. It is the sin which, more than any other, caused the crucifixion of Jesus. The Christians of early times were willing to undergo martyrdom rather than to be guilty of idolatry by worshiping Caesar. The threat of authoritarianism, therefore, is a deadly serious threat which deserves to be emphasized.

Totalitarianism, with emphasis on the "total," conflicts with the Christian doctrine of man. Christianity teaches that man was made in the image of God and that God so loved mankind that he gave his only begotten son to save it. It teaches that man's destiny is to glorify God and enjoy him forever. How, then, could totalitarianism with its view that man's whole significance is derived from the state be reconciled with Christianity? God can claim the whole of a man because he is perfect, but dictators who are so conspicuously imperfect cannot. All the old arguments against legal slavery as man-stealing apply to the kind of control exercised by the totalitarian state over its subjects. Even the willing submission to the totalitarian yoke is no justification because we are not our own to dispose of as we see fit. "On the contrary," says Calvin, "we are God's; to him, therefore, let us live and die." [28] In the heat of conflict with the Nazis, Martin Niemoeller drew the same conclusion, pointing out that just as the tribute money bore Caesar's image and superscription and therefore belonged to Caesar, so we bear God's image and superscription and therefore belong to God.[29] Totalitarianism thus turns out to be a consequence of authoritarianism. Idolatry still leads to slavery, as it did in Old Testament times.

There is one point on which Christianity gives some support to the totalitarian position. When the totalitarians reject the liberal distinction between internal and external aspects of human life as a method of divorcing one from the other, they agree with Christianity. Beliefs do affect behavior, and the inner life of man is the wellspring of his life in its external manifestations. Christ recognized the connection when he interpreted the commandments against murder and adultery by tracing these sins back to anger and lust. On numerous occasions Christ attacked a merely external compliance with the law as hypocrisy and a perversion of the law's intent. He spent much time teaching and preaching, and he instructed his disciples to do the same. Teaching and preaching are activities directed primarily to the mind and the heart where the control of behavior resides. He was warning us that inner conversion and not outward conformity is the key to genuine righteousness. The entire missionary effort of the church from the apostles to the present is predicated on this truth.

If Christianity is right in this analysis, then John Stuart Mill is wrong. What God has joined, i.e., the inner and outward life of man, liberalism cannot tear asunder. It does not follow, however, that the Christian must agree with the totalitarians about thought control. He cannot agree with them, because he believes in the providence of God, whereas the totalitarians do not. What government cannot and should not control is not thereby left unregulated if God is the Ruler of nations and the Lord of history. For that reason faith in God is the foundation of spiritual, intellectual, and civil liberty. If that faith is true, thought control by government is unnecessary and noxious, and it will not be sought by those who hold that faith. But if that faith is false, thought control by government is logically necessary, will be attempted, and will result in either tyranny or anarchy.

THE MODERN LIBERAL CONCEPT OF THE STATE

Modern liberalism was built upon the foundation of classical liberalism. The two share a common belief in individual liberty, representative institutions, constitutionalism, majority rule. A long history of struggles to wrest civil rights from absolute monarchs, to clear away the special privileges and burdensome restrictions of feudal lords, to establish the supremacy of elected representative bodies over lawmaking and taxation, to subject the executive power to the rule of law, to broaden the suffrage, and to provide universal education at public expense binds the two kinds of liberalism together and constitutes the world's liberal heritage. Because these monumental achievements are indeed a heritage, they are accepted and loyally supported by conservatism. There is still controversy, of course, but it is concerned with interpretations and does not call into question the liberal achievements themselves. In addition to these achievements, the two kinds of liberalism share a common outlook which includes an optimistic view of human nature, a belief in intellectual and social progress, and a high regard for science and technology, which borders on faith.

In spite of common background and common outlook, liberalism has changed so much that it is wise to differentiate between classical liberalism as exemplified by Thomas Jefferson and modern liberalism as exemplified by Franklin D. Roosevelt. The difference between them is not concerned with the structure but with the functions of government. Classical liberalism believed in laissez faire, whereas modern liberalism believes in government intervention and direction. While it would not be inaccurate to say that modern liberals are socialistic, it would be misleading because socialism has so many connotations that do not apply to liberalism. Modern liberalism is completely non-Marxist, does not accept the class struggle, and is not interested in promoting any dogmas about the nationalization of the means of production. To call the modern liberal state a welfare state would be essentially accurate but confusing on account of the association which a relentless and well financed propaganda has established between the terms "welfare state" and "police state." The police state is anathema to all liberals and is in no way connected either by design or by necessary consequence with the welfare state. In view of the many pitfalls produced by ambiguous usage and partisan propaganda, the term "modern liberal state" seems to be most neutral and least ambiguous.

The split between classical and modern liberalism was caused by changed conditions. In Jefferson's day the liberation of man, especially the common man, meant a weak and decentralized government. The individual could take care of himself. Land was plentiful; business did not require huge outlays of capital; entrance into the professions did not impose a prolonged and expensive education; workers could change jobs without much difficulty or go west and make a new start. What the individual needed above all else was equal opportunity. In colonial times the main obstacle had been government, which sanctioned large landholdings and primogeniture, imposed property restrictions on voting and officeholding, and granted monopolies and other special economic privileges. Under these conditions, liberals naturally viewed government as a threat to individual liberty.

In our day the situation is radically different. In an economy dominated by huge corporations it is not possible for small independent producers to defend themselves without the aid of government. The size of the capital outlay necessary to start a new business is prohibitive for large numbers of people. Capital outlay for the conquest of space and the forthcoming space-based enterprises is beyond the reach of everybody but the federal government. The kind of education required for entrance into the professions is lengthy and costly. Labor needs large and powerful unions to protect itself against management, but union members also need protection against bossism, and many workers remain unorganized. Problems of unemployment and obsolescence arise from technological progress and automation. All but a few investors lack the training and knowledge to protect themselves from exploitation and fraud, and wise investments in complex far-flung enterprises are increasingly matters for specialists. Farmers are dependent on prices they are unable to control and lack the knowledge and facilities needed to cope with weather hazards, erosion, and insect pests. Most people do not earn enough to protect themselves against the danger of prolonged illness when medical care is so expensive, not to mention the disabilities of old age and the possibility of extended periods of involuntary unemployment. Consumers cannot adequately defend themselves against misleading and uninformative advertising, nor are they in a position to bargain with large business units about high prices. Everywhere we turn we see an increasingly sensitive and complex economy, which all but very few people can manage or understand. Businessmen, professional men, farmers, workers, investors, depositors, and consumers are all at the mercy of war, revolution, and economic collapse anywhere in the world.

These many developments have forced a profound change in the attitude of liberals toward government, especially the federal government. It is evident that the federal government is the only agency which has the financial resources and the political power to protect the people against the hazards of modern life and to promote by positive cooperative action the welfare of all the people. Even the federal government may have to be supplemented by some degree of international control if the trend toward world economic interdependence continues to grow. The old classical liberal concept of the state is an anachronism in the kind of world we live in. Roosevelt's New Deal was a success because it recognized these facts of modern life and revised its concept of the state accordingly, and the Republican party has been denied for thirty years the opportunity to govern the country because it refused to recognize these facts and because it clung to an outdated conception of federal power.*

The electoral judgment which entrusted the government of the United States to the Democratic party during all these years was essentially a moral judgment. It condemned the kind of attitude symbolized by Herbert Hoover, i.e., when he smugly proclaimed in his 1928 campaign that America alone had finally solved the age-old problem of poverty and could not see the impending Great Depression; when he obstinately refused to see economic collapse when it came and kept seeing prosperity "around the corner"; and when his heartless and rigid cast of mind engendered only belated and ineffective remedial measures. On the other hand, electoral judgment endorsed the kind of attitude symbolized by Franklin D. Roosevelt, i.e., the warm responsiveness to human need, the willingness to experiment and to take bold measures to solve pressing problems, the determination to see that the federal government should act for the benefit of all the people and not just the favored few, the realism which understood the importance of international relations and the futility of isolationism, the discernment which correctly appraised the menace of fascism and took effective steps to overcome it. Most of us who are old enough to have lived through the transition from Hoover

* The Eisenhower victories were strictly personal, not party, victories.

to Roosevelt and the ensuing years in which the internal challenge of the Great Depression and the external challenge of fascist aggression were both successfully met remember the Roosevelt era as one of deliverance, adventure, and achievement.

The modern liberal idea that governmental power should be exercised for the good of all the people and should do for individuals and groups what they are unable to do for themselves is definitely in line with Christian teaching. There is no basis in the Old Testament for the narrow view which ascribes moral responsibilities to individuals alone and denies these responsibilities to the nation. One of the most persistent themes of prophets like Isaiah and Amos was that the nation and its rulers are bound by the moral law and have a moral mission to perform. The prophets demanded that the nation and its rulers be concerned with economic and social justice, relieve suffering and distress, promote temperance and good morals. They did not hesitate to hold kings personally responsible before God for meeting these demands and to tell them so to their face.

Classical liberals and some modern conservatives sometimes try to contrast the Old Testament with the New, arguing that national responsibilities in the social and economic field disappeared with ancient Israel and that Christ replaced these with a purely individualistic gospel. They argue from the premise that it is wrong to help people because people should help themselves. Such a premise is Emersonian, not Christian. When John the Baptist sent his disciples to inquire whether Jesus was really the Messiah, Jesus' reply was a total rejection of the Emersonian premise. Jesus merely pointed to what he had done for afflicted people. He was doing good to these people and did not suppose that he was making them less self-reliant. He sent out his disciples and instructed them to do likewise. There is no evidence that Jesus exempted anyone from discipleship on the ground that he was a government official. Furthermore, modern individualists forget that ancient Israel was succeeded by the New Israel, which is the church, and that the prophets' demand for social justice and welfare was not lost but transferred to the New Israel.

Many critics of modern liberalism substitute an individualistic gospel for the gospel of Christ. They say that the farmer, the worker, the depositor, the investor, the aged, the sick, the unemployed, the small businessman, and the consumer ought to look out for their own welfare. If the difficulties of these people are their own fault, moral responsibility is destroyed unless they suffer the full weight of the consequences. If they do not know enough, they should learn. If they make mistakes, they should pay for them. If they make their bed, they should lie in it. Critics of modern liberalism who pronounce such judgments so lightly and so easily look upon their government as though it were the incarnation of Cain, whose memorable words were: "Am I my brother's keeper?" [30] And yet many of these critics pray the Lord's Prayer every Sunday, including the petition: "And forgive us our debts, as we forgive our debtors." [31] They listen to the words of Paul: "We then that are strong ought to bear the infirmities of the weak, and not to please ourselves." [32] They hear the story of the good Samaritan and are told about the grace of God which no man deserves. They read in the Bible that a government official "is the minister of God to thee for good." [33] Surely there is a deep inconsistency here between religious profession and political philosophy.

In spite of the great affinity which exists between modern liberalism and Christianity about the duty of the state to promote the general welfare by taking positive action in economic and social affairs, no Christian should give to modern liberalism his unqualified support. The greatest weakness of modern liberalism has been and still is philosophical aridity. Modern liberals do not have the kind of philosophy which their program requires. They are consistently secular in their outlook, espousing both relativism and positivism. When they are challenged to produce some guiding principle, the best they can do is to offer that shallow slogan of the English utilitarians—the greatest good for the greatest number. The slogan does not define good, and the modern liberals often do not know that it is based on a crude pleasure-and-pain calculus. Neither does it give any explanation why the lesser number's good should not also be included.

The modern liberal's approach to the decisions of our day is subjective. Fearing "dogmatism" and "indoctrination," he makes everything a matter of personal likes and dislikes. He avoids making value judgments about likes and dislikes by counting them. For instance, if you cannot decide whether so-called "right-to-work" laws are sound public policy, you can count personal likes and dislikes on the subject in an election. If the subject was not an issue in the last election, the pollsters and survey research centers will be glad to come up with a calculated guess and advise the members of Congress or the state legislatures accordingly. The common good is redefined as the temporary adjustment of group pressures. Why? Because the common good demands evaluation, whereas group pressures lend themselves to computation. If the liberal gets into a controversy with other people, he will not say, "I am right," but, "That is the way I feel about it." You can argue about being right, but to do so about how someone feels is futile. Such an approach to life and politics is sheer escapism: you escape from the duty to commit yourself to a position and from the duty to think a problem through to a defensible solution. The first deficiency is moral, and the second is intellectual.

The failure of the New Deal to develop an adequate philosophy explains why its success was so short-lived, why in ten years' time dedicated New Dealers became "tired" New Dealers, why modern liberalism is more nostalgic than dynamic. Let us take agricultural policy as an example. The New Deal could meet the agricultural crisis of 1933 on a short-term basis with the Agricultural Adjustment Act. The farmer had to be saved, not tomorrow or the day after tomorrow, but right now. The obvious solution was to cut production, make parity payments, and raise prices. But is such a temporary expedient sound as a permanent policy? It is not. It makes no rational sense to stimulate agricultural productivity with one policy and curtail it with another policy, and it makes no moral sense to reduce farm output when so many people in the world suffer from starvation and malnutrition.

A sound long-range agricultural policy would require that the welfare of the farmer be achieved in terms of his place in a healthy economy with due regard to the welfare of business, labor, and other domestic interests. It would require that we solve the problems inherent in the difference between need (what people should have for their well-being) and demand (what people are actually able and willing to buy). It would require that the position of the United States in the world, including the moral obligations of leadership as well as the necessities of power politics, be considered. These requirements raise many difficulties which cannot be met by hastily devised compromises among whatever internal pressures happen to be the greatest at the moment. Basic theoretical questions have to be answered first. What is meant by a healthy national economy? Do you mean only full employment and the elimination of the business cycle or do you include such considerations as distributive justice and the ability of an economy to provide a great enough variety of employment and incentives to accommodate many different kinds of talents? We know what demand is, but what is need? Is it what people want or what they should want? To what extent is need physical, psychological, social, moral, and spiritual? The politicians as adjusters of individual and group pressures cannot answer these questions. The conventional research teams and task forces cannot answer them. Behavioral survey research centers cannot answer them. Electronic computers cannot answer them. Modern liberalism cannot answer them—it does not even ask them! To answer such questions, one has to have a comprehensive philosophy of government which, in turn, is a special application of a philosophy of reality. In other words, one has to have a theology. Even a bad theology or a pseudo theology is better than none, as the longevity and vitality of communism so unfortunately prove.

Modern liberalism is defective from a Christian standpoint in still another way. The defect is the optimistic view of human nature which it inherited from classical liberalism. Both kinds of liberalism postulate that man is inherently good. If liberals are confronted with the undeniable existence of evil as exemplified in jealousy, greed, cruelty, exploitation, and fraud, the reply is that society is responsible. How society "got off the track," so to speak, remains unexplained. What keeps it off the track receives several unsatisfactory answers.

Liberals share the old Greek belief that ignorance is the source of all evil and that if men knew enough, they would always be good. In that case the answer is simple and can be stated in one word—education. So liberals have gone all out for education from kindergarten to graduate school. Now they are extending their efforts and enthusiastically embracing adult education, TV courses, audio-visual aids, teaching machines, correspondence courses, bookmobiles, and short institutes. These efforts are doubtless laudable, and it would be a rare individual who championed illiteracy and ignorance. But too much is expected of education, and the reason is that the underlying assumption that knowledge and goodness are inseparable is false. Education is a two-edged sword which makes both the good and the wicked more effective. The Germans were among the best educated people in the world, yet that fact did not prevent them from supporting Hitler. If the liberals were right about education, it would follow that the most learned people in our country would also be superior in moral and civic conduct. No very close acquaintance with scholars is needed to know that this is not the case. To admit the limitations of education and scholarship is not being anti-intellectual, nor is it an invitation to close schools, burn books, and persecute scholars. It is just being truthful.

The other answer which liberals, both classical and modern, give to the problem of evil is that society is responsible. They are strict environmentalists. If we could get rid of economic insecurity and poverty, if everyone had enough to eat and to wear, if there were no city slums and rural shacks, if physical disease and mental illness could be cured by physicians and psychiatrists, there would be no evil in the world. If this is true, it is only a matter of time before our scientists and technicians relegate the problem of evil to the archives. But the fallacy of this extreme environmentalism is only too evident. All one has to do to see this fallacy is to take a look at the rich. They have fine food, fine clothes, and fine housing. Their wealth protects them from worries about unemployment and old-age insecurity, and it commands the best medical and psychiatric service available in the country. But is good moral and civic conduct inseparable from wealth? Few indeed are those who would say so.

The liberals never appreciate the depth of evil, and one even wonders sometimes if they believe in its reality. It would seem that two world wars, the atrocities perpetrated by the fascist and communist regimes against their own subjects, the systematic murder of six million Jews, the bloody repression of Hungary by the Soviet Union, the brutal conquest of Tibet by Red China, the terror and torture in Algeria, the riots in Little Rock and New Orleans, the plastic bombs in Paris, the firing squads in Cuba, and countless other examples of man's inhumanity to man would demolish once and for all any easy optimism about the inherent goodness of human nature. But the liberal illusion dies hard. Had liberalism been Christian, there would have been no such illusion because Christianity has always made allowance for the existence of demonic forces and placed the source of wickedness in the human heart and will. The Christian doctrine of original sin asserts that in every human being there is a rebellion against God which affects all his faculties. Power can repress but not cure it; reason cannot reach it and is twisted into rationalization; emotion is corrupted by selfishness and pride; and the will is imprisoned by sin and the effects of sin. Only the grace of God can bring salvation, regeneration, and sanctification. Law and politics are consolidating and manipulative forces, but they are not creative forces. There has to be something already there to be consolidated, and you cannot manipulate what does not exist. The missionary precedes the jurist and the statesman.

Liberals have generally looked with distaste upon Christian teaching concerning human nature. Such teaching was deemed unfashionable, prescientific and unscientific, a remnant of medieval superstition, a dying vestige of an unenlightened Puritanism. Above all it was deemed academic and irrelevant. The facts, however, confute the liberals. If an extensive liberal welfare program is entrusted to morally corrupt and spiritually unenlightened government officials, the results will be disastrous. You will get stealing, favoritism, inefficiency, and abuse of power. These results will be even more predictable and pronounced if the citizenry's moral standards are similarly low, for in that case there will be no protest and therefore no improvement. Public opinion will then overlook the stealing, acquiesce in the favoritism, condone the inefficiency, and endure the abuse of power. Worse still, the public will begin to get in on the gravy train and thus become accomplices. Under such conditions a welfare program is itself a corrupting influence which will metastasize like cancer in the body politic. Reform becomes incredibly difficult, if not downright impossible, because too many people are involved and are sure to resist exposure with every means at their disposal. The logic of sin takes over and the harsh but accurate diagnosis of Scripture applies: "And this is the condemnation, that light is come into the world, and men loved darkness rather than light, *because their deeds were evil*. For every one that doeth evil hateth the light, *lest his deeds should be reproved.*" [34] When conditions have reached a level so low that moral integrity is extinguished and conscience is stone dead, the only possible hope for recovery lies with an outside force. In the case of one of our states, that force can only be federal intervention, but what if the whole nation should succumb? The answer given by history in such an extremity is foreign conquest (e.g., the conquest of the Roman

Empire by the Germanic tribes) or national extinction (e.g., the enslavement and destruction of the Ten Tribes of the Northern Kingdom of Israel by the Assyrians).

We are not suggesting that the American body politic is now in the grip of so advanced a stage of moral illness, though there is moral illness enough to cause grave concern. Neither are we attempting to justify those critics of modern liberalism who misuse the Christian doctrine of man to block and discredit all social reform. The important point to establish is that moral integrity and welfare programs are interdependent and that social reform cannot succeed beyond the moral capacity of both government and people to sustain it. Secularism prevented the modern liberals from perceiving the connection. They met with some success because they were drawing on the moral capital accumulated by centuries of Christian life, but they neither created this capital nor replenished it.

The foregoing discussion of classical liberalism, conservatism, totalitarianism, and modern liberalism proves that the Christian faith has much to say concerning the state. What it has to say, moreover, is by no means vague and overly general. The many specific points of political doctrine, current and traditional attitudes, movements and policies which have been singled out for analysis and evaluation stand as conclusive evidence that realities which are concrete and alive have been dealt with in a meaningful way. The outcries of readers whose toes have been stepped on will testify as to that aspect of the matter. Christianity cannot be identified with any one of the particular political ideologies or systems. It cannot, therefore, be a front for capitalism, democracy, the American way of life, or any of even the highest achievements of man. On the other hand, the confrontation of political realities with the Christian faith reveals that the results are positive as well as negative. What emerges has enough substance to be grasped by the human mind, whether secular or Christian, and utilized as a standard for thought and action.

Nevertheless, a great deal of the Christian teaching about politics remains shadowy and lacking in precision. This shortcoming is partially the effect of confining our analysis to the state, which is itself a very general concept. A more definite picture can be drawn if we proceed to re-think in Christian terms some of the particular concepts for which the state is a generalized composite. We need to know what Christian thought can do with concepts like constitution, citizenship, and representation. Only then can many details come into clear focus and the broad outline of the Christian teaching concerning politics acquire the necessary definiteness.

Chapter IV

CHARTER AND CHOICE

IMPORTANCE OF THE CONSTITUTION IN AMERICAN THINKING

FEW concepts are more important to Americans than the concept of constitution. At no time in our history have we lived otherwise than under written constitutional law, for all the thirteen colonies had charters which were constitutions. Even before the Pilgrims landed on the shores of North America, they drew up a rudimentary constitution known as the Mayflower Compact. When the followers of Thomas Hooker moved beyond the jurisdiction of Massachusetts, they drew up and adopted the Fundamental Orders of Connecticut, which was their constitution and which the King later sanctioned. When settlers crossed the mountains into what is now Tennessee and found themselves beyond the reach of the government of North Carolina, they drew up constitutions—the Articles of the Watauga Association in East Tennessee and the Cumberland Compact in Middle Tennessee. When North Carolina ceded its western claims to the United States without consulting the inhabitants involved, the people of East Tennessee revolted, adopted a constitution, and formed the state of Franklin which unsuccessfully sought admission to the Union. When Texas became an independent republic, it adopted a constitution. No new state has ever joined the Union without first proposing a constitution which was scrutinized by Congress. Even Puerto Rico, which is not a state but an "associated commonwealth," did not receive its present status until Congress had approved the Puerto Rican constitution, and this approval was no perfunctory matter. The United States as a nation has always had a written national constitution, the Articles of Confederation from 1781 to 1789 and the Constitution from 1789 to the present, except for the short period of the Continental Congress from 1776 to 1781. Some critics say that we have a mania for constitutions. It has been suggested that if three Americans were shipwrecked on a desert island, the first thing they would do would be to adopt a constitution under which there would be a president, vice-president, and secretary-treasurer. There is scarcely any private organization which does not have a "constitution." Even if this document is lost, forgotten, ignored, or not taken seriously, the members would feel uncomfortable without the thought that there is one somewhere.

The Constitution of the United States is taken very seriously, often to the point of reverence. No official, federal or state, can hold office without swearing an oath to uphold it. When a citizen applies for a passport, he must swear to uphold and defend the Constitution against all enemies, foreign and domestic, without evasion or reservation. Aliens who seek American citizenship must demonstrate a knowledge of and affection for the Constitution. No important bill or policy is adopted without considerable discussion of its constitutionality, so much so that the merits and demerits are sometimes actually forgotten. The tendency to think in constitutional terms is so strong that the American's instinctive reaction, when he does not like something, is to say, "It's unconstitutional."

In view of the central importance assigned to the Constitution by Americans, it is appropriate to go into the question of what a constitution is. Political science has an embarrassingly rich literature on this question, as we found to be the case when dealing with the concept of the state. Constitutions have been classified as substantive and formal, rigid and flexible, written and unwritten. They have been related to state forms and classified accordingly (e.g., liberal, socialist, national). Sometimes it is their origin (or supposed origin) which is used as the principle of classification, and we speak of a constitution as a social compact among individuals, as a contract between states, as the enactment of a people, or as the grant of a sovereign authority. Sometimes constitutions are treated as statements of the values actually honored and observed in a country and therefore regarded as law (e.g., in the United States). At other times constitutions are treated as statements of national aspirations rather than national practice and are therefore more properly regarded as political rather than legal documents (e.g., in many Latin American countries). The variety and richness of constitutions have a number of sources, among which different national backgrounds and the experience of different historical periods are the most important. It will simplify the discussion if we concentrate on American experience and bring in from time to time such comparative and historical insights as are needed for clarification and amplification.

In the American mind a constitution is first of all a written document which contains a preamble, a bill of rights, a framework of government, an amending clause, and such amendments as have been added to the original document over the years. The preamble identifies the source from which the constitution derives its authority and states the purposes which it seeks to fulfill. The bill of rights is a catalogue of substantive and procedural restraints on government and is designed to protect persons. The framework of government sets up organs, agencies, and units of government, both territorially and functionally, and defines, as-signs, and limits their powers. The amending clause provides a special procedure or procedures whereby the original document may be changed or revised. In addition to the written document, it is understood that the interpretations and usages which have been sanctioned by time and general consent are to be regarded as part of the constitution conceived in a broad sense as being a "living" document. Finally, a constitution is regarded as positive law, a set of obligatory forms which courts will recognize and enforce.

CONSTITUTIONS
AND NATIONAL VALUES

Now that we have briefly outlined the American conception of what a constitution is, we must turn to an analysis of its meaning and implica-tions. We shall begin with an examination of the Constitution of the United States, which sets the standards of the traditional American conception of a constitution, as the embodiment of the values of the American people. The placing of these values in the constitutional text sets them apart from other values which may enjoy considerable sup-port among the people. Placing them in the Constitution means that they are well-nigh universally held. They are shared by no mere 51 per cent majority but by a consensus approaching unanimity. Nor are these values the passing fancy of a temporary enthusiasm, for they are the enduring moral convictions of the people over many generations through many periods of crisis and strain. The fact that they are embodied in the Constitution further means that the people are formally committed to them and that government officials are pledged to support and pro-mote them.

A clue to the selfhood of the people whose values are embodied in a constitution is usually found in the preamble. Because the preamble is not considered law by the courts, there is an inclination to pay little attention to it. The inclination is strengthened by familiarity often in-duced by the practice of memorizing the preamble and thereby making it a matter of unthinking repetition. The outcome is a feeling that the preamble could not be anything else than what it is. How else could it read?

It is not until we apply a little historical perspective that the possibil-ities become visible. There was a time when preambles clearly stated that the constitution was the grant, magnanimously and graciously handed down, of a sovereign monarch. The pattern for this type of preamble was set by the charter of 1814 granted by King Louis XVIII. Another type of selfhood was reflected in the old Hohenzollern empire. The pre-amble of the German constitution of 1871 made it plain that the German Reich was a dynastic pact. The transformation of the German Reich from a dynastic federal to a democratic unitary basis was accurately mirrored in the preamble of the Weimar constitution of 1919.* The preambles of all the Soviet constitutions reflect the class basis and Marxist orientation of their makers and commit the state to the communist ideology.

There has been much argument about the historical accuracy of the conception of selfhood embodied in the Preamble of our own Constitution. The debates in the Philadelphia Convention of 1787 leave no doubt that the framers were vigorously nationalist and that the language of the Preamble was not adopted by inadvertence. Among themselves the framers consistently used the word "national." Their substitution of the word "federal" during the ratification campaign was a clever propaganda move. On the other hand, the two words became synonymous and the viewpoint of Hamilton, Marshall, Webster, and Lincoln triumphed. Whatever doubts one might entertain about the accuracy of the Preamble in 1789, American history has made it true. It is now well established that the Constitution is not a contract between sovereign states but the enactment of the American people, from which *both* the federal government and the states derive their authority. Whether or not the framers who wrote the Preamble were good historians, they were very good prophets. Our customary use of plural subject and singular verb in speaking of our country—i.e., the United States *is*—symbolizes the supremacy of political reality over grammatical purity.†

In many modern constitutions the selfhood of the people is conveniently spelled out in what is called the "dogmatic" part of the constitution. What is meant thereby is a series of propositions which commit the state to certain positions. The short-lived Spanish constitution of 1931 was an unusually good illustration. The first seven articles stated, among other things, that Spain was a democratic republic (i.e., neither monarchical nor Marxist), "integral" territorially (i.e., something between unitary and federal), secular religiously, Castilian linguistically, and committed to peaceful and legal methods internationally.[1] What happened to that Spanish constitution shows that the values of its makers were not in fact the values of the Spanish people or, at least, did not reflect anything like the national consensus which a constitution is supposed to symbolize.

In keeping with our Anglo-Saxon dislike for abstractions, the Constitution of the United States contains no "dogmatic" section, though there are "dogmatic" propositions scattered throughout the document

---

* In spite of the unitary preamble, the Weimar constitution set up a federal republic.

† Even states' rights agitators lapse into this usage. Similarly, it takes a real effort to say "War Between the States" for "Civil War," and it is not the length but the political unreality which is responsible for the effort.

(e.g., the requirement that the states have a republican form of government, the general declaratory statements which begin the first three articles and incorporate the theory of separation of powers). The task of reconstructing the values to which the Constitution commits us as a people is a difficult one. We shall try to sketch the broad outlines without introducing tedious references to particular articles, sections, and paragraphs.

According to the standards set by the Constitution, we believe the purposes for which government is instituted are union, justice, domestic tranquillity, the common defense, the general welfare, and the blessings of liberty. In other words, our national order should be stable, just, and free. The right of human personality to grow and to reach full maturity, regardless of race or creed or class, should be guaranteed by legal provisions to protect privacy, conscience, association, oral and written expression of thought and feeling. Special privileges such as titles of nobility or special disabilities such as slavery should not be allowed, and all individuals should be equal before the law and entitled to whatever standing in the community they have earned for themselves. No person should be deprived of life, liberty, or property without due process of law, a rule which commits us to the proposition that the end does not justify the means. Rights which have been validly acquired under the law and in good faith are vested rights which should not be impaired by retroactive government action. All persons should enjoy the equal protection of the laws, which means that public authority should have neither favorites nor victims but should exercise the power which belongs to all for the benefit of all. The right to vote should belong to all citizens, except in cases where the common good indicates that it should be denied for defendable reasons such as infancy, insanity, or crime.

Government should be based on the consent of the governed, to which end the chief policy makers should be elected by and responsible to the people; the military should be subordinate to civil authority; the levying of taxes and the expenditure of public money should be for the public good as determined by the elected representatives of the people; local matters should be settled on the basis of local standards of what is right and expedient, and national matters settled on the basis of national standards. Government officials should be responsible to the people for the exercise of power but should follow the dictates of their conscience and judgment during their term of office and not be bound by instructions or harassed by procedures which undermine their representative character, such as the referendum, the initiative, and the recall. The powers of government should stay in the branches (legislative, executive, judicial) and units (federal and state) where the American people have placed them and not be abdicated, usurped, or redelegated in such a way as to impair the integrity of the functional and territorial distribution of power laid down in the Constitution.

The foregoing cursory survey of our national values as embodied in the Constitution can be summarized by saying that our country is committed to peace, justice, and liberty, together with those means which our national experience as specified in the Constitution holds to be necessary to the fulfillment of those ends. These constitutional ends and means are the official standard of our national values.

NATIONAL VALUES
AND CHRISTIAN APPRAISAL

Many centuries ago, Augustine wrestled with the problem of passing judgment on earthly states. He started from Cicero's definition of the state as a people bound together by mutual interest and consent to law. Cicero made it clear that by law he meant the legal embodiment of justice, defining justice as giving to everyone his due. What troubled Augustine was that there is always a gap between law and justice. "Justice being taken away, then," he exclaimed, "what are kingdoms but great robberies? For what are robberies themselves, but little kingdoms?" [2] This is particularly true where the people do not give God his due. "Where, then," he asked, "is the justice of man, when he deserts the true God and yields himself to impure demons?" [3] On this basis a true state is impossible, and you have only "some promiscuous multitude unworthy of the name of people." [4]

Augustine solved his problem in the following way:

> But if we discard this definition of a people, and, assuming another, say that a people is an assemblage of rational beings bound together by a common agreement as to the object of their love, then, in order to discover the character of any people, we have only to observe what they love. Yet whatever it loves, if only it is an assemblage of reasonable beings and not of beasts, and is bound together by an agreement as to the objects of love, it is reasonably called a people; and it will be a superior people in proportion as it is bound together by higher interests, inferior in proportion as it is bound together by lower.[5]

On this basis Augustine concluded that the Roman people formed a true state and identified the "object of their love" as power and glory. These two objects were not, of course, by any means the highest possible. Yet Augustine found some merit in them: "Nevertheless, they who restrain baser lusts, not by the power of the Holy Spirit obtained by the faith of piety, or by the love of intelligible beauty, but by the desire of human praise, or, at all events, restrain them better by the love of such praise, are not indeed yet holy, but only less base." [6] The relative merit

of the Roman standard (the love of power and glory) explains Roman
success. On the other hand, the fact that this standard is spiritually defective explains the eventual fall of the Roman Empire.* The true standard of man is to glorify God and not to seek human praise. Augustine
referred to Christ's observation in the Sermon on the Mount that those
who pray, fast, or give alms to be seen of men have their reward already.
God gave the Romans what they wanted. Whose fault was it that the
reward proved unsatisfying and ephemeral? "There is no reason," Augustine concluded, "why they should complain against the justice of the
supreme and true God—'they have received their reward.' " [7]

If we apply the Augustinian test to the United States, the constitutional
standard we have outlined becomes "the object of our love" and therefore the measure of our righteousness. In the light of that standard, we
do better than the ancient Romans because peace, justice, and liberty
are higher Christian values than power and glory. There is no doubt
that Augustine would concur in this judgment, for he taught that peace
and justice are the proper end of temporal states and that liberty is the
consequence of righteousness. In spite of the dream of an "American
Empire" by a few founding fathers like Hamilton, a passing enthusiasm
for "Manifest Destiny," and a period of economic imperialism around
the turn of the nineteenth century, national power was never one of our
central values. As a nation we were never committed to world conquest
like the German Fascists, to world revolution like the Russian Communists, or to carrying "the white man's burden" everywhere in the world
like the British imperialists. Even in our struggle with the Soviet Union,
we have allies but no satellites. We took in our western territories as
states on an equal footing with the original thirteen states; we gave the
Philippines their independence; we did not annex the countries of Central
America and the Caribbean in which we used to intervene; and we gave
American citizenship and self-government to the Puerto Ricans. National
glory was even less appealing, in spite of occasional Fourth of July
oratory.

On the other hand, there is a national value which is not mentioned,
at least not as such, in the Constitution but which many friends and foes
of our people think is typically American. That value is called by various
names such as wealth, material prosperity, the "American standard of
living," or money. Its constitutional anchor, if one there must be, is the
reference to the general welfare in the Preamble. To many people the

---

* It should be noted that the sacking of Rome by the Goths was the event
which caused Augustine to write *The City of God*. The pagans blamed this catastrophe on the spread of Christianity and the consequent anger of the ancient
Roman gods. Augustine undertook to show that it was the inadequacy of these
ancient gods which engendered the moral decay and military weakness that led to
the sacking of Rome.

term "general welfare" is synonymous with material prosperity. There is nothing wrong with material prosperity as such, but there is very much wrong with treating it as an idol, as an object of worship, as the supreme value of life. It stands on a lower plane than peace, justice, and liberty as an "object of love." Scripture is full of warnings against this particular form of idolatry. Perhaps the most often quoted (and misquoted) warning is that of Paul in the First Epistle to Timothy: "For the love of money is the root of all evil: which while some coveted after, they have erred from the faith, and pierced themselves through with many sorrows." [8] But the warning runs through the Bible from the denunciations of the prophets to the strictures against the rich in the Epistle of James. In spite of all warnings, the inroads of this particular form of idolatry are considerable and amount to a serious corruption of our national constitutional standard. Too often we find Americans who are loyal to the Constitution only because they attribute our material prosperity to its beneficent provisions, thereby debasing our national values and undermining the stability of our constitutional order by linking it with the business cycle. In view of our national material prosperity, which is unequaled anywhere in the world and without precedent in all history, one cannot help but wonder if the fate of Rome awaits us. Like the ancient Romans, we modern Americans have gotten what we wanted. Will some modern Augustine arise and say to us: Do not complain to God about your precarious international position and possible national destruction, for have you not had your reward?

CONSTITUTIONAL LAW
AND NATIONAL MORALITY

The discussion of our constitutional standard, i.e., the Augustinian "object of our love," leads quite naturally to the relationship between law and morality. The problem arises because the constitutional standard is obviously a moral one and because it characterizes itself as "the supreme law of the land." Among the many current opinions which are most commonly expressed on the subject are two which deserve more than a passing mention: (1) that the law embodies the average morality of a people, (2) that people cannot be made good by law.

The first opinion is expressed in various ways. Most frequently it is said that the law embodies the minimum standards of a people. If by "minimum" one means that there are no moral standards lower than those sanctioned by the law, the statement is false. There are people who do not believe that cheating and stealing are wrong, but they certainly do not have the law on their side. It would be better to say that the law embodies the lowest *common* denominator of the community in the area of morals. This would recognize that there are people whose moral standards are not a common moral denominator because those who live up to them are uncommonly good. It is the mission of those people to raise the moral level of others to the point where the higher standards become the common standards. In the meantime, all that the morally superior people have a right to ask of the law is liberty—liberty being defined in the luminous words of Montesquieu as "the power of doing what we ought to will, and in not being constrained to do what we ought not to will." [9]

The second opinion, i.e., that people cannot be made good by law, is frequently voiced with great conviction by some and received as a truism by others. This opinion contains both truth and error, depending on what one means by it, and therefore should not be accepted uncritically. If by it one means that true righteousness is an inner quality of the spirit which external compulsion cannot adequately reach, the opinion is sound. There are occasions when we need to be reminded of the freedom of the spirit, which lies beyond the jurisdiction of positive law. Thus, when the people of East Tennessee wrote the constitution of the abortive state of Franklin and provided that all liars be disfranchised, they overreached themselves. They were right in believing that it makes a vast amount of difference politically whether the electorate is given to truth or falsehood, but wrong in thinking that the constitutional requirement was administrable and could take care of the situation.

On the other hand, we must not go too far by denying all connection between positive law and the inner life of man. When the law defines first-degree murder as premeditated killing, it is certainly joining the external fact of killing with the internal factor of premeditation. The law differentiates between the taxpayer who underpays by inadvertence or honest mistake and the one who does so knowingly and deliberately. The law speaks of malicious intent, of good faith, of sanity and insanity. In all these and many other cases the law recognizes the existence of intangible realities and attaches consequences to them. The difficulty in ascertaining and assessing these realities does not justify confining the law to external behavior: it only means that there are limits beyond which positive law is not effective and therefore should not overextend itself. What is involved here is the difference between what is just and what is quixotic. Experience and wisdom are needed to tell the difference, and even these are by no means infallible.

To say that people cannot be made good by law is misleading, and it is wrong if we fail to admit, as is frequently the case, that people can be improved through law. Let us consider an example. The Constitution provides that no state shall "deny to any person within its jurisdiction the equal protection of the laws." [10] This provision does not create a new ethical norm, for this norm was already ethically valid before it was incorporated in the Constitution. The effect of putting it in the Constitution is to make this ethical norm a legal norm as well. The immense prestige of the Constitution is thrown on the side of the ethical norm which, by itself, had not proved sufficiently persuasive to enough people. The ethical norm now receives an honored and official place where it is clearly visible and not easily ignored, and respect for the Constitution brings with it a substantial accretion of supporters. Those who previously opposed the ethical norm or one of its applications, who approved or condoned violations of it by their state governments, are now in a quandary. Many of those people will now experience a sense of guilt which will eventually swing some of them to the right side.

Another consequence of putting this ethical norm in the Constitution is that the power of the federal government is involved. Individual defiance of federal court orders is a very serious business which means fines and jail sentences. Organized resistance is even more serious and means the intervention of federal marshals and, if necessary, of the armed forces of the United States. When face to face with a situation of this kind, most people will comply with the law whether resignedly, reluctantly, or indignantly. The moral value of that kind of compliance is small, but there is some moral value nonetheless. In the course of time, new habits become established and grudging compliance is transformed into something better when it is apparent that the dark forebodings on which much of the opposition was based were groundless. Furthermore, the supporters of the ethical norm who were silenced by intimidation and a police-state atmosphere are encouraged and strengthened by the protection of their government. They can be much more effective now that they can act and speak in the open, and they can win over those who did not adhere to the ethical norm because the case for it had never been presented to them. The situation has changed to one in which reasoned argument and moral persuasion are once again feasible means of communication. A new countervailing force is born which can mobilize the conscience of the local people and deliver the state government from the clutches of men of ill will.

Even with all the advantages which flow from incorporation in the Constitution, the road ahead is not at all easy and short. The point to be understood here is not that constitutionalizing an ethical principle and enforcing it with federal power is a 100 per cent effective remedy. The point is that a great deal of moral progress can be achieved through law. Court orders are only a beginning. One may concede that they are not the best kind of beginning, but they are a beginning, and they are not the end. When all qualifications have been made, the one basic and irremovable fact remains that law is a very powerful and significant educational force, and nothing should be allowed to make us forget it.

THE CONSTITUTION
AND OBJECTIVE NORMS

There is another line of thinking about the Constitution with which we must deal in some detail. It is essentially a cynical line which holds that the Constitution is not a body of objective intelligible principles and rules capable of serving as a guide to citizens and officials. At stake is the traditional belief that our government is one of laws and not of men.*

A very good example of this line of thinking can be found in the following statement by Lawrence Dennis:

> The oath to uphold the Constitution really amounts to nothing more or less than an oath to uphold what the courts may pronounce the Constitution to be. A rational oath of allegiance or of office must be an engagement to uphold the sovereign will or might of the people as made explicit by a duly authorized leader or representative of the people. A person can intelligently swear to obey and uphold the commands of a king or a supreme council or leader. But one cannot intelligently pledge one's self to uphold a document which one is incompetent to interpret, a Court interpretation of which one cannot obtain to settle a given doubt, and all the thousands of court interpretations of which no finite mind—not even that of a Philadelphia lawyer—can possibly encompass.[11]

It would be comforting if these words could be dismissed as the isolated view of one of those very few Americans who openly praised fascism and recommended that our country follow the example of Hitler and Mussolini. Unfortunately, this is not the case. Many highly respected and much more influential people share the same position with regard to the nature of law, constitutional or otherwise.

There is, for instance, K. N. Llewellyn. Speaking of judges, sheriffs, jailers, and lawyers he says: *"What these officials do about disputes is, to my mind, the law itself."* [12] In other words, law is official behavior. Llewellyn believes that official behavior exhibits certain regularities which can be generalized into "rules" which make prediction and manipulation possible—particularly the latter. He thus comes to the following conclusion: "And *rules*, through all of this, are important so far as they help you to get judges to do something. That is their importance. That is all their importance, except as pretty playthings." [13]

Another even more distinguished advocate of this point of view is Thurman Arnold. He, too, looks at law as behavior. The main difference with Llewellyn is that Arnold lays more stress on the "pretty playthings" as mythology. "We may define jurisprudence or the science of

* Some qualifications are needed to make this belief completely valid, but these will be made later on.

law in our present day," says Arnold, "as the effort to construct a logical heaven behind the courts, wherein contradictory ideals are made to seem consistent." [14] In other words, folk law is folklore. But folklore is important. Arnold explains why: "Courts owe their prestige to the idea that they are constantly making the law more certain. They owe their power to the fact that they never clarify total situations. They leave the cases which are just around the corner always undecided, and thus compel businessmen and legislators to be constantly in fear of their judicial veto. This is characteristic of judicial government. *Without it we would scarcely have what people call a government of law.*" [15]

The behavioral approach to law has a multitude of roots, and many people, sometimes of very different backgrounds, have contributed to it. There is the crude behaviorism of the psychologist John Broadus Watson, which reduces all realities to matter and motion (e.g., reading is equated with eye movements and thinking with incipient throat movements). There is the philosophy of Henri Bergson with its strictly instrumental view of intelligence as a fabricating tool useful for the adjustment of means to ends but useless for the perception of truth. There is the philosophy of pragmatism so succinctly expressed by Dennis: "If it works, it survives, and if it survives, it works." [16] There is the Sorelian concept of the social myth, which has been avidly espoused by so many social scientists. There is the positivism of Auguste Comte and its naive conception of science.

It would be futile for our purposes to go into an extended discussion of these ideological origins of the behavioral approach to constitutionalism. These origins are mentioned only to show that the views of people like Dennis, Llewellyn, and Arnold are not isolated instances which can be dismissed as idiosyncrasies. They are deep-seated aberrations which confuse reasoning with rationalization and deny objectivity to all but empirical realities. They are utterly destructive of constitutional government because once constitutional norms have been denied an independent existence, there is nothing left to guide either citizen or official except subjective desires. Nothing is intelligible, and everything is visceral.

It so happens that the constitutional issues raised by behaviorism were thrashed out long ago in the history of the Christian church. The consensus of Christian thought is incompatible with behaviorism and points to the way in which a constitution should be conceived and interpreted. Let us first consider the testimony of Scripture. The Bible itself is a written, objective, intelligible, meaningful standard given by God to direct man's thought and conduct. "All scripture," says Paul, "is given by inspiration of God, and is profitable for doctrine, for reproof, for correction, for instruction in righteousness: That the man of God may be perfect, thoroughly furnished unto all good works." [17] The intelligibility and objectivity of the law is repeatedly affirmed in the Old Testament. A rather vividly worded instance of this quality is the following:

> For this commandment which I command thee this day, it is not hidden from thee, neither is it far off. It is not in heaven, that thou shouldest say, Who shall go up for us to heaven, and bring it unto us, that we may hear it, and do it? Neither is it beyond the sea, that thou shouldest say, Who shall go over the sea for us, and bring it unto us, that we may hear it, and do it? But the word is very nigh unto thee, in thy mouth, and in thy heart, that thou mayest do it.[18]

This same quality of the law is frequently described in the Psalms: "The law of the Lord is perfect, converting the soul: the testimony of the Lord is sure, making wise the simple. The statutes of the Lord are right, rejoicing the heart: the commandment of the Lord is pure, enlightening the eyes." [19] In the Book of Proverbs we read: "When thou goest, it shall lead thee; when thou sleepest, it shall keep thee; and when thou awakest, it shall talk with thee. For the commandment is a lamp; and the law is light; and reproofs of instruction are the way of life. . . ." [20] The power of Scripture is also acknowledged in many places in the New Testament as, for instance, in Luke's comment on the superiority of the people of Berea: "These were more noble than those in Thessalonica, in that they received the word with all readiness of mind, and searched the scriptures daily, whether those things were so." [21]

It is clear that there is no support whatever in Scripture for the idea that law is official behavior. Quite the contrary: it is the standard by which official behavior, as well as all other behavior, is judged. This standard is not identical with men's wishes and preconceptions. Indeed, it often clashes with them. Nor is this standard a compilation of isolated and unrelated rules, precepts, stories, prophecies, letters, and poems. There runs a design or pattern through the books of the Bible which ties all the parts together into a single whole. The Christian church has affirmed that the unity of the Bible, written as it was over many centuries through the prism of many different personalities under a great variety of circumstances, is attributable to divine authorship. God was its author, not its editor. Certainly no one laid greater emphasis on this point than historic Protestantism. A typical statement of the historic Protestant position is to be found in the Confession of Faith of the Presbyterian Church in the United States: "The authority of the Holy Scripture, for which it ought to be believed and obeyed, dependeth not upon the testimony of any man or church, but wholly upon God (who is truth itself), the author thereof; and therefore it is to be received, because it is the word of God." [22]

There are critics who argue that even if we concede the divine authority of Scripture, the meaning and applicability are of doubtful certainty and clarity. They say that even Satan quotes Scripture, that you can prove anything by Scripture, and that the guidance you get from the Bible is as ambiguous and therefore as useless as that of the Delphic oracle. The objection is not at all new and, consequently, has been answered many times. Calvin answered it by asserting that the Bible is self-authenticating and that its essential meaning is plain and obvious to all who seek to understand it.

Wherefore, when the Church receives it, and seals it with her suffrage, she does not authenticate a thing otherwise dubious or controvertible; but knowing it to be the truth of God, performs a duty of piety, by treating it with immediate veneration. But, with regard to the question, How shall we be persuaded of its divine original, unless we have recourse to the decree of the Church? this is just as if any one should inquire, How shall we learn to distinguish light from darkness, white from black, sweet from bitter? For the Scripture exhibits as clear evidence of its truth, as white and black things do of their colour, or sweet and bitter things of their taste.[23]

The plain and objective meaning of Scripture, however, is not effective unless the reader or hearer is ready to receive it rather than reject or distort it. Recognizing this, Calvin observes: "It is necessary, therefore, that the same Spirit, who spake by the mouths of the prophets, should penetrate into our hearts, to convince us that they faithfully delivered the oracles which were divinely intrusted to them." [24]

One of the greatest Calvinists, John Milton, stated the same position on the plainness and directive efficacy of Scripture in words even more precise and beautiful, which deserve to be quoted in full:

It is true, there be some books, and especially some places in those books, that remain clouded; yet ever that which is most necessary to be known is most easy; and that which is most difficult, so far expounded itself ever, as to tell us how little it imports our saving knowledge. Hence, to infer a general obscurity over all the text, is a mere suggestion of the devil to dissuade men from reading it, and casts an aspersion of dishonour both upon the mercy, truth, and wisdom of God. We count it no gentleness or fair dealing in a man of power amongst us, to require strict and punctual obedience, and yet give out all his commands ambiguous and obscure; we should think he had a plot upon us; certainly such commands were no commands, but snares. The very essence of truth is plainness and brightness; the darkness and crookedness is our own. The wisdom of God created understanding, fit and proportionable to truth, the object and end of it, as the eye to the thing visible. If our understanding have a film of ignorance over it, or be blear with gazing on other false glisterings, what is that to truth? If we will but purge with sovereign eyesalve that intellectual ray which God hath planted in us, then we would believe the Scriptures protesting their own plainness and perspicuity, calling to them to be instructed, not only the wise and the learned, but the simple, the poor, the babes; foretelling an extraordinary effusion of God's Spirit upon every age and sex, attributing to all men, and requiring from them the ability of searching, trying, examining all things, and by the spirit discerning that which is good; and as the Scriptures themselves pronounce their own plainness, so do the fathers testify of them.[25]

The great thinkers of historic Christianity, while convinced of the authority and plainness of Scripture, have always admitted that the relevance of scriptural truth to particular conditions and problems requires intellectual effort. Scriptural truth demands interpretation. For this reason the Christian church has formulated creeds to assist its members in performing this necessary effort. Some present-day denominations such as the Baptists are nonconfessional, but in this respect they lie clearly outside the main stream of historic Christianity. The Eastern Orthodox, Roman Catholic, Lutheran, Anglican, and Reformed communions all have insisted on the necessity for creeds, and these communions comprise the overwhelming bulk of all Christians in both past and present. The creeds have developed to meet particular errors, problems, and challenges which have arisen from time to time. The most universal and famous of them all, the Apostles' Creed, is a very good illustration of the function of creeds. Practically every word in it is in the nature of an answer to some specific and usually recurring situation, e.g., affirming that God is the maker of earth as well as heaven against the Gnostics who taught the contrary, affirming the divinity of Jesus Christ against humanists and skeptics who believe he was a mere man, affirming the humanity and historicity of Jesus Christ against the Docetists, who made Jesus Christ into a spirit whose incarnation was unreal and unimportant.

The creeds, however, are not on the same level with Scripture. They are interpretations of it, not substitutes for it. They should not be regarded as unalterable. The Protestant tradition has been especially insistent on this point, differing in this respect from both the Eastern Orthodox and Roman Catholic traditions. The Protestant tradition holds that there is a continuing duty to test the accuracy of creeds as the distilled essence of scriptural truth. "The infallible rule of interpretation of Scripture," says the Confession of Faith of the Presbyterian Church in the United States, "is the Scripture itself; and therefore, when there is a question about the true and full sense of any scripture (which is not manifold but one), it may be searched and known by other places that speak more clearly." [26] The matter of accuracy is influenced by the amount of historical knowledge available at the time a creed was written, by the controversies now gone or subsided which influenced the phrasing, by the depth of spiritual experience and firmness of faith of those who wrote it. Moreover, the problem of relevancy is also to be considered. New errors and confusions, or variants of old ones, arise and require theological answers. Then there is the problem of language: changes in the meaning of words necessitate explanations or new formulations.

All these processes are fraught with some danger. Greater historical, linguistic, and archeological knowledge may serve to clarify and deepen the meaning of Scripture to us, but it may also be used to undermine Scripture, so that the most learned commentators are not necessarily the best interpreters. Efforts to make scriptural truth relevant to current problems may result in dilution or in the substitution of purely secular doctrines and prejudices. Changes in language may be more than verbal and introduce error in the substantive meaning. These are risks which must be taken, however, and they have been. As a rule, creedal changes can be made only by special procedures designed to make as sure as possible that a change represents the settled and considered judgment of the whole church and not the opinion of a small group supported by a bare and perhaps temporary majority.* In all this, the Protestant tradition relies on the promise of Christ and the guidance of the Holy Spirit to protect the church from error and lead it to truth. Roman Catholicism also relies on the promise of Christ and the guidance of the Holy Spirit, but it insists that these are infallibly applicable only through the Papacy. Protestantism, on the other hand, does not presume to restrict the freedom of the Holy Spirit to choose his own channels and modes of expression. It believes that the most authoritative church is the "holy catholic church" of the Apostles' Creed, which includes all true believers in Christ throughout all ages and throughout all the branches and visible churches of the ecumenical household of faith. The continuing core of basic Christian doctrine which has come down to us from the apostles and has withstood almost every conceivable attack and survived all manner of errors stands as an impressive witness to the reliability of the Protestant belief in the "holy catholic church."

It may seem that the foregoing theological discussion is a digression far removed from the American conception of the Constitution. Actually, however, it is no digression at all. There is a direct, logical, and historical connection between the Protestant conception of scriptural truth and the American conception of constitutional government. In this secular age we easily forget that our forefathers were trained and nurtured in biblical thinking and concepts. *It was from the Bible that they learned what it means to govern one's life in accordance with a written standard.* They had 150 years of experience in doing this throughout the colonial period, which in turn was preceded by another one hundred years among their Protestant ancestors in Great Britain, France, Holland, Germany, and Switzerland. Believing the Bible to be the one infallible rule of faith

---

* For example, the Book of Church Order of the Presbyterian Church in the United States prescribes that any change in the Confession of Faith must receive a majority vote of one General Assembly, a majority vote in three-fourths of the presbyteries, and another majority vote in the next General Assembly.

and practice, these Protestants built schools wherever they went, for what good can the Bible do if you cannot read it? They read and reread it, meditated upon it, memorized large portions of it, argued about it, listened to innumerable sermons expository of it. They were so filled with it that their vocabulary and their literary style bore an unmistakable biblical stamp. In colonial Connecticut the Bible was accepted as a basis for decisions by civil courts. In their churches they were accustomed to living under written confessions of faith and written church constitutions.

During all these formative years our forefathers learned the habit of adjusting thought and conduct to written law, and they were familiar with the problems associated with this habit. They knew that written standards have to be interpreted and therefore will sometimes be misinterpreted, but they did not for that reason become cynical about the standards themselves. They knew that interpretation is a creative and cooperative enterprise and that sound interpretation is as much a matter of spirit as it is of knowledge and dialectical skill. They knew that living by a written standard is a complex venture which requires that all parts be given their due weight and be understood in terms of the general design. They knew that interpretation is partly individual and partly institutional, necessitating a proper balance between liberty and authority, and there was due process in the church before it existed in the state. All that was necessary to achieve constitutionalism in government was to transpose their experience from the religious to the political sphere. American constitutional government as we know it would have been impossible without this transposition.

In the light of Christian experience with Scripture, therefore, a number of errors in contemporary thinking about the Constitution become evident. One of these errors is the idea that interpreting the Constitution is purely a matter of technical knowledge. The American Bar Association, quite naturally perhaps since its members are professional lawyers, is particularly enamored of the idea. New recruits have appeared lately among conservatives who do not like Chief Justice Warren's opinions because they think he is "soft on communism," and segregationists who resent his decisions in the field of race relations. These several groups believe (or profess to believe) that long years of judicial experience would eliminate all erroneous interpretations of the Constitution.[27] They assume that if our judges were walking storehouses of adjudicated cases, the courts would always know what the Constitution means. But this is to confuse knowledge with understanding, and the confusion arises from the mistaken supposition that the Constitution is a mere legal code instead of the charter of our national values. Carried to its logical conclusion in an age of automation, this supposition would result in government by computers. Christian experience should certainly deliver us from so great an absurdity, for it has long been established that the greatest biblical scholars are not necessarily the best interpreters of Scripture, and during certain periods of history they have actually been among the worst—as were the learned scribes in Jesus' own day. This is not, of course, an invitation to appoint ignoramuses to our seminaries or to our Supreme Court. It is a salutary—and apparently necessary—reminder that insight is more essential than knowledge and statesmanship is more important than craftsmanship.

Another contemporary error is the idea that because we believe that our government is one of laws and not of men, the Constitution is somehow self-executing. This is pure verbal magic, if we mean that men can be dispensed with. Citizens have to obey it and rulers to implement it. There must be acceptance by all concerned. This again is a biblical idea: "And Moses came and called for the elders of the people, and laid before their faces all these words which the Lord commanded him. And all the people answered together, and said, All that the Lord hath spoken we will do. And Moses returned the words of the people unto the Lord." [28] This covenant was the source of the social contract theories which became the basis of modern constitutionalism and is the assumption behind the oath to support the Constitution which is required of all officeholders. The effect is to join firmly together the rule of law and the freedom of man and is known in British politics as constitutional morality.

Our customary reliance on the courts tends to obscure the importance of constitutional morality. We thrust upon the judges the duty of preserving the integrity of constitutional norms, forgetting that judges cannot perform it alone. Sometimes they cannot perform it at all. An example of such an instance is the matter of the qualifications of members of Congress, the determination of which is assigned by the Constitution to each house. It would be unconstitutional for a state to elect as United States senator someone who was less than thirty years old or who was resident of another state. If this happened, however, no court would take cognizance of the matter. It would be up to the constitutional morality of the Senate itself to refuse to seat such a person. Not to be overlooked in such an eventuality would be the low level of constitutional morality which would cause the people of a state to elect a disqualified person. Such a case, of course, is very unlikely to happen.

Unfortunately, there are actual cases which reflect a deplorably low level of constitutional morality on the part of state legislatures and the people who elect them. Among these none is more widespread than the failure of state legislatures to reapportion themselves every ten years as required by explicit provisions in their own state constitutions. A remedy may now have been found in a case involving Tennessee, whose legislature has not been reapportioned since 1901, by bringing the issue

under the equal protection clause of the Fourteenth Amendment and
thereby making it a federal matter. What this means is that we are trying
to correct immorality at the state level by drawing upon the greater
morality of the federal judiciary. A specific evil may thus be corrected,
but we are still left with the deeper problem which is inherent in the
immorality of the members of state legislatures who violate their oath
to abide by the state constitution and the immorality of voters who keep
returning them to office.

The extreme seriousness of constitutional morality was emphasized
as far back as 1645 by John Winthrop, the first governor of colonial
Massachusetts. He pointed out that magistrates are not professional people in the same sense that technicians are, such as architects and ship-
builders, who can be held to strict account for their mistakes. Magistrates
work in the area of policy and discretion, where errors of judgment are
unavoidable, and "therefore you must run the hazard of his skill and
ability." [29] Mistakes of this kind, says Winthrop in truly Calvinistic
language, should be borne patiently and compassionately inasmuch as
"you have continual experience of the like infirmaties in yourselves and
others." [30] It is also a matter of agreement: "The covenant between you
and us is the oath you have taken of us, which is to this purpose, that
we shall govern you and judge your causes by the rules of God's laws
and our own, according to our best skill." [31] Quite different is the case
if moral failing is involved: "If it fall out that the case be clear to common apprehension, and the rule clear also, if he transgresses here, the
error is not in the skill, but in the evil of the will: it must be required
of him." [32] An enormous distance separates John Winthrop from those
contemporary lawyers who ascribe first importance to legal craftsmanship, public administrators who see the guarantee of good government
in better civil service rules and better courses in personnel management,
social scientists and newspaper editors who pay scant attention to moral
integrity among public officials and in the electorate. The many technical
improvements in governmental procedures and the growth of specialized
knowledge are truly noble achievements, but they presuppose that moral
foundation of all constitutionalism which John Winthrop so greatly
stressed, or else they will come to naught.

THE SUPREMACY CLAUSE
OF THE CONSTITUTION

The next topic to which we should turn our attention is that part of
the Constitution commonly referred to as "the supremacy clause." Article
VI states that the Constitution "shall be the supreme law of the land." It
is clear from the context that the framers were primarily interested in
what C. J. Friedrich calls "effective regularized restraint" on governmental power.[33] They wanted to make sure that all governments in the

United States would stay within the limits, substantive and procedural, assigned to them. Their intent to restrain the federal government is clearly seen in the specification that those laws of the United States shall be supreme which are "in pursuance" of the Constitution. Their intent to restrain the states is even clearer since they spelled out the meaning of supremacy so that no one could misunderstand. The judges in every state are required to put the Constitution, valid federal laws, and treaties of the United States first and give them effect, "anything in the Constitution or laws of any State to the contrary notwithstanding." The third paragraph of Article VI completes the supremacy clause by requiring *all* officials, federal *and state,* to take an oath to support the Constitution.

It is apparent that the whole effectiveness of the supremacy clause rests on two conditions which we have previously disposed of in this chapter, namely: (1) the intelligibility and objectivity of constitutional norms which exist independently of the behavior or wishes of those to whom they apply, (2) the moral capacity of officials to abide by their oath to support the Constitution. Without the first condition, the Constitution would have no meaning or its meaning would be too uncertain to guide anybody. Without the second condition, the Constitution would be an ineffective piece of paper.

Since the supremacy clause is concerned with restraining the federal and state governments, the inference would seem to be that the framers of the Constitution meant to leave certain questions open, notably the relation of the nation to the world and the relation of constitutional law to natural law or what is colloquially known as "the higher law." In other words, the Constitution is an exercise of national sovereignty, but it is not an affirmation of national sovereignty as a dogma excluding the claims of international law or natural law.

The attitude of the framers of the Constitution on the subject of international relations may be inferred from the provision they made in the supremacy clause for treaties. Treaties are one of the three types of laws which are declared to be the supreme law of the land. In the absence of this inclusion, treaties would be binding internationally. They would not, however, be binding domestically until Congress had passed an enabling act making the treaty obligatory on American citizens and enforceable in our courts. The effect of including treaties in the supreme law is to bypass this extra step and to curtail the embarrassment inherent in the distinction between international and domestic effects. The embarrassment is curtailed rather than eliminated because the courts have held that in case of conflict between a federal statute and a treaty, whichever is the most recent overrides the other. There is the possibility, therefore, that Congress could abrogate a treaty *domestically* by passing a law contrary to it. Such a law would not abrogate the treaty internationally, but it would put the United States in the very awkward position of breaking a commitment and inviting retaliation by the other signatories. The eventuality is not likely, however, because Congress is usually concerned with the honor and good name of the nation in the world. Furthermore, the President, who is the country's chief spokesman in foreign affairs, would probably veto any bill which violated a treaty, and the necessary two-thirds vote to override his veto would be more than usually difficult to muster. The inclusion of treaties as part of the supreme law of the land, therefore, was a very long step forward in making the United States a responsible member of the family of nations.

It is also noteworthy that whereas the supremacy clause specifies that all laws of the United States must be "in pursuance" of the Constitution, the specification is not repeated with regard to treaties. The clause says "and all treaties made, or which shall be made, under the authority of the United States, shall be the supreme law of the land. . . ." Do the reference to *all* treaties, the failure to repeat the phrase "in pursuance thereof," and the use of the phrase "under the authority of the United States" mean that a treaty could violate the Constitution and still be valid law? The framers were silent on the question, and yet it seems probable that they, who were such careful draftsmen, had a sound reason for the phraseology they used. It is likely that they meant to leave the federal government a free hand in negotiating with foreign powers without having to worry over questions of constitutionality. To have come right out and said that a treaty does not have to be constitutional would have been impolitic; so in this case as in many others where strong opposition was foreseen, they left the matter somewhat vague and used language which merely pointed in the direction they hoped the government would follow. The risk involved in taking this course was not ignored, for the framers put a severe check on the treaty power by requiring that the Senate approve treaties by a two-thirds vote before the President can ratify them.

The intention of the framers with respect to treaties has been given effect by the courts in the same guarded but significant manner. By taking jurisdiction in cases involving treaties, the Supreme Court has by inference asserted the right to review and, presumably, to invalidate them. On the other hand, whereas many federal and state statutes have been invalidated by the Supreme Court in the entire history of the United States, on the issue of whether a treaty could violate the Constitution the Supreme Court has been circumlocutory and unclear, taking the position that it was unnecessary to settle a point which was not actually before them. The general trend of court decisions in cases involving foreign relations has been markedly latitudinarian. In several leading cases, the Supreme Court has ruled that the treaty power is broader than the legislative power, that the Tenth Amendment does not apply to treaties, that the rule of the nondelegation of legislative power does not extend to foreign relations, that executive agreements have the same force and effect domestically as treaties. Early in our history Chief Justice Marshall ruled that international law is part of the law of the United States. There have been several attempts to reverse this latitudinarian trend initiated by the framers and followed by the Supreme Court. One of these, the Bricker Amendment, would have even turned the clock back to the Articles of Confederation. All these attempts, however, have failed.

Fortunately, we have some of the thinking of one of the framers of the Constitution, James Wilson, on the relation of international law and domestic law. It is true that this is the thinking of one man, but we must remember that Wilson was one of the chief architects of the Constitution. He took a leading part in the legal arguments with Great Britain which eventually led to the Revolution, was a signer of the Declaration of Independence, was an important figure in national politics under the Articles of Confederation, represented Pennsylvania in the Constitutional Convention of 1787 in Philadelphia, and was appointed to the original Supreme Court by President Washington. He was one of the most effective participants in the debates which took place on the floor of the Convention and was a key member of the Convention's Committee on Detail, which prepared the first draft of the Constitution. We happen to have a rather full record of his views on law because he delivered a series of lectures on jurisprudence at the University of Pennsylvania. Because of his important role during this formative period in our history, his views deserve careful consideration.

James Wilson's position was that all law ultimately derives its authority from the will of God. The following passage from his lecture *Of the General Principle of Law and Obligation* spells out the different categories or forms of laws as he understood them:

> That law, which God has made for man in his present state, that law, which is communicated to us by reason and conscience, the divine monitors within us, and by the sacred oracles, the divine monitors without us. This law has undergone several subdivisions, and has been known by distinct appellations, according to the different objects which it respects.
>
> As promulgated by reason and the moral sense, it has been called natural; as promulgated by the holy scriptures, it has been called revealed law.
>
> As addressed to men, it has been denominated the law of nature: as addressed to political societies, it has been denominated the law of nations.
>
> But it should always be remembered, that this law, natural or revealed, made for men or for nations, flows from the same divine source: it is the law of God.[34]

Wilson criticized Grotius for teaching that international law derives its authority from the consent of nations. His criticism was in the following terms: "The law of nations, we see, he traces from the principle of universal consent. The consequence of this is, that the law of nations would be obligatory only upon those by whom consent was given, and only by reason of that consent. The farther consequence would be, that the law of nations would lose a part, and the greatest part, of its obligatory force, and would also be restrained as to the sphere of its operations." [35] Wilson defined the law of nations as "the law of states and sovereigns" which, like all law, is obligatory and not optional.[36] But he departed from the traditional idea that international law is addressed only to governments and does not include individuals in its scope. In effect, he nationalized and individualized international law. In his lecture, whose title *Of Man as a Member of the Great Commonwealth of Nations* is significant, he said: "It has been already observed, that the maxims of this law ought to be known by every citizen of every free state. Reasons, and very sufficient ones, were suggested, why this should be the case. A new reason, striking and illustrious, now appears why the maxims of this law ought to be particularly known and studied by every citizen of the United States. To every citizen of the United States, this law is not only a rule of conduct, but may be a rule of decision." [37]

The foregoing line of thinking establishes the fact that James Wilson did not regard the supremacy clause as an assertion of national sovereignty understood as the source of all law binding on Americans. By rejecting Grotius' idea of national consent as the source of international law, Wilson rejected the anarchistic conception of the world as a lawless congeries of peoples ruled by force and expediency. The will of God becomes the bridge which establishes communications between peoples and cultures, the common ground on which compatible constitutional edifices may be erected, and the common objective toward which the participation of nations may converge. Conceived in these terms, national sovereignty ceases to be a principle of international anarchy and returns to its earlier position as a principle of order, i.e., political power under law and therefore limited by law. As James Wilson so clearly foresaw, this conception of sovereignty was destined to be a peculiarly American phenomenon. As Americans we have long been accustomed to living under several levels of law in a system which provides for both federal and state sovereignties. Looked at in this light, American citizenship has become a training ground for world citizenship. The framers of the Constitution could construct a national edifice along these lines. They could not construct a similar international edifice, because the will and the instrumentalities were not available. But they could and did build a national edifice in such a way that it would not impede the construction of a larger edifice at a later period if and when world conditions became favorable.

The importance of this aspect of the framers' handiwork for our time can scarcely be exaggerated. We are now living in a world which is economically so interdependent that the prosperity of one nation is inseparably connected with that of other nations. The lethal nature and widespread distribution of armaments mean that there can be no such thing as national security in an insecure world. There is a growing mutual interpenetration of domestic and international politics everywhere. Modern communications transmit ideas everywhere, with all the consequences which ideas can have, and effectuate innumerable intercultural contacts. The ecumenical movement is reaffirming the common bond of faith which unites all Christians and the love of God which encompasses all men, Christian and non-Christian, in all parts of the world.

From these facts of modern life arises the necessity for new ideas and new institutions. No one could be more deeply concerned with this necessity than the Christian, and it is incumbent upon him to interpret his own national tradition in such a way that it will not be an obstacle to the constructive work of statesmanship in foreign affairs. It is his duty to fight proposals like the Bricker Amendment and campaigns like the one which was waged against status-of-forces agreements several years ago, because they are just such obstacles. In the Christian faith he has the spiritual resources that are indispensable to generate the dynamics of a new world order, i.e., the good will without which nothing lasting can be accomplished. It was the thought of Luke when he wrote the words: "Glory to God in the highest, and on earth peace, good will toward men." [38] The three things are interlocking. In the Christian faith, too, he has the insight needed to invent, design, mold, and construct the instrumentalities which may some day give us a viable world order, as was demonstrated by Woodrow Wilson when he initiated the movement toward collective security with his League of Nations.

The second question which is left open by the supremacy clause is that of the "higher law." The clause mentions the Constitution, federal laws, treaties, and the constitutions and laws of the several states. It neither affirms nor denies the existence of a higher law. It is completely silent on the subject, and yet we know that a belief in a higher law was very general at that period in our history. The Declaration of Independence is explicitly based upon it, and several of its signers were also framers of the Constitution. Many of the framers expressed that belief unmistakably and frequently in other places. In his lecture *Of the General Principle of Law and Obligation,* James Wilson explained his own position thus: "Nature, or, to speak more properly, the Author of nature, has done much for us; but it is his gracious appointment and will, that we should also do much for ourselves. What we do, indeed, must be founded on what he has done; and the deficiencies of our laws must be supplied by the perfection of his. Human law must rest its authority, ultimately, upon the authority of that law, which is divine." [39]

Another very important testimony is that of Gouverneur Morris. He too was a most influential member of the constitutional convention not only because he took such an active part in the debates but more especially because he was the key member of the Committee on Style. The final draft of the Constitution was his phrasing and language. Morris' testimony is significant in yet another way. He was a polished, sophisticated, hard-headed conservative, who was critical of organized religion and was widely, though erroneously, believed by his contemporaries to be irreligious and atheistic. Yet it was this same Gouverneur Morris who affirmed the supremacy of the higher law, which he called "the precepts of religion." In his inaugural address as president of the New York Historical Society in 1816, he said:

> But the most important of all lessons is, the denunciation or ruin to every state that rejects the precepts of religion. Those nations are doomed to death who bury, in the corruption of criminal desire, the awful sense of an existing God, cast off the consoling hope of immortality, and seek refuge from despair in the dreariness of annihilation. Terrible, irrevocable doom! loudly pronounced, frequently repeated, strongly exemplified in the sacred writings, and fully confirmed by the long record of time. It is the clue which leads through the intricacies of universal history. It is the principle of all sound political science.[40]

These declarations, and many others like them which could be cited, make it evident that the supremacy clause was not intended to assert a superior validity to the Constitution over the higher law. As is well known, the belief in a higher law persisted in our history, even after the Constitution had ceased to be regarded as a Federalist Party product and had become a universally revered document. That belief is still evident in the thinking of Daniel Webster, whose conception of the Constitution was closest to that of the framers. In his historic reply to Senator Hayne of South Carolina on January 26, 1830, Webster said: "If the gentleman had intended no more than to assert the right of revolution for justifiable cause, he would have said only what all agree to. . . . I admit that there is an ultimate violent remedy, above the Constitution and in defiance of the Constitution, which may be resorted to when a revolution is to be justified." [41]

The reason why the supremacy clause is silent on the higher law is that the framers did not think that the higher law could be reduced to anything like a comprehensive code. The Constitution was itself about as much of an implementation of the higher law as practical wisdom would recommend. The recognition of that law, however, is implicit in the broad language of the Constitution which allows the organs of government to interpret that language in the light of the higher law as perceived from generation to generation. Most of all, it is implicit in the amending clause. When one remembers that the inclusion of amending clauses was not yet the universally established custom among constitution-makers and that the members of the Constitutional Convention of 1787 were very modest about the excellence of their handiwork, the relation of the amending clause to the higher law becomes clear. A legal way was provided to correct whatever mistakes more adequate conceptions of the higher law might from time to time indicate, mistakes which could not be corrected by normal interpretation.

James Wilson again provides us with a clue to the thinking of the framers. In his defense of the Constitution before the Pennsylvania ratifying convention, he said: "As our constitutions are superior to our legislatures; so the people are superior to our constitutions. Indeed the superiority, in this last instance, is much greater; for the people possess, over our constitutions, control in act, as well as in right." [42] Wilson's point is embodied in the last part of the Tenth Amendment, a part which often passes unnoticed and which we therefore italicize: "The powers not delegated to the United States by the Constitution, nor prohibited by it to the States, are reserved to the States respectively, *or to the people*." The eagerness of some conservatives to find a constitutional basis for states' rights has caused them to forget that the Tenth Amendment embodies something much more important: the constitutional recognition of the sovereignty of the American people.

Popular sovereignty, however, was not understood by the framers of the Constitution as divine omnipotence or as a license to violate the higher law. Their meaning in this matter was accurately expressed many years later in Abraham Lincoln's Gettysburg Address. When Lincoln spoke of the new birth of freedom which was in store for the American people, he qualified his statement with the words "under God." The Constitution was intended as a restraint upon all governments in the United States. Although it was also understood as a standard of conduct for Americans, it in no way excludes the authority of the higher law. The kind of popular sovereignty envisaged by the framers of the Constitution was sovereignty *under God*. This kind of sovereignty is a principle of creative freedom which prevents the Constitution from being turned into a legal straitjacket, and a principle of responsibility which makes room for the directives of Divine Providence and the rightful claims of mankind beyond our national boundaries. By virtue of popular sovereignty conceived in this manner, the Constitution receives the only kind of supremacy which it is right for the basic charter of any people to possess.

THE CONSTITUTION AND
THE SCRIPTURAL CONCEPT OF LAW

There is much significance, from a Christian point of view, in the fact that the Constitution is law. For law is an important scriptural concept.

Law, notably the Decalogue, is presented as the will of God for his own glory and for the good of man. It specifies the kind of conduct which God expects of man, and that conduct, in turn, is an expression of the kind of being which God intended man to be. It is, therefore, essentially normative. In one sense it is self-enforcing. There is a price to be paid for violating it. People who lie, steal, kill, covet, and commit adultery set into motion a chain of consequences which are personality-shattering and socially destructive. On the other hand, the law is not self-fulfilling because it demands perfect obedience, which is humanly impossible. This is true in a behavioral sense and still truer in the spiritual sense which Christ placed upon it. There is no such being as a righteous man because every man breaks the law with every breath he takes. By the law, man is condemned. "O wretched man that I am!" exclaimed Paul, "who shall deliver me from the body of this death?" [43]

Paul's experience is not solely an individual one. It can also be a national experience. The Bible records such an experience when the book of the law, which had been lost, was found and read to King Josiah: "And it came to pass, when the king had heard the words of the law, that he rent his clothes." [44] The reason for his anxiety is not far to seek, "for great is the wrath of the Lord that is poured out upon us, because our fathers have not kept the word of the Lord, to do after all that is written in this book." [45] In order that his personal experience should be a national experience, King Josiah next called "all the people, great and small: and he read into their ears all the words of the book of the covenant that was found in the house of the Lord." [46] What happened is easy to understand: it was not until the law was read to them that the king and his people realized how far they had fallen. As long as imperfection compares itself with imperfection, there is not much cause for alarm or sense of guilt, though people do wonder why "things are in such a mess." They suffer the consequences of lawbreaking without understanding the cause of their suffering, and above all they do not feel personally responsible for the evil which holds them in its grip. It is only when imperfection is confronted with perfection, when what one is stands in the light of what one was meant to be, when what one does is contrasted with what one ought to do, that man realizes his predicament and stands self-convicted. The realization may burst upon him with the suddenness of a flash of lightning or it may grow upon him little by little. In either case it is a shattering experience because man then understands that he cannot blot out the deeds of the past, erase the stain of the present, or meet the law's demands in the future. He knows that he is morally impotent and spiritually insolvent. The law is a mirror, mercilessly accurate and unflattering, in which he sees his own face as it really is and which no human artistry can make attractive.

This agonizing experience is not the prank of a sadistic God. It is a necessary stage in the spiritual redemption and growth of man, for it is the point at which he may throw himself on the mercy of God. When he does so, he begins to understand that God loves him in spite of all guilt and ugliness, that Christ has paid the price of sin and thereby met the demands of justice, that a new supernatural power has entered his life which can do for him what no man can do for himself, that reconciliation has taken the place of alienation, that he has been born into a new life which even death cannot extinguish. By the grace of God, he has been saved through faith.

Let us now turn back to the Constitution and look at it in the light of the scriptural concept of law. As soon as we do this, we realize that constitutional norms reflect unattainable ideals. This is what makes them norms. They do not so much tell us what the behavior of citizens and officials is as what it ought to be, and there is always a gap between legal norm and actual practice. The difference between the United States and a country like Argentina, therefore, is only one of degree, important though the degree may be. In neither case do we find law-abiding citizens and officials in any full sense. This is especially true if we look beyond the strict letter of the constitutional norm and take into account the spirit to which the letter points.

The Constitution contains several provisions on religion, and their plain intent is that there shall be religious liberty in the United States. Nevertheless, the provision of Article VI which prohibits religious tests for holding public office did not prevent many Protestants from voting against John F. Kennedy for President solely because he was a Roman Catholic, nor many Roman Catholics from voting for him solely because of his religion. A narrow legalistic interpretation of Article VI exonerates those voters from technical guilt, but they most assuredly violated its spirit in that they did by ballot what they are forbidden to do by law. And the Christian knows, with the apostle Paul, that "the letter killeth, but the spirit giveth life." [47] The record is worse if we move from such political and governmental instances to the social sphere. Many forms of religious discrimination, sometimes blatant and sometimes muted, are all around us. They are not unconstitutional in a legal sense, but they are so in a moral sense.

The record is no different in the case of other constitutional norms. The Constitution forbids suffrage restrictions based on race and enjoins the states from denying to any person the equal protection of the laws, but resourceful and determined resistance is seriously jeopardizing the application of these constitutional norms. The Constitution sets freedom of opinion and due process of law as standards for government agencies, but persons who could not have been convicted in court are sometimes subjected to "exposure" by federal and state legislative committees and irreparably damaged in their reputations and employment opportunities.

The intent of the full-faith-and-credit clause of the Constitution is that whatever is legally valid in one state should be legally valid in all states. This constitutional norm is respected in business contracts, marriage certificates, divorce decrees, and title deeds to property. But there are areas in which it is not respected, notably in the professions like law and medicine. The intent of the commerce clause is that state boundaries should not be trade barriers, but some barriers are erected nonetheless under the guise of the states' police power.

Just as the church found that Scripture cannot be understood by the exegesis of isolated passages without reference to the whole, so the jurists have found that one constitutional norm cannot be interpreted without reference to other norms and to the general design of the Constitution. Thus, the federal government's power over interstate commerce and the states' police power are both constitutionally valid. Neither one should be used to nullify the other. The necessity of reconciling these two creates many legitimately difficult borderline cases, but it also affords fruitful opportunities for the machinations of the unscrupulous.

The gap between constitutional norm and national practice is the analogue of sin in the Christian religion. Just as intellectual difficulties are not the fundamental obstacle to acceptance of the Christian faith but rather symptoms of a much deeper trouble, so many legal arguments about the Constitution are not the real cause of the gap between constitutional norm and national practice but rather symptoms of a refusal to accept the constitutional norms themselves. It is much easier, however, to hide this basic kind of refusal from oneself by smothering it with elaborate and intricate constitutional arguments. It is also much more respectable and expedient from the standpoint of public opinion. Constitutional arguments about states' rights often have this character. They are usually a cloak for the retention of racial segregation or for the rejection of further government regulation of business. Arguments about the constitutionality of foreign aid frequently have the same character. They can be the product of deep frustration about the cold war, of intolerant nationalism, of a conspiratorial psychology, or of other attitudes which one would be ashamed to avow publicly. It would be absurd, of course, to suggest that all constitutional arguments are hypocritical attempts to deceive oneself and others. Some constitutional arguments are sincerely and unselfishly meant, sound in fact as well as in logic, and thoroughly in keeping with the spirit of the Constitution. The difference between the two kinds can be exceedingly difficult to determine. In a surprising number of cases, however, it is easy to tell the difference. But even in those cases, proof is generally unobtainable and the best one can hope for is moral certitude. The quality which helps us most here is what the apostle Paul calls the discerning of spirits.

In a Christian sense, therefore, the Constitution functions as a mirror for the national conscience. The confrontation of constitutional norm and national practice has the same kind of effect which the rediscovery of the law had on King Josiah and his people. The effect is not as pronounced as it should be because a clear and forceful confrontation is seldom made. The general public is astonishingly unfamiliar with the Constitution, and those who have studied American government and constitutional history have been smothered by the sheer weight of judicial precedents and technical details from which normative elements have been diligently removed in the name of "scientific objectivity." Despite these unfavorable circumstances, there has been enough confrontation to produce an uneasy conscience. It is the task of the church acting through its members who are political scientists, constitutional historians, practicing politicians, and community leaders to make this confrontation vivid and clear, thereby restoring to the Constitution one of its primary functions as the mirror of the national conscience.

To perform this task effectively raises three problems. The first and most immediate is a heightened sense of national guilt. Such a sense would be disturbing, not comforting. It would bring with it all the usual retinue of apologizing, rationalization, acrimonious argument, character assassination, and outright resistance. The church would be fighting against the trend of the times, which emphasizes peace of mind and frowns on "troublemakers." The church would lose members, money, and prestige. It would acquire new enemies. Would the turmoil to the country and the loss to the church be worth the effort? If we adhere to the teaching of Scripture, the answer must be in the affirmative. The same experience which was necessary to ancient Israel is equally necessary to modern America. Just as the presentation of the gospel requires a personal decision on the part of the individual, so the presentation of constitutional norms requires a decision on the part of the people. The Constitution is the charter of our national values. We can choose to live up to it or to live it down. A choice has to be made. It is the same kind of choice, though on a lower scale, which was presented to the people of Israel: "I call heaven and earth to record this day against you, that I have set before you life and death, blessing and cursing; therefore choose life, that thou and thy seed may live: That thou mayest love the Lord thy God, and that thou mayest obey his voice, and that thou mayest cleave unto him: for he is thy life, and the length of thy days. . . ." [48]

The second problem involved in the confrontation of constitutional norm with national practice is the relative character of all constitutional norms. Our national values, judged by the standard of the Christian faith, are superior to those of the ancient Romans and the contemporary Russians, but they are not final or absolute. The Christian must not make a religion out of the American way of life. He must remember that no national charter is an ultimate reality, and the church must press for improvement at the same time that it presses for commitment and compliance or else be guilty of idolatry. Failure to remember this truth means that decline and fall will follow national fulfillment, and as Augustine pointed out to the Romans, we shall have had our reward. We shall then appreciate the meaning of the words of Ecclesiastes: "I have seen all the works that are done under the sun; and, behold, all is vanity and vexation of spirit." [49]

The third problem raised by the confrontation of constitutional norm and national practice is one of dynamics: where do we get the power to escape from the burden of guilt which such confrontation inevitably thrusts upon us? We know from Scripture that this power does not reside in the law. As Paul explained at length in the Epistle to the Romans, the law convicts but does not save. This problem, however, will be postponed until a later chapter because it involves a thorough discussion of the transposition of Christian teaching to another aspect of political life.

Chapter v

LAW AND LIBERTY

O NE of the most basic and most controversial topics in political science as well as in current politics is civil rights. Every introductory course in American government devotes a considerable amount of time to this topic. In spite of the many controversies which rage around the concept of civil rights, there is much that can be regarded as "given" and beyond argument. Let us begin by outlining what is generally accepted and clarify it further by limiting the discussion primarily to the American context.

THE NATURE OF CIVIL RIGHTS

The first thing to observe is that civil rights belong to the category of positive law. They are not, therefore, written by the hand of the Creator "in the heart of every man" where they may be read by "right reason" but written by human hands in specific authoritative legal documents where they may be read and interpreted by minds professionally trained in the law. They can be looked up and quoted. Most of the federal civil rights are to be found in the first ten amendments (i.e., the so-called "Bill of Rights"), but several others are in the original Constitution (e.g., Article I, section 9) and in the post-Civil War amendments (e.g., the Fourteenth Amendment). There are also civil rights under state law, which can be located in state constitutions. Civil rights bind all branches of government and must be interpreted and implemented by these branches. It is understood that the judicial branch has a general superintendence over civil rights, but the legislative and executive branches are also involved in the process of recognizing, honoring, interpreting, and implementing civil rights. The resulting involvements mean that the constitutional provisions give rise to a vast body of statutes, administrative decisions, judicial determinations, and court orders which definitely bring civil rights within the realm of behavioral reality. No one questions, therefore, the assertion that civil rights belong to the category of positive law.

The second thing to observe is that civil rights are rights of persons. The word person is specifically used in the all important due-process-of-law clauses of the Fifth and Fourteenth Amendments, and it is the assumed subject of all civil rights, except where the Constitution specifies

citizenship. Civil rights depend on jurisdiction, not citizenship, and therefore belong to aliens as well as citizens. There are people nowadays who
think that civil rights ought to belong only to citizens, but such is not
the law of the United States. It is also noteworthy that, beginning with
Chief Justice John Marshall, the word person has been interpreted to
include not only natural persons but corporations such as business com-
panies, churches, colleges, and universities. This interpretation has been
challenged by Justice Black, but unsuccessfully. The justification for the
use of the legal concept of person, which is broader than the ordinary
concept denoting natural persons only, is that in many cases natural
persons can be effective chiefly through organization. Chief Justice Marshall gave constitutional recognition to what was already a fact of life.
This broad conception of the word person does raise many thorny problems about which there is much disagreement, but there is no doubt
whatever that this conception is part of the established law of the United
States.

The third thing to be observed is that civil rights are conceived as
restraints on the power of government. The restraints are specific and
numerous, both substantive and procedural, addressed to particular units
(e.g., to states as in Article I, section 10), or to particular branches of
one government (e.g., to Congress as in the First Amendment), or to
all branches of all governments (e.g., as in the due-process-of-law clause
in the Fifth and Fourteenth Amendments). Their presence in the Constitution is the product of a long evolution which began in Great Britain
many centuries ago. The problem originally was to curb royal power,
which was often exercised in an arbitrary manner inimical to the liberties
and welfare of the British people. In Great Britain these legal restraints
were never extended to Parliament because Parliament, unlike the
Crown, was regarded as the spokesman of the people, and Parliament's
interest therefore was not deemed alien or hostile to the people. In the
United States, however, the restraints were extended to all branches of
government, including the representative legislative branch, on the theory
that the people needed to be protected against representatives who might
not be true to their trust, and against popular majorities which could be
as arbitrary as any monarch. The Articles of Confederation contained
no Bill of Rights because the powers of the central government were too
weak to be a threat and because those powers, such as they were, did
not operate directly on individuals but through the state governments
which, in turn, were limited by bills of rights in state constitutions. But
when the Constitution creating a powerful federal government authorized
to act directly on individuals was submitted for ratification, there was
a great outcry that the liberties of the people were endangered by the
inadequacy of the restraints provided.[1] The result was the prompt en-

actment of the first ten amendments. There is no intrinsic reason, as some of the most recent postwar constitutions in Europe plainly show, why a Bill of Rights should be conceived in negative terms, solely as restraints upon government rather than as objectives of government. The reason it is so conceived in the United States is a matter of constitutional history and the product of the power of the Jeffersonian liberal ideology whose concurrence had to be obtained if the Constitution was to be ratified.

The fourth and last thing to be observed is that the idea of liberty is the heart and core of the Bill of Rights. The many and detailed provisions applicable to persons accused of a crime—e.g., indictment by grand jury, trial by jury, the right to be informed of the nature of the accusation, the right to counsel, the right to confront witnesses, the right to compulsory process to obtain witnesses on one's own behalf, the right not to testify against oneself, the prohibition against excessive bail and excessive fines, the prohibition against bills of attainder and *ex post facto* laws, the rule against double jeopardy, the right to a writ of habeas corpus and the restrictions imposed on its suspension—all assume that any intereference with individual liberty by government should be fully justified and rigorously proved, and that even justified intereference with such liberty should be conducted with a minimum of inconvenience to the individual. These detailed provisions all assume that personal liberty is normal and right, i.e., that every person is entitled to choose and change his residence, to choose a mate and raise a family, to choose or change his occupation and to work at it, to dispose of his leisure time as he sees fit, and in general to engage in the pursuit of happiness in his own way. Personal liberty is not to be totally terminated by capital punishment, directly and severely curtailed by imprisonment, or indirectly burdened by fines or other economic penalties except for a just cause meticulously established. Even those civil rights which deal with property are not unrelated to liberty since all liberty presupposes a proper economic foundation.

The idea of liberty, so central to the Bill of Rights as a whole, finds its most far-reaching embodiment in the First Amendment: "Congress shall make no law respecting an establishment of religion, or prohibiting the free exercise thereof; or abridging the freedom of speech, or of the press; or the right of the people peaceably to assemble, and to petition for a redress of grievances." Being caught in criminal proceedings is, after all, an exceptional situation, but the freedoms involved in worship, speech, press, assembly, and petition are not exceptional situations. They are normal, constant, fundamental, and all-encompassing. There are and have been justices of the Supreme Court who, recognizing this special significance of the First Amendment, have propounded the so-called "preferred position" doctrine which ascribes a peculiar sanctity to the

First Amendment not shared by other parts of the Bill of Rights, a sanctity which would mean that any governmental act interfering with First Amendment freedoms is presumed to be invalid. This doctrine has never been fully accepted by a majority of the Supreme Court, but it nevertheless exercises an appreciable influence on judicial thinking. The fact that First Amendment freedoms are generally classified as substantive rather than procedural rights might be regarded as something of a step in the direction of the "preferred position" doctrine.

It is well to remember that civil rights are included in the Constitution itself and thus become part of the supreme law of the land. All other laws must conform to them, and there is no unit or branch or level of government which is not obligated to respect them. Sovereignty in the British sense of a legally unrestricted determinate authority does not exist in the United States. The position of civil rights in the highest level of positive law created by the American people imparts an impressive eminence to the idea of liberty.

The foregoing discussion outlined four characteristics of civil rights which are beyond dispute. It is a matter of record, however, that the topic of civil rights is frequently the subject of widespread and acrimonious disagreement. The Supreme Court itself is not of one mind on civil rights, as frequent concurring and dissenting opinions amply testify, and a number of its decisions have unleashed several successive storms of controversy in the general public. Cases involving communist activities, racial segregation, and the place of religion in public life have been especially troublesome.

Conflict about civil rights is inevitable for several reasons. To some extent it is a matter of language. The meaning of terms like "due process," "equal protection," "probable cause," "excessive bail," "cruel and unusual punishment," "involuntary servitude," and "privileges and immunities of citizens of the United States" is not automatically obvious and fixed even among fair-minded and informed people. These terms are loaded with values, and the content of values is partly a matter of philosophy and partly of context. A word like "democracy" means one thing in the communist ideology and quite another in the Western tradition, and even in the United States it has changed its meaning considerably since the days of George Washington. The constitutional provisions in which our civil rights are embodied could have perfectly clear and fixed meanings only if there were complete agreement about values and if the context were always the same. Neither of these conditions being fulfilled, it is a necessary consequence that there will be conflict over civil rights.

Another reason for conflict arises from the fact that the Constitution is a complex document embodying a great deal more than civil rights.

The Constitution is indeed a charter of liberties, but it is just as certainly an instrument of government. There are many values in the Constitution besides liberty, and these must likewise be honored and given effect, which means that they must be reconciled. It is impossible to adhere to a literal interpretation of the First Amendment and give full effect to the Preamble. And every student of American government knows that to maintain the civil rights of persons and the police power of the states, both of which are constitutionally valid, raises a multitude of difficulties and imposes on the courts the necessity of making adjustments in concrete cases in such a way as to save as much of both constitutional values as possible.

If our courts are going to clarify terms in a reasonably consistent manner and reconcile competing constitutional values, a guiding philosophy is needed. The balancing of whatever forces happen to bring pressure upon the courts at the moment cannot impart to constitutional law that measure of intelligibility and predictability which is essential to all law. Furthermore, it is necessary that the guiding philosophy be widely shared by the general public, or else court decisions will encounter too much misunderstanding and resistance.

The intellectual effort required by the development of a guiding philosophy is blocked by several obstacles. Lawyers and political scientists who specialize in the field of civil rights get lost in the vast accumulation of court decisions. They are so engrossed in the process of mastering technical details that they seldom pause to think about fundamentals and ask themselves what it all means. A large section of the general public, predisposed in favor of a technical approach to every problem, naively believes that all we need is better trained and more experienced craftsmen of the law. The traditional bent of the American mind is practical and pragmatic, unaccustomed and unwilling to grapple with philosophical and theological categories.

The greatest single cause of intellectual torpor is probably the reverence in which the Constitution is held. As long as we are satisfied with the provisions of positive law, why should we bother ourselves about any higher law? Thus, the Constitution becomes an obstacle to basic thinking. We need to ask ourselves what we would think if the Constitution were abolished. This is the question which Walter Berns raised in his criticism of the American Civil Liberties Union:

> The Union is morally neutral, tolerant of everything except suppression of liberty, asking only that change be peaceful, because the organization lacks any moral standards. . . . And since the Union makes no pretense of following the seventeenth-century natural rights doctrine of Hobbes and Locke, it follows that the only possible basis of civil liberties is civil authority, or in this case, the First Amendment to the Constitution. If the First Amendment were to be repealed, the ACLU could pursue one of two courses: it could

dissolve itself as an organization, or it could confine its activities to agitating for a reinstatement of the Amendment. Without the Amendment it could not assert that civil liberties were basic, but only desirable.[2]

It is our misfortune that the predicament of the American Civil Liberties Union is also that of far too many of our fellow citizens.

The best approach to developing a philosophy of civil rights would appear to be in terms of a conception of human nature or, as the theologians call it, the doctrine of man. What makes such an approach especially fitting is that civil rights refer to people. Not everyone has a theory of human nature on the conscious articulate level, but everyone necessarily assumes such a theory (often without being aware of doing so). There are many theories of human nature; so a corresponding philosophy of civil rights could presumably be constructed on any of them. Some theories, however, are obviously ill-adapted to such an enterprise. Notable among these is the theory that man is an animal like the ox, differing from the ox in complexity but not in kind. People who think in these terms can hardly be expected to worry themselves about a philosophy of civil rights. Oxen simply do not have civil rights! The question is pretty well divided between the individualists and the collectivists. Most arguments about civil rights, once we pierce through the legalistic armor in which they are usually encased, are discovered to hinge on individualism or collectivism. We shall therefore first analyze each of those ideologies for their theory of human nature and consequent teaching on civil rights, and criticize them from a Christian standpoint. Secondly, we shall analyze the Christian doctrine of man and develop its implications for civil rights.

INDIVIDUALISM, HUMAN NATURE, AND CIVIL RIGHTS

Individualism is one aspect of classical liberalism. Of the two terms, liberalism is the broader because it includes theories about government, economic systems, education, religion, and society as well as about the nature of man. However, individualism is the heart and core of classical liberalism because classical liberalism is man-centered or "humanistic."

It is axiomatic with the classical liberals that man is by nature free. By "free" they mean that he is under nobody's control but his own. The family would seem to bring up something of a problem when it comes to defending the thesis that man is born free. The great liberal thinkers meet the challenge boldly by treating the family as the exception which proves the rule and establishes the thesis. John Locke regards the family as a temporary arrangement imposed by the long period of dependence of children. "The bonds of this subjection," he says, "are like the swaddling clothes they are wrapped up in and supported by in the weakness of their infancy. Age and reason as they grow up loosen them, till at

length they quite drop off, and *leave a man at his own free disposal.*" [3]
Rousseau takes the same position:

> The most ancient of all societies, and the only one that is natural, is the
> family: and even so the children remain attached to the father only so long
> as they need him for their preservation. As soon as this need ceases, the
> natural bond is dissolved. The children, released from the obedience they
> owed to the father, and the father released from the care he owed his chil-
> dren *return equally to independence.* If they remain united, they continue so
> no longer naturally, but voluntarily; and the family itself is maintained only
> by convention.
> This common liberty results from the nature of man. His first law is to
> provide for his own preservation, his first cares are those which he owes to
> himself; and, as soon as he reaches years of discretion, he is the sole judge
> of the proper means of preserving himself, *and consequently becomes his own
> master.*[4]

It is obvious that if thinkers like Locke and Rousseau thus grudgingly
concede a temporary and limited authority to the family, they are hardly
likely to make greater concessions to other institutions. Indeed, they do
not make any. It is significant that, in the passage just quoted, Rousseau
says that the family is "the only one which is natural," and even the
family becomes voluntary as soon as the children have reached adult-
hood.[5] All other institutions rest on "convention" (Rousseau) or "consent" (Locke), including even the state and the church, for which special
authority independent of the members has often been claimed throughout Western history. Perhaps the most radical and passionate assertion
of this same individual liberty, conceived as emancipation from all institutional dependence and from any authority other than self, came
from the pen of Ralph Waldo Emerson:

> The appearance of character makes the State unnecessary. The wise man is
> the State. He needs no army, fort, or navy,—he loves men too well; no bribe,
> or feast, or palace, to draw friends to him; no vantage ground, no favorable
> circumstance. He needs no library, for he has not done thinking; no church,
> for he is a prophet; no statute-book, for he has the lawgiver; no money, for
> he is value; no road, for he is at home where he is; no experience, for the life
> of the creator shoots through him, and looks from his eyes.[6]

The whole drift of classical liberal thinking is in the direction of extricating man from all external claims upon him and making him autonomous and sovereign. Man is self-validating. When Thomas Paine
sought to justify his participation in the American Revolution, he wrote:
"I saw an opportunity in which I thought I could do some good, and I
followed exactly what my heart dictated. I neither read books, nor studied
other people's opinions. I thought for myself." [7] What is involved here
far exceeds the basic hostility toward government, great as it is, characteristic of classical liberalism. The aim, in Rousseau's words, is to
secure man "against *all* personal dependence." [8] Quite consistently, there-

fore, Rousseau excoriates "factions" and "partial associations" as inimical to individual liberty and demands "that each citizen should think only his own thoughts. . . ." [9]

Sheldon Wolin is one of the very few—if not the only one—of contemporary students of the stream of political thought to have noticed and given due weight to the rejection of personal dependence in classical liberalism. He goes on to observe that "the liberal was eager to surrender to impersonal power, power which seemingly belonged to no specific individual. The entity which satisfied these longings was society. Its power was impersonal and was directed against all of the members indifferently." [10] There is much to be said in favor of this comment, and Wolin makes a strong case for it. There is no doubt, for instance, that both John Locke and Thomas Paine had high regard for society, held that man is by nature social, spoke of common interests, and extolled the virtues of "humanity." If one were looking for a proof text embodying what Wolin is talking about, it would be Rousseau's trenchant statement: "Finally, each man, in giving himself to all, gives himself to nobody. . . ." [11]

Nevertheless, there is a tendency in classical liberal thinking toward rejecting or, at least, minimizing individual dependence on even impersonal power. It was no accident that Thomas Paine called his book "The Rights of Man" and not "The Rights of Men" or "The Rights of Humanity." The source of the rights of man, sometimes identified with the Creator and sometimes with Nature, would seem to be external to man. However, the Creator and Nature are often conceived as internal to man, written in his heart and perceived by his reason. In a sense they are not impersonal powers that stifle man's longing for independence from the outside. In another sense, of course, they are both transcendental, one theological and the other metaphysical, and therefore to that extent independent of man. There resides in classical liberal thought an ambiguity on this point, an ambiguity which is doubtless due to the fact that absolute individual independence is neither possible nor even conceivable.

Does man deserve this kind of independence? The classical liberals are quite sure that he does. For one thing, adult man is rational. "Thus we are born free," says Locke, "as we are born rational; not that we have actually the exercise of either: age that brings one, brings with it the other too." [12] He has an innate love of goodness and truth: "No man is prejudiced in favour of a thing knowing it to be wrong." [13] He is inherently wise and good: "A man is the façade of a temple wherein all wisdom and all good abide." [14] It would be tedious to multiply testimonials by great liberal thinkers to illustrate their optimistic view of human nature. Surely a creature so good, so rational, and so wise as man can safely be entrusted with absolute liberty by the Creator!

By the time we reach John Stuart Mill, the transcendental sources of individual liberty have been eroded by skepticism. Mill does not believe in natural rights and is not at all sure about the nature of truth and the capacity of man to grasp it. The most that Mill concedes is that the extent to which truth may be discovered and grasped depends on the ceaseless competition of ideas, that all operational truth is born of conflict. But his optimism about human nature continues unabated, and so does his longing for personal independence. That he would not go along all the way with Wolin's comment that "the liberal was eager to surrender to impersonal power" is evident in Mill's denunciation of public opinion. In his classic *Essay on Liberty* Mill was concerned with much more than setting forth limits on state control of individual thought and behavior: he was protesting against the tyranny of public opinion and social pressures. These forces are surely predominantly impersonal and nonpolitical, and yet Mill found great fault with them.

The more one studies the teachings of classical liberalism on human nature, the more one realizes how individualistic they are. For it is man in his separateness that the classical liberals revere. All national, racial, religious, social, and cultural moorings and colorings have been abstracted away. Man has been stripped of whatever his physical and social environment may have conferred upon him because environment cannot be regarded as an individual achievement.

God made no two individuals alike, and the classical liberal wants to improve on God's creatures by making them still more unlike. The process of liberation is conceived as one of individualization, i.e., differentiation. "I do not believe that any two men," says Thomas Paine, "on what are called doctrinal points, think alike, *who think at all.*" [15] For Paine, to think is to disagree. The same idea is expressed by John Stuart Mill: "He who lets the world, or his own portion of it, choose his plan of life for him, has no need of any other faculty than the ape-like one of imitation." [16] Mill's meaning becomes unmistakable when we see him praise eccentricity: "Precisely because the tyranny of opinion is such as to make eccentricity a reproach, it is desirable, in order to break through that tyranny, that people should be eccentric. Eccentricity has always abounded when and where strength of character has abounded; and the amount of eccentricity in a society has generally been proportional to amount of genius, mental vigour, and moral courage it contained." [17] What is an eccentric? Someone who is different, so different that there is no one else like him. Mill's thought is echoed by Emerson: "Whoso would be a man, must be a nonconformist." [18]

Individualism has been enormously popular in the United States. The classical liberal philosophy in which it was expressed has pretty largely fallen into oblivion as far as the average American is concerned, but its meaning lives on in nonphilosophical ways. It lives on in the popular admiration for the Lone Ranger who successfully fights for justice single-handed, without owing anything to organized government or community support. It lives on in the image of the self-made man who has built up and governs his own industrial empire by his own unaided efforts. It lives on in the idea that the self-educated graduate of "the University of Hard Knocks" is superior to the formally educated graduate of Harvard University. It lives on in the minister who gets his call direct from God without the intermediary of the church and without the benefit of a seminary education. It lingers in the tradition which looks for presidential timber in the Log Cabin.

It is true, of course, that the old liberal individualism has been on the wane in the United States. The Lone Ranger is now confined to radio and television, and he would speedily find himself in jail were he to try to practice his calling. The self-made businessman is being displaced by the much more sophisticated organization man. A degree from the University of Hard Knocks does not impress the personnel division of a modern corporation. The minister whose seminary is accredited only in Heaven will have a hard time finding a church. We do not look for presidential candidates in log cabins, and if, perchance, we did find one in such a place, the cabin would doubtless be prefabricated.

A waning force though it may be, individualism continues to wield a considerable influence. That influence is nowhere more clearly visible than in the field of civil rights, especially among those most dedicated liberals who are known as libertarians. For the effect of the individualist philosophy on civil rights, we do not have to wade through a mass of Supreme Court decisions and treatises on constitutional law, and the reason why we are thus spared is that Justice Black condensed it all in a recent public interview.[19] Justice Black is widely and correctly acknowledged to be the most libertarian member of the Supreme Court, so that what he says in that interview has a representative and authoritative character.

Justice Black asserts in fluent fashion the conviction that there are absolutes: "Now, I have read that every sophisticated person knows that you cannot have any absolute 'thou shalt nots.' But you know when I drive my car against a red light, I do not expect them to turn me loose if I can prove that though I was going across that red light, it was not offensive to the so-called 'universal sense of decency.' I have an idea there are some absolutes." [20] The absolute in question here is the idea of liberty which he finds embodied in the Bill of Rights and most especially in the First Amendment. "I confess," he says somewhat sarcastically, "not only that I think the Amendment means what it says but also that I may be slightly influenced by the fact that I do not think Congress *should* make any law with respect to these subjects. That has become a rather bad confession to make in these days, the confession that one is actually for something because he believes in it." [21] Two years before, he had explained that the "balancing" of different parts of the Constitution so as to save and give effect to all parts did not apply to the First Amendment because its authors believed it to be an absolute, and by putting it in the Constitution, intended to exempt First Amendment freedoms from the erosions of the balancing technique.[22] Again and again he reiterates his conviction that when the First Amendment says "Congress shall make no law," it means exactly that, and nothing less than that.

Justice Black tolerates no exceptions and consistently rejects all those that are brought up to him. Obscenity is no exception: "My view is, without deviation, without exception, or whereases, that freedom of speech means that you shall not do something to people either for the views they have or the views they express or the words they speak or write." [23] Libel is no exception: "I have no doubt myself that the provision, as written and adopted, intended that there should be no libel or defamation law in the United States under the United States Government, just absolutely none so far as I am concerned." [24] Sedition is no exception: "My answer to the statement that this Government should preserve itself is yes. The method I would adopt is different, however, from that of some other people. I think it can be preserved only by leaving people with the utmost freedom to think and to hope and to talk and to dream if they want to dream. I do not think this Government must look to force, stifling the minds and aspirations of the people. Yes, I believe in self-preservation, but I would preserve it as the founders said, by leaving people free. I think here, as in another time, it cannot live half slave and half free." [25] When asked whether he subscribed to the Court's clear-and-present-danger test, he replied tersely: "I do not." [26] Commenting on Justice Holmes's famous illustration that no one has the right to shout "fire" in a crowded theatre, Justice Black agreed that it was "a wonderful aphorism" and upheld it on the curious ground that the property right of the theatre owner would be violated by such conduct.[27] This way of handling the difficulty is as ingenious as it is strained, but it does enable the learned judge to be consistent in refusing to allow government to curb speech under any circumstances.

Several revealing statements conclusively show that Justice Black's interpretation of civil rights stems from the kind of individualist philosophy we have been outlining. For example: "I am not going to say any more except this: I was asked a question about preserving this country. I confess I am a complete chauvinist. I think it is the greatest country in the world. *I think it is the greatest because it has a Bill of Rights.*" [28] Clearly, the idea of individual liberty is central to all his thinking, and he reconciles it with the idea of national security by a complete identification of the latter with the former. Individual liberty, to him, is the quintessence of America. Any lingering doubt about his meaning would be dissipated by the terms in which he expressed his pride at being "a member of what I consider the greatest Court in the world. *It is great because it is independent. If it were not independent, it would not be great.*" [29] By characterizing the Court as "independent," he refers to more than the fact that the Court is coordinate with and not subordinate to the legislative and executive branches of the government. In words reminiscent of Thomas Paine's remark that no two people think alike who think at all, Justice Black adds the following clarification: "If all nine of those men came out each Monday morning like a phonograph speaking one voice, you could rest assured it would not be independent." [30]

We have now reached a point in our discussion when we must appraise liberal individualism in the light of the Christian faith. That appraisal will have to be negative, even though we must recognize the greatness of liberalism's political, economic, and cultural achievements. There are four main points of conflict between liberal individualism and Christianity.

The first point concerns the transcendental base from which the early liberal individualists tried to derive the value of man. Insofar as that base was theological, the God involved was Deism's Creator and not the God of the Christian faith. Deism's Creator is not a living person who loves, judges, chastises, and redeems men. Neither is he an historic person who freely chose Israel to be his people, who was incarnate in Jesus Christ, who as the Holy Spirit preserves and guides the church which is the New Israel. He is rather a principle or concept which is necessary to account for the beginning of the universe and explain its rationality. He is either absent from his creation or is present but imprisoned by it (i.e., he cannot deviate from "the laws of his own nature"). Such a conception rules out the supernatural and turns prayer into either a soliloquy or a human meditation upon inanimate truth. There is some inconsistency in the fact that Deists believed in Providence and spoke of "the Arbiter of the Universe." The inconsistency may be explained as a vestigial remnant of the Christian faith or as a species of determinism which is not Christian. If it be asked whether such a conception makes any practical difference, the answer is that it has the effect of eliminating God as "an ever present help in time of trouble" and throwing man entirely on his own unaided and meager resources.

The other transcendental base was Nature. This was a metaphysical base calculated to spare the sensitivities of people who thought themselves too "enlightened" to have anything to do with religion but who understood that the positive realm of behavioral reality is not enough. In essence, Nature is a frozen reality, a kind of petrified forest of abstract laws and principles, immutable and eternal, which man can understand but neither abrogate nor modify.

A second point of conflict is classical liberalism's unduly optimistic view of human nature. Since we have already criticized it in our discussion of classical liberalism in Chapter III and will deal more in detail with the Christian doctrine of man later in the present chapter, it is unnecessary to dwell upon this particular point of conflict. Suffice it to say that the classical liberal view of man rejects original sin, ignores the depravity of human nature, and pays scant attention to the finiteness of human reason.

A third point of conflict centers on the classical liberal concept of the individual. Christianity values originality and creativity, but not eccentricity. We cannot assume that to be different is the aim of existence. If we were to push this idea to its ultimate conclusion, it would mean that the ideal society would be a society of freaks, which would be no society at all. It is true that God made no two individuals alike, but neither did he make them totally unlike or sentence them to cosmic isolation and perpetual social quarantine. Man was made for community, for fellowship with God and man. Furthermore, whereas classical liberalism stresses individual disentanglement, Christianity commands involvement. The Incarnation itself was an involvement, i.e., the involvement of the divine with the human. When God became flesh, he became a particular man, among a particular people, in a particular place, and at a particular time in history. When Jesus of Nazareth walked the earth and met people, he did not abstract away whatever physical, social, and moral traits characterized them and thus leave bare individuals stripped of everything but ghostly natural rights. He took them as they were, healed their bodies and their minds, and gave new life to their institutions (e.g., matrimony). The point was not to dissolve the ties—physical and social—which bind men into community and therefore individual interdependence, but to transform and glorify those ties. To remove them is to produce alienation, loneliness, and rootlessness. If pushed far enough, this process leads to insanity and eventually to death itself, which is the most complete dissolution of ties known to man.

The fourth point of conflict arises from the place of the idea of liberty in liberal individualism. To set up the idea of liberty—indeed, any idea—as the ultimate reality is to construct an idol. If special attention is paid to the way liberal individualism conceives liberty as personal independence, we get a species of polytheism wherein every individual is a god. In either case the result is idolatry. Only God is absolute, and all other gods are false, transitory, and self-defeating.

The effects of the liberal individualist philosophy on civil rights are not hard to see. Because freedom is treated as an absolute, all other values tend to be completely excluded or only partially reintroduced under the false theory that these other values are necessarily by-products of freedom. Moral considerations are particularly hard hit. "The one inexpiable sin," Walter Berns points out, "is for government to get into the business of distinguishing good from evil." [31] Actually, the Supreme Court has not maintained a strict libertarian position. The Court will approve governmentally imposed limits on freedom if the government can establish that there is "a clear and present danger of a substantive evil which Congress has a right to prevent." The reference to a substantive evil amounts to an admission that freedom is not an absolute and reintroduces moral considerations in the judicial determination of controversies. The clear-and-present-danger test is a compromise between the radical libertarian position of Justice Black and the collectivist-oriented "dangerous tendency" test. However, as Berns so ably and conclusively proved, the concession decidedly leans in the libertarian direction and embroils the Court in serious difficulties because the clear-and-present-danger test affirms in theory what it denies in practice, and the Court has no ethical theory to guide the practice.

The effects of the liberal individualist philosophy are not limited to the judicial process but color the attitudes of the citizenry. There is a marked tendency to overemphasize the rights of persons and underemphasize—if not actually to ignore—the duties and responsibilities of persons. A pall of selfishness hangs over the land which does not improve with multiplication. Continual insistence on one's rights and the habit of litigation are not Christian traits and were severely castigated by the apostle Paul and by Christ himself. In the name of liberty we have citizens who obstruct the realization of justice in race relations, businessmen and farmers who decry high taxes but demand government contracts and price supports, workers who assert the right not to join unions but insist on receiving the material benefits obtained by unions. All these things, and more, are defended in the name of the right to liberty, and the resulting concentration on rights impedes the general welfare, burdens the courts, and lowers the moral stature of individuals.

COLLECTIVISM, HUMAN NATURE, AND CIVIL RIGHTS

Just as individualism starts with the individual, so collectivism starts with the group (i.e., state, people, nation, government, social order, or whatever name the collectivity happens to have). Collectivism is more difficult to discuss because it is not a popular concept. Individualism has been so dominant in the United States that one can scarcely find a leading figure in either past or present who thinks of himself as a collectivist, and he would not admit it if he did. In our country, to say that the state exists for the individual and not vice versa is received as a truism. Collectivism has ugly overtones in American ears and suggests some form of totalitarianism. We have visions of police states, brainwashing, and regimentation. We think of Nazi Germany, Fascist Italy, the Soviet

Union, Red China, and the pathetic satellite states in the Eastern bloc. Now it is true enough that collectivism, if pushed to its logical conclusion, does mean totalitarianism. The trouble is that collectivism in this country is never pushed that far and exists in more respectable intermediate forms which have the effect of disguising its true nature. What is needed, therefore, is an analysis of the logic of collectivism, especially with respect to its teachings concerning human nature and civil rights.

To do this, we shall go back to the seventeenth century and analyze the thought of the English philosopher Thomas Hobbes. Hobbes was an extremist, but that very fact is a great advantage because extremists plunge in where many more circumspect people are headed and do not know it. That Hobbes was a foreigner and lived a long time ago is also an advantage, for it lifts the discussion out of a context in which our emotions and commitments might make it more difficult for us to think clearly. It is true that there are and have been forms of collectivism not all of which travel quite the same paths that Hobbes did. Nevertheless, after due allowance has been made for differences in conceptual tools and in context, the fact remains that the essence of all collectivism is rendered especially clearly in the thought of Thomas Hobbes.

Part I of Hobbes's *Leviathan* is devoted to psychology, and that psychology is rigidly materialistic and mechanistic.[32] He takes great pains to show that everything begins with sense perception. Man is a physical organism which receives external stimuli through its five senses and responds to them. All reality is contained in stimulus and response. What is commonly thought of as the higher processes of the mind constitutes no exception, for these are only more complex responses to stimuli. Imagination and memory denote various stages of "decaying sense," and experience is "much memory." [33] Reason is "Adding and Substracting of the Consequences of generall names agreed upon," [34] is "attayned by Industry," and consists "in apt imposing of Names." [35] What Hobbes calls "the passions" is defined as "the small beginnings of Motion, within the body of Man," [36] and the passions are classified as desire (motion toward an object) and aversion (motion away from an object).[37]

Happiness is defined as "a continuall progresse of the desire, from one object to another; the attaining of the former, being still but the way to the later." [38] The pursuit of happiness inescapably engenders conflict so that Hobbes concludes that there is "a generall inclination of all mankind, a perpetuall and restlesse desire of Power after power, that ceaseth onely in Death." [39] Power is defined as a man's "present means to obtain some future apparent Good." [40] Consequently: "The Value, or Worth of a man, is as of all other things, his Price; that is to say, so much as would be given for the use of his Power. . . ." [41] Hobbes finds that men by nature are substantially equal in power, at least to the extent that "the difference between man, and man, is not so considerable, as that one man can thereupon claim to himselfe any benefit, to which another may not pretend, as well as he." [42] The consequence is that all men are by nature at war with one another, and war consists not only in actual fighting "but in the known disposition thereto." [43] In Hobbes's often quoted words, the life of men is "solitary, poore, nasty, brutish, and short." [44]

If we say that the picture is horrible, Hobbes will readily agree. If we say that it is unrealistic in the sense that human beings could not possibly live this way and in fact never have, Hobbes will agree again. His point is that the picture describes how men would live if it were not for the civilizing power of government, and it is not possible to live without government. This point is so important that Hobbes takes care not to leave the consequences to be inferred by the reader. There is no spiritual reality, for "the seed of Religion" exists in man only,[45] proceeds from anxiety engendered by a curiosity concerning causes which can never be satisfied but which can be camouflaged and allayed by the invention of a fictitious Deity.[46] The same applies to the moral realm: "The notions of Right and Wrong, Justice and Injustice have there no place." [47] Nor is law a natural phenomenon, and even the "Laws of Nature" to which Hobbes pays considerable attention are not true laws at all but only dictates of reason. "These dictates of Reason," he explains, "men use to call by the name of Lawes; but improperly: for they are but Conclusions, or Theoremes concerning what conduceth to the conservation and defence of themselves. . . ." [48]

As every student of the history of political thought knows, the Social Contract is Hobbes's solution to the war of all against all. By its terms, each individual agrees with every other individual to transfer all his power to some person or persons, i.e., the Sovereign, on condition that everyone do the same. The Sovereign, being the recipient of all this power and not himself a party to the contract, has unlimited authority and a civil commonwealth is thus instituted.

Hobbes's solution seems individualistic and democratic because it appears to establish government on the basis of the consent of the governed through individual agreement. Actually, however, it is nothing of the kind. The erroneous impression comes from Hobbes's use of the contract device, which was one of the favorite conceptual tools of his time. But Hobbes's contract is not a true contract, for the individuals who are parties to it really have no choice—unless you consider an option between civilized living and personal extinction a genuine choice. The idea that man in a State of Nature (which is another conceptual tool characteristic of the time) had at least enough reason to see why the Social Contract is the only way out of the war of all against all is also illusory. To Hobbes, reason is not the natural possession of man but the product of civilization. The reason which tells man that security of life and civilized existence depend on the Social Contract is neither sight nor foresight but hindsight.

The groundwork has thus been laid down by Hobbes with the utmost care for the proposition that everything which human beings value and which makes them human beings is the offspring and creation of government. Do you believe in the Christian religion? The only reason is that you were taught from infancy so to believe by the commonwealth.[49] Do you believe in the kingdom of God? That kingdom and the civil commonwealth are one and the same.[50] Do you believe there is a difference between right and wrong? The difference is a creation of the civil (i.e., positive) law emanating from the command of the Sovereign.[51] Do you believe in property and care about the economic system under which you live? They are the product of the commonwealth.[52] Do you believe in law and order? These are the handiwork of the Sovereign.[53] Do you believe in truth? Truth is a matter of definition over which the Sovereign has a monopoly.[54] Do you believe in industry, agriculture, the arts, the sciences, and all the accomplishments that go to make up what we call culture? All these things are created by the Sovereign and would not exist without him.[55] Everything that we are and can become is determined by the commonwealth. To Hobbes, the commonwealth is God on earth, the supreme and ultimate reality and authority in which we live and move and have our being.

Much, if not most, of these Hobbesian conclusions are distasteful to contemporary collectivists. They do not like the psychological foundations of the Hobbesian man, and they bristle at the deification of government. What these collectivists fail to see, however, is that logic is on Hobbes's side. The ultimacy which they deny to government is ascribed to race, nation, social order, community, or some other collective entity. It is implicit in the motto "my country right or wrong," in the designation of all that is right as "American" and all that is wrong as "un-American," in the philosophy of many professional educators that the sole proper objective of education is "adjustment to the group," in the pressure for conformity, in many conceptions of "loyalty" and "disloyalty." The ultimacy is there. Our collectivists usually prefer not to admit it, at least not in so many words. The implicit is more comfortable than the explicit because the need to account for the ultimacy thus does not have to be faced, and the psychological foundations of collectivism do not have to be explored. Whether government or some other collective entity is chosen as the embodiment of this ultimacy does not really make a great deal of difference, except that Hobbes is more logical because he recognizes the role which power must play in any kind of collectivism. It ill behooves collectivists to balk at sovereignty, which necessarily means the supremacy of government. They affirm the end while denying the means.

Is there a place for liberty in the collectivist ideology? There is, although liberty is conceived in a special and characteristic way. Here again, Hobbes is very helpful. He defines natural liberty as "the absence of Opposition," by which he means the absence of "externall Impediments of motion." [56] Freedom is mobility, the power to move. If you cannot move, you are not free—in fact, Hobbes would say you are dead. Now it is obvious that, in view of individual weakness and the multitude and strength of "impediments," natural liberty is small indeed. Significant liberty is civil liberty, which can exist only in a commonwealth. What man could not do by his own unaided means, he can do by drawing on the power of the Sovereign. Men are free to do those things which the Sovereign has made it possible for them to do, such as "the Liberty to buy, and sell, and otherwise contract with one another; to choose their own aboad, their own diet, their own trade of life, and institute their children as they themselves think fit; & the like." [57] Hobbes therefore reaches the conclusion that our liberty consists in our subjection to the Sovereign.[58] This conclusion looks like a contradiction in terms until we remember that, to Hobbes, liberty is another word for power. Only the powerful are free (to the extent of their power), and the weak are unfree.

The collectivist conception of liberty destroys all civil rights in the traditional American sense of legal restraints on government, for to limit the power of government is to diminish the source from which individual liberty is derived. What is left of civil rights is something quite different: those rights which the government has found it expedient for its own aggrandizement to confer upon individuals and groups. Those are rights which individuals and groups have against each other, but never against government. Although it is not improper to refer to them as "civil rights," the preferred term is "civil liberties" because the latter implies something which is granted as a matter of expediency rather than of obligation.

A case for a large amount of individual liberty can be made from a collectivist point of view, though not all collectivists are by any means inclined to make it. For example, it can be argued that a wide distribution of private property and economic liberty should be granted on the ground that such a condition fosters national productivity and industrial efficiency more than monopolistic and centralized bureaucratic control. Freedom of thought, inquiry, and research can be defended on national security grounds because it leads to a maximum of scientific and technical progress at a time when national survival may well depend on the extent and rate of such progress. It can be argued that freedom of speech and press strengthens government because the glare of publicity tends to curb inefficiency and corruption. It has been argued as far back in history as Polybius that freedom of association, including political opposition, is more conducive to national power than dictatorship on both empirical and psychological grounds. It can be argued that a meticulous respect for the procedural rights of persons accused of crimes enhances the morale of the people and therefore the power of the government. In every case, however, liberty is justified because it benefits the collectivity (e.g., state, nation, social order, government) and not because it benefits the individual. The individual is expendable, a brief and mortal instant in the long span of relatively immortal collective life, a unit valuable only for what it can contribute to the whole. Liberty, therefore, is strictly a matter of policy.

The effect of the collectivist philosophy on the Bill of Rights is easily predictable. Whenever the police power of the state and the civil rights of a person clash, the tendency is to resolve the conflict in favor of the police power. In cases involving charges of subversion, the tendency will be to prejudge them in favor of the government. The way in which the First Amendment is phrased does give a little trouble, for the statement "Congress shall make no law" is certainly categorical, and there is no disposition to credit Congress with omniscience or omnipotence. But while collectivist-oriented thinkers are unwilling to entrust Congress with unlimited power, they have no such reservation concerning the American people. Nothing must be allowed to interfere with the sovereignty of the nation. What this attitude means in practice is that the collectivists are willing that Congress should make a law in the areas forbidden by the First Amendment, provided that they agree with Congress that the security of the nation demands it. Their support of the clear-and-present-danger test and still greater support of the dangerous-tendency test do not stem from a recognition of the need to give effect to all the values embodied in the Constitution but from their adherence to the Hobbesian concept of sovereignty.

Collectivism is, of course, incompatible with the Christian faith. The collectivist theory of sovereignty violates the First Commandment, and the collectivist concept of human nature conflicts sharply with the Christian doctrine of man. The extent of the incompatibility will now become increasingly evident as we discuss the Christian approach to civil rights.

THE CHRISTIAN DOCTRINE OF MAN AND CIVIL RIGHTS

The Christian doctrine of man is God-centered (theocentric). It is not man-centered (anthropocentric), whether we take man in his separateness as in individualism or in a group as in collectivism. It is the theocentric dimension which differentiates Christian humanism from secular humanism. All humanism might be said to be pro-man in intent, but the Christian variety asserts that any doctrine of man which is not theocentric is man-destroying. The secular variety intends one thing and achieves its opposite. The theocentric dimension is necessary

not only to achieve the good of man but also to understand him. Without a knowledge of God, there is no way to account for the uniqueness
of the human creature which distinguishes him from all other creatures.

Man and the image of God

Scripture teaches that man was made in the image of God: "And
God said, Let us make man in our image, after our likeness. . . . So
God created man in his own image. . . ." [59] The account in Genesis
makes it clear that the expression "God's image" does not mean a dis-
embodied spirit. Man was given a physical body: "And the Lord God
formed man of the dust of the ground, and breathed into his nostrils the
breath of life, and man became a living soul." [60]

Because God made man's body, it will not do to look upon the physical
or animal side of man as evil. "And God saw everything that he had
made, and, behold, it was very good." [61] Furthermore, when God breathed
"the breath of life" into the human body, he sanctified it. Life is from
God and of God. "In him was life," says the apostle John, "and the
life was the light of men." [62] The apostle Paul described the body as
"the temple of the living God" [63] and urged the Christians in Rome to
"present your bodies a living sacrifice, holy, acceptable unto God, which
is your reasonable service." [64] Christ himself showed great concern for
the body and bodily needs. He felt compassion for physical suffering,
fed the hungry, healed all manner of physical illness, including leprosy,
blindness, paralysis, fever, and bleeding. To go out and heal the sick
was one of Christ's directives to his disciples. An even more compelling
reason for thinking that the Christian faith does not regard the body as
evil or as the cause of evil is the affirmation of the Apostles' Creed: "I
believe in the resurrection of the body." The basis of the Creed on this
point is the resurrection of Jesus Christ which, despite the equivocations
of some modern theologians, was a physical resurrection. All four Gospels
teach it in the plainest terms, and Paul bluntly says that to disbelieve
it means that "our preaching is vain, and your faith is also vain." [65]

Yet the body is not itself the image of God but only an appropriate
frame for it. Among all of God's creatures, man is the only one endowed
with reason by which he can perceive order and truth, and with the
capacity to distinguish right from wrong. He alone was given dominion
over all other living creatures. He was also instructed to subdue the
earth, and so well has he done this that he is now reaching into outer
space to subdue the great beyond in God's creation. He was made for
freedom and immortality. He has imagination and partakes of the divine
creativity. He differs from all other creatures in that he alone has transcendence. Man is part of his environment, but he also transcends it in
that he can set himself apart from it, judge it, modify it, and remove him-

self to another environment. He is even self-transcendent in that he can look at himself as though he were somebody else and pass judgment upon himself with a surprising amount of objectivity. All these traits are attributes of divinity. They do not make him God; they do make him God-like. It was this perception of the nature of man as God intended him to be which caused the Psalmist to be filled with awe and say: "For thou hast made him a little lower than the angels, and has crowned him with glory and honour." [66]

Anyone who believes this account of man's origin is impervious to the Hobbesian claim that man owes to the commonwealth everything that makes him noble and truly human. Man is indebted to the commonwealth for much that he has, as Christ acknowledged when he instructed us to render unto Caesar what is Caesar's, but not for what he is. The characteristic reaction of the Christian when confronted with collectivist claims is on the order of that so eloquently expressed by Milton:

Our liberty is not Caesar's; it were a blessing we have received from God himself; it is what we are born to; to lay down at Caesar's feet, which we derive not from him, were an unworthy action; of a degrading of our very nature. If one should consider attentively the countenance of a man, and not inquire after whose image so noble a creature were framed, would not any one that heard him presently make answer, That he was made after the image of God himself? Being therefore peculiarly God's own, and consequently things that are to be given to him, we are entirely free by nature, and cannot without the greatest sacrilege imaginable be reduced into a condition of slavery to any man, especially to a wicked, unjust cruel tyrant.[67]

Reactions such as Milton's make us realize that the scriptural teaching is not a politically irrelevant theological proposition but, on the contrary, a vital force in practical politics.

The Christian doctrine of man also accounts for the fall of man and affirms the depravity of human nature. The story in Genesis relates that the cause of man's downfall was disobedience. The disobedience arose from man's desire to deify himself ("ye shall be as gods") [68] and from his contempt of the lawmaker which all disobedience implies. When we try to make other people into our own image, use ourselves as the yardstick of what is right and wrong, and "play God," we are repeating the original sin of Adam and Eve. Let it be noted, too, that the sin in question was basically a thing of the spirit, something all-pervasive and fundamental which could not be compartmentalized in any one part of man such as the body. Adam and Eve did not want to eat the fruit of the tree of the knowledge of good and evil because they were hungry and had nothing else to eat, and it was not until temptation had had its impact that it occurred to Eve that the tree was "good for food" and "pleasant to the eyes." [69] The spiritual conceit which knows neither the love nor the fear of God caused not only disobedience but disbelief ("Ye shall not surely die").[70] To disobey and disbelieve the Creator is to alienate oneself from him, to break the bond of fellowship which was intended to link Creator and creature, and to cut oneself off from the source of eternal life.

A chain reaction followed the alienation of man from God. First Adam and Eve sought to cover up (they "made themselves aprons"); [71] then they sought to hide (they "hid themselves from the presence of the Lord God amongst the trees of the garden").[72] Next came the attempt to pass the blame to somebody else ("And the man said, The woman whom thou gavest to be with me, she gave me of the tree, and I did eat").[73] Even those who do not believe in the historicity of the Genesis story must admit that, in all this, the reactions of Adam and Eve were the prototype of the reactions of all men, e.g., of the child who disobeys his parents and is caught, of the traitor who sells his country and stands trial for his life, of the corrupt politician who steals and is confronted with investigation and exposure, of the power-mad dictator who seeks to escape from domestic tensions he has caused and resorts to a diversionary foreign war. Alienation from God initiates the disruption of human fellowship and thrusts man into an endless series of truly vicious cycles. He is in a bind from which he is powerless to liberate himself.

His trouble is partly the consequence of the evil he has done and partly the impact upon him of the evil which other people have done. His chief trouble, however, is within himself. He has lost control. His reason is dimmed; his emotions are warped; his will is impaired. Every fugitive from justice can testify to the constant dread, the rationalizing, the alternation of self-accusation and self-justification, the hiding and the fleeing, all of which form the basic pattern of the guilt-stricken man. To some extent a partial and temporary relief may be obtained by going to the physician, the psychiatrist, the social worker, and the lawyer. The relief is partial and temporary because it does not go to the root of the trouble, i.e., the alienation from God. The world's first fugitive from justice, Cain, saw this well enough and gave the correct diagnosis: "Behold, thou hast driven me out this day from the face of the earth; and from thy face shall I be hid; and I shall be a fugitive and a vagabond in the earth; and it shall come to pass, that every one that findeth me shall slay me." [74]

Man is by no means always conscious of his alienation from God, but it is radical and fatal nonetheless. It is one of the most fallacious popular aphorisms which says: "What you don't know won't hurt you." Cancer is not less fatal because a man does not know he has it. Sin is personality-shattering in the same way and leads to death regardless of the sinner's lack of awareness. The rich young ruler who came to Jesus was righteous by the accepted standards of his contemporaries. He knew something was wrong, but he did not know what it was. Whatever it was, he understood only that it was somehow spiritually crippling and that it denied him eternal life. His story shows that there is no salvation in ignorance. It is one of the errors of Roman Catholicism to make sin dependent on its being done knowingly and voluntarily. The Roman Catholic overlooks the fact that all men sin by inadvertence and by necessity as well as by deliberate choice, and in concentrating on the depraved deed, he forgets the depravity of the doer. Calvin is much more correct when he says: "Original sin, therefore, appears to be an hereditary pravity and corruption of our nature, diffused through all parts of the soul, rendering us obnoxious to the Divine wrath, and producing in us those works which the Scripture calls 'works of the flesh.' " [75] Corruption is not localized in the mind or the will but pervades and stains the whole person. For that reason Paul asserts that no man is righteous [76] and that "the natural man receiveth not the things of the Spirit of God: for they are foolishness unto him; neither can he know them, because they are spiritually discerned." [77]

The natural man may acknowledge that he is unable to cope with his condition and turn to professional people such as psychiatrists, physicians, lawyers, guidance counselors, or social workers in the hope that they can do for him what he cannot do for himself. The amount of help which these people can give is limited. They may make life tolerable and livable, but they cannot make it abundant and glorious. They may bring about a truce, but they cannot give peace. A broken fellowship with God is beyond their ability to mend, and as long as this fellowship remains broken, human fellowship remains disrupted. What the natural man needs is forgiveness and reconciliation, and these only God can give.

The Christian faith teaches that this need of the natural man for forgiveness and reconciliation has been met in the birth, life, death, and resurrection of Jesus Christ. What only God could give, God has given. The motive is love; the object is the salvation of man; and the condition is faith in Christ. No more concise a statement of these terms can be found than in John: "For God so loved the world, that he gave his only begotten Son, that whosoever believeth in him should not perish, but have everlasting life." [78] Forgiveness has been accorded, but not at the expense of justice because Christ has paid the price of sin. With conversion a new creature is born whose course through many vicissitudes is guided by the Holy Spirit toward a new level of life. The Christian, like the natural man, is still a sinner, but he is headed in a different direction. He is like a sick man who, though he is still suffering and his faculties are still impaired, has found that his sickness is no longer in-

curable, because he knows a physician who can and will relieve his suffering, improve his present condition, and eventually restore him to the
fullness of health. Martin Luther explained it thus:

Brother, it is not possible for thee to become so righteous in this life, that
thou shouldest feel no sin at all, that thy body should be clear like the sun,
without spot or blemish; but thou hast yet wrinkles and spots, and yet art
thou holy notwithstanding. But thou wilt say: How can I be holy, when I have
and feel sin in me? I answer: In that thou dost feel and acknowledge thy
sin, it is a good token; give thanks unto God and despair not. It is one step
of health, when the sick man doth acknowledge and confess his infirmity. But
how shall I be delivered from sin? Run to Christ the physician, which healeth
them that are broken in heart, and saveth sinners.[79]

The vicious circle which imprisoned the natural man in bonds of steel
has been broken, and he now finds himself in a different chain reaction,
i.e., the chain reaction of love initiated by grace and transmitted among
men from faith to faith. The vertical fellowship of man to God has been
restored through reconciliation, and consequently the horizontal fellowship of man to man can also be restored.

Once these vertical and horizontal relationships have been set aright—
and it is God's purpose that they should be—man is well on his way to
fulfilling his destiny, which is so to live that all that he does and all that
he is will give glory to God. By grace he is able to do what God intends
that all men should do but not all men can do: "Let your light so shine
before men, that they might see your good works, and glorify your
Father, which is in heaven." [80]

We conclude, therefore, that man escapes the claims of collectivism by
virtue of his destiny as well as by that of his origin. The jurisdiction of
the state over human beings is always relative and limited. The state did
not create man, and man does not live for the state. It is likewise apparent that liberal individualism is ruled out by the Christian doctrine of
man, and for the same reason: man did not make himself, and he does
not live unto himself or for himself.

Christianity and natural law

Before moving from the Christian doctrine of man to the Christian
idea of liberty and its consequences for civil rights, it is necessary to
take up the problem of natural law. We cannot dispense with a discussion of this knotty problem, because God is the Father and Ruler of
all men, both Christian and non-Christian. Does God expect anything
of unbelievers or is his love confined only to Christians? The question
has become more important than ever in this pluralist world where Christians are in a minority, a world in which peace and survival depend
on the discovery and acceptance of a common ground among men, a

world in which some states do not concede civil rights to men. Furthermore, Christians are sinners even though forgiven and called unto perfection, hence the question is of concern to them also. Then there is the fact that historically civil rights grew out of natural rights or, at least, what their supporters took to be natural rights. Almost to a man, the founders of this country believed in natural law. For all these reasons, we cannot escape the question: does God expect anything of men, regardless of their belief or unbelief?

The classic answer to this question has been in the affirmative and has taken the form of a belief that there is a natural law which is universal, immutable, eternal, and antecedent to all political and social organization. The answer is unpopular in the United States today and finds few supporters. Prominent among the reasons is the number of different versions of natural law which history records, beginning with the Stoics, who first developed it. There have been Christian and non-Christian versions. Even among Christians, there have been many disagreements. The divergences have been so numerous and significant that even John Courtney Murray, a dedicated champion of natural law, felt a certain amount of sympathy with its critics and said: "For my part, I would not at all mind standing with them, tearless, at the grave of any of the shallow and distorted theories that they mistake for the doctrine of natural law." [81]

Among those Christians who most decisively assert the doctrine of natural law and defend it with consistent vigor are the Roman Catholics. Their espousal of the doctrine is so well known and of such long standing that it has come to be identified with them in the American public mind. "It is sometimes said," admitted Father Murray, "that one cannot accept the doctrine of natural law unless one has antecedently accepted 'its Roman Catholic presuppositions.' This, of course, is quite wrong. The doctrine of natural law has no Roman Catholic presuppositions." [82] Father Murray's denial is correct in that a person could subscribe to the Roman Catholic version of natural law and not be a Roman Catholic. The Roman Catholic version sees in natural law a number of principles which can be perceived by natural reason and "are susceptible of verification." [83] Even a non-Christian could subscribe to it, provided he believed in God. A Marxist or a positivist, however, could not because the Roman Catholic version is theocentric.

For a statement of the Roman Catholic version, we shall follow Father Murray rather than St. Thomas Aquinas despite the fact that the latter carries a greater weight of authority. The thought of Aquinas is cast in a forbidding scholastic mold which is difficult for the American mind to understand. The thought of Father Murray, on the other hand, while still Thomist in substance, is readily understood by contemporary Americans. It is readily understood not only because he is an American but because, in his recent book *We Hold These Truths: Catholic Reflections on the American Proposition* he assigned himself the formidable task of proving that Roman Catholicism and the American tradition are compatible. So ably and persuasively did he perform this task that he would almost have us believe that the American tradition, including its great formative and constitutive documents like the Declaration of Independence and the Constitution, was the work of Roman Catholics! In addition, his literary style is lucid, elegant, forceful, and witty, reflecting the kind of sophistication which comes only from a thorough assimilation of the best of man's cultural heritage in all its breadth and depth. If any man can make natural law palatable to present-day Americans, that man is John Courtney Murray.

After stating that the doctrine of natural law has no Roman Catholic presuppositions, Father Murray goes on to explain: "Its presupposition is threefold: that man is intelligent; that reality is intelligible; and that reality, as grasped by intelligence, imposes on the will the obligation that it be obeyed in its demands for action or abstention. Even these statements are not properly 'presuppositions,' since they are susceptible of verification." [84] Although man's reason is admittedly limited, it is not so limited but what it can perceive that "what is good is to be done and what is evil is to be avoided," grasp the meaning of good and evil as primary principles in basic situations such as parent and child relationships, and know "basic moral laws of human life" such as the Ten Commandments.[85] No special revelation and no great amount of education are needed for these three achievements: "These three achievements requiring, as they do, only common human experience and only a modicum of reflection and reasoning are within the powers of human intelligence as such, at least *ut in pluribus,* in the case of most men." [86]

That Father Murray means by "reason" a great deal more than being adept in the use of deductive logic is evident in what he calls "a fourth area of achievement open to the moral reason of man." [87] In that area a heavier demand is made on rational human nature, a demand which involves qualities that are not widely shared by normal men. "The further the human mind advances toward apprehending the particulars of morals, the greater the part that knowledge, experience, reflection, and dispassionateness of judgment must play." [88] Elitist consequences flow from this heavier demand: "This area is reserved for those whom St. Thomas calls 'the wise' (*sapientes*)." [89]

The rational activity of ordinary people and of the "wise" leads to the discovery and formulation of a body of principles of order or propositions regulative of human behavior. A number of them have been fairly specific and controversial, notably those dealing with birth control and the family. Nevertheless, Father Murray makes rather modest claims for them. Natural law is not a blueprint, a straitjacket, or the imposition of a set of half-truths and dated prejudices on a rebellious public. "It can claim to be," he says, "only a 'skeleton law,' to which flesh and blood must be added by that heart of the political process, the rational activity of man, aided by experience and by high professional competence." [90] The efficacy of natural law in furthering individual and social welfare is presented with a like circumspection: "It does not show the individual the way to sainthood, but only to manhood. It does not promise to transform society into the City of God on earth, but only to prescribe, for the purposes of law and social custom, that minimum of morality which must be observed by the members of a society, if the social environment is to be human and habitable." [91]

Father Murray's account is, of course, strongly theistic. Man's reason is not left hanging in a spiritual vacuum. Natural law "supposes a natural theology, asserting that there is a God, Who is eternal Reason, *Nous,* at the summit of the order of being, Who is the author of all nature, and Who wills that the order of nature be fulfilled in all its purposes, as these are inherent in the natures found in the order." [92] Father Murray, following the line laid down by Aquinas, derives natural law from the "eternal law" which "is the Uncreated Reason of God" and which the rational creature apprehends through participation.[93] All this is very good Stoicism and Deism, but is it Christian?

Father Murray admits that the question has been raised: "Finally, there is the charge that natural-law doctrine is not 'Christian.' If it be meant that the doctrine in structure and style is alien to the general Protestant moral system, in so far as there is such a thing, the charge is true enough." [94] The disparaging remark about Protestantism is, of course, beside the point. The point is not whether the doctrine of natural law is Protestant or Roman Catholic but whether it is Christian. As a matter of fact, Father Murray does deal with it anyhow, and with considerable skill. His argument is not centered on the Bible, although he does say: "It would not, of course, be difficult to show that the doctrine is, in germinal fashion, scriptural." [95] His only reference to the Bible in this part of the discussion is to the story of the rich young ruler, and this story neither affirms nor denies the existence of natural law. What it does prove, Father Murray believes, is that the Christian gospel exceeds rather than abrogates the type of righteousness which natural theology indicates God expects of man. "The Christian call is to transcend nature, notably to transcend what is noblest in nature, the faculty of reason. But it is not a call to escape from nature, or to dismantle nature's own structure, and least of all to deny that man is intelligent, that nature is intelligible, and that nature's intelligibilities are laws for the mind that grasps them." [96]

We must now turn to Protestant teaching on natural law. Father Murray thinks that this teaching can be nothing other than negative. His appraisal reads thus: "For the Protestant, on the contrary, the whole doctrine of natural law is a challenge, if not an affront, to his entire style of moral thought and even to his religiosity. The doctrine is alien to him, unassimilable by him. He not only misunderstands it; he also distrusts it." [97] Father Murray's appraisal is a mixture of truth and error or, at the very least, an overstatement. The fault is not altogether his own, because Protestantism, unlike Roman Catholicism, is not subject to the control of an authoritarian ecclesiastical bureaucracy claiming infallibility unto itself. Protestant unity is unity in diversity and therefore can be, at times, difficult to grasp. Moreover, the diversity is not hidden beneath the impressive mantle of an official position. But Father Murray is right in thinking that some Protestants do reject natural law altogether and that others have misgivings about the Roman Catholic teaching on natural law.

Among the Protestants who reject natural law, we must dismiss those who do so because they have espoused positivism, relativism, or some other brand of secular ideology. To the extent that they have surrendered to such ideologies, they have ceased being Protestant. Let us point out in passing that this sort of deviation is by no means peculiar to Protestants. Roman Catholics are similarly smitten, as is illustrated by the Frenchman who, when asked what his religion was, answered: "Personally I am an atheist, but naturally I am a Catholic." If it be replied that such a person is not a good Roman Catholic, we must readily agree —and hasten to add that he would not be a good Protestant either. This manner of identifying oneself with a religious communion is spiritually spurious and offensive to the Christian faith, for it reduces both Protestantism and Roman Catholicism to mere cultural patterns divested of theological convictions, spiritual power, and the responsibilities of churchmanship.

Among the Protestants who deserve the name and who reject natural law outright, Karl Barth is one of the most eminent. Barth's rejection of natural law is the inevitable consequence of his general position on revelation, which is that the Bible is the word of God, authoritative and all-sufficient, independent of and unrelated to any human philosophical systems and church pronouncements, and that the word of God was made flesh in Jesus Christ absolutely, totally, exclusively, and finally. "The Gospel," says Barth, "is not a truth among other truths. Rather, it sets a question-mark against all truths." [98] Any Christian position must therefore be scriptural and Christ-centered, or it is not Christian. It is not enough that a position does not contradict anything in Scripture: there must be definite warrant for it in Scripture.

Barth does not think that natural law meets this test: "By 'natural law' we mean the embodiment of what man is alleged to regard as universally right and wrong, as necessary, permissible, and forbidden 'by nature,' that is, on any conceivable premise. It has been connected with a natural revelation of God, that is, with a revelation known to man by natural means." [99] Barth does not accept any revelation of that kind, for "it would mean that the Christian community was sharing human illusions and confusions. It is bad enough that, when it does not risk going its own way, the Christian community is widely involved in these illusions and confusions. It should not wantonly attempt to deepen such involvement. And it would be doing no less if it were to seek the criterion of its political decisions in some form of the so-called natural law." [100]

It is indeed difficult to accept the doctrine of natural law as a Christian doctrine if the Barthian test is used as the criterion. The nearest thing to a scriptural endorsement of natural law is the following passage in one of Paul's epistles: "When the Gentiles, who have no knowledge of the Law, act in accordance with it by the light of nature, they show that they have a law in themselves, for they demonstrate the effect of a law operating in their own hearts. Their own consciences endorse the existence of such a law, for there is something which condemns or commends their actions." [101] The passage is certainly clear enough and might be used to satisfy the Barthian test. However, to do so would make the acceptance of an important doctrine hinge on a single passage of Scripture when no other passage can be used for such a purpose without subjecting it to considerable strain. We would still have to explain why Paul, who was thoroughly at home in the Greek world, would pay so little attention to this major contribution of the then widely current Stoic philosophy. If Paul did believe in natural law, he was not much concerned with it or he would have commended it for the guidance of Christians. A fair conclusion of the matter would seem to be that if the doctrine of natural law is nonscriptural, it is at least not unscriptural. This conclusion, needless to say, does not meet the Barthian test.

The Barthian test has considerable appeal to all Protestants, even to those who do not subscribe to it. The reason is not far to seek: it is the centrality of Scripture which was the basis of the Reformation and has been the life of true Protestantism ever since. From the very beginning with Luther and Calvin, Protestants have been impressed with the reliability of scriptural truth and the unreliability of extrascriptural truth. They have seen too much of the tendency to compromise principle, to magnify the outlook of one age into the universal truth for all ages, to confuse the institutional interests of ecclesiastical bureaucracies with the imperatives of the Christian faith, and in short to engage in "teaching for doctrines the commandments of men." [102] Against such tendencies stand the integrity and stability of the written word, "the sword of the Spirit" [103] in the hand of everyone who sincerely and assiduously seeks to ascertain the will of God regardless of all personal prejudices and involvements. Calvin's voice was the voice of Protestantism when he said: "For, if we consider the mutability of the human mind,—

how easy its lapse into forgetfulness of God; how great its propensity to errors of every kind; how violent its rage for the perpetual fabrication of new and false religions,—it will be easy to perceive the necessity of the heavenly doctrine being thus committed to writing, that it might not be lost in oblivion, or evaporate in error, or be corrupted by the presumption of men." [104]

Nevertheless, the Barthian test is unsound and an extreme position which is not typical of the mainstream of Protestant thought. To affirm the authority and supremacy of scriptural truth over all truth is one thing, but to do so in such a way as to exclude all other truth is quite another. Calvin asserted that God revealed himself "in every part of the world," [105] praised "heathen writers" and "ancient lawyers" for the excellence of their work, which cannot be disregarded "unless we wish to insult the Spirit of God," [106] and urged us to avail ourselves of the contributions of the secular arts and sciences "lest, if we neglect to use the blessings therein freely offered to us by God, we suffer the just punishment of our negligence." [107] In the main, and with due allowance for differences in emphasis, Calvin thus stated the classic Protestant answer regarding the position of the Christian toward extrascriptural truth. All truth is of God and we must accept it "wherever it shall appear." [108] Scripture is a necessary corrective for human reason and secular learning, but it is not a substitute for them. It was this position which caused Protestantism to dot the United States with schools and colleges long before public authority became seriously interested in education and to insist that Protestant ministers receive a good liberal as well as theological education.

Because of this broader position toward truth, Protestantism has traditionally believed in natural law. Even Martin Luther accepted it, though he did not think in terms of law and was as distrustful of secular learning as he was well versed in it. In advising princes, for example, he urged them to make wise decisions and recommended "the law of nature, of which the reason is full" [109] and much preferred it to an abundance of positive law which he dubbed "a rank growth." [110] Calvin accepted it in no uncertain terms: "Now, as it is certain that the law of God, which we call the moral law, is no other than a declaration of natural law, and of that conscience which has been engraven by God on the minds of men, the whole rule of this equity, therefore, must alone be the scope, and rule, and end, of all laws." [111] The Protestant founders of our country and their Protestant ancestors in Europe believed in natural law, and the importance they ascribed to it can be seen in the amount of space which James Wilson devoted to natural law in his lectures on jurisprudence. The most outspoken contemporary defender of the historic Protestant position on natural law is the Swiss theologian Emil Brunner. He does this so well that we shall quote his words at some length:

Either there is a valid criterion, a justice which stands above us all, a challenge presented *to* us, not *by* us, a standard rule of justice binding on every state and every system of law, or there is no justice, but only power organized in one fashion or another and setting itself up as law. Either there exist eternal, indefeasible rights of man, or there are merely the opportunities of the lucky and the lack of opportunity of the unlucky. Either there is a sacred law, which can be appealed to against every inhuman, unjust social order, against any caprice or cruelty on the part of the state, or that sacred law is a mere dream and law is nothing but another name for the chance products of the actual elements of power in a political field of force.

But if there is no sacred, eternal, divine, absolute law, there is no possibility of denouncing any form of law or polity or national act as unjust. If the positivistic theory of law is right, there is no possibility of waging war against the totalitarian state as a monster of injustice. Nor can we even say—it is unjust—but only it does not suit me, I do not like such things.[112]

In view of the above record, it is plain that Father Murray is mistaken in his belief that the doctrine of natural law is "an affront" to the Protestant's "entire style of moral thought and even to his religiosity." [113] What he should have said is that Protestants object to certain aspects of the Roman Catholic version of natural law on the ground that they are not Christian or not sufficiently Christian. The Protestant objections are that the Roman Catholic version makes insufficient allowance for the distortion of human reason by sin and that it overemphasizes reason at the expense of the will. As a matter of fact, the two objections are closely related. The failure to give due weight to the pervasiveness of sin and its corruption of human reason leads to unduly confident formulations of natural law propositions. The chances of error, even among Aquinas' *sapientes,* are much greater and more common than Roman Catholicism supposes. A less offensive as well as more accurate way to approach this problem would be to adopt the policy of Richard Niebuhr: "If we cannot say anything adequately, we can say some things inadequately." [114] It is better to be honestly and modestly tentative in matters of natural law lest we legislate where we should only discover and advise.

The other Protestant objection is directed at the related Roman Catholic failure to give the will its due. The will is more fundamental than reason, for it is the will which has the power to ignore or discard the findings of reason and to change reasoning into rationalizing. Father Murray is right in saying that men are intelligent, but the issue is frequently not one of intelligence. The world is full of intelligent people who are not amenable to reason. Good will and ill will are the controlling factors. Would it have done any good to reason with the leaders of Nazi Germany or Red China about the atrocities they perpetrated? If it be objected that these were exceptional cases of people corrupted by the possession of too much power, it is easy enough to find examples closer to home among ordinary people. What would Father Murray do, for instance, with a Louisiana barber who propounded with the utmost seriousness the theory that Negroes are descended from sheep? The evidence offered for his theory was this: "You just put your hand on their head. That's not hair, that's wool! And take a look at their nose. Don't it look like a sheep's nose? Besides, they breed like rabbits." The trouble with this kind of man is not intelligence, however much it may seem like it in this case, for he can be quite rational on other subjects. The basic trouble is ill will, which no amount of reasoning can touch. The Bible sometimes calls this condition hardness of heart and sometimes possession by an evil spirit, but never an error in reasoning. Neither can we say that the *sapientes* are necessarily exempt from this kind of flaw, as anyone who has attended faculty meetings or meetings of his professional society can testify.

Father Murray's magnifying of reason at the expense of the will extends to the divine sphere itself. It is significant that he emphasizes God as "Uncreated Reason" and thereby imprisons God in his own legislation. The Protestant, on the other hand, while acknowledging the reason of God, emphasizes his will. God is a free agent who can change his mind and intervene in human and cosmic affairs according to his pleasure. Because God is free, man can be free also and always has a way out of every social necessity and physical determinism in which he is enmeshed. Once again, Emil Brunner makes the needed corrections:

Natural laws are not absolutes; behind and above them there is divine freedom. Natural laws are not ultimates, they are instrumental to God's purpose. They do not determine the purposes of God. They are organs, servants of His will. God's purposes can never be understood in terms of law. The law in every sense of the word has a subordinate, although a very important and indispensable function in God's economy. It has always to be reckoned with as a means of God, but it is never to be taken as an ultimate expression of God's will and purpose. It is therefore questionable whether we are justified in speaking of "eternal laws." All laws, whether natural or moral, belong to the created world. God's own will can never be expressed ultimately in terms of law, because the freedom of His love as well as of His holiness is above them. If theology speaks of the law of God's own being, we must take care that we are not caught in our own words, putting abstractions above God's free will.[115]

The Christian concept of liberty

We are now ready to take up the Christian idea of liberty and its consequences for civil rights. First of all, let us recognize that liberty is not an absolute, for only God is absolute, and man is not God. Liberty is not God either. Liberty is an attribute of God and cannot be detached from his other attributes. We have to single them out and discuss them separately for purposes of analysis because that is the way the human mind works. We cannot talk about everything at once. There is such a thing as the direct spiritual experience of reality, but intellectually we can grasp reality only through its manifestations. All of God's attributes are inseparable aspects of the single divine reality, and any attempt to isolate any of them takes them out of their spiritual context and results in distortion. Omnipotence is not to be had without omniscience nor liberty without benevolence. For man to claim absolute liberty unto himself is sheer insolence and sheer nonsense.

Man can lay only a very limited claim to liberty on the basis of his origin. He was made in the image of God, but no image is anything more than a pale reflection of the original. Neither can it be a substitute for the original, though there are people who would like to treat it as such. Even in the Garden of Eden, man was given only a measure of freedom. He had his instructions: "to dress" and "to keep" the garden,[116] to be "fruitful and multiply" and have dominion "over every living thing that moveth upon the earth," [117] and to refrain from eating of the fruit of the tree of the knowledge of good and evil.[118] Whatever limited claim man had to liberty by virtue of his origin was largely lost through sin. It was not wholly lost, because man is still in the image of God, though the image is distorted and scarcely recognizable. Fallen man can no more have a rightful claim to the same measure of liberty which belonged to him in his state of innocence than a poor copy of a great painting can command the same price as the original.

This scriptural language will not impress secular-minded people since they do not believe in original sin. Some of them do not believe in any sin whatsoever and will admit only to "mistakes." Even these people, however, recognize the substance which the scriptural language conveys when they agree that criminals are not entitled to liberty and should be confined to the penitentiary. Thieves, murderers, perjurers, arsonists, and dangerous maniacs cannot be entrusted with freedom. What Scripture does, and secular-minded people refuse to do, is to assert that the criminal elements do not have a monopoly over evil but that there is evil in every one of us. "The actual sins of the individual man," Barth points out, "are the means by which the general situation is more or less clearly made known. Particular sins do not alter the status of a man; they merely show how heavily the general dominion of sin presses upon him." [119]

The logic of sin being what it is, the denial of freedom of movement which imprisonment assures cannot be the only restriction. We must recognize that the denial of liberty is coextensive with sin. No man, in the name of freedom of speech, has a right to spread malicious gossip, false rumors, and misinformation. No man, in the name of freedom of the press, has the right to disseminate vicious propaganda, to write inflammatory editorials calculated to incite lawlessness, and to publish articles that debase the morals of his readers. No man, in the name of academic freedom, has the right to defy logic in his lectures, to teach anything as a fact which is contrary to the evidence in his possession, to pretend to be an authority in a field he knows nothing about, and to plagiarize or otherwise take credit for what is the work of others. No man, in the name of religious liberty, has a right to propagate heresy and schism or impose by force or fraud even the right convictions on other people. No man, in the name of personal liberty, has the right to play fast and loose with the affections of other people, to become an alcoholic or a drug addict, to commit suicide, or to live by the false maxim that "every man has the right to go to hell in his own way."

All these activities violate natural law, as Father Murray would probably express it, or are contrary to the will of God, as a Protestant would prefer to put it. Whichever way you choose to express it, the fact remains that what is morally right is not optional but mandatory and that which is morally wrong is not optional either but forbidden. No positive law—not even constitutional law—can alter this fact or detract from its normative character in any manner, because the will of God "must alone be the scope, and rule, and end, of all laws." [120] Of all the definitions of civil liberty which most closely respect this imperative of the Christian faith, we would choose Montesquieu's, which says that "liberty can consist only in the power of doing what we ought, and in not being constrained to do what we ought not to will." [121]

This reasoning will be painful to liberals and anathema to libertarians, but they should at least concede that this is what the Christian faith requires. It is not only God and Mammon whom we cannot both worship and serve. We cannot worship the Goddess of Liberty and the God who was incarnate in Jesus Christ either. There is no Christian version of the old Roman Pantheon where a collection of gods can sit together as equals. Polytheism to the contrary notwithstanding, no man can worship and serve more than one deity at a time. Man must choose and take the consequences or, to use the current vernacular, each of us must make an existential decision.

We have now shown that no man can claim absolute liberty for himself because such liberty is an attribute of God alone. Human liberty, therefore, is a relative thing. We have further shown that what relative liberty man can possess under natural law is diminished because of his corrupt nature. Sin is servitude, and there is not much liberty in servitude. The true source of human liberty is not man's origin but his destiny. That destiny is to glorify God and enjoy him forever. That is man's destiny because it is what God intends that all men should do. Emil Brunner makes this point very well: "Thus the origin of the dignity shared equally by all mankind is not to be sought in abstract reason, nor in a general order of being, but in the will of the living God, who addresses every man as 'thou' and summons him to responsible being, to life in communion, in the love with which He first loved man." [122] By the grace of God which enfolds all men in his love, in spite of their corrupt nature, many of the deeds of non-Christians and nominal Christians have served to glorify God, as Calvin recognized with a readiness, fairness, generosity, and broad-mindedness with which his critics seldom credit him. God has been glorified in the achievements of every civilization and in the lives of those who performed them, and this is the true basis of the natural liberty which belongs to all men.

For the Christian, to glorify God and enjoy him forever has a special and more specific meaning: to grow into the likeness of Jesus Christ. Because Jesus Christ was the only begotten Son of the living God, the unique incarnation of the divine in the human, and because he lives in the hearts and minds of those who believe in him, the destiny of man is most fully achieved in the Christian. Because of God's forgiveness given for Christ's sake, because of the atonement whereby Christ substitutes himself for us at the bar of judgment, and because of the sanctification which accompanies the growth of the Christian in the likeness of Christ, the last and innermost bastion of servitude, i.e., sin, is breached and crumbles. With this change a new kind of liberty is born, Christian liberty, which far exceeds natural liberty. The Christian is now a new creature whose liberty will not become the cause of harm and grief to himself and to other men but, on the contrary, will be a blessing to those whose lives he touches. Furthermore, Christian liberty is in a sense his inheritance since he partakes of Christ's liberty to the extent to which he is Christ-like, for "where the Spirit of the Lord is, there is liberty." [123]

The connection between the destiny and the liberty of man is that there can be no glorifying of God which is not free. When Christian theology tells us that man was created for fellowship with God, it means that there had to be some common ground between them. Some reciprocity had to be possible, for no true fellowship was ever based on one-way communication. You cannot have fellowship with an inanimate object, however much you might be attached to it, and fellowship with an instinct-bound animal is minimal at best. Slavery, too, is incompatible with fellowship. The case of the slave Onesimus is most instructive on this point. Onesimus had robbed and fled from his master, Philemon, and had been converted by the apostle Paul, Paul sent Onesimus back to Philemon with a letter which said in part: "It occurs to me that there has been a purpose in your losing him. You lost him, a slave, for a time; now you are having him back for good, not merely a slave, but as a brother Christian." [124] Legal slavery, which is a property relationship, was supplanted by Christian brotherhood, which is a personal relation-

ship and a form of fellowship. The spirit of Christ abolished the slave
status in fact, and tradition has it that Philemon later abolished it in
law by emancipating Onesimus.

Furthermore, when we speak of glorifying God as the destiny of man,
we need to remember that all glorifying is in essence a form of giving,
and giving requires freedom. A gift which is not free is no gift at all
but a tax. The New Testament raised the whole concept of stewardship
to the level of freedom for that very reason. The glorifying of God in
church is no longer to be supported by the ancient Jewish tithe, which
was a tax, nor should it be supported by the business practice of charg-
ing for services or making money out of bazaars or the like, but by the
voluntary response of grateful beings seeking to honor God. Paul stated
the matter thus: "Every man according as he purposeth in his heart, so
let him give; not grudgingly, or of necessity: for God loveth a cheerful
giver." [125]

The right to witness

Because of man's destiny, therefore, both natural and Christian liberty
are entitled to respect by government. When this respect is translated
into positive law, we have civil rights. But there is another line of
Christian thought which has a bearing on the matter of civil rights,
and that is the relationship which exists between the depravity of human
nature and the power of government. Not every restriction on the natural
liberty of man has the effect of conferring jurisdiction on government.
The reason is that government officials, being human, are tainted with
the same depravity which afflicts the people over whom they rule, and
the possession of political power increases opportunities for evil. If the
natural liberty of the governed needs to be restricted, so does that of
the government, and the need is even greater. To say that no man has
a right to propagate heresy and schism, for example, does not give government officials the competence to define these terms and mete out
temporal penalties. That a professor has no right to teach anything as
a fact which is contrary to the evidence in his possession does not give
the government the right to control teaching. Even in a state university
there should be no such right. For the state legislature to attempt to
control teaching would deny the *raison d'être* of any university by placing
the control of the learned in the hands of the ignorant.

The traditional American conception of civil rights as legal restraints
applicable to all units, branches, and levels of government is therefore
sound from a Christian point of view. We need to know, however, what
practical effects the Christian doctrine of man has on the interpretation
of civil rights, particularly the First Amendment freedoms of religion,
speech, press, assembly, and petition. To determine what these effects
are, it is necessary to reject the libertarian position of Justice Black be-

cause it makes freedom an absolute. Walter Berns is right: government agencies have to get into the business of distinguishing good from evil. There are obvious risks in doing this, but there are equally obvious risks in not doing it. Let us first distinguish between the positive and negative aspects of governmental action in dealing with good and evil.

If we turn the clear-and-present-danger test from its negative phrasing, i.e., "a substantive evil which Congress has a right to prevent," and recast it in positive form, we shall be speaking of "a substantive good which Congress has a right to promote." This reformulation has the merit of conceding to government the right to witness. The right to witness by churchmen to their faith, by university people to the truth, and by physicians to health is a natural right which is part of the destiny of man since there can be no glorifying God without this kind of witnessing. The right to witness is universal and inalienable, inherent as it is in the will of God, and cannot legitimately be taken away from government officials either in their individual or corporate capacity, and neither can it be denied to the people as a political community. If one seeks a constitutional anchor for this right, we point to the Ninth Amendment, which reads: "The enumeration in the Constitution of certain rights shall not be construed to deny or disparage others retained by the people."

On Christian grounds, the case for defending the right to witness is even stronger, for when Christ instructed us to seek "first the kingdom of God, and his righteousness," [126] he did not exclude government officials and thus make them religious eunuchs and amoral beings. That the apostles understood Christ's meaning to include government officials can be seen from Peter's conversion of the Roman centurion Cornelius and from Paul's witnessing before Felix and Festus, who were Roman officials. Certainly, no one took this right as applied to magistrates more seriously than John Calvin,[127] and it was echoed by John Dickinson, one of the framers of the Constitution, when he wrote that "it is the duty of government, with the utmost attention and caution, to promote and enforce the sublime and beneficial morality, as well as theology, of Christianity. . . ." [128] The right to witness not only by appropriate pronouncement but by effective action creates responsibilities. Emil Brunner points out that the early Christians had to live with the evil of slavery as long as they were a minority and that they could abolish it only as a spiritual fact within their own Christian fellowship. However: "The situation was, of course, radically altered as soon as Christianity became a predominant factor in the shaping of public order, as it was from the time of Constantine onward. In this new situation, the Christian was no longer a mere object of the law; *he was at the same time its source. Hence he was partially responsible for its substance.*" [129]

Our constitutional history has exemplified the right to witness by the people and their government, as shown by the Thanksgiving proclamations of the President of the United States, the motto on our coins, the chaplains in our Congress and our armed forces, state recognition of diplomas and certificates from denominational colleges and universities, federal assistance to denominational educational institutions in the form of grants and scholarships and research contracts, the exemption of church property from taxation, the exemption of conscientious objectors from military service, and the prayers with which the sessions of the Supreme Court are opened. The extensive welfare activities of state and federal governments are an expression of the right to witness in the field of morals. Government sponsorship of private and public research activities, supervision of advertising, and protection of patents and copyrights are an expression of the same right in the field of truth.

It will be objected that government witnessing to what is right involves the risk of witnessing to what is wrong, and that the resources available to government are so great as to make all government witnessing an awesome thing. The objection has merit but is mitigated by three reasons. First, a natural right is not less of a right because it can be abused. To run the risk of being wrong is part of mature manhood, and we do not want immature people in charge of our public affairs. As Oliver Ellsworth so truly said in defending the Constitution during the ratification campaign: "If, my countrymen, you wait for a constitution which absolutely bars a power of doing evil, you must wait long, and when obtained *it will have no power of doing good.*" [130] Second, a natural right applies to all men, not just to Christians alone; hence all witnessing is entitled to respect. It is not the expression of faith (witnessing) but its suppression (censorship and persecution) which is politically injurious and which the First Amendment seeks to prevent. Third, as long as the right to dissent is respected and the customary democratic avenues of change are kept open, there is a built-in chance to recuperate from what may be wrong in community witnessing.

We have now said that it is necessary for government to go into the business of distinguishing good and evil, and we have further established that the positive side of the problem is covered by the right to witness. Let us now turn to the negative side and establish criteria which government should follow in dealing with evil. These criteria are two in number.

The first criterion is that government should not deal with evil per se, out of context, directly as such. This is not because there is a natural right to tolerate evil but because government has neither the power nor the wisdom to cope with evil in that form. The restriction is a necessary consequence of the depravity of human nature. However, evil is not thereby left unchallenged. Christians, in particular, have other weapons at their disposal than governmental power, weapons which are appropriate for the purpose. Martin Luther made this point concretely and vividly: "Heresy can never be prevented by force. That must be taken hold of in a different way, and must be opposed and dealt with otherwise than with the sword. Here God's Word must strive; if that does not accomplish the end it will remain unaccomplished through secular power, though it fill the world with blood. Heresy is a spiritual matter, which no iron can strike, no fire burn, no water drown." [131] What Luther said here about religious heresy applies with equal force to political, social, and economic heresy.

The second criterion, which we shall call the principle of aggravated evil, considers evil in the context of circumstances which are in themselves punishable, such as a riot. Evil in general and out of a particular context puts too great a strain on official discernment, but evil in the context of a specific situation is more clearly visible and manageable. It is partly for this reason that our federal courts have traditionally refused to give advisory opinions and to take jurisdiction over hypothetical or "moot" cases. When we speak of "aggravated evil," we mean that the evil situation is aggravated by the evil spirit or principle which may be involved in the situation, and not the other way around. We mean to move from tangible effects to the intangible cause, from the symptoms to the disease. We mean to recognize in political life the validity of what Christ said about all of life, namely, that it is the things which "proceed out of the mouth" and "come forth from the heart" which "defile the man." [132]

It is not enough to say with John Stuart Mill that disorder, being an objective behavioral reality, is something which falls within the purview of government but that the cause of the disorder should not be taken into account.[133] The cause of the disorder, though it lie in the intangible area of the written or spoken idea, is relevant to the situation and must be adjudged good or evil. Thus, if some Nazi or neo-Nazi denounces the Jews in vituperative language, making false allegations of fact, using spurious logic or no logic at all, under circumstances which precipitate violence or which make violence an immediate prospect, there is just ground for restraint and punishment by government. The evil does not consist only in the fact of violence. It is aggravated by the viciousness of the speech itself, and that viciousness is part of the situation. We cannot agree with the libertarian position on civil rights which would grant the protection of government to that kind of speech.

On the other hand, if a Southern moderate were to make a reasonable and nonabusive speech advocating racial justice and respect for federal law in a Southern city at a time of racial crisis, the result might well be a riot in which considerable damage would be done. Here again we have disorder, but the cause is just and needs to be heard. The government should protect that speaker in this case. For the government to do otherwise would mean giving every rabble-rousing group a veto over every speech. The rightness or wrongness of a cause is a factor which cannot be ignored when First Amendment freedoms are translated into behavior. We have civil rights in order that we might be free to glorify God by furthering what is good and not by perpetrating what is evil.

The principle of aggravated evil is not as unprecedented as it may seem to some liberals. Actually, it is not different from the law which treats malice aforethought as relevant in murder cases, considers malice and falsehood as the decisive elements in libel cases, and refuses to give effect to racially discriminatory clauses in housing agreements. All we are doing is extending these precedents to First Amendment cases. The principle of aggravated evil does confront government officials with the necessity of making moral decisions, but the necessity is always present. Officials may refuse to admit it, hide it from themselves, or try to hide it from others, but it is there nonetheless. It is unavoidable.

Under these circumstances, the moral stature of government officials becomes very important. That, too, is unavoidable. Some accommodation to the moral level of government officials and the people they represent (or over whom they rule) may be made, as we acknowledge when we say that the British and Swiss governments need fewer checks than the Argentine and South African governments. The accommodation, however, can operate only within fairly narrow limits, for there are levels of morality so low that checks are futile and amount to nothing more than what several of the framers of the Constitution characterized as mere "parchment barriers."

On this matter of moral stature, the Christian faith can make a great and decisive contribution in two ways: (1) by setting up a standard of what true moral stature is, (2) by giving people the power to go a long way toward attaining that stature. The standard, of course, is Jesus Christ and those noble figures throughout history who have exemplified in their lives the mind and spirit of Christ. The power comes from the faith which Paul referred to when he said: "I can do all things through Christ which strengtheneth me." [134] The process of converting and reconstructing human nature, i.e., what we sometimes call "character building," is a task which belongs pre-eminently to the church, and upon the success of the church in performing it depends the liberty of man. This is a fact which no cliché about "a government of laws and not of men" can becloud. No constitutional system will ever be devised which can take the place of good men or make high moral stature superfluous.

Chapter VI

PARTICIPATION
AND POLITICS

W E are now ready to inquire what light the Christian faith can shed on the concepts of citizenship and representation. The essence of both citizenship and representation is participation in politics, hence the title of this chapter.

SECULAR CONCEPTS OF CITIZENSHIP

As a concept of political science, citizenship has had a long history. In the Greek and Roman world the accent was on participation. Aristotle denied that citizenship is a matter of residence or parentage, and he did not think it should be confused with the legal status of a freeman. A freeman was no slave, but he was not necessarily a citizen either (e.g., he might be a foreigner). Indeed, Aristotle specifically defined citizenship as participation in politics. He did not regard participation as an end in itself, however, but held that it should be granted or denied on the basis of individual sharing in the state's dominant value. Thus, citizenship was made to depend on the form of the state, e.g., a person who was a citizen in a democracy would not be one in an oligarchy.

The Romans continued to think of citizenship as participation, but they dropped the ethical and sociological approach of the Greeks and replaced it with a legalistic approach more congenial to the Roman mind. Citizenship was now a legal status conferring the right to participate in politics, and that status was no longer dependent on the form of the state. A Roman was as much a citizen under the empire as he was under the republic. To this right to participate in politics were added certain other rights and privileges not concerned with voting or holding public office but which had to do with the civil law, originally thought of as an exclusively Roman product and only later extended to persons not of Roman origin. It was this latter essentially civil rights aspect of Roman citizenship which the apostle Paul invoked when he berated the magistrates at Philippi for beating and imprisoning him and his associates without a trial [1] and again when he raised the question of jurisdiction and appealed to Caesar.[2]

In monarchical Europe the idea of participation was dropped from the concept of citizenship and replaced by that of allegiance. The essence of the idea of allegiance—the obligation to obey—was of feudal origin. It was this feudal origin which saved the idea of allegiance from being completely one-sided, for reciprocity was central to all feudal thinking. The duty of the vassal to obey his lord was balanced by the duty of the lord to protect the vassal. So in monarchical Europe allegiance and protection became reciprocal. But the idea of participation was lacking, and thus monarchs were said to have "subjects." This terminology is still retained as a vestigial remnant of the past, though not as a reality of the present, by the history-minded British when they speak of British subjects and never British citizens. Because the monarchies of Europe were mainly and increasingly national, allegiance and nationality came to be synonymous terms and continue to be so used in international law. Also associated with allegiance was inalienability, as illustrated by the old maxim of British law "once an Englishman, always an Englishman," which played a part in causing the war of 1812. If you were born an Englishman or a Frenchman, you could never be anything else. The right of expatriation and naturalization came later, but even so, it was and still is considered in law as a concession which the sovereign may or may not grant and whose terms are determined solely by the sovereign.

Then came the French Revolution and with it the reintroduction of the term "citizen," to which the ancient idea of participation in politics was once more indissolubly linked. A sharp distinction was made between civil rights (*droits civils*) and political rights (*droits politiques*), which has become classic in continental Europe. The former belonged to persons as human beings while the latter were reserved to persons as participants in the political process and who were known as citizens. In traditional monarchical Europe the very word "citizen" had a radical ring and was quite as disturbing as the word "comrade" later became in bourgeois capitalism. In revolutionary France, however, "citizen" was not only a legal status but a mode of address, which sounded like a title of nobility and denoted a true fellowship in which participation in politics was based on a common loyalty to the ideals of the French Revolution. Monarchical sovereignty became national sovereignty. For a while, usage differentiated between "subjects" and "citizens." Monarchies had subjects, and republics had citizens. It was in line with this usage that the term "citizen," in spite of its radical overtones, was adopted by the conservative framers of our Constitution. By now the distinction between subject and citizen had vanished with the disappearance of monarchies and exists only as an historical curiosity.

The American concept of citizenship bears the marks of the long evolution we have been outlining. In many ways that concept is not too felicitous an amalgam of older ideas, all of which are involved in varying degrees and cause a good deal of ambiguity. From monarchical

Europe we get the idea of allegiance, which is an essential component of American citizenship, as we recognize in the last and decisive step in naturalization which is the oath of allegiance. As we have seen, allegiance implies protection but not necessarily participation. During the years when the Philippines were a dependency of the United States, Filipinos were nationals of the United States but never American citizens. They owed allegiance to the United States and were entitled to the protection of the American government but were otherwise in the position of aliens.

From Rome we get the idea that citizenship is a matter of law. Anyone who qualifies under the Fourteenth Amendment definition or under congressional legislation on the subject is a citizen. All he needs to establish his status is a valid birth certificate or a certificate of naturalization. And yet, in practice we are not altogether satisfied with this Roman legalistic idea. We have also inherited from the Greeks and from the French Revolution the feeling that citizenship ought to have something to do with shared ideals and that participation without such sharing is ethically reprehensible and politically unwise. We give vent to this feeling when we say of someone: "He is legally an American citizen, but he is not really an American." We feel that an American monarchist would be a caricature of a citizen and that an American Nazi or Communist is not truly a citizen either, the law to the contrary notwithstanding. What we mean when we react in this manner is that citizenship is more than a legal bond and that such people do not and cannot share with us what we consider to be the presuppositions of citizenship. Citizenship means membership in a community, and how can there be community without a common loyalty to shared ideals? This feeling has found its way into our naturalization laws which prescribe not only a willingness to defend the United States but also an understanding of and affection for the Constitution. However, these laws cannot affect citizenship by birth. In the latter case, either American parentage or birth on American soil is deemed sufficient proof that citizenship in law is citizenship in fact, which is probably a sound assumption in the great majority of cases but which is not necessarily so and may become less so if the ideologies should make large inroads on the American mind.

The distinction between civil rights and political rights is recognized in the United States, but not without considerable blurring. On the one hand, the Constitution speaks of the "privileges or immunities of citizens of the United States," and jurists tell us that voting and officeholding are privileges rather than civil rights. The point is important because a civil right is something of which we cannot be deprived, whereas a privilege may be denied or withdrawn on grounds of public policy. On the other hand, popular usage insists on speaking of the right to vote and to hold office, and the courts have given some support to popular

usage by handling voting cases under what are clearly civil rights provisions of the Constitution, such as the due process and equal protection
clauses of the Fourteenth Amendment. The ambiguity gets us into con-
tradictions. For example, we believe that resident aliens should be taxed
but should not vote, and we also believe that taxation without representation is unjust.

THE CHURCH
AS A POLITICAL SOCIETY

It comes as a surprise to many Christians to be told that there is
such a thing as Christian citizenship. Years of infiltration by the liberal
individualist philosophy have taught them otherwise. Religion, they believe, is a private matter, a wholly personal relationship between man
and God. What a man believes is his own business, is not a fit subject
for discussion, and is best honored by respectful silence. The same goes
for church membership. These Christians hold that the church is a voluntary association of like-minded people. One can be a good Christian
without being a church member. Now that the church has generally ceded
most of its erstwhile education and welfare functions to public authority,
church membership is more optional than ever. Furthermore, the American tradition of separation of church and state requires that the state
keep out of church affairs. A widely accepted corollary says that the
church should stay out of politics as a kind of *quid pro quo*. A further
corollary, which is reinforced by the long dominant liberal individualist
philosophy and by the popular notion that all politics is evil, holds that
the church has no political aspects. Against a background of this kind,
for anyone to say that the church is a political society whose members
are citizens comes as something of a shock. We must get over the shock
and resolutely lay aside the secular incrustations which are responsible
for it. We must go back to Scripture and those who have been Scripture's
most faithful interpreters over many years of Christian history.

If we go back to the scriptural record, we are struck by the emphasis
which Christ placed on the kingdom of God. Again and again he stressed
the kingdom as absolutely central to his mission. He opened his ministry
with the declaration: "Repent: for the kingdom of heaven is at hand." [3]
His model prayer included the petition: "Thy kingdom come." [4] He instructed his disciples to seek the kingdom ahead of anything else.[5] The
kingdom was the central theme of almost all his parables. In his conversation with Nicodemus it was simply assumed that the kingdom was
the most important thing in the world. He discussed it in all sorts of
connections, e.g., in relation to the rich, the poor, children, scribes,
Pharisees, prostitutes, publicans, disciples, and Gentiles. He spoke of
it with that spontaneity, naturalness, informality, and frequency which
one reserves for an ever present reality and central concern. It was a

reality which transcended history (e.g., "My kingdom is not of this world") [6] and yet is in history (e.g., "behold, the kingdom of God is within you").[7] He thought of it as an immediate present available now, and also as a future fulfillment in history and beyond history, in life and beyond death into life everlasting. The apostles understood their Lord's meaning and sought to further the kingdom on earth. Any perusal of a good concordance shows that the Epistles are full of references to the kingdom, and to the New Israel, which continued the Old Israel that had been a kingdom (theocracy) even before Saul and David.

In view of all this emphasis, what right have we American Christians to disregard or minimize the kingdom of God and to substitute for it an individualist nonpolitical gospel? Of course, not everybody has disregarded or minimized the kingdom. Unfortunately, among those who concern themselves with it, there have been serious misinterpretations from the "right" and from the "left."

On the right we have the premillennialists who make the kingdom an exclusively eschatological reality. They make everything hinge on the Second Coming of Christ after which Christ will reign on earth for a thousand years. They scan, peep, speculate, and calculate, awaiting Armageddon with breathless trepidation and trying to discern occult "clues" in Scripture and match them up with "the signs of the times"—in spite of Christ's explicit and repeated warning not to engage in that kind of thing. They thereby read the full Gospel out of life and become irresponsible and unprofitable Christians.

On the left we have the advocates of what was known in the twenties and thirties as the Social Gospel. Their foremost representative, Walter Rauschenbusch, tried to establish the Social Gospel by sharply differentiating kingdom from church: "Jesus always spoke of the kingdom of God. Only two of his reported sayings contain the word 'Church,' and both passages are of questionable authenticity." [8] It is Rauschenbusch's contention that immediately after Christ's death the disciples formed and attached themselves to the church and forgot the kingdom: "But the Kingdom was merely a hope, the Church a present reality. The chief interest and affection flowed toward the Church. Soon, through a combination of causes, the name and idea of 'the Kingdom of God' began to be replaced by the name and idea of 'the Church' in the preaching, literature, and theological thought of the Church. Augustine completed this process in his *De Civitate Dei*." [9]

From this dissociation flows a marked hostility to the church (e.g., "The Kingdom of God breeds prophets; the Church breeds priests and theologians").[10] It appears, however, that Rauschenbusch's belittling of the church is based not so much on his reading of Scripture as it is on his reaction to the failure of the organized church of his day to support him in his denunciation of economic exploitation, colonialism, and militarism. However natural his reaction may be, it does not justify the dissociation. Augustine was right: the apostles did—and rightly—identify the church with the kingdom of God. Consider, for instance, the words of Peter: "But ye are a chosen generation, a royal priesthood, an holy nation, a peculiar people; that ye should shew forth the praises of him who hath called you out of darkness into his marvelous light: Which in time past were not a people, but are now the people of God: which had not obtained mercy, but now have obtained mercy." [11] Of course, we must remember that the apostles were using the word church in its New Testament sense of the community of believers across all man-made barriers and both in and beyond time. Rauschenbusch failed to understand apostolic teaching on this subject because of his un-Protestant view of Scripture, which led him to ascribe error to the apostles and conveniently to question the authenticity of passages which do not harmonize with his thesis.

Even the most individualistic Christian will have to admit that the word kingdom is a political term. A kingdom is a political society governed by a king. That is what the term meant when Christ used it, and that is what it has always meant before and since. We might draw the inference from Christ's use of the term that monarchy is the only legitimate form of government. But let us remember that it is God who is King, and not some fallible earthly mortal. Indeed, because God is King, absolute monarchies are usurpations of the divine sovereignty, and even constitutional monarchies are suspect. The Old Testament account of the institution of monarchy in ancient Israel makes this point unmistakably clear: "And the Lord said unto Samuel, Hearken unto the voice of the people in all that they say unto thee: for they have not rejected thee, *but they have rejected me, that I should not reign over them.*" [12] The Old Testament account goes on to spell out with a wealth of detail the evil consequences which would and did follow the adoption of monarchy. In another age and setting Calvin was to pass a similarly unfavorable judgment on monarchy: "The vice or imperfection of men, therefore, renders it safer and more tolerable for the government to be in the hands of many, that they may afford each other mutual assistance and admonition, and that if any one arrogates to himself more than is right, the many act as censors and masters to restrain his ambition." [13]

It would be incorrect to suppose that these judgments are applicable only to ancient Israel or to temporal states. We have it on Christ's own authority that monarchy is not a proper form of government for the church. His comment was occasioned by the demand of James and John for first place in the Kingdom, a demand which provoked dissension among the disciples. "But Jesus called them to him," Scripture records, "and saith unto them, Ye know that they which are accounted to rule over the Gentiles exercise lordship over them; and their great ones exercise authority upon them. But so shall it not be among you: but whosoever will be great among you, shall be your minister: And whosoever of you will be the chiefest, shall be servant of all." [14] The application of Christ's teaching to church polity is concisely expressed in the Presbyterian Confession of Faith: "The Lord Jesus Christ is the only head of the church, and the claim of any man to be the vicar of Christ and the head of the church, is without warrant in fact or in Scripture, and even anti-Christian, a usurpation dishonoring to the Lord Jesus Christ." [15]

To the secular-minded, the kingdom of God is inconceivable. How can you have a kingdom, they ask, without a king? What makes the kingdom conceivable and real to those on the inside is that they do not accept the secularist assumption that Christ is dead. Christ died but was resurrected, and he lives in the church and rules over it. There lurks in the thinking of secularists another equally unwarranted assumption, namely, the assumption of visibility. And yet they know that millions of people have been governed by kings, czars, emperors, and sultans whom they have never seen in all their lives. Moreover, the fact that in our day television and rapid transportation have largely changed this situation is not altogether an advantage. It is not necessary for the reality of government that a ruler be visible but only that he exist and that he govern.

Christian teaching on the kingdom of God leaves no doubt that the central fact is the fact of divine government, the tremendous reality which is conveyed by the word "election." It was God who chose the people of Israel, and not the other way around. At first glance, it seems a peculiar choice. The Jews were not gifted in military matters like the Assyrians, nor in art and philosophy like the Greeks, nor in science and mathematics like the Babylonians, nor in law and government like the Romans. They were by nature a singularly undistinguished people. They were a kind of national edition of Job in that they were stripped of all those endowments and aptitudes which might have tempted them to think of themselves as the makers of their own destiny. They had to rely on God because there was nothing else on which they could rely. All they had was their religion, but that religion was their claim to greatness and glory.

The entire Old Testament is built on this central theme of divine election and government. God chose Abraham. God turned the selling of Joseph as a slave into the agency through which the Jews were saved from starvation, thereby transforming evil into good. It was God who liberated the Jews from slavery in the land of Egypt, and he did it in such a way that no Jew could think of claiming credit for it. How indeed could a minority group, sunk in the status of slavery, without weapons and military training, without organized government, without economic resources, and without a conscious cultural tradition, possibly hope to liberate itself from the yoke of one of the most powerful and civilized peoples in antiquity? On the other hand, what reason could the Egyptians have for depriving themselves of a useful and cheap labor force? The liberation of the Jews was literally a miracle. So was their survival in the wilderness and so was their successful invasion and conquest of the Holy Land against fortified cities where they were outnumbered by well-armed peoples filled with the fervent zeal that goes with the defense of hearth and home. If we went into the details of these events or followed the rest of the story of the Jews through the vicissitudes of the judges, the monarchy, the captivity, the restoration, and the dispersion, we would reach the same fact, namely the awesome reality of divine election and government which no human combination of forces can withstand.

Attempts to explain away these events in naturalistic terms have been ingenious. Taken individually and separately, some of them are plausible, but taken together, they are thoroughly unconvincing. There is a limit beyond which coincidences cease to be coincidences and happenstance becomes destiny. There is no other way to explain the history of ancient Israel otherwise than the Bible does it, i.e., as the mighty acts of God, because the Jews were quite powerless to perform them. The Jews were not only powerless: they were unwilling. Times without number they rebelled, disobeyed, dragged their feet, wandered off in different directions, became unresponsive and insensitive, suffered from blindness and forgetfulness. But always came the will of God who gave them a law beyond their wisdom, an ethic beyond their reach, and a religion beyond their understanding. God pleaded, cajoled, entreated, and reasoned with them. When these appeals failed came military defeat, civil strife, foreign rule, bondage, and dispersion so that changed conditions could do what argument and sentiment could not do. There could be no doubt that a king really and truly did govern his people.

It has not been otherwise with the New Israel. The Greek word for church, *ecclesia,* means "those called out," those who have assembled by God's direction. As the Book of Acts puts it: "And the Lord added to the church daily such as should be saved." [16] Once again the human material was unpromising. Who were the disciples? ignorant and impetuous fishermen like Peter, violent and vindictive men like James and John, corrupt tax collectors like Matthew, narrow-minded zealots like Saul of Tarsus. That the apostles were an unimpressive group by worldly standards was well recognized at the time. When the apostles addressed crowds after Pentecost, the audience was "amazed" and "marvelled" at the performance by ignorant Galileans,[17] and not being able to deny the evidence confronting them, some of the listeners attributed it to drunkenness.[18] Commenting on this startling contrast between the insignificance of the human material and the magnificence of the accomplishment, Paul was later to say:

For ye see your calling, brethren, how that not many wise men after the flesh, not many mighty, not many noble, are called: But God hath chosen the foolish things of the world to confound the wise; and God hath chosen the weak things of the world to confound the things which are mighty; And base things of the world, and things which are despised, hath God chosen, yea, and things which are not, to bring to nought things that are: That no flesh should glory in his presence.[19]

Once more we see the mighty will of God directing and governing the church, often overruling its members. The earliest church was composed entirely of Jews who would have been perfectly willing to remain a Jewish sect. But a necessity stronger than their inclination ruled otherwise. Being Jews, they tried to conform to the observances of Judaism. Being Christians, they also had their own observances. Being both proved inconvenient and burdensome.* Furthermore, the Christians' interpretation of the common religious heritage was now different from that of the Jews with whom they endeavored to worship. There was also the fact that the Jews were not mission-minded whereas the Christians were.

Any hope that the Christians could remain a Jewish sect or convert the bulk of the Jews was destroyed by the hammer blows of persecution. The result was to propel procrastinating Christians into an earlier fulfillment of the Great Commission to go unto all nations and preach the Gospel. As a hurricane strikes a seed pod and disseminates the seeds over the land to sprout and grow into new plants, so persecution tore the Christians loose from Palestine and scattered them far and wide over the Roman Empire to form new churches wherever they went.

The consequent influx of Gentiles into the church soon confronted the Jewish Christians with a basic problem: could the Gentiles be accepted as brothers in Christ on equal terms with the original disciples without regard to differences in racial and national backgrounds? Did the commandment to love one another as Christ loved us apply to these people also? As usually happens in such cases, the issue arose out of a specific context. That context was the Lord's Supper, which was then not a token but a real meal and was the most sacred of Christian observances. On the one hand was Christ's direct command to eat this bread and drink this cup. On the other was the strict rule that Jews and Gentiles should have no social relations, especially partaking of meals which implied acceptance and fraternization. Christ or culture, that was the choice before them. No evasion was possible. Either you ate and drank, or you did not. Being Christians, they chose Christ. When they did, the age-old barrier between Jew and Gentile was broken.

---

* The Jews observed Monday, Thursday, and Saturday. The Christians added Sunday (Jesus' resurrection), Wednesday (Jesus' arrest), and Friday (Jesus' death). To observe all these days would have left Tuesday as the only normal day of the week.

Many other problems arose involving the relations of law to faith, of Greek philosophy to Christian theology, of pagan morals to the Christian ethic. In all these cases, the will of God took effect, often against the inclination, beliefs, will, and sometimes even the resistance of the church members. In the New Israel as in the Old, there was this ever present and imperious Will, "wholly Other," as Barth was to overstate it later, asserting itself with decisive, often surprising, always disturbing, and sometimes shattering impact. The church was no fortuitous collection of individuals or pluralistic juxtaposition of groups but a genuine kingdom, the kingdom of God on earth.

Many present-day Americans do not realize that the church is a kingdom, but the pagan Romans realized it clearly. The Romans did not believe in Christ as either Lord or Savior, but they knew a kingdom when they saw one. They recognized an empire within an empire and feared it accordingly. From its very beginning, the Christian church has presented a political problem, which can be traced through the persecutions by Roman authorities, the conversion of Constantine, the long struggle between pope and emperor during the Middle Ages, the wars and revolutions of the Reformation period, and the present controversies in several countries over the relations of church and state. If it be objected that the kingdom of God has suffered from disunity, disloyalty, rebellion, particularism, regionalism, sedition, and secession, we must of course agree. The kingdom of God has indeed suffered from all these ills, and it still does. What kingdom has not? These ills do not disprove that it is a kingdom but only show that it has not yet reached complete fulfillment. The kingdom of God is on earth, but not yet on earth as it is in Heaven.

We have had to discuss at some length the reality of God as a political ruler because the idea is so uncongenial to our contemporary mentality. Contemporary man is in one respect kin to the apostle Thomas: he wants to see with his physical eyes and feel with his hands before he can believe, and his whole inclination is to say that an invisible and intangible ruler is no ruler at all. Some Christians find it a little easier to believe that God can rule through a representative because the representative, at least, is visible and tangible. They rationalize their weakness by arguing that it is inconceivable that God could have founded a kingdom and not left somebody in charge. They cannot bring themselves to believe that God can look after his own kingdom and that not even his most important ministers are indispensable men. They should remember and weigh the words of Christ to Thomas: "Thomas, because thou hast seen me, thou hast believed: blessed are they that have not seen, and yet have believed." [20]

Just as contemporary man finds an invisible and intangible king unreal, so he finds the description of God as a political ruler disturbing and even shocking. With his mouth he recites the catechism which affirms that

Christ "executes the office of king" [21] and sings hymns which pay homage to Christ the King, but his mind is not involved. And yet, how can anyone—even Christ—be a king and not be in politics? The reticence, not to say indignation, which such a thought unleashes is no fault of Christian theology but has its source in the prevailing association of the word politics with graft and corruption, narrow partisanship, bossism, personal self-aggrandizement, and betrayal of principle. It is high time that we liberate ourselves from the domination of this conception of politics. The word political was originally the adjective form of the Greek word *polis* (i.e., city, state, or city-state). Anything is political, therefore, which affects the *polis* and implies the existence of a good which is common to all members and which requires cooperative action for its attainment. The term *polis* has changed many times over the centuries as it moved from one language group to another and from culture to culture, but the reality denoted by it remains the same. The term "kingdom of God" as applied to the church has also changed (e.g., Augustine's *civitas Dei* and Barth's "Christian community"), but the reality behind it has remained intact.

The kingdom of God as it emerged from the Old Testament to the New Testament went through a formative period in which certain basic decisions, essentially constitutional in nature, had to be made. In this respect, the kingdom of God was not unlike other kingdoms. For example, it had to have a name for its people. Some called them the New Israel, thus pointing to the continuity with the Old Israel. This, of course, would not mean much to Gentile Christians. Others, usually non-Christian Jews, called them Nazarenes. This name emphasized the carpenter-prophet from Nazareth and denied, at least by implication, the Messiah-King born in Bethlehem. However, it did have the merit of bringing out that Christ was an actual historical person and not a mythical figure or the figment of an overheated imagination. Another name was Followers of the Way, thus emphasizing the Christian ethic and manner of life which characterized the disciples. Somehow or other, none of these names took. The name which did take and was destined to endure, "Christian," was first used in Antioch, probably because in that city the Christians were so mixed in background and origin that being followers of Christ was the only common factor which outsiders could detect. In any case, the name was appropriate, simple, and truthful.

There was also the matter of symbolism to be determined. Every political community has a symbol (e.g., the Moorish crescent, the Chinese dragon, the Communist hammer and sickle, the Nazi swastika), which serves as a focus of loyalty and a center of meaning. It was necessary that the kingdom of God should have a symbol too. For a while the lamb and the fish were in competition for first place, and there was something to be said for each. Nevertheless, neither one took hold. The lamb was too closely associated with Jewish history to be very meaningful to Gentiles, implying as it did familiarity with the Jewish sacrificial system. The fish was too circumstantial, being associated with the nonessential fact that several of the original disciples happened to be fishermen. Soon the church adopted the Cross as its symbol and has retained it ever since.

Now the Cross was the most radical, improbable, and audacious symbol that could have been chosen. To the Roman world in which the first Christians lived, the cross was the symbol of the most cruel and ignominious form of execution reserved for the worst non-Roman criminals. It meant death and dishonor. Even the disciples could not, at first, shake off the weight of these associations. It was a disheartened little group who watched Christ die on the Cross, for they thought it meant the tragic end of all their hopes. It took a while for them to think through the event and understand that the Crucifixion meant salvation from sin, reconciliation with God, and the gateway to life everlasting. When they did think it through, the Cross became an altogether different symbol significant of a total reversal of values and indissolubly linked with the kingdom of God. Aside from its deep spiritual merit, the Cross as a symbol also had the lesser practical merit of being simple in construction, easily seen and easily reproduced.

Like all kingdoms, the kingdom of God developed its own rituals and ceremonies, such as baptism and communion, and its own special days, such as Sunday, Christmas, and Easter. The kingdom also developed its own doctrines and creeds. These we call theology, but from the point of view of the kingdom as a political society, it could be regarded as its "public philosophy" (to borrow Walter Lippman's phrase), i.e., a body of truth supported by a consensus of people who have knowledge of it and live by it. As we have previously noted, Peter did not hesitate to characterize the kingdom in political terms as "an holy *nation*" and "a peculiar *people,*" holy because it was sanctified by the Holy Spirit and peculiar because its symbols, observances, and doctrines were their distinctive possessions not shared by non-Christian peoples.

All political societies, kingdoms included, have some sort of governmental structure. The kingdom of God is no exception. Again, we do not ordinarily think of the church in those terms. This is partly because Christ showed no interest in structure, leaving the problem to be solved organically in response to changing needs. It is due even more to our tendency to think in terms of written constitutions, organization charts, and unitary forms of government. Finally, we are hypnotized by the obvious divisions of the church along national, denominational, and sociological lines. The proliferation of the church universal into autonomous visible churches does preclude us from classifying it as unitary in structure. Neither can we classify it as a confederation, because in a confederation the member states are sovereign. The visible churches are autonomous, but they are not sovereign. Christ is the Lord and Head of the church of which the visible churches are but branches and segments. The category of political science which comes closest to describing the structure of the kingdom of God is federalism, for federalism maintains the integrity of sovereignty while allowing a great variety of group life and political structure. This was the structure of the ancient (pre-Roman) Catholic Church and has continued to be characteristic of it. The most ambitious attempt to do away with the federal or conciliar structure was made by Roman Catholicism, but at no time has the attempt been successful. The Eastern churches never acknowledged the authority of the Bishop of Rome, and the Roman church lost its boldest bid for monopoly in the West with the advent of the Reformation. The federal structure is the only one which encompasses all Christians as members of one body.

The fact that the structure is so loose, fluid, and unsubstantial does not disprove its existence or represent an attempt to read preconceived ideas into reality. If anything, it is our secular political scientists and jurists who have erred in the latter direction. Written constitutions as instruments of government are never completely accurate descriptions of the actual distribution of power and frequently hide many deviations and exceptions. Administrative organization charts can be even more deceptive in the very field of political science where we expect the greatest definiteness and concreteness. As our public administration specialists are increasingly willing to admit, the facts of administrative life may well nullify the provisions of an organization chart or operate in a manner unforeseen by the law, e.g., when subordinates because of expert professional knowledge or stronger personalities in fact overrule and control the officials who are supposedly their superiors or when one agency does the work assigned by law to another agency.

We have only one more element in the traditional political science concept of the state to consider in connection with the kingdom of God, and that is the element of territory. This element is obviously lacking in the kingdom of God. The kingdom of God has no territorial limits in the sense of an exclusive jurisdiction over a fixed portion of the earth's surface and separated from other jurisdictions by sharp, identifiable, and impermeable territorial boundaries. But is traditional political science right in insisting that territory is an indispensable element of statehood? The answer is no. The addition of the territorial element was a contribution of feudalism, which developed to stabilize what the Germans so aptly call the era of the Wandering Peoples (*Voelkerwanderung*) when Germanic tribes roamed belligerently and restlessly over the corpse of the Roman Empire. It was retained as a principle of order to circumscribe the points of friction between peoples. As such the element of territory is still useful, but it is defective as a description of political reality. The menace of German fascism and Russian communism with their fifth columns and their satellites has taught us that jurisdiction extends wherever there are people who accept it. It is the fact of allegiance, not residence, which is decisive. From this more realistic point of view, we can say that wherever there are people who acknowledge Christ as their Lord, there is the kingdom of God, regardless of where they live, regardless of what positive law may provide, and regardless of Iron Curtains, Bamboo Curtains, or any other kind of curtains or Walls of Separation which men try to interpose between themselves and God.

CHURCH MEMBERSHIP
AS CITIZENSHIP

The kingdom of God, like all states, has citizens. The apostle Paul does not hesitate to say so: "Now therefore ye are no more strangers and foreigners, but *fellowcitizens* with the saints, and of the household of God. . . ." [22] In this citizenship, as in all citizenship, the one indispensable feature is allegiance—in this case, allegiance to Jesus Christ. The ecumenical movement has rediscovered this feature and has made it the test of membership in the National Council of Churches and the World Council of Churches. The Unitarian bid for membership in the National Council was turned down because the Unitarians do not acknowledge Jesus Christ as Lord.

One of the peculiarities of the kingdom of God is that it has no natural-born citizens. "Except a man be born again," said Jesus to Nicodemus, "he cannot see the kingdom of God." [23] The same point is succinctly made by Augustine: "There none are born, for none die." [24] The reason is that all men are born sinners. It takes the grace of God to save and forgive them, thus making them fit for citizenship in the kingdom. All citizens of the kingdom are such by naturalization only.

Scripture prescribes baptism as the naturalization procedure. Once again we rarely, if ever, think of baptism in that way, and yet the evidence is compelling. We have it on Christ's own authority: "Except a man be born of water and of the Spirit, he cannot enter into the kingdom of God." [25] It is repeated by Peter when, in answering the query of his listeners as to what they should do, says: "Repent, and be baptized every one of you in the name of Jesus Christ. . . ." [26] Peter's formula actually amounts to an oath of allegiance. To repent is to renounce one's previous allegiance to another sovereign, whoever he may be, and the use of water is symbolic of the washing away of the imprint of that other sovereignty. To believe in Christ is to commit oneself to him as Lord and to put one's trust in his protection as all allegiance implies. It is a personal decision involving the reorientation and restructuring of one's whole personality. It is also a public act performed in the presence of witnesses. Both personal and public aspects are important. In the case of infant baptism, the personal decision is not waived but postponed until such time as he becomes a communicant member (or is "confirmed," as some churches put it) and is completed by a public profession of faith. Whatever the name and procedure may be, inner conversion and outward commitment are essential and constitute a true oath of allegiance.

Just as a citizen of the United States goes through a process of Americanization, so the citizen of the kingdom of God goes through a process of Christianization. An unassimilable citizen is a contradiction in terms. "Therefore if any man be in Christ," says Paul, "he is a new creature: old things are passed away; behold, all things are become new." [27] How new is he and what is he like? For the answer we must turn to the Sermon on the Mount where is to be found the most complete statement of what is generally called the "Christian ethic."

The Sermon on the Mount opens with the well-known Beatitudes. In these, Christ calls "blessed" certain types of people: the poor in spirit, those that mourn, the meek, those that hunger and thirst for righteousness, the pure in heart, the peacemakers, those persecuted for righteousness' sake, and those persecuted for Christ's sake. In each case, Christ affixes a promise. This is not the place to dwell on each of the Beatitudes at length. Innumerable sermons have been preached and books written about them. Our concern here is limited to their political significance. The Beatitudes are a kind of preamble to the spiritual constitution of the kingdom of God. They do not, like the Preamble of the Constitution of the United States, approach the matter of objectives in terms of abstract concepts such as union, justice, defense, welfare, and liberty. Instead, they speak in terms of certain types of people which it is the object of the kingdom to produce and to sustain. Christian truth is truth embodied in persons, truth incarnate and therefore living truth.

The Sermon on the Mount proceeds to elaborate the characteristics of the citizen of the kingdom. He meets the demands of the moral law, fulfilling the spirit as well as the letter. He is accommodating in his relations with others, coming to terms with his adversary and going well beyond what he is asked to do. He is charitable in construing the motives of other people and generous in responding to their needs. He does not take offense, whether offense is intended or not, and neither keeps score nor "evens" the score. He has a Christ-like capacity for love which enfolds all men, regardless of their deserts and regardless of reciprocation. His word is absolutely dependable and his answers are straightforward, simple, and clear. In him there is no pretense or ostentation, no egocentric pursuit of publicity, no hypocrisy. He is not censorious and faultfinding but fair-minded and kind. He is not anxious for the morrow and experiences no "existential dread" (*Angst*), because his Christian faith tells him that God loves him and will look after him. Nothingness (*le néant*) does not exist for him because God fills every part of the universe. His life is built upon a Rock, and he knows it.

Other parts of the Gospels and the Epistles elaborate still further. The citizen of the kingdom is moved by faith, not fear or doubt, and therefore does not condemn himself "in that thing which he alloweth." [28] When he is concerned with appearances it is only for the sake of other people. He is sensitive and responsive; so his capacity for suffering is tremendous. But his suffering is ennobling rather than debasing or debilitating and permits him to share with other people and therefore to help them. He is "all things to all men" [29] because his capacity for fellowship is as broad as humanity, but no "fence-straddler," because he erects no fences and he takes away those which other people erect. He enjoys the quiet strength of real conviction and has the intellectual stability which goes with knowledge of the truth, for he is not "tossed to and fro, and carried about with every wind of doctrine." [30] He has learned the secret of contentment and knows "both to abound and to suffer need." [31]

The Christian ethic, when presented to men, has always exerted a peculiar fascination and provoked almost every type of reaction except indifference. Some reject it outright as slave morality born of the resentment of impotence and as a sinister plot to rob the strong and successful of what is rightfully theirs. Others dismiss it as silly nonsense. Still others regard it as the highest and most beautiful ethic conceivable, but impractical and irrelevant to human life in this corrupt world. Finally, there are those who accept it enthusiastically and think it easy to apply. "All you have to do," they say, "is to do what it says." All these reactions are faulty, but this last one is the shallowest of them all. The others at least have the merit of understanding the Christian ethic enough to know that it is contrary to human nature. Men do not naturally turn the other cheek, walk the second mile, love their enemies, lend and give generously, enjoy freedom from worry, avoid censoriousness and ostentation. It is Christ, not the natural man, who calls qualities like meekness and purity of heart blessed. In the eyes of the world, the meek are insignificant and mousy, and the pure in heart are naive and inexperienced. Only one man ever lived the Christian ethic to the full. That man was Jesus of Nazareth, and he could do it only because he was the Son of God. Even deeply committed and mature Christians, still being sinners, cannot live it to the full. There is always a gap between profession and practice, reach and grasp, aspiration and achievement. And this gap makes hypocrites of us all.

Nevertheless, though the gap cannot be completely bridged in this life, it can be narrowed to an impressive extent. Evangelical Christians know that the transformation involved is not to be had by simply working at it in accordance with the maxim that "practice makes perfect" but by the effectual intervention of the Holy Spirit apprehended through faith. What many of even these evangelical Christians overlook, however, is that the Christian ethic attains a real fullness of meaning and is translated into human lives only in the kingdom, for it is the ethic of the kingdom.

When Christ delivered the Sermon on the Mount, he was not addressing all mankind. He was addressing his disciples and those who were to be his disciples in the years to come. He assumed, and his disciples understood, that much of the kind of life he was urging them to lead was possible only in the Christian community. Take the following instance: "Give to him that asketh thee, and from him that would borrow of thee turn not thou away." [32] In what kind of context would this rule receive its fullest meaning and application? Would it not be in the kingdom of God? It is in the kingdom that he that asketh would neither be nor feel like a beggar because in a close fellowship there is no such thing as begging but only the joy of giving. We ask many things of family and close friends which we would not think of asking of strangers. In this kingdom no one would ask for more than the giver can or should give because both parties are considerate of each other's capabilities and needs. In this kingdom the giver would know that his gift will not be put to wrongful use. In this kingdom the borrower will not borrow unnecessarily or unwisely, and the lender will know that he is not encouraging laziness in the borrower or endangering his own power to help others in the future.

In a context other than the kingdom of God the rule is not wholly inapplicable, but its application has to be modified to include several considerations. Outside of the context of Christian fellowship, asking easily turns into imposition, giving into an affront. You have to refuse to give when you know that the gift will be put to evil use. You have to turn away from a borrower if lending means encouraging him to "sponge" and to become a parasite. It is only in the kingdom that asking and giving, borrowing and lending, are a bond and a joy instead of a painful headache, a heavy burden, and a risky responsibility. It is only in the kingdom that property transactions of this kind can be communal without being communistic, simultaneously and alternatively private and public.

The rule which enjoins you to be reconciled with your brother if he "hath ought against thee" [33] has the same presupposition. It takes at least two to be reconciled. In the kingdom reconciliation is possible and can be initiated by either side. Reconciliation may or may not involve restitution, but it always includes forgiveness. It does not take much experience of life to know that both extending and accepting forgiveness are difficult and sometimes impossible. In the kingdom, however, both are natural and normal. The joy of reconciliation is most fully felt and understood in the kingdom because personal experience is reinforced by observation, and the experience of each is multiplied by the experience of all.

The blessedness of purity of heart is another case in point. Its meaning cannot be understood by introspection alone. Where else but in the kingdom can one see what it means not to have to worry about mixed emotions, ulterior motives, calculating natures, selfishness disguised as altruism, rudeness camouflaged as honesty, and love adulterated by possessiveness or corrupted by selfish gratification? Take purity of heart out of the context of the kingdom, and what happens is that the pure in heart are imposed upon and cheated in business, in politics, in love, and even in academia.

Some rules do imply relations primarily with the outside. Loving your enemies is one of these because in the kingdom one has no enemies. Even in this case, however, the existence of the kingdom is an efficacious help. The reason is that in the world, to love one's enemies is not a rule of life. Loving one's enemies will not be believed or else it will be taken for cowardice, weakness, or just plain stupidity. The one thing the Christian can be sure of is that he will be misunderstood and unappreciated. But if there is another world, the world of the kingdom of God, to which he can go for understanding, appreciation, encouragement, and inspiration, the Christian is in quite a different situation. He has a place to which he can turn to replenish his spiritual resources and to know that, after all, he is not alone and foresaken. Those Christians who think they can practice a rule like loving one's enemies solely by individual will power or autosuggestion overestimate their own strength and neglect one of the greatest sources of strength which Christ made available to them when he founded the church. It is right and proper for a man to resort to private prayer to God, but let him not forget that God most frequently answers through the voice of fellow Christians. As it is said in Genesis, "It is not good that the man should be alone," [34] and the application of the statement goes far deeper than the need for feminine companionship which was its specific context. Without the fellowship of other Christians, the individual who tries to practice the rule to love his enemies is alone though he be caught in the hustle and bustle of an immense crowd. There can be no citizen without fellow citizens.

The Christian ethic is not only born into and sustained by the kingdom: it also grows with it. The group effect has always been of decisive importance. The appearance here and there of an individual who exemplifies the Christian ethic to an unusual degree can always be dismissed by the secular-minded as an exception. It may indeed be regarded as the exception which proves the rule that the Christian ethic is impractical and meant to be dreamed rather than lived. Curiously enough, the Christian may have a similar reaction. He, too, may feel an individual's ethical stature is an exception, something so unique that it is unattainable by all but the rarest few. But when an entire group lives the Christian ethic, the effect is arresting and compelling, especially so because many of the people in the group are not unusual in social standing, native intelligence, level of education, and worldly goods. The secular humanist who feels drawn to the Christian ethic and the professed Christian who wistfully looks at it as something beyond his reach both gaze at this group and say to themselves: if these people can live by it, why not I?

It was the Christian fellowship aspect of the church which proved so appealing to the jaded citizens of the disintegrating Roman Empire. They were confronted with the fact of personal and group experience, a fact that was in many ways mystifying but as undeniable as it was attractive. When Peter spoke of being called "out of darkness" into Christ's "marvelous light," [35] he was not exaggerating. He was only putting into words what all on the inside experienced and what those on the outside could see even when they could not understand. The power of group witness is just as compelling today as it was in the early days of the church, but it is not as easy to see because the church is cluttered up and weighted down by nominal Christians. Church membership has been allowed to lapse into a merely technical and fictional citizenship sought for worldly reasons. Especially on the congregational level, real Christians are hidden from view by a dense crowd of nominal Christians.

However, the real Christians are still there, and their magnetic attraction continues to exert its gravitational pull wherever a number of them get together. Anyone who has traveled for a denominational board and compared the experience with traveling for a business establishment or a government agency knows the difference. Anyone who has attended top-level church conferences and compared them with business conventions or professional meetings knows the difference too. Anyone who has lived a few weeks (or even a few days) in a town like Montreat, North Carolina, and compared it with normal towns of the same size knows the difference. Anyone who has traveled abroad and compared the way of life of missionaries with that of tourists, businessmen, military personnel, and diplomatic circles cannot help but know the difference. Roman Catholicism recognized the difference when it gave birth to its numerous monastic orders, and even now Roman Catholic terminology revealingly distinguishes "secular" and "religious" clergy.

What is the difference? It is the difference between hard-headed business "deals" and mutually rewarding common tasks, loneliness in a hotel room or bar and full companionship in a home, scholarly competition for professional recognition and a common search for the will of God, externally induced excitement and inwardly surging joy and gaiety, a town where civic order rests on impersonal forces and one where it springs from mutual trust and shared truth, a world dedicated to pleasure or profit among people alien to each other and a world dedicated to un-

selfish service among people where identification has abolished alienation. Basically, it is a difference in jurisdiction. The kingdom of God is
ruled by the spirit of Christ, and you cannot help but feel it in spite of
all the imperfections which cling to everything human.

This rule does no violence to personality, for personality is neither
abolished nor absorbed but transformed. Peculiarities of position, place,
national custom, and social status do not give way to a drab uniformity
but retain their existence, except that they no longer obscure the vision
of man because they have become transparent and even translucent.
"Behold," we read in Scripture, "I make all things new." [36] Yet newness
of things does not mean strangeness, for we recognize them as the disciples recognized Christ when he was transfigured on the mountain top and
when he was resurrected after the Crucifixion. If this be magic, it is the
kind of magic which enables a great novelist to see a small town as an
arena pulsating with the drama of the human spirit struggling to find
itself, while another person sees only the sleepy, narrow, boring stagna-
tion of dull people to whom nothing of interest ever happens.

CHRISTIAN CITIZENSHIP
AND SECULAR CITIZENSHIP

The existence of the kingdom of God means that every Christian has
dual citizenship. The notion of dual citizenship is not hard for Americans to understand because we are already accustomed to it by the coexistence of federal and state citizenships. We know what it means to
manage more than one claim on the loyalty of persons. The citizens of
the kingdom are related to each other by faith. To that extent the kingdom is an exclusive fellowship which does not include non-Christians.
However, Christian citizenship is not thereby divisive, because the Christian is tied to non-Christians as well as to other Christians by the bond
of love. As Martin Luther put it: "We conclude, therefore, that a Christian lives not in himself, but in Christ and in his neighbor. Otherwise he
is not a Christian. He lives in Christ through faith, in his neighbor through
love. By faith he is caught up beyond himself into God. By love he de-
scends beneath himself into his neighbor." [37] Luther makes it clear that
by "neighbor" he means any neighbor, for the Christian "does not distinguish between friends and enemies or anticipate their thankfulness or
unthankfulness, but he most freely and most willingly spends himself and
all that he has, whether he wastes all on the thankless or whether he gains
a reward." [38] Calvin also emphasizes this bond of love in the following
passage:

Whoever, therefore, is presented to you that needs your kind offices, you
have no reason to refuse him your assistance. Say that he is a stranger; yet
the Lord has impressed on him a character which ought to be familiar to

you; for which reason he forbids you to despise your own flesh. Say that he is contemptible and worthless; but the Lord shows him to be one whom he has deigned to grace with his own image. Say that you are obliged to him for no services; but God has made him, as it were, his substitute, to whom you acknowledge yourself to be under obligations for numerous and important benefits. Say that he is unworthy of your making the smallest exertion on his account; but the image of God, by which he is recommended to you, deserves your surrender of yourself and all that you possess. If he not only has deserved no favour, but, on the contrary, has provoked you with injuries and insults,—even this is no just reason why you should cease to embrace him with your affection, and to perform to him the offices of love. He has deserved, you will say, very different treatment from me. But what has the Lord deserved? who, when he commands you to forgive men all their offences against you, certainly intends that they should be charged to himself. This is the only way of attaining that which is not only difficult, but utterly repugnant to the nature of man—to love them who hate us, to requite injuries with kindnesses, and to return blessings for curses. We should remember, that we must not reflect on the wickedness of men, but contemplate the Divine image in them; which, concealing and obliterating their faults, by its beauty and dignity allures us to embrace them in the arms of our love.[39]

It is necessary to stress this bond of love because so many secular humanists strenuously object to what they consider to be the exclusivist attitude of the Christian. Most of all they object to evangelism. What right, they ask, have missionaries to interfere with the lives of non-Christian peoples in Africa and Asia? Let us note, in passing, that there seems to be no objection to interfering with foreign peoples for the purpose of making profits, or furthering the national defense of the United States, or immunizing them against communism, or inculcating them with a favorable image of the American way of life. It is only in the case of religion that "interference" takes place. It is ironical that secular humanists should single out missionaries for criticism because, of all fields of human activity, the mission field is the least exclusive and the most unselfish.

The heart and core of missionary work is indeed witnessing, but it is witnessing based on service motivated by love. No medical missionary makes conversion to Christianity a condition for treatment. His ministrations are extended to all who need his services regardless of creed, color, language, or culture. A missionary who teaches English, science, or mathematics does not require that his pupils be Christians before he imparts these valuable skills to them. He teaches all who will come to him. A missionary who is an agronomist does his best to help farmers to improve their land, their farming methods, and their standard of living on the same nondiscriminatory basis. Of all the people who reside abroad, no one identifies himself more completely with his neighbors than the missionary, for he does so to the point of accepting hardship, jeopardizing his health, and making their language and customs his own. His respect for the culture of the people among whom he lives is no mere academic respect for a way of life he neither knows nor shares but a lifelong identification with what he has made his own. The missionaries were engaged in Peace Corps work long before there was a Peace Corps, doing the work at much lower cost, devoting their entire lives to it instead of a short term, and knowing exactly why they were doing it. Respect for the integrity of personality and culture is an essential part of the Christian way of life and was pointed out as far back in history as Augustine. "This heavenly city," says Augustine, "then, while it sojourns on earth, calls citizens out of all nations, and gathers together a society of pilgrims of all languages, not scrupling about diversities in the manners, laws, and institutions whereby earthly peace is secured and maintained, but recognising that, however various these are, they all tend to one and the same end of earthly peace. *It therefore is so far from rescinding and abolishing these diversities, that it even preserves and adapts them,* so long as no hindrance to the worship of the one supreme and true God is thus introduced." [40]

The effect of Christian citizenship is to raise secular citizenship far above the accident of birth and the changing provisions of positive law. Beyond birth certificates and certificates of naturalization lies the spiritual fact of loyalty to country, and a rich ethical content fills the dry husk of legal provisions. The negativism which sees only rights in citizenship cannot stand the searchlight of a Christian conscience. If, as Luther says, the Christian is the "perfectly dutiful servant of all" and "subject to all," [41] there will be no room for a passive conception of citizenship which accepts everything and contributes nothing. For the Christian and those whom he influences, citizenship and participation in the public life of the country are inseparable. There is a consequent duty to be informed, to think, and to act so as to promote the common good of all. To evade serving on juries, to contrive not to testify in court, to neglect to vote, and to avoid public office are types of behavior which are incompatible with the solidarity of the Christian with all his countrymen. To vote for candidates because they promise benefits for oneself or one's friends when such benefits are injurious to the public or for policies calculated to enhance special privilege is likewise a violation of the Christian ethic. To use the spoken or written word in such a way as to violate due process of law in spirit while managing to stay within the letter of the law is also unthinkable.

The Christian conception of citizenship prevents secular citizenship from degenerating into narrow nationalism because the ecumenical aspects of the kingdom of God keep the channels of communication with other peoples and cultures open and because the allegiance to Christ keeps open the access to a wisdom which is more than human. By virtue of the Christian dynamism in its midst, the secular political community cannot surrender to an isolationist philosophy and seal itself off from the vertical and horizontal sources of enlightenment and renewal which keep it healthy. Americans would be more disposed to appreciate the liberating influence of Christian citizenship among them if they paused to reflect on the somewhat similar influence of federal on state citizenship. A citizen of one of our states is a much better citizen of that state than he would be if he were not also a citizen of the United States, just as any of our states would be much poorer in all respects if it were independent. Without the federal tie (one sometimes feels like calling it the federal life line), state citizenship would soon shrink and move in the direction of what the French so picturesquely call "belfry patriotism" (*patriotisme de clocher*), i.e., a patriotism that extends only as far as the local church steeple can be seen. The corrective and broadening influence of federal citizenship would be gone, and every state would suffer for it.

The idea that Christian citizenship demands that we turn our backs on our country, that we cannot be "citizens of mankind" without renouncing our national citizenship, and that a higher allegiance abrogates a lower one, is not a Christian idea. The Christian faith demands transformation, not secession, disloyalty, expatriation, or flight. The Incarnation itself is the most conclusive witness of this characteristic demand of the Christian faith. The love of God was not love in the abstract, a sort of generalized benevolence brooding over all men and touching none, but love made flesh and particularized in a specific historical person. Jesus himself during his years in Palestine proceeded in the same manner. He took individuals like Zaccheus, accepted them as they were, and then transformed them so that they, in turn, were so suffused with the redeeming love of Christ that it spilled over and inundated all who came into contact with them. This is how the technique of redemption works. It is a truly remarkable technique which does no violence to personality. It is unlike that of the Greek myth of King Midas who supposedly turned to gold everything he touched. In that case, every object was denatured by becoming something else than what it was. It is equally unlike that of Hinduism in which personal identity is extinguished by being merged in a vast impersonal reality. The Christian technique neither denatures nor extinguishes identity but glorifies it. The application of this technique to politics means that secular citizenship is similarly glorified. For that reason Christian citizenship is never subversive, even when it has to be nonconformist, and has nothing in common with brainwashing, standardization, or any other technique which has the effrontery of trying to strike all individuals and nations off of the same mold.

The significance of this peculiarity of the Christian faith of respecting the integrity of that which it glorifies will be especially appreciated, once it is understood, by the new nations of Asia and Africa which are wor-

ried about westernization, by liberal humanists who are anxious to preserve individuality and cultural differences, and by patriots who do not
want their country to be subjugated by world Caesarism or dissolved
into some kind of political Brahma-Atman. If Christianity were just an
ideology or just one more religion among many religions, its claim to
universal allegiance would be offensive, and it could not serve as the
foundation of a decent and stable world order because the inevitable
result would be cultural and political tyranny. But Christianity is nothing of the kind. Whoever shall lose his life in the service of others for
Christ's sake shall find it again, and he shall find it more abundant and
more fit to exist than he ever thought possible. Conversion is the fulfillment of selfhood, not its destruction, dissolution, or absorption.

If American citizenship is to be rescued from the paltry, legalistic, negative, selfish, and narrow reality which it much too often is, Christian
citizenship must permeate American political life. The American people,
therefore, have a vested interest in the growth and health of the kingdom
of God, which no Jeffersonian Wall of Separation should be allowed to
nullify. The vitality of federal citizenship depends on that of Christian
citizenship, just as the vitality of state citizenship depends on that of
federal citizenship. This dependence is true in all forms of government,
but nowhere is it more visibly true than in a democracy because in a
democracy the choice of the rulers rests with the citizenry. The stature
of the citizens determines the wisdom of the choice, and it also determines what is possible and what is impossible for the rulers to accomplish.

REPRESENTATION:
SECULAR AND CHRISTIAN CONCEPTS

The reference to rulers brings up the subject of representation. No subject is more important to democracy since democratic government is
representative government almost by definition. Clarity of thought about
representation, however, is not commensurate with its importance. Several theories have dominated political thought, and each has had its adherents. Of these theories, four deserve special attention: (1) the medieval, (2) the Burkean, (3) the individualist, (4) the fascist.

The medieval theory is organic and institutional in nature and does
not rely on voting or any other mechanical process to achieve representation. There was voting in the Middle Ages, of course, as we soon realize
when we think of the Electors in the Holy Roman Empire. However,
even these instances show that voting assumed rather than produced representation. Representation went with position. It was assumed that the
notables of a kingdom could speak for the people under them because
immemorial tradition and an unchanging network of personal and institutional ties guaranteed an identity of interest, a mutuality of feeling, and

a correspondence of views. The idea of quality was also involved since the notables were thought to be abler, more enlightened, and more responsible than the people lower down in the hierarchy of medieval society. In our rapidly changing and mobile society so different from the tradition-bound society of the Middle Ages, the medieval concept of representation seems strange and unreliable. Nevertheless, there are traces of it left here and there. When someone wants to put on a drive or campaign in a city and calls together (if he can) the key businessmen, clergymen, educators, public officials, and professional men, he is relying on the medieval concept of representation. These key people are assumed to be representative not because anybody voted for them (which would rarely be the case) but because of the responsible and influential positions they hold in the community. It is supposed, and not always incorrectly, that as those people go, so will the city.

The Burkean theory is generally known as virtual representation. We are calling it "Burkean" here because Edmund Burke was its most famous defender and eloquent expositor. In a celebrated speech to his constituents in the English city of Bristol, he gave the theory its classic expression:

Certainly, gentlemen, it ought to be the happiness and glory of a representative to live in the strictest union, the closest correspondence, and the most unreserved communication with his constituents. Their wishes ought to have great weight with him; their opinion, high respect; their business, unremitted attention. It is his duty to sacrifice his repose, his pleasures, his satisfactions, to theirs; and above all, ever, and in all cases, to prefer their interest to his own. But his unbiassed opinion, his mature judgment, his enlightened conscience, he ought not to sacrifice to you, to any man, or to any set of men living. These he does not derive from your pleasure; no, nor from the law and the constitution. They are a trust from Providence, for the abuse of which he is deeply answerable. Your representative owes you, not his industry only, but his judgment; and he betrays, instead of serving you, if he sacrifices it to your opinion.

My worthy colleague says, his will ought to be subservient to yours. If that be all, the thing is innocent. If government were a matter of will upon any side, yours, without question, ought to be superior. But government and legislation are matters of reason and judgment, and not of inclination; and what sort of reason is that, in which the determination precedes the discussion; in which one set of men deliberate, and another decide; and where those who form the conclusion are perhaps three hundred miles distant from those who hear the arguments?

To deliver an opinion, is the right of all men; that of constituents is a weighty and respectable opinion, which a representative ought always most seriously to consider. But *authoritative* instructions; *mandates* issued, which the member is bound blindly and implicitly to obey, to vote, and to argue for, though contrary to the clearest conviction of his judgment and conscience,—these are things utterly unknown to the laws of this land, and which arise from a fundamental mistake of the whole order and tenor of our constitution.

Parliament is not a *congress* of ambassadors from different and hostile interests; which interests each must maintain, as an agent and advocate, against other agents and advocates; but parliament is a *deliberative* assembly of *one* nation with *one* interest, that of the whole; where not local purposes, not local prejudices, ought to guide, but the general good, resulting from the general reason of the whole. You choose a member indeed; but when you have chosen him, he is not member of Bristol, but he is a member of *parliament.*[42]

The Burkean theory is the accepted theory of British politics and, to a large extent, the established British practice as well. Any Briton may run and be elected in any constituency without regard to his residence; no member of Parliament can be bound by instructions or held to electoral promises and bargains; there is no referendum or recall; and elections are held at such intervals as Parliament itself determines unless the Crown shortens them by calling an election before the expiration of a statutory term. The amount of trust which is placed in members of the British Parliament staggers the American imagination. What American would be willing to let the members of his state legislature fix their own salaries and terms of office, exempt their acts from judicial review and executive vetoes, and trust them to speak for all the citizens of the state instead of merely those in their districts? Yet that is precisely what our British cousins do, and they suffer no dire consequences for it (which does not mean that the citizens of our states would be as fortunate if they tried to do the same).

The individualist theory is much more restrictive. Representation in this case is a minimal trust given grudgingly and necessitated by the fact that direct democracy is impracticable except in very small and homogeneous towns. The representatives are really delegates or agents—bellhops for their constituents, if one wishes to use a derogatory term. Great reliance is placed on political machinery to insure that the representative will do and say only what his constituents want him to do and say. Where the individualist theory holds sway, you find the practice of instructing and recalling representatives, frequent elections, a multitude of elective rather than appointive positions, and rotation in office. Its high point of popularity in the United States was during the Confederation period, but it had roots in colonial New England where it was encouraged by the Congregationalist rather than Presbyterian form of church polity. It continues to live in the requirement that the representative be a resident of the district which elects him, the expectation that he "nurse his constituents," and the growth of techniques of direct democracy such as the initiative, the referendum, the recall, and the direct primary. The development of modern techniques of opinion measurement curtails still further the representative's freedom of action and gives the pollsters something of a political commissar's power of intimidation.

The fascist theory has been a reaction against the individualist theory. To the fascist, representation is another word for power.[43] You cannot represent those whom you do not control. To be sure, there exists an identity of opinions and sentiments between a representative and his constituents, but this identity is no accident. From the fascist viewpoint, it is the result of the political skill of the representative who has made his constituents want what he wants, think what he thinks, feel what he feels, and act as he wants them to act. It is this political skill of the representative ranging from emotional appeal and reasoned argument to bribery and coercion which substitutes unity for diversity. "For it is the *Unity* of the Representer," Hobbes argued, "not the *Unity* of the Represented, that maketh the Person *One*. And it is the Representer that beareth the Person, and but one Person: And *Unity,* cannot otherwise be understood in Multitude." [44] The representative does not reflect unity: he makes it; hence all representation is personal. As such it is a composite of native gifts, specialized knowledge, and practical experience which some people possess and others do not. The fascist theory differs sharply from its rivals and is too radical to find much acceptance. Even in the military profession, where a fascist philosophy is most likely to take root and flourish, there are points of resistance such as the emphasis on rank (e.g., a captain is a captain, whoever he may be).

All these theories of representation are defective in a number of ways, and their greatest defect is that they bog down on procedure and neglect the substance. If we look at the word "represent," we note that its literal meaning is "to present again" (i.e., to *re*-present), and that it carries the idea of presence. Immediately we wonder: who is present, and why again? The usual and practically automatic answer is: the people, of course! But this is not a helpful answer. At best, it fits only a democracy, and there are other forms of government besides democracy. Moreover, it does not cover other situations, such as when an attorney is said to represent his client in court. Neither does it tell us what is meant by "presence," except that we understand that physical presence is not involved (e.g., the people of the United States are not physically present when their representatives assemble in Congress). A little reflection adds the thought that all representation, in essence, concerns persons. It is true that we sometimes speak of interests (e.g., pressure groups) or will (e.g., the will of the people), but these are abstractions which conceal the centrality of personality since only persons have interests and will. Once again, we are confronted with the basic question of selfhood to which we allude when we speak of self-government and the self-determination of peoples.

Insofar as we get any answers to the question of selfhood in connection with representation, the most common one is that the self involved is the average self. It is implied in the frequent references to "the common man" and fostered by the pollsters with their concept of an adequate sample or cross section. It is more than implied in electoral campaigns when a candidate is assiduously recommended to the electorate by his managers and friends as not too bright and not too dull, neither refined nor crude, neither overly proud nor unduly meek, but as just a plain ordinary American with whom any of us would feel completely comfortable and at home. One candidate for high office was so nondescript and colorless that a critic caustically remarked: "He is the kind of a man who is lost in a crowd of three." The electorate is reassured by the thought that the candidate, if elected, will be quite "safe" and do in office exactly what we would do if we were in his place. There is a counterpart to this kind of political thinking in the economists' concept of marginality, according to which all units, being supposedly identical, are interchangeable without affecting the value. We have an echo in family life whenever parents "praise" a child by saying that he is in no way exceptional but completely "normal." All this kind of thinking is nothing less than the cult of mediocrity and therefore jars the Christian conscience which aspires to perfection.

Perhaps we can get at the transforming power of the Christian faith over the idea of representation by asking why anybody should have to be re-presented, i.e., presented a second time. Why is not the first time enough? because he is not presentable. Presentable to whom? To God, of course, for God is the Sovereign of all kingdoms. The people who deny or ignore his sovereignty in normal times remember it in times of national extremity when their prayers surge forth inarticulate and incoherent but instinctive, irrepressible, and fervent, as "the Spirit itself maketh intercession for us with groanings which cannot be uttered." [45] As a saying current during World War II described the situation, there are no atheists in foxholes. No man or group of men, unforgiven and unredeemed by the grace of God, is presentable. The weight of corruption is too great; the stain of sin is too indelible; the impact of guilt is too incapacitating. To say that a man is not presentable is equivalent to saying that he is unrighteous. It is in recognition of this fact that Christian theology teaches that Christ is our intercessor and mediator—in other words, our representative. He presents us again as new creatures made presentable by the indwelling Christ who covers us with his righteousness. Christ can do this because he was what we are not, i.e., the incarnation of the living God, and because he is present in those who believe in him.

This theological concept of representation is not as strange and remote from secular life as we might at first think. Why, for instance, does an attorney represent a client in court? because the attorney has status in that court, a status which comes from a kind of specialized knowledge and experience which his client does not possess. In a complicated legal battle in court, a client who proceeded on his own would be paralyzed by objections at every turn, would literally not know what he is doing, would soon find himself in contempt of court, and would of course lose his case. The attorney does for his client what his client cannot do for himself. He stands in the place of his client. This, in effect, is substitutionary atonement, but the parallel with theology goes even further. No attorney can represent a client unless the client has engaged him and has confidence in him. Confidence in this context is but another word for faith, i.e., trust in his attorney's ability and integrity, and commitment to his guidance. The client places his liberty and property and sometimes his very life in the hands of his attorney. That is what we mean when we say that an attorney represents us.

The concept of representation in Christian theology can be carried over into the field of politics just as well, and great would be its redemptive effect if it were. When we say that a congressman represents his constituents, we mean that the congressman is better than they are, or else he should not be in Congress, and his representation is a sham. What is it that makes a true representative? It is a certain presence. If secular states were identical with the kingdom of God, that presence would be nothing less than the presence of God. Secular states, however, are very far from being identical with the kingdom of God. The presence involved in these states is something which, for want of a better term, we shall call national ideals as these are embodied in persons.

We are aided in this domain by the availability of much symbolism. There is, for instance, Uncle Sam who is one of our national symbols. It is no coincidence that Uncle Sam should look so much like Abraham Lincoln, for Lincoln was in many respects the embodiment of our national ideals. He was physically tall and vigorous but never brutal, a very practical and pragmatic man who nevertheless held a high conception of the Union and had a deep understanding of American history, a man of faith but no bigot, charitable and kind but not weak, folksy and witty without being common or vulgar. There is also John Bull who symbolizes the British nation. John Bull is stocky and massive, slow to start and hard to stop, a tenacious person who never gives up, a moral man through and through, a responsible citizen, a reliable and honorable businessman. It seems eminently fitting that Winston Churchill, the statesman who saved his country in the most desperate crisis of its history, should look—even physically—so much like John Bull.

When we look at a national symbol like Uncle Sam and John Bull, we are looking at a representative figure. But it is not representative in the sense of being average. Quite the contrary. The national symbol represents what the people would like to be, what they consider their very best selves. When a Lincoln or a Churchill appears on the political horizon, their compatriots recognize in him the embodiment of their national symbol, and it is this feature alone which makes him their representative. Representation is incarnation. The people, however, do not always recognize a representative when they see one. It is necessary that their national ideals be vital and widely shared. People who have no ideals can have no representatives, regardless of all titles and legal terminology. People in that condition will put into office politicians like Warren G. Harding, but not even a landslide vote can make them representative.

The process of nominating and electing candidates for public office in a democracy is intended to achieve representation, and we would not think of doing away with it. Nevertheless, it does not always work well, and many times it does not work at all. Unrepresentative people do get elected. Conversely, there are people in and out of office who are representative though no ballot was ever cast for them. In our secularism we have forgotten that election is also a theological term. God elects, and the people, if they have enough spiritual discernment, recognize the fact by their exercise of the suffrage. To understand this truth has the immediate effect of relegating secular theories and practices dealing with representation to the realm of relativity where they properly belong.

When the medievalist argues for organic representation, he is pointing to the fact that representation may go with position, and his argument is a salutary corrective for the opinionated individualist who insists that no one can be representative who did not receive a specified number of votes. But the medievalist errs when he believes that representation always goes with position, for he is in effect trying to freeze the Holy Spirit into what is an ephemeral structure. When the individualist defends the electoral process as a tried and tested method of weeding out impostors and finding truly representative persons, he makes a strong point. But he errs when he tries to make an absolute out of the electoral process, for techniques are as relative and ephemeral as institutions. He too is trying to imprison the Holy Spirit in man-made channels and to achieve the impossible, which is to routinize spiritual life. When the fascist emphasizes the part played by personality in representation and objects to the deification of institutions by the medievalist and of machinery by the individualist, he is right. But he errs when he ignores the sinfulness of the representative and when he would have political leaders usurp the place of God by presuming to stamp their own image upon their followers.

It is the Burkean theory of representation which comes closest to the Christian conception. Burke's insistence that a representative's conscience and judgment come from Providence rather than from his constituents is sound, and so is his conclusion that the representative should therefore be allowed a large measure of freedom. The reasons for Burke's position on representation, however, were more constitutional than theological, and from this fact comes a certain lack of depth. The theological dimension is needed to give the Burkean theory its maximum fullness of meaning and also to point up its limitations.

The theological dimension which is implicit in the Burkean theory of representation becomes explicit in the Presbyterian Church. For that reason, it will help to clarify matters if we pay some attention to the Presbyterian system of government. A Presbyterian minister does not accept "offers": he responds to calls. The congregation does not "hire" its minister when it elects him: it affirms its belief that God has called this particular minister to this particular church at this particular time. A Presbyterian minister preaches the word of God as God has given him to understand it; hence he is not supposed to confine himself to what his congregation wants to hear, and he may (and sometimes must) make his people uncomfortable and even angry. He is not even a member of the church whose pastor he is. He is a member of the presbytery. He is a free agent because his allegiance is to Christ and not to the congregation.

Similarly, a Presbyterian elder is chosen by the congregation only in the sense that the people recognize in him a depth of knowledge of the Christian faith, a level of Christian morality, and a range of Christian influence which come closest to embodying (i.e., representing) what every member of the congregation aspires to be. He is chosen by the congregation because he is representative already, and not representative because the congregation chose him. It is because of this representative quality that the congregation cannot instruct the elders individually as elders or collectively as a session. Similarly, the session cannot tell its representatives in presbytery what to say or how to vote. In the Presbyterian system, the relation between representation and freedom is clearly drawn: ruling elders (members of the session) have the awesome responsibility of representing Christ and have been adjudged by the congregation to be sufficiently successful in meeting that responsibility to occupy the position they hold; hence they should be free not only to think and to speak but to govern.

The Presbyterian system does not assume perfection and infallibility on the part of its officers. It provides checks, but the checks are applied by the more mature Christians in presbytery in the case of ministers, and in the session in the case of elders with appeals to the higher church courts in both cases. In no case are the checks applied by the less mature Christians in the congregation. No informed Presbyterian, of course, argues that there may not be mature Christians who are not elders and immature Christians who do get to be elders. What he does say, however, is that the right to govern and the fact of representation are indissolubly linked, that whoever embodies the mind and spirit of Christ is to that extent entitled to the freedom of Christ, that the right to judge is an attribute of Christian maturity and not a numerical matter. The system does no violence to the congregation, for its members would not have it any other way. If they had not thought the elders sufficiently representative of Christ to be fit to govern the church, they would not have voted for them.*

The Burkean theory of representation was dominant in the minds of the framers of the Constitution, and their handiwork shows it. The electorate can neither instruct nor recall the President or the members of Congress; there is no provision for the initiative or the referendum; all federal officials are paid by the federal treasury and not by the states; the rules on rotation in office which were characteristic of the Confederation period were swept away, and all federal elected officials were made indefinitely re-eligible; the disciplining of the members of Congress was vested in the respective bodies to which they belonged. The government of the United States was made uncompromisingly representative with no concession whatever to direct democracy. The framers of the Constitution were reacting strongly against the individualist mood of the Revolutionary and Confederation periods. They were nationalists who felt about the United States much as Burke felt about the British Empire. They were also turning away from the Deism which was fashionable among the upper classes and going back to Christianity in which they found the theological presuppositions of Burkean representation.

It was their expectation that the personnel of the new federal government would possess a degree of ability and integrity that would justify the large measure of power allotted to them. Hamilton thought that United States senators, especially, would be of great moral, intellectual, and political stature because the very size of national concerns would lift them out of the narrow contacts, petty animosities, and limited horizons of state and local politics.[46] Edmund Randolph, the Governor of Virginia and leader of the Virginia delegation in the Philadelphia convention, voiced this expectation thus: "Greater talents, and a more extensive reputation will be necessary, to procure an election for the federal, than for the state representation. The federal representatives must therefore be well known for their integrity, and for their knowledge of the country they represent. We shall have ten men thus elected. What are they going for? Not to consult for Virginia alone, but for the interest of the United States collectively." [47] James Wilson of Pennsylvania was of the same mind: "It is the duty of a nation to intrust the management of its affairs only to its wisest and best citizens." [48] It was his hope that the new federal government would achieve this aim and deliver the country from what "is often and lamentably transformed into a scene of the vilest and lowest

---

* I am well aware of the human weaknesses which affect the operation of the Presbyterian system, such as the worldly motives which intrude in the selection of elders and the mechanical way in which the election of commissioners to the General Assembly is passed around the churches. I do believe, however, that the Presbyterian system as such is sound and that it works well in spite of the human weaknesses which Presbyterians share with other Christians.

debauchery and deception." [49] Roger Sherman, a signer of the Declaration of Independence who represented Connecticut at the Philadelphia Convention, rejected the whole idea of instructing a representative: "Should his instructions, therefore, coincide with his ideas on any
measure, they would be unnecessary; if they were contrary to the conviction of his own mind, he must be bound by every principle of justice
to disregard them." [50] Another impressive defense of the freedom of
the representative was given by another one of the framers of the Constitution, John Dickinson, when he was a member of the colonial legislature of Pennsylvania in 1764. "A good man *ought* to serve his country," said Dickinson, "even though she *resents* his services. The great
reward of honest actions is not the fame or profit that follows them, but
the *consciousness* that attends them. To discharge on this important occasion the *inviolable duty* I owe the public, by obeying the *unbiassed
dictates* of my *reason* and *conscience,* hath been my sole view; and my
only wish now is that the resolutions of this House, whatever they are,
may promote the happiness of *Pennsylvania." [51]* These last four men,
who were among the most influential members of the convention, were
also dedicated conservative Christians with no Deistic sympathies. From
Christianity came the high conception of representative government and
the realization that higher and more inclusive loyalties attract higher
types of people to government service than lesser and more exclusive
loyalties.

Our country was fortunate in that the most important part of our formative period, the making of the Constitution, should have been in the
hands of men who held this high conception of representative government because we were soon to lose much of it. Had this conception not
been anchored in a providentially rigid Constitution, our national political life might have gone the way of our states with their mania for doing
by constitutional amendment what should be done by state statute and
local ordinances, their nonconsecutive gubernatorial terms, their crippling restrictions on legislative power, their earmarking of taxes, their
constitutionally imposed ceilings on state borrowing, their use of the
referendum and the recall, their irresponsible constitutional boards and
commissions, their little baronies built around constitutionally impregna-
ble offices, their delusion that responsible government is directly proportional to the length of the ballot and the number of offices filled by popular election, and their false notion that government gets purer and better
as you get down to the "grass roots."

When the essential nature of representation was obscured, an engulfing
secularism magnified the mechanical and numerical significance of voting.
The voice of the people is the voice of God (*vox populi, vox Dei*); so
went an ancient and overambitious saying. Defective though the saying
is as a statement of what happens when the people speak, it is still su-

perior to the modern idea that the voice of the people is the voice of Univac. It is generally overlooked that the greatest defender of majority rule, Jean Jacques Rousseau, never asserted the unqualified sovereignty of numbers. He imposed qualitative conditions on voting: (1) that every citizen be civic-minded and vote only for his conception of the common good and not his selfish individual or group interest, (2) that every citizen should be an active participant in politics and contribute to the state whatever insights and judgment his participation gave him, (3) that pressure groups and political factions not be able to substitute their thinking and their will for those of the voters, (4) that there be full information and full discussion of issues available to the voters.

Without these conditions, you do not get the General Will but only a combination of selfish interests which Rousseau calls "the will of all." Rousseau insisted that majority rule has spiritual and moral presuppositions, and his retention and advocacy of these presuppositions may well have been derived from the Calvinistic atmosphere of Geneva in which he grew up. "Those who know Calvin only as a theologian," said Rousseau, "much under-estimate the extent of his genius. The codification of our wise edicts, in which he played a large part, does him no less honour than his *Institute*. Whatever revolution time may bring in our religion, so long as the spirit of patriotism and liberty still lives among us, the memory of this great man will be for ever blessed." [52] Rousseau's General Will closely resembles the Holy Spirit; his description of the Legislator fits the person of Christ to a striking extent; and his comments on the necessity for changing human nature virtually mean that conversion is the indispensable prerequisite of citizenship.

Following out the logic of the Christian concept of representation as incarnation, we find that service to one's fellow man is the necessary consequence. Christ himself set the norm when he said he came not to be ministered unto but to minister [53] and when he told his disciples that "whosoever of you will be the chiefest, shall be servant of all." [54] Faith is not to be barren but fruitful. "Not every one that saith unto me, Lord, Lord, shall enter into the kingdom of heaven," he warned, "but he that doeth the will of my Father which is in heaven." [55] Christ did not mean that doing the will of the Father is to be understood only as a matter of worshiping, praying, preaching, meditating, singing hymns, and partaking of the sacraments. Neither did he mean that Christians should confine themselves to "church work" in the narrow sense. The service he had in mind was an all-inclusive thing which touches every phase of life and every type of person. After having talked of taking care of the hungry, the thirsty, the naked, the sick, prisoners, and strangers, he added the following significant conclusion: "Inasmuch as ye have done it unto one of the least of these my brethren, ye have done it unto me." [56]

From this fusion of divine and human service demanded and exemplified by Christ, Protestantism drew the conclusion that the medieval distinction between secular and sacred was a false distinction as far as a Christian is concerned. Luther proclaimed the doctrine that every believer in Christ is a priest and that within the priesthood of all believers there are only differences of function. Calvin taught the same thing, calling it the doctrine of Christian vocation, which imparted a sacramental quality to even the most menial of tasks and raised all occupations to the level of spiritual significance.

If we use the yardstick of service to man and apply it to politicians, we may be surprised to discover that these much criticized people come out rather well. T. V. Smith went so far as to call them "secular priests" and "secular saints." T. V. Smith was a professor of philosophy who served in the Illinois legislature and the national Congress, and it was his experience in practical politics which led him to reappraise the role of the politician. Smith's general thesis is stated thus: "Democracy is government by politicians for citizens who too often reward them with disdain. This disdain of politicians is a dangerous disease. It is peculiarly dangerous for a democracy. Politicians are the secular priests of our common faith in one another. Either they attend to our joint business or that business gets neglected. If it gets neglected, then democracy fails from inefficiency." [57]

The case for T. V. Smith's thesis is much stronger than the usual popular attitude would lead us to believe and hinges mainly on two central arguments. The first is that running for elective office is a broadening and liberating experience because "it forces upon the politician a fairly painful discipline that nearly everybody else is able to avoid. It forces him to break out of his own group and to adjourn a good many prejudices." [58] The Protestant discovers that Roman Catholics and Jews are good people too; the professional man who has the usual prejudice against organized labor learns to make friends with union officials; the "egghead" finds that his opinion of businessmen must be revised; the white man soliciting Negro votes comes to realize that race makes less difference than he had thought; the Anglo-Saxon learns to appreciate the virtues of fellow Americans of different national origins. The politician may not, at first, give up his prejudices, but he is likely to get rid of most of them in the end. In order to get votes, it is necessary to get acquainted with all sorts of people, to listen to them whether he thinks they make sense or not, to understand their problems, and to convey to them the impression that he likes them. It is possible, of course, to be a hypocrite and to pretend. But hypocrites are not usually convincing, even if they happen to be exceptionally good actors, because their real attitude shows through and because the stress and strain of campaigning will sooner or later cause a politically fatal slip. Furthermore, the politician does not

run only once or twice but is the veteran of many campaigns as well as
many years in office. It is much easier—and safer—to be sincere than
to simulate. The politician is forced by the range of his contacts and the
varied pressures that are exerted on him to enlarge his interests, broaden
his knowledge, reach out beyond the limited social circles in which most
people live out their entire lives, and think hard about a multitude of
problems most of which would never occur to him if he were not a politician. By necessity, the politician acquires something of the Christian
virtues of understanding and compassion. He does not often get the
credit for this attainment, because it is generally inexpedient to show it
in dealing with people who have not gone through similar experiences,
but the attainment is there nonetheless.

The second argument concerns the function of the politician in society. That function is intercessory in nature. Few people see as much
human sin as the politician. He is constantly confronted with hate, greed,
jealousy, malice, falsehood, selfishness, narrow minds, and narrower sympathies. These traits crop out in unexpected places, e.g., among his friends
who try to take selfish advantage of their friendship and among highly
respected people who push for decisions which border on the unethical
and the illegal. He cannot ignore these ugly aspects of human nature, because they affect the decisions he has to make and to get other people to
make. Neither can he afford the luxury of being shocked and thus lose
his intellectual and emotional balance to the extent of forgetting that
good coexists with evil. Above all, he has to do something about the
tensions which sin produces in society. He goes to one group and listens
to their recriminations and denunciations, and the outbursts help them
to calm down a bit. And he listens with sympathy, thereby gaining their
confidence. He makes comments and suggestions. In time he brings the
group to the point where they are willing to talk and perhaps to negotiate
with the opposite group. In the meantime, the politician has repeated the
process with that other group. He brings the two groups together, and by
much hard work of mediation and conciliation, he persuades each side
to make concessions and agree on a reasonable compromise. The leaders
of the two groups then go back to their followers and face heavy criticism
because the followers have not gone through the same educational process. In each group the compromise is eventually accepted on the basis
that the "betrayal" involved in the compromise is blamed on the machinations of "that crooked politician." Like the goat in ancient Israel
who was saddled with the sins of the people and turned loose in the
wilderness, so the politician carries the blame for the sins of other people.
He gets a bad name, but life has become tolerable and livable. This kind
of thing is nothing less than intercession in a very Christian sense, and
intercession is part and parcel of representation. By his work of inter-

cession, the politician has made the people more presentable than they would otherwise have been.

The case for T. V. Smith's thesis, therefore, is very strong and deserves to be heard and understood. Nevertheless, there are flaws in it from a Christian standpoint. There is a limit to the moral progress which can be achieved by serving one's fellow man without drawing on the resources of the Christian faith. For the politician, there is the danger of self-righteousness, which threatens whenever salvation by works is assumed. He needs to heed Luther's warning: "Our faith in Christ does not free us from works but from false opinion concerning works, that is, from the foolish presumption that justification is acquired by works." [59] For the public, there is the danger that the "secular saints" will be too secular and too few. Being too secular means that in the absence of faith in Christ, the politician will not have the inner strength to push his work of intercession far enough. More important is the certainty that there will be too few of even the secular kind of saint. Nomination and election machinery are necessarily confined in their effectiveness to the people who are willing to run for elective office, for behind elections is Election. If the people who have the talents, moral integrity, social contacts, and personal prestige are unwilling to enter politics, the electoral machinery is helpless; and less able and commendable people will monopolize the field.

When we inquire why the most desirable people refuse to run for office, we discover several reasons not one of which can be touched by election laws, nominating devices, or any other species of gadgetry. One reason is that these people are unwilling to accept the loss of income which leaving their occupations would entail. A second reason is that they are repelled at the prospect of having their reputations besmirched by the unprincipled attacks that go with politics. A third reason is that they realize that being in office means being put "on the spot" where painful decisions will have to be made, painful because every one of them to some extent involves committing evil and condoning injustice. The first reason means sacrifice; the second means accepting blame without guilt; and the third means accepting both blame and guilt. The combination spells virtual crucifixion. Now a man whose faith is vital and strong might shrink from virtual crucifixion, but he will go through with it for Christ's sake in order that other people may live. He is a Christian saint. A man whose faith is weak and nominal may overlook the first two reasons for staying out of politics, but he will balk at the third reason. He will take a beating for others, but not virtual crucifixion. He is a secular saint. All around these Christian and secular saints is the amorphous mass of people who do not want to be saints of any kind.

To summarize the mission of the kingdom of God with its vivifying concepts of citizenship and representation projected into the secular states of this world, we could not improve on the words of Milton: "To make the people fittest to choose, and the chosen fittest to govern . . . ." [60] These words are unusual not only in their clarity and conciseness but in their adequacy, for they are directed at both the rulers and the governed. They might well become the motto of the church as it contemplates its mission in the arena of politics.

Chapter VII

SEPARATION
AND STABILITY

R ELIGION is once again a matter of conscious public concern in the United States. The rise of church membership to the highest point in our history, the increase in financial contributions to religious causes, the growing volume and popularity of books and articles dealing with religious topics and themes, and the emergence of a new relationship between psychiatry and religion arising out of a common interest in mental health are all indications of this concern.

Although its roots lie deep in the crisis of our Western civilization, this concern has very definitely erupted into the realm of the political. It has appeared via the Fourteenth Amendment in cases involving the reciprocal relations of state police power and personal freedom of worship. Other cases dealing with the teaching of religion in public schools have also occupied the courts and led to a general discussion of the merits and demerits of a purely secular education. The issue of racial segregation is forcing a widespread reconsideration of old arguments regarding the Christian's duty to obey constituted authority and also his duty to challenge constituted authority on grounds of conscience and the higher law. Segregation is also precipitating conflicts within our Southern churches on matters of church polity touching the nature and extent of the authority of church organs over their members. One of the most recent sources of religious concern is the rise of Roman Catholics to high public office, even to the presidency of the United States. The latter, especially, has stirred up ancient and bitter arguments about the proper relations between religion and politics.

These several developments call into question one of the most basic tenets of our American heritage: the so-called "separation of church and state." Most Americans today probably accept it as one of our country's great contributions to Western civilization, but we are having to reinterpret and reassess it. Already, during the last decade, a remarkable number of important books have been published which deal with this basic tenet, the most thorough and comprehensive of which is Anson Stokes' three-volume work *Church and State in the United States*.[1] A much shorter but excellent book is Loren Beth's *The American Theory of Church and State.*[2] In spite of these publications, however, there remains much to be said on the subject, particularly from a Christian standpoint.

A great deal, if not most, of the discussion on church and state relations centers on the problem of stability. A typical example can be found in a recent editorial in *The Christian Century* expressing approval of the Supreme Court decision in the New York Regents' Prayer case and voicing the hope that the Court will rule against the Maryland and Pennsylvania laws which provide for the reading of Scripture in public schools. The editor contends that "any other decision would not only breach the church-state wall but would also open the doors of the public schools to practices which abrogate the rights of minorities and which tend to embroil the churches in bitter, insoluble controversy."[3] Avoidance of controversy is the mainspring of this editorial, and it is clear that the editor believes that separation of church and state is the price of peace. Separation and stability are but two sides of the same coin.[4] The editor of *The Christian Century* does not consider whether separation might not mean instability in the long run. He makes not the slightest attempt to define or explain what he or anybody else means by stability. What he does, instead, is simply to assume that stability means the avoidance of trouble—a very debatable proposition! As one might expect from *The Christian Century,* the editor rests his argument not on theological but on wholly secular grounds, namely, the intent of the framers of the Constitution and the First Amendment. While awaiting the decision of the Supreme Court on the Maryland and Pennsylvania laws, he made the following characteristic recommendation: "The American people might well spend the interim exploring their political and religious origins, saturating themselves in the nation's treasured documents, and discovering again why our forefathers, profiting from tragic experiences, were determined to push and keep church and state forever apart. Such a refresher course in American and in church history will make us ready for any Supreme Court decision which hews to the line of the First amendment."[5]

Since this recommendation is typical not only of *The Christian Century* but also of most contemporary thinking about the relations which should exist between church and state, it is necessary that we give detailed consideration to what the framers of the Constitution and the First Amendment did intend with regard to this problem. In doing so, we do not in any way concede what the editor of *The Christian Century* obviously assumes, namely, that the American tradition is infallible. What the framers intended is not conclusive as to what is right, but it has a good deal to do with what is likely to be accepted. For tactical reasons, therefore, we must first ascertain what the framers thought in order to determine on whose side they were, and then proceed to a discussion of the issue on its merits.

CHRISTIANITY
AND THE FIRST AMENDMENT

When we go back to this formative period of our history, we are struck by the absence of the now current phrases "separation of church and state" and "wall of separation." The key word was "establishment," and it is the word which found its way into the language of the First Amendment. For twentieth-century Christians, establishment is a strange word so remote from our experience that we scarcely know what it means. For eighteenth-century Americans, however, the situation was quite otherwise. Establishment was then no speculative term: it was a descriptive term rooted in European and colonial experience and imbedded in the living present.

Establishment was based on the conviction that the state should be officially committed to one of the Christian denominations, should promote that religion actively, and should suppress or at least discourage all opposition to it or deviation from it. This policy was conceived to be essential to the well-being of the state and to the preservation of religious truth. It was the policy in force, in varying degrees, in all the colonies except Rhode Island. While the general thesis of establishment was clear and easily understood, its implementation was complex and ever changing. It meant that financial support for ministers and church buildings came from public funds. It could mean that voting was restricted to members of the established church, as was true for a time in colonial Massachusetts. It usually disqualified Roman Catholics, Jews, agnostics, and some Protestants from public office. In colonial Connecticut, for a while, it meant that pastors elected by the congregation had to be confirmed by the legislature acting as a presbytery and that no new church could be organized without the consent of the legislature. It could mean, as in some of the southern colonies, that marriages and funerals could not legally be conducted by any ministers other than those of the established church. It generally meant the prosecution and punishment of unlicensed preachers. Sometimes a state attempted to establish a particular religion without establishing a particular church. Thus, the South Carolina constitution of 1778 declared: "The Christian Protestant religion shall be deemed, and is hereby constituted and declared to be the established religion of this State. All denominations of protestants in this State . . . shall enjoy equal religious and civil privileges." [6] Since a provision of this kind inevitably raises questions as to what the Christian Protestant religion is, this South Carolina constitution proceeded to incorporate an amazingly lengthy and detailed creed which followed very closely the Thirty-Nine Articles of the Episcopal Church. The long and protracted struggles ending in disestablishment are too complicated to follow here, but they do illustrate the ingenuity and inventiveness of the contestants. The central thesis of establishment was simple enough, but its modalities were infinitely complex and varied.

The original Constitution implied by its omission of the then customary reference to God in the Preamble, by the absence of any religious language in the oath of office prescribed for the President in Article II, and by the provision in Article VI prohibiting religious tests for holding public office, that there was to be no *national* establishment in the historical and contemporary sense familiar to eighteenth-century Americans. What was implied in the original Constitution became explicit in the First Amendment. That is what the framers meant, and that is all that they meant. James Madison, who piloted the amendment through the House of Representatives, tried to say so in so many words but was blocked by opposition to the word "national." The story of what happened when the First Amendment was being considered by the House of Representatives is most enlightening.

As first presented to the House by Madison, the amendment read: "No religion shall be established by law, nor shall the equal rights of conscience be infringed." [7] This formulation ran into immediate opposition. Roger Sherman, a member of the Connecticut delegation to the Constitutional Convention at Philadelphia, had already objected in the Convention to a similar proposal by the South Carolina delegation on the ground that it was unnecessary. "The State Declarations of Rights," he argued, "are not repealed by this Constitution; and being still in force are sufficient." [8] He now repeated his objection on the floor of the House of Representatives: "Mr. Sherman thought the amendment altogether unnecessary, inasmuch as Congress had no authority whatever delegated to them by the constitution to make religious establishments; he would, therefore, move to have it struck out." [9] Other congressmen, however, were not so sure. Congressman Huntington objected that Madison's language might have the effect of disestablishing religion in the states and voiced the hope that "the amendment would be made in such a way as to secure the rights of conscience, and a free exercise of the rights of religion, *but not to patronize those who professed no religion at all.*" [10]

Madison's reaction to these objections is recorded as follows: "Mr. Madison thought, if the word national was inserted before religion, it would satisfy the minds of honorable gentlemen. He believed *that the people feared one sect might obtain a pre-eminence,* or two combine together, and establish a religion to which they would compel others to conform. He thought if the word national was introduced, it would point the amendment directly *to the object it was intended to prevent.*" [11] Madison's comment is thoroughly revealing of the situation existing at the time, all the more so because he himself was what one might call a radical separationist in the manner of Jefferson, Justice Black, the American Civil Liberties Union, and *The Christian Century*. He realized that his personal position was strictly a minority position for which there was no chance of adoption at that time. After all, there were only two states, Rhode Island and Virginia, which had no religious requirements of any kind when the First Amendment was being debated in Congress, and even Virginia's separation of church and state was only four years old.[12] Madison therefore yielded to pressure with that facility which always came so naturally to him. It was plain as could be that in a multi-denominational country the new federal government ought not to be used by one Christian church to victimize or seek special advantage over other Christian churches as had been the case, with varying degrees of severity, in all the colonies except Rhode Island.

Even so, Madison's suggestion that the word national be inserted did not meet with favor. The reason, however, had nothing to do with religion. The word national in those days was loaded with political dynamite because it conveyed the idea of one amalgamated people and consolidated government, which offended the champions of the states. Congressman Elbridge Gerry, one of the three members of the Philadelphia Convention who had refused to sign the Constitution, was on his feet to denounce the offensive word. The record then gives us a characteristic bit of Madisonian duplicity: "Mr. Madison withdrew his motion, but observed that the words 'no national religion shall be established by law,' did not imply that the Government was a national one. . . ."[13] Madison then tried to reach the states directly by inserting a provision that "no State shall infringe the equal rights of conscience," but that provision was rejected by the Senate.[14]

The final outcome was the adoption of the First Amendment in its present form: "Congress shall make no law respecting an establishment of religion, or prohibiting the free exercise thereof." The careful phrasing meant that the Madisonian-Jeffersonian separationist doctrine had failed. The nation refused to impose not only separationism but even disestablishment on the states. Mark DeWolfe Howe was quite correct, therefore, when he said: "The religious clauses of the First Amendment adopted the negative principle of liberty in order to achieve what was then conceived to be an appropriate division of power between the nation and the states. For those who ratified, if not for those who framed, the First Amendment, it bespoke a theory of federalism rather than a theory of freedom."[15]

We should not conclude, however, that the Madisonian-Jeffersonian separationist doctrine had won on the national level. The very language of the First Amendment specifies only that the nation was to have no religious establishment in the historically determined sense of giving federal support to any one of the Christian denominations which included virtually the entirety of the population. That no separation in the Jeffersonian sense was intended is clear from the many evidences of Christian commitment (e.g., Thanksgiving proclamations, chaplaincies in the armed forces and in the houses of Congress, etc.) to which Justice Potter Stewart appropriately referred in his dissenting opinion in the New York Regents' Prayer case. The foremost authority on church and state relations in the United States, Anson Stokes, concludes that our constitutional provisions made the nation "nonecclesiastical" but not "nonreligious" [16] and that America was "mainly Christian in origin, character, and purpose," in sharp contrast with the Soviet Union which is really and truly secular.[17]

John Courtney Murray, the distinguished Roman Catholic spokesman of the American tradition, likewise rejects the separationist interpretation of "the nation's treasured documents," in which the editor of *The Christian Century* says we should be "saturating" ourselves. Pointing to the great multiplicity of Christian denominations which was as evident to Americans in the eighteenth as in the twentieth century, Father Murray looks upon our constitutional provisions dealing with religion as "articles of peace" rather than "articles of faith." [18] In one sense, of course, he is right. To have established any one church, even if feasible (which it was not), would have led straight to endless discord. He, too, shares the concern for stability which animates Loren Beth and the editor of *The Christian Century,* but unlike them he does not posit stability as the highest good to be expected. There was more than a cold grasp of existing political realities by practical men involved in the rejection of establishment by the First Amendment. There was the right of the church to be, to grow, and to carry out its redemptive mission among sinful men, a right which does not originate with public authority but which public authority recognized and undertook to guarantee. Under the First Amendment, the Roman Catholic Church has prospered remarkably, and for that Father Murray is properly grateful. But there is a further spiritual significance which Father Murray cannot be expected to admit, namely, a profoundly Protestant understanding that no visible organized church has the right to identify itself with the Church Universal, i.e., the Holy Catholic Church of the Apostles' Creed. It is only natural that this spiritual significance should exist, since the Constitution and the First Amendment were the work of Protestants.

The First Amendment meant that long and painful experience in Europe and in the colonies had taught us the lesson that ecclesiasticism is promoted by establishment and that ecclesiasticism is a perversion of the Christian faith. Our country was not to be Presbyterian, Congregationalist, Methodist, Episcopal, Baptist, Lutheran, or Roman Catholic. But the framers of the Constitution and the First Amendment understood that it was and would continue to be a Christian country. The only official document which Stokes could find that states the contrary was the Treaty of

Peace and Amity of 1797 between the United States and Tripoli, in which it was declared that "the government of the United States of America is not, in any sense, founded on the Christian religion. . . ." [19] This bit of appeasement addressed to a Moslem country did not ring true and was significantly omitted when the treaty was renegotiated in 1805.[20]

RELIGIOUS VIEWS OF THE FRAMERS OF THE CONSTITUTION

We shall now turn to an examination of the religious views of the framers of the Constitution to determine whether these views harmonize best with disestablishment or separationism. In order to narrow the investigation, we shall confine ourselves to those founding fathers who took part in the Constitutional Convention of 1787 in Philadelphia.* First, we shall make a brief survey of those framers who were not particularly influential in the Convention but whose views are interesting in themselves and whose presence formed the setting within which the more important members had to operate. Second, we shall analyze the views of those framers who were the key architects of the Constitution.

*The religious views
of the less influential framers*

Let us now consider those framers who were definitely Christian. In the New England states we find Caleb Strong of Massachusetts, "a sober Calvinist" and the author of a collection of speeches entitled *Patriotism and Piety*.[21] Rufus King, then of Massachusetts and later of New York, was an Episcopalian who served as Warden of Trinity Church in New York and was instrumental in the establishment of the General Theological Seminary of the Protestant Episcopal Church in New York.[22] He declined a position as Manager of the American Bible Society to which he had been elected, but in doing so he expressed his "approbation" of the Society's work and explained that he declined on the advice of his bishop, who felt that the Bible should be distributed through church channels in conjunction with the Book of Common Prayer.[23]

In the Middle Atlantic states, David Brearly of New Jersey "was a delegate to the Episcopal General Convention of 1786, and was one of the compilers of the prayer-book." [24] His colleague William Livingston, governor of New Jersey as well as delegate from that state to the Convention, was a Presbyterian. He believed in revelation, looked upon the Bible as authoritative, and stated his creed in the *Independent Reflector* of which he was editor.[25] Because his religious views were in some re-

---

* Many more people were involved in making the First Amendment, of course, but the First Congress was controlled by the Federalists among whom the framers occupied positions of leadership. The Bill of Rights was an extension of the original Constitution, and the passage of both was, in essence, a single continuous act.

spects unconventional, he was accused of being a Deist by some of his contemporaries. He denied the charge vehemently. In an essay entitled "Deism" which was published in the *New Jersey Gazette* of June 12, 1786, Livingston ridiculed any man who argued that natural reason unaided by revelation could suffice as a guide for conduct in this life or as proof of the immortality of the soul. "Have you ever seen such a man, sir?" he asked, "why then you have seen a—blockhead." [26] John Dickinson of Pennsylvania was a life-long Quaker who contributed heavily to Quaker educational causes.[27] Thomas FitzSimons of Pennsylvania, a Roman Catholic, "was the largest contributor to the erection of St. Augustine's Church in Philadelphia. . . ." [28] Richard Bassett of Delaware was "an enthusiastic Methodist and life-long friend of Bishop Asbury" and "paid one-half the cost of the First Methodist Church in Dover." [29] His colleague George Read was a believer in the strict observance of Christian practices such as keeping the Sabbath. "Believe me," he wrote to a kinsman, "it is dangerous to indulge ourselves in *small* breaches of that duty we owe to the Divinity, as *one* is apt to bring *others*. . . ." [30] There is also some evidence that his religious thinking was doctrinal as well as behavioral. "There can be no difficulty," he wrote, "I apprehend, in meeting with or discovering one another in the other world." [31]

In the southern states, Edmund Randolph, Hugh Williamson, Charles Cotesworth Pinckney, William Few, and Abraham Baldwin were definitely Christian. Edmund Randolph of Virginia started out as a Deist and was converted to Christianity during the fight to disestablish the Episcopal Church in Virginia.[32] His father had been a Deist too and rejected twice as Visitor of the College of William and Mary because he was not a Christian.[33] The decisive factor in Edmund Randolph's conversion to Christianity was his wife. He himself gave the following account of it: "When we were united I was a deist,—made so by my confidence in some whom I revered, and by the labours of two of my preceptors who, though of the ministry, poisoned me with books of infidelity. I cannot answer for myself that I should have been brought to examine the genuineness of holy writ if I had not observed the consolatory influence which it brought upon the life of my dearest Betsey. . . ." [34] By the time he attended the Philadelphia Convention, Randolph had been for a number of years a practicing and fervent Episcopalian.*

---

* The quality of Randolph's spiritual life may be seen in a prayer entitled "A Prayer for My Family" which he wrote at the time of his wife's death: "O God, whose mercies have hitherto covered us from the most grievous afflictions to which the condition of human life is exposed, hear us, we beseech thee, in this hour of distress. We bow with pious resignation to thy late decree which tears from us her whom we all loved, and, so far as the gospel suffers, even adored. Pour into our hearts the balm of thy holy spirit; that, if this dispensation of thy providence was drawn upon us by our sins, we may sincerely repent, and thus

Hugh Williamson, raised and educated in Pennsylvania but representing North Carolina where he had become an influential figure, was a Presbyterian. He studied theology in Pennsylvania and Connecticut, was admitted to the presbytery of Philadelphia, and preached for about two years.[35] He left the ministry partly for reasons of health and partly because of theological battles between the adherents and opponents of Whitefield, and turned to medicine.[36] He never departed, however, from his Presbyterian faith. Charles Cotesworth Pinckney of South Carolina was an Episcopalian who served for fifteen years as president of the Charleston Bible Society.[37] William Few of Georgia was a Methodist who "was a staunch believer in revealed religion. . . ."[38] Abraham Baldwin, who represented Georgia, was a Connecticut Congregationalist who studied theology at Yale, was licensed to preach by the New Haven Association of Ministers, and served as chaplain in the revolutionary forces in Connecticut until the end of the war.[39] As Connecticut was not the scene of much military activity, Baldwin managed to eke out time to study law and was admitted to the bar in Fairfield in 1783.[40] He declined a position as Professor of Divinity at Yale [41] and moved to Georgia in 1873.[42] Four years later the legislature of the sovereign state of Georgia sent this Connecticut Yankee preacher as delegate to the National Constitutional Convention in Philadelphia. Times do change.

The position of these Christian framers on establishment is not available in every case and often cannot be inferred. It would appear that George Read, Alexander Martin, John Dickinson, and Abraham Baldwin leaned toward establishment in the states, though there is no evidence that they favored national establishment. Against any establishment were the two Pinckneys, Williamson, Randolph, and Livingston. Rufus King's position is doubtful.

George Read was president of the convention which adopted the Delaware constitution of 1776 and chairman of the committee which presented this constitution to the convention. In the original draft of that constitution in Read's handwriting is Article 22 "requiring all officers,

---

secure forgiveness. Keep her example ever before our eyes, that in nothing we may offend against thy law; and by daily recalling to our view those virtues by which we believe her to have ascended into a seat of eternal bliss, we may become worthy of being known to her at our awful change. May we estimate the world as she did, merely as affording an opportunity of performing our respective duties, of manifesting a Christian-like temper and conduct to all mankind, and of preparing ourselves for obtaining that reward which our beloved Saviour has promised to those who feed the hungry, clothe the naked, and visit the sick. Thou, O Lord, to whom her heart was open, who knowest it to be spotless, except with inseparable human frailty, protect our family affection; that neither misconduct nor dissension may make this agonising event a source of disunion, or the cause of our falling off from each other; but teach us to consider every breach of family harmony as it would have been considered by her while living, an interruption to that heavenly peace of soul which she enjoyed." Quoted in Conway, *Omitted Chapters of History in the Life and Papers of Edmund Randolph,* 390.

before entering on the execution of their offices, to make and subscribe a declaration of their faith in the doctrines of the trinity in unity, and the divine inspiration of the Holy Scriptures." [43] Alexander Martin, delegate from North Carolina, had recommended as governor the "public support of ministers, regardless of denomination" to the legislature.[44] Abraham Baldwin introduced a bill in the Georgia legislature in 1785 "for the regular establishment and support of the public duties of religion." [45] This bill proposed to levy a tax for the support of ministers regardless of denomination and was based on the premise that "the Knowledge and practise of the principles of the Christian Religion tends greatly to make good Members of Society as well as good Men." [46]

John Dickinson was in favor of religious freedom, opposed test oaths for holding office, and spoke against a resolution of the colonial assembly requesting that Pennsylvania be turned into a royal colony lest the Church of England be established therein.[47] On the other hand, Dickinson favored the support of Christian ministers by taxation. He asserted that "it is the duty of government, with the utmost attention and caution, to promote and enforce the sublime and beneficial morality, as well as theology, of Christianity; and, considering them as connected with government, how can this be done better than by employing men of wisdom, piety, and learning to teach it,—and how can they be so employed unless they are properly supported,—and how can they be supported but by the government that employs them? Let impositions be laid for this purpose." [48] It is clear that Dickinson regarded the promotion of the Christian religion in both its ethical and doctrinal aspects as a legitimate function of government but opposed the establishment of any particular Christian denomination.

Rufus King opposed establishment in 1785 when he expressed misgivings about the appointment of an Anglican bishop in America because he thought the bishop would be "the channel of improper information to his spiritual head, the King of England." [49] On this occasion, he did not want the clergy to "have their influence on the Government." [50] In 1798, however, King was worried about immigration from Ireland and suggested that all immigrants should be required "to bring with them Certificates from the religious Societies to which they belonged. . . ." [51]

On the side of disestablishment were the two Pinckneys of South Carolina, who were most responsible for the constitutional provision of Article VI prohibiting religious tests for holding office, and Hugh Williamson of North Carolina, who severely castigated establishment in his two-volume *History of North Carolina*. Edmund Randolph was also for disestablishment. He compared the vitality of the Presbyterians in Virginia with the stagnant complacency of the Episcopalians and blamed the latter on establishment.[52] He defended the Constitution in the Virginia convention against those who criticized it for not guaranteeing religious liberty. His argument was that control over religion was not one of the delegated powers of Congress, and he saw in the variety and number of denominations a healthy situation which would make religious tyranny impossible.[53]

The most dedicated foe of establishment in the Convention was probably William Livingston of New Jersey. He was engaged in a vigorous controversy from 1767 to 1770 to prevent the appointment of an Anglican bishop in the colonies [54] and fought another fight to prevent King College (later Columbia University) from becoming identified with or controlled by the Church of England.[55] He opposed a proposal to incorporate a recognition of Christianity in the Articles of Confederation because it was a state matter, for such a provision would lay "the foundation of endless altercation and dispute," and though he believed in "true piety," he said, "I should not be willing that any human tribunal should settle its definition for me." [56]

It is now time to turn to those other framers of the Constitution who were likewise not decisively influential in the Convention and who were non-Christian either because they were Deists or because they were indifferent to religion. In this group we find Langdon, Hamilton, Franklin, Washington, Mason, Wythe, Davie, and Blount. It may seem surprising to find Hamilton, Franklin, and Washington in this category. Although they were political giants during the formative period of our history, they were not giants in the Convention. Hamilton was too far to the right; Franklin was too far to the left and too old; and Washington was presiding officer.

John Langdon of New Hampshire, says his biographer, was not "what one would call a religious man." [57] He did not become a member of a church until 1806 toward the end of his life. Alexander Hamilton of New York appears to have had religious interests early in life,[58] but his whole career was one of coldly secular ambition. According to his colleague in the Convention, Jonathan Dayton of New Jersey, Hamilton greeted Franklin's suggestion that the sessions of the Convention be opened with prayer by caustically remarking that the personnel of the Convention was able to cope with any situation and "that therefore he did not see the necessity of calling in *foreign aid!*" [59] Franklin's views on religion are, of course, very generally known and were those of a Deist. Washington, too, was a Deist with a strong sense of Providence and religious feeling, but there was nothing specifically Christian about his convictions. George Mason of Virginia was a vestryman in the Episcopal Church, but as was the case with so many leading Virginians of that period, he was nevertheless a confirmed Deist.[60] One of the central passions of his life was liberty of conscience, and he was closely associated with Madison and Jefferson in the successful fight to disestablish the Episcopal Church in Virginia. George Wythe, also of Virginia, was another Episcopalian who was a Deist. He became a vestryman in 1769 [61] but went through two periods of complete skepticism, one in his youth and one in middle age, from which he never fully recovered.[62]

In the North Carolina delegation William Richardson Davie appears to have been neither a Christian nor a Deist. His early background was Presbyterian. He was brought up by his uncle, the Reverend William Richardson, who educated Davie "to be his successor as the pastor of the Waxhaw Presbyterian Meeting House." [63] He also studied under John Witherspoon in Princeton.[64] All this early Presbyterian training, however, was ineffective and the reason probably was an environment hostile to Christianity. President Caldwell of the University of North Carolina, who had been brought down from Princeton and had unsuccessfully tried to convert Davie, described this environment thus: "The State appears to be swarming with lawyers. It is almost the only profession for which parents educate their children. Religion is so little in vogue, that it affords no temptation to undertake its cause. In New Jersey it had public respect and support. In North Carolina, and particularly in the part east of Chapel Hill, every one believes that the way of rising to respectability is to disavow as often and as publicly as possible the leading doctrines of the Scriptures." [65]

William Blount, also of North Carolina, seems to have ignored religion altogether. He was the living embodiment of the economically centered man whom Charles A. Beard saw in the Constitutional Convention. His correspondence is full of references to financial transactions, tobacco shipments, land deals, business ventures, and constitutes one big intellectual and spiritual desert. That his conduct was in keeping with his correspondence is suggested by a letter of one Thomas Hart who remarked: "What a Sett of Atheisticall fellows must there be in Newbern that thinks there is Neither God nor Devil to punish them in a Nother World, for their usury. . . . I wonder trully how many poor Sons of Bitches with tears in their Eyes have I seen within these Six weeks past, Coming from your place. . . ." [66]

One member of the Convention who defied classification from a religious standpoint was Luther Martin of Maryland. He was well known, of course, as a vociferous and unsuccessful advocate of states' rights, who alternately irritated and exhausted his colleagues with long-winded speeches. But not much is known about his religious views and affiliations. There is an entry for April 5, 1813, in the diary of one Reverend Dr. James Millmore in which he refers to the conversion of Luther Martin, who is described as "an eminent lawyer in Baltimore, advanced in years, who had been equally celebrated for his powerful eloquence at the bar, and for his notorious sacrifices at the shrine of Bacchus." [67] After remarking on the "fervor and sublimity" of Martin's religious testimony on that occasion, Dr. Millmore added the comment: "Thanks be to God,

His power is infinite." [68] After he had joined the Episcopal Church, Luther Martin had trouble keeping up payments on his pew rent so that the pew was eventually turned over to somebody else. His biographer says of him: "Next to intemperance, gross carelessness in money matters seems to have been his prevailing fault." [69] In the light of this curious religious background, it is surprising to discover Luther Martin taking a stand for establishment of the Christian religion nationally. In a long speech denouncing the Constitution before the Maryland House of Delegates, Martin singled out Article VI in these words:

The part of the system, which provides that *no religious test* shall ever be required as a qualification to any office or public trust under the United States, was adopted by a great majority of the convention, and without much debate,—however, there were some members *so unfashionable* as to think that *a belief of the existence of a Deity,* and of a *state of future rewards and punishments* would be some security for the good conduct of our rulers, and that in a christian country it would be at *least decent* to hold out some distinction beween the professors of christianity and downright infidelity or paganism.[70]

The religious views
of the more influential framers

It is now time to examine the views of those framers who were most influential in the making of the Constitution. Determining which ones fall in that category is, of course, largely a matter of judgment and, to some extent, of conjecture. A reasonable basis would be participation in the general debates in the Convention and service on the several "grand committees" which were appointed from time to time to handle difficult questions, on the Committee on Detail, and on the Committee on Style. On this basis, Rutledge, Johnson, Sherman, Ellsworth, Madison, Wilson, and Gouverneur Morris are of decisive importance.

Although John Rutledge of South Carolina is important, there is very little information available on his views. The main reason is that he was the kind of person who did not like to write or make speeches but was adept in manipulating people behind the scenes. From 1761 to 1789 he was in control of affairs in South Carolina, whether in office or out of it. His work in the Convention was done in committees and at informal meetings when the Convention was not in session, which was easy since all the delegates were in prolonged and close physical proximity. His biographer, Richard Barry, says that Rutledge was an Episcopalian who steadfastly refused all church offices such as vestryman because he did not believe in mixing religion and politics, and he claims that Rutledge helped to write the clause in Article VI forbidding religious tests.[71] Whether or not Rutledge was sincerely religious, he made a remark during the Convention which indicates quite clearly that he thought religion is politically irrelevant. The topic under discussion was slavery, and his comment, as reported by Madison, was the following: "Religion and humanity had nothing to do with this question. Interest alone is the governing principle with nations." [72]

William Samuel Johnson of Connecticut was an ardent Episcopalian, son of an Episcopal clergyman, and himself trained for the Episcopal ministry. [73] In spite of his theological studies and his father's wishes, Johnson was never ordained. He decided upon a military career but encountered immovable opposition from his father, so they compromised on law. [74] Johnson never wavered in his devotion to the Episcopal Church and was in the forefront of the fight to persuade the British Government to send an Anglican bishop to the American colonies. [75] He was silent on the issue of establishment, perhaps because he was an Episcopalian in a Congregationalist state.

Roger Sherman of Connecticut was brought up in the strictest Congregationalist tradition and served his church in many capacities such as deacon, moderator, and chairman of the committee on pulpit supply. [76] "Along with his Calvinistic belief," says one of his biographers, "went an abhorrence of the Roman Church and a thorough distrust of the Episcopal system." [77] As might be expected, Sherman took a strong stand against the proposal to establish an American episcopate. [78] His sympathies were on the side of establishment, though there is no record of his having advocated it for the nation. However, he defended the propriety of Thanksgiving proclamations by the President and based it on Old Testament precedents. [79] As we have already noted earlier, he opposed the First Amendment in the House of Representatives and a similar proposal in the Convention itself. As United States Senator he voted against the confirmation of Gouverneur Morris as Minister to France on the ground that Morris was "an irreligious and profane man" and that it was contrary to sound public policy to appoint to office any but "godly and honest men." [80]

Oliver Ellsworth of Connecticut was a Congregationalist who studied theology but turned from the ministry to law. [81] Throughout his life he was active in the church, an orthodox Calvinist in his thinking, a strict practitioner of family religion, and the owner of a library in which more than half of the books were works on religion. [82] He favored establishment for Connecticut, and as member of the legislature, he led in the rejection of a Baptist petition to disestablish the Congregational Church. His argument was that "particularly in a republican government, good morals are essential," that morality depends on religion, and that therefore state support of religion is no more open to question or exception than state support of education. [83] On the other hand, Ellsworth rejected test oaths as ineffective and criticized England "where every person who holds a public office, must either be a saint by law, or a hypocrite by practice." [84] He defended Article VI by pointing out that in a multi-denominational country, the establishment of any one denomination "would incapacitate more than three-fourths of the American citizens" and that "the majority of our citizens would never submit to this indignity." [85] Nevertheless, his endorsement of religious liberty for the nation as a whole was not altogether free of reservations. He contended that "the civil order," by which it would appear from the context that he was referring to Congress, has the right to enact "laws against drunkenness, profane swearing, blasphemy, and professed atheism." [86]

James Madison was a Deist, but even deism was hardly central to his thinking. In the numerous and voluminous pronouncements he made on the subject of religion, it is difficult to find anything that looks like a definite theological conviction. In a letter to a minister written in 1825 long after his retirement from public life, Madison did affirm that "the belief in a God, all powerful, wise, and good, is . . . essential to the moral order of the world, and to the happiness of men," but this conclusion was based on a purely philosophical type of reasoning which leaves no room for revelation and which is not in any way specifically Christian.[87] A number of Christian beliefs can be found in Madison's famous *Remonstrance* to the Virginia legislature against a bill to establish "Teachers of the Christian Religion," but Madison was making a case to a legislature dominated by Episcopalian Christians for whom exclusively secular arguments would have been ineffective. Another document, a petition asking for the repeal of a law incorporating the Episcopal Church of Virginia, also contained many Christian sentiments, but here again Madison was not speaking for himself but for petitioners identified as "We, the subscribers, members of the Protestant Episcopal Church."

The real passion of Madison's life was what he conceived to be religious liberty. He vacillated and wobbled on most questions, including such important ones as the Bill of Rights and centralization of power; he was a follower of Hamilton and later of Hamilton's archenemy Jefferson, but on the issue of religion he was consistent and unwavering. He objected to the word "toleration" because it implied granting as a matter of grace what was a matter of right.[88] "Religious bondage," he declared, "shackles and debilitates the mind, and unfits it for every noble enterprise, every expanded prospect." [89] He objected to a bill in the Confederation Congress to allocate public land in the territories for religious purposes.[90] He thought Congress had no right to have chaplains at public expense and that Congressmen should have "contributed for the purpose a pittance from their own pockets." [91] He had qualms about his own presidential Thanksgiving proclamations even though they were "absolutely indiscriminate, and merely recommendatory. . . ." [92] He opposed the teaching of religion in state universities, even on a nonsectarian basis, because he thought it implied establishment, and the professors would be "theological gladiators." [93]

James Wilson was brought up in Scotland as a Presbyterian and at the age of twenty-three came to Pennsylvania, where he studied law under the Quaker John Dickinson and was influenced by a friend to join the Episcopal Church.[94] He was definitely an evangelical Christian all his life. Wilson was a strong believer in natural law, which he identified as the law of God considered in three aspects: natural law "as promulgated by reason and the moral sense," revealed law "as promulgated by the holy scriptures," and the law of nations "as addressed to political societies." [95] The source of obligation for this law in all three aspects was not the consent of man but the will of God.[96] He believed that the purpose of life, both for individuals and for nations, is to discover the will of God [97] and that the revelation of that will in the Bible is "supereminently authentick." [98] But he did not think of scriptural teaching as self-interpreting and self-enforcing. Using "reason, conscience, and the holy scriptures," he held that it is the function of human government to apply this will of God to concrete situations through the various levels of positive law.[99] In spite of the strongly theological foundations of his political thought, James Wilson was unmistakably on the side of disestablishment, praised "the celebrated Locke" for his doctrine of toleration, and condemned establishment in Great Britain.[100]

Gouverneur Morris of Pennsylvania is almost as hard to classify as Luther Martin. Most of his countrymen thought of him as a foe of the Christian religion, if not of all religion. An extreme reactionary in politics, he was worldly and sophisticated in social relations and gifted with a sharp wit and a sharp tongue. He was not a churchman, had no patience for ritual, and heaped scorn on many current beliefs which he regarded as superstitions.[101] He also offended his more conventional contemporaries in the realm of conduct. One of his biographers attributes Morris' mastery of the French language not to the tutors with whom his parents had supplied him but to a French mistress which he is said to have kept.[102] He had quite a reputation as a ladies' man and did not get married until he was fifty-seven years old.[103] When he broke a leg and had to have it replaced by a wooden one, a friend tried to console him by suggesting that the misfortune would at least put certain temptations beyond his reach, whereupon Morris replied: "My dear sir, you reason so convincingly and you show me so clearly the advantage of being without legs, that I feel almost tempted to get rid of the other one." [104]

In view of this background and the frequent charges of atheism, it comes as a surprise to discover that Gouverneur Morris had some very pronounced religious views that coincide with several conservative Christian positions. He was far from being an atheist and asserted that "irrevocable doom" is the fate of nations which do not believe in God and immortality as taught in the Bible, and he characterized this belief as "the principle of all sound political science." [105] Robert Sherman himself could not have assigned a greater authority to the Bible than did Morris. "The reflection and experience of many years," said Morris, "have led me to consider the holy writings, not only as most authentic and instructive in themselves, but as the clue to all other history. They tell us what man is, and they, alone, tell us why he is what he is: a contradictory creature that, seeing and approving what is good, pursues and performs what is evil. All of private and public life is there displayed. Effects are traced, with unerring accuracy, each to the real cause." [106] Morris was on the side of disestablishment, but unbelief was obviously not the reason. It was not Christian truth which he feared but rather the misrepresentation and misconception of it by church and government officials and ignorant bigotry by the rank and file.

The intent of the framers
and establishment: a summary

Our survey of the religious views of the framers of the Constitution does not lend support to the radical separationist doctrine of Madison and Jefferson. The evidence shows that the majority, both numerical and effective, of the delegates at the Philadelphia Convention were committed Christians and that practically all the rest were Deists. Now Christians and Deists had three politically important religious convictions in common, namely, (1) that God rules the world and guides peoples and their governments with his providence, (2) that morality is rooted in religion and cannot long survive without it, (3) that political stability and strength depend on morality and nowhere more so than in a constitutional republic. In the light of these convictions, the framers would have been shocked by the modern idea that government can be neutral toward its own foundation. Gouverneur Morris voiced the mind of practically the entire Convention when he spoke the following words: "But *the most important of all lessons is, the denunciation or ruin to every state that rejects the precepts of religion.* Those nations are doomed to death who bury, in the corruption of criminal desire, the awful sense of an existing God, cast off the consoling hope of immortality, and seek refuge from despair in the dreariness of annihilation. Terrible, irrevocable doom! loudly pronounced, frequently repeated, strongly exemplified in the sacred writings, and fully confirmed by the long record of time. It is the clue which leads through the intricacies of universal history. *It is the principle of all sound political science.*" [107]

The evidence also shows that the great majority of the Convention favored disestablishment nationally and that an only slightly smaller majority favored disestablishment in the states by state action. Disestablishment was intended to guarantee the freedom of the church, and the framers had come to believe that this meant the freedom of the churches. There is no doubt that both Christians and Deists believed in religious liberty, but theirs was no negative Jeffersonian conception of liberty. Their thinking followed the line marked out by one of the philosophers they admired most, Montesquieu, when he said: "The political liberty of the subject is a tranquillity of mind arising from the opinion each person has of his safety. In order to have this liberty, it is requisite the government be so constituted that one man need not be afraid of another. . . ." [108] It seems more than a coincidence that Montesquieu's felicitous word tranquillity should have found its place among the stated objectives of the Preamble, i.e., "to insure domestic tranquillity." Now tranquillity is not an attribute of negation, doubt, neutrality, weakness, or timidity. It is an attribute of strength, a strength which is sure of itself and therefore respects the convictions of others. It is a positive force, not the absence of force.

It is not generally understood by the public that the radical separationist interpretation of the First Amendment has only recently become semiofficial, as a result of the progressive secularization of the United States in the twentieth century. What is probably a majority of the American people now mistakenly believe that the views of Madison and Jefferson have always been accepted without question. Even less generally understood is the fact that the intrusion of radical separationism in the thinking and decisions of the Supreme Court is still more recent and therefore by no means hallowed by usage. As Loren Beth reminds us: "It was not until the so-called 'Roosevelt Court' in the 1940's that the religious clauses of the First Amendment were specifically applied against the states under the wording of the Fourteenth." [109] The Supreme Court, using the due process clause of the Fourteenth Amendment, has been imposing the Madisonian-Jeffersonian negative view of religious liberty on the states. Mark DeWolfe Howe of the Harvard Law School explains this recent development thus:

Conceding that the states may not deny religious freedom to any person, one may still want to know whether the liberty thus protected has the dimensions of positive freedom—permitting state encouragement of accepted truth—or the limited dimensions of a simple immunity from state-imposed burdens. Though the Supreme Court has not dealt with the issue in these terms, it has, in effect, decided that the Fourteenth Amendment compels the states to abandon the concept of positive religious freedom and substitute the negative, Jeffersonian concept. [110]

Howe goes on to observe that by its decisions the Supreme Court has "created national policy" and questions "whether its creation by judicial decision was an appropriate exercise of judicial power." [111]

THE LOGIC
OF RADICAL SEPARATIONISM

Having ascertained that the radical separationist position on church and state relations finds little support in either the thinking and handiwork of the framers of the Constitution and the First Amendment or in the American tradition until very recent times, we must turn our attention to the merits of the issue. For the issue of constitutionality and tradition is secondary while that of merits is fundamental and primary. Now it should be obvious that the merits of any issue cannot be satisfactorily discussed except by reference to a standard of some kind. Without such a standard, discussion merely increases rather than dispels confusion of thought. But to choose a standard is a personal commitment, and in every commitment there are two elements: the honesty which consists in acknowledging to oneself and to others what that commitment is instead of denying or disguising it, and the courage to think through the theoretical and practical consequences of that commitment. The commitment of this book is to the Christian faith; therefore, the problem of church and state relations will be analyzed in Christian terms.

This is not to deny that the problem can be analyzed in other terms such as positivism, liberalism, Marxism, or Americanism. As a matter of fact, it is in those other terms that the problem is usually analyzed. This procedure is quite permissible—for a positivist, liberal, Marxist, or superpatriot. But it is not all right for the Christian because he supposedly has already chosen another standard. We may disagree with a scholar like Loren Beth who openly and admittedly writes from the standpoint of cultural pluralism tinged with a liberal philosophy, but we must admire his honesty and be grateful for his craftsmanship in delineating the consequences of that standpoint for church and state relations. We have a right to expect a like honesty and craftsmanship among those who profess the Christian faith. Unfortunately, we are often disappointed. It is only very rarely true, however, that any insincerity is involved. What usually happens is that there is a substitution or mixture of standards, generally on the subconscious level, which results in confused, ambiguous, and not infrequently contradictory thinking.

One of the most important current attempts to analyze the merits of the problem of church and state relations is to be found in a report of a special committee of the United Presbyterian Church in the United States of America.[112] This report is important for several reasons. It is not the isolated thinking of one individual but the collective thinking of a group of distinguished churchmen. It is intended as advice and counsel by a Christian church for the guidance of its members. Submitted to the 174th General Assembly, the report was discussed and then referred to the sessions, presbyteries, and synods of the United

Presbyterian Church for their appraisal. It was approved with minor changes by the 175th General Assembly in 1963. This means that the report carries the weight of one of the most influential Protestant denominations in America.

It is a real pity that this report, which is a much needed and courageous attempt to guide the thinking of the numerous and influential members of a great church on a critical issue, should so fully exemplify the kind of substitution and mixture of standards to which we previously referred. Since clarity is often enhanced by contrast, we shall engage in a detailed criticism of the UPUSA Report and use it as a convenient vehicle to spell out a position on church and state relations which is truly based on and consistent with the Christian faith.

The key conceptions of the report are neutrality and extrication, neutrality by the state and extrication by the church. These conceptions mean that the report has adopted the radical separationism of Madison and Jefferson and commends it to the membership of the United Presbyterian Church.

Political neutrality

On the subject of neutrality, the report offers the following definition: "A true state, in the light of the first amendment to the American Constitution, is one which neither favors church or sect nor is hostile toward religion." [113] What this definition means is amplified thus:

On religious matters, that is, matters of faith, dogma, indoctrination, government must be neutral. It is this order of government which Presbyterians endorse. That government shall not be hostile to religion has been affirmed as often and as decidedly in recent Court decisions as that it shall favor no religious group above another. In a state such as this, religious commitment brings no advantage. Once profession of religion becomes a worldly advantage, danger of impure love of Christ is increased. Such a state is the kind of political order in which Presbyterians wish to live, teach, and evangelize.[114]

Let us note, first of all, the substitution of standards. How is a "true state" determined? It is determined "in the light of the first amendment to the American Constitution," not in the light of the Christian faith. Why should government not be hostile to religion? Is it because such conduct is contrary to Christian teaching? The report does not say so, but it does look for support "in recent Court decisions." If we move beyond the two statements quoted above, we find further corroboration of the report's liberal secularism in the rejection of the idea of a Christian state, which "history" shows to be "as dangerous for true religion as for civil liberty." [115] Natural law is likewise rejected, this time in the name of Christ. "It is to Christ that the church bears witness," says the report, "not to a theological articulation of the place of the political order in the structure of reality. This is why the celebrated theory of natural law, so dominant for medieval Christendom, may not figure in contemporary Christianity's discussion of the doctrine of the state." [116]

Since we have already explained our position on the concepts of state and natural law in chapters III and IV, we shall simply refer the reader to them. However, we cannot help wondering how a church is going to bear witness to an inarticulated Christ since it is through our theological articulations of his spirit in political, economic, social, and cultural life that we can bear witness at all. Furthermore, we question the adequacy of dismissing natural law by the easy process of tagging it with medievalism, especially since the Western world has believed in natural law for at least eighteen hundred out of the last two thousand years.

Whether the authors of the report like it or not, the fact is that in this country the "profession of religion" is already "a worldly advantage." It is common knowledge that candidates for public office have found church membership a political asset and avowed hostility to religion a political liability. None should appreciate this fact of politics better than Presbyterians, for their involvement is as definite as it is one-sided. As the distinguished president of a theological seminary once remarked: "Too often the United Presbyterian Church is only the Republican party at prayer." Nor is this involvement to be regarded solely in the light of a narrow conception which limits politics to party affiliation. Who does not know that to be a Presbyterian is a badge of respectability in American society? To be a Presbyterian elder, especially, is taken to mean that one is a solid citizen, a reputable businessman, a good financial risk, a safe man for your daughter to marry, a socially desirable next-door neighbor, a fitting sponsor of worthy causes, and a good trustee for the old Alma Mater. The authors of the report rightly look upon this kind of situation as a danger, but they should also perceive that it is a great opportunity. In any case, the involvement is already here, unavoidably, and it is sheer delusion to suppose that separation of church and state can put an end to it. Extrication is not the answer. The need is for an involvement which is total instead of one-sided and which, above all, is redemptive. But involvement will be less and less total and redemptive as government becomes more and more pervasive of life, if government is sentenced to religious neutrality by the law of the land with the connivance of the church.

The report's nearest attempt to give its position a scriptural basis occurs in the following passage:

"Render to Caesar the things that are Caesar's and to God the things that are God's" is a quotation often applied to church-state relations. This quote *does not* have direct application to the series of problems before our Church! The New Testament denies such application. The issue is not "What is

Caesar's and what is God's." Caesar has no autonomy over against God, whether he knows it or not! The issue is, what does it mean to follow a Lord who, when confronted with a double-edged question, silenced his antagonists with a double-edged answer? We cannot concern ourselves with the legalistic question of what is God's and what is Caesar's.[117]

The comment about double-edged questions and double-edged answers is extraordinary, to say the least, since Christ is commended to us as a tricky debater. The other comment, that Caesar has no autonomy against God, is sound enough but conflicts with the earlier statement that Christ's famous reply has no direct application to church-state relations. Since government officials, being human, bear God's image and superscription, they too must render unto God what is God's, namely, themselves. No neutrality is contemplated or allowed here.

Scripture makes it very clear that no Christian, whether in or out of government, has any business being neutral. Government officials, like other men, must decide whether to serve God or Mammon. "He that is not with me," said Jesus "is against me; and he that gathereth not with me scattereth abroad." [118] People who do not like this verse sometimes quote another where Jesus said, "For he that is not against us is on our part." [119] But there is no contradiction here, once the context of those two verses is taken into account. In the first instance, Jesus was speaking of confrontation with evil. In the second instance, he was speaking of someone who was doing good—and in Christ's name—but who did not associate with the little band of disciples. What the second passage means, when applied to us now, is that one does not have to be a Presbyterian or out of public office to be on Christ's side, but one does have to be on his side. The advocates of neutrality might profitably ponder over another saying of Jesus: "Whosoever therefore shall confess me before men, him will I confess also before my Father which is in heaven. But whosoever shall deny me before men, him will I also deny before my Father which is in heaven." [120] In the Book of Revelation we find these words: "I know thy works, that thou art neither cold nor hot: I would thou wert cold or hot. So then because thou art lukewarm, and neither cold nor hot, I will spue thee out of my mouth." [121] Could neutrality receive a more scathing indictment?

Tax exemption

Following out their theme of neutrality and extrication, the authors of the UPUSA Report recommend that the United Presbyterian Church "begin the process of extricating itself from the position of being obligated, or seeming to be obligated, to the state by virtue of special tax privileges extended to it." [122] Their point is that tax exemption is a form of support, and so it is. The state, by granting the exemption, is saying that it is in the public interest that the churches should flourish and therefore chooses this way of encouraging them as a matter of public policy, just as it does in the case of educational and charitable institutions and for the same reason. Who is to say that the state is wrong in this judgment? An agnostic, a Marxist, or a positivist might say so with good logic, but for a Christian church to say so is to question the value of its own redemptive mission.

How far can the state go in giving encouragement to the churches? The answer to this question cannot be a matter of pure logic. If we took the radical separationist view that any encouragement or support is unconstitutional, we would have to go a great deal further than the UPUSA Report does. We would have to insist that the churches generate their own electricity, secure their own water supply, and employ their own police force, because receiving these services from government puts the churches in a position of dependence. We would have to insist that the Post Office discontinue handling church bulletins and publications, because this service is of great value to the churches. We would have to deny the churches the use of public highways, because highways are financed by government and can be used to further evangelistic work, thereby tending toward an establishment of religion. Of course, pushing the principle of separation to such extremes would be absurd, and even the Southern Baptists and the POAU,* for all their dedication to radical separationism, would not go this far. Furthermore, such extremism would also be unconstitutional because it would amount to prohibiting the free exercise of religion.

We have already gone too far in the direction of radical separationism. In an era when universities are tax exempt and receive federal and state grants, industry is protected by tariffs, agriculture receives price supports, labor is guaranteed minimum wages, bank deposits are insured by government, the unemployed receive unemployment compensation, home owners receive federal financial assistance, authors are given copyrights, and inventors receive patents, why should the churches be the only ones denied the assistance of government? Are the churches so polluted and subversive that they must be hermetically sealed off from all contact with government lest the nation be contaminated? It was this aspect of recent Supreme Court decisions which prompted Mark DeWolfe Howe to protest against the inequity involved. "The believer," he pointed out, "living in a society which has come to look upon its liberties as claims rather than immunities, finds it hard to see why the most important of his freedoms must still be looked upon as a mere immunity." [123] Strange as it may seem, radical separationism would put the churches in the same sort of position in the United States which it occupies in the Soviet Union.

* POAU is an abbreviation for a pressure group known as Protestants and Other Americans United for the Separation of Church and State.

On the other hand, neither can we go to an extreme in the opposite direction and say that it makes no difference how much support the churches receive from government. Again, this is not a matter of pure logic. There is no difference in logic between direct support by way of outright financial grants and indirect support by way of tax exemption. Both are forms of support, and the difference between them is one of degree. Few people, if any, would deny that outright grants by government to churches as churches would constitute the kind of establishment forbidden by the Constitution. When financial assistance, whatever its form, is carried to a point where churches cease to be supported by their members and look to government for their continued economic existence, the independence of the churches is undermined, and with it the purity and vitality of the Christian message are compromised.

Public office

With regard to interlocking ecclesiastical and governmental structures, the UPUSA Report is silent because there is no such interlocking in the United States and nobody argues that there should be. Church and government organizations are completely separate and independent of each other, and the churches, especially, are amazingly diverse in matters of polity. There is universal agreement that it is important for the purity and vitality of the Christian faith that party politics and personal political advancement should play no part in the selection of church leaders. In the light of history, including our own colonial history, this *de jure* and *de facto* separation of ecclesiastical and political bureaucracies is one of the monumental achievements of American civilization.

There is only one point left about which a considerable measure of disagreement continues to exist, namely the extent to which religious affiliation and commitment should enter into the evaluation of candidates for public office. No question of legality is involved, because Article VI of the Constitution is understood to mean that neither the federal government nor the states may legally disqualify anyone from public office on grounds of religion or irreligion. The question is whether the people should do by ballot what they may not do by law. On this point the UPUSA Report takes the position that a candidate's religious convictions are politically relevant. A criterion is therefore needed. The report offers the following: "The sole political criterion for the evaluation of the fitness of a candidate for public office is his competence to govern constitutionally, thus safeguarding and implementing the liberty which is the heritage of the free people who form his constituency and whose public servant he seeks to be." [124] The authors of the report emphasize this criterion by repeating it in the form of a recommendation: "Candidates for public office be evaluated strictly on the basis of their competence to govern constitutionally." [125]

The report's criterion is another striking illustration of the undiscerned substitution of secular for Christian standards. By this criterion mediocrity in public office is acceptable because mediocrity is not unconstitutional. By this criterion Christians could support candidates pledged to the repeal of the Social Security Act, the liquidation of TVA, the withdrawal of the United States from the United Nations, the conquest and annexation of Cuba or Mexico on national security grounds. Measures such as these would be disastrous, but who can deny that they would be constitutional? The inadequacy of the criterion is so obvious that one wonders how a church committee could seriously offer it for the guidance of Presbyterian Christians.

The immediate reason for this criterion, however, is only too clear from the context. The authors of the report fear Roman Catholicism. One would think that scriptural teaching would have protected a group of distinguished churchmen from such an error. Particularly relevant here is Paul's principle, to which we have referred several times, that whatsoever is not of faith is sin. Fear—whether of Roman Catholics, Communists, Fascists, or any other group—is sin and therefore unacceptable as a basis for the construction of either national or church policy. In this case, the authors of the report have put themselves in the position of rejecting any Roman Catholic candidate for public office (in spite of the fact that Roman Catholics are "on our part" [126] because they are Christians) unless he gives satisfactory proof that he adheres to "what seems to be an indigenously American type of Roman Catholic thought." [127] This is a secular criterion, if there ever was one! The effect of this criterion goes beyond doing an injustice to those of our fellow citizens who are Roman Catholics. Competence to govern constitutionally is a formula which hides the real problem, which is competence to govern righteously and wisely. But to solve the real problem demands an answer which is sure not to meet with anything like the degree of unanimity which the test of constitutionality confers. Surely, the membership of the United Presbyterian Church is entitled to a better guidance inspired by the Christian faith, not by the secular fears, of its leaders.

Military service

The UPUSA Report also turns its attention to problems created by military service and proceeds with its policy of extrication. It recommends that "The Church recognize that the continuation of the present practice whereby its ministers serve as military chaplains, paid by the state, raises serious questions in the light of separation of church and state, and that its policies in this connection be thoroughly reexamined." [128] The problem here is much like the one raised by tax exemption. The presence of chaplains in our armed forces means that the government of the United States recognizes the moral and spiritual needs of its military personnel and, as a matter of national policy, draws on the resources of the churches to satisfy those needs. In the armed forces, men of every description, cultural attainment, social position, race, and occupation are thrown together in close proximity, torn loose from their families, their church, their occupation, their neighbors, their friends. In wartime, there is the added tension which comes from the hazards of battle such as capture, physical and mental injury, and death. Under the strain of these conditions, men need to be reminded of the eternal verities of the Christian faith even more than in civilian life. At its lowest level, our national policy with regard to chaplains is a matter of morale which everyone, whether secularly or religiously oriented, recognizes as a proper governmental concern. At its highest level, this policy is an official acknowledgment that man is a moral and spiritual being. It seems incredible that a Christian church, of all institutions, should cast doubt on the propriety of such a policy in the name of an idol called "the principle of the separation of church and state."

The UPUSA Report also recommends that "Ministerial candidates and ordained clergymen, like other Americans, claim exemption from military service only on grounds of conscientious objection, and that the historical support our Church has given to conscientious objectors be reaffirmed." [129] We are faced here with another instance of an attitude which should be thoroughly familiar by now. The government has always asserted its right to determine under what conditions the national interest requires that certain categories of people (e.g., workers in essential war industries) be exempted from military service. The exemption of ministerial candidates and clergymen is based on the judgment that it is in the national interest that ministers remain on "the home front." This judgment may be questioned and debated. It may be a faulty judgment. But how can a church say so without undermining its own *raison d'être?*

The one surprising aspect of this last recommendation is the support given to conscientious objectors. It is surprising because it is utterly inconsistent with the strict separationism of the report as a whole. The exemption of conscientious objects is granted by Congress solely to those who object on religious grounds. Philosophical, moral, or political grounds are unacceptable. In the light of the principles followed by the report, exemption of conscientious objectors ought to be denied as constituting an establishment of religion.

United Presbyterians will be even more confused by recommendations three, four, five, and six, which unexpectedly present the government with a set of demands on behalf of the church, e.g., that "mature pastors" be permitted to enlist in the armed forces "at a rank commensurate with their maturity and experience." [130] The recommendations in themselves are sensible and justified, but they are not compatible in spirit or logic with radical separationism.

Education

Another area in which we should examine the position taken by the authors of the UPUSA Report is the important and controversial area of religion and public education. As a preface to their detailed recommendations, the authors of the report offer the following standard: "Public schools are creations of the whole society operating through civil authority and justify their existence solely in terms of their usefulness to the society." [131] By way of explanation, they add that "public schools should not ignore the personal beliefs in God which are part of the life of its pupils, but should recognize and respect such beliefs." [132] The next sentence makes it clear that what is meant by recognizing and respecting is the previously encountered principle of neutrality. How restrictive the principle of neutrality is becomes evident in their specific recommendations. The report recommends, for instance, that students be "allowed sufficient time" to celebrate their religious holidays "away from public school property," that religious holidays are "foreign to the purpose of the public school," and that clergymen be allowed to speak in public schools "provided their speaking does not constitute religious indoctrination or their presence form a part of a religious observance." [133] Any form of federal or state financial assistance, direct or indirect, to parochial schools should be opposed.[134]

Once again we observe the intrusion of a secular standard, i.e., "usefulness to society." Adhering to such a standard, even though recommended by a church, is not witnessing to Christ: it is surrendering to Caesar. What if the society concerned were communist or fascist? Would the authors of the report still advocate that public education should be useful to that society? Replying that the report presumably refers to American society does not help much, unless one is ready to assert that American society is everything that it should be. If by "usefulness" one means improvement, a higher standard is implied, and the implication should be recognized and developed. The church should remind society that there are conditions and practices to which Christians should not adjust and that public education should motivate and equip young people to change these conditions and practices.

It should be pointed out that there are two respects in which radical separationism conflicts with the report's standard, defective as it is, of usefulness to society. The first is that American society and the Western cultural heritage generally cannot be understood without reference to Christianity. English literature, for example, is full of references to the Bible and to Christian doctrine. The settlement and growth of our country, to take another example, would have been very different without the Reformation. How can anyone who is ignorant of the Christian contributions to Western civilization claim to be liberally educated?

The second respect in which radical separationism defeats the announced standard of usefulness to society concerns the matter of adjustment so dear to professional educators. As the secularists keep telling us, we live in a religiously pluralist society. A religiously pluralist society is one in which people of many different persuasions must live together in peace and concord, or else it will be more of a menagerie than a society. The strongest basis for peace and concord is mutual respect. Now mutual respect presupposes understanding, and understanding is partly an objective matter, which comes from being informed, and partly a subjective matter, which comes from appreciating how another person feels about his convictions because you know how you feel about yours. Mutual respect is not the product of ignorance, and neither does it thrive in an atmosphere of awkward silence and apologetic attitudes, which reduce communication to the level of noncontroversial platitudes.

Minority groups should not be compelled to accept religious convictions they do not share, but they should be acquainted with them. It is a real disservice to minority groups not to prepare them to understand and appreciate what they are going to have to live with for the rest of their lives. And a preparation which consists in the dehydrated presentation of "value systems" camouflaged as academic objectivity is an inadequate preparation. What minority groups will meet in adult life is not bloodless abstractions but full personally held convictions. The validity of this point is by no means limited to religion. It applies to political convictions just as well, for example. Moreover, it also applies to majority groups. How can majorities be expected to respect that which they have not been taught to know and to understand? The time to begin the acquisition of mutual respect based on knowledge and sympathetic understanding is in school, but it will not be acquired through an artificial antiseptic world of make-believe. If we continue to proceed on the general theory that stability is promoted by running away from controversy instead of learning to cope with controversy in a decent and civilized manner, instability is what we will get.

These two arguments against radical separationism, i.e., that a secular education is not complete and that maturity comes from learning how to handle controversial issues, can be supported by non-Christians as well as Christians. Jews, Unitarians, agnostics, Protestants, and Roman Catholics therefore all have a common interest in opposing a radical separationist interpretation of religious liberty as it relates to public education. But Christians should oppose it for deeper spiritual reasons.

Radical separationism means the progressive secularization of American life. We must not be misled by seemingly liberal statements that

"Ministers, priests, and rabbis should be free to speak in public schools" when there is a proviso that they must avoid the one thing which makes them what they are and in which they have specialized professional training. To invite a Roman Catholic priest or a Jewish rabbi to speak on his hobby of ornithology to a local high school and pretend that the invitation is a good example of religious liberty is "for the birds," as one might say under the circumstances. The invitation ignores the educational principle that speakers should be invited on the basis of their professional competence, and on that basis no minister, priest, or rabbi could speak in public schools if religion is taboo. The UPUSA Report recommends Bible reading in public schools only in connection with literature, history, or related courses.[135] This is to deny that the Bible has more than literary or historical value for purposes of education and invites Presbyterians to cultivate one attitude toward the Bible in church and another in school, a dualism which is good for neither church nor school. Even so, the authors of the report are less radical than the editor of *The Christian Century,* who rhetorically asks: "Is the Bible a talisman, a cabalistic charm?"[136] The editor might be surprised to be told that the Bible is something much better than a talisman or cabalistic charm, namely, that it is the word of God, the sword of the Spirit. Many people on the mission field and at home have been gripped and converted by its message without benefit of interpretation or comment, and they did not worry about which version they were reading.

If the authors of the UPUSA Report would press their radical separationism further, the religious consequences might be more apparent to them. They would have to eliminate any use of religious terminology and any reference to the Middle Ages or the Reformation lest someone should give a sectarian explanation. They would have to eliminate any reference to God lest some sensitive agnostic or atheistic child or parent be offended. History and literature would have to be expurgated lest "objectivity" be lost. Zoning regulations would have to be revised so that churches, like saloons, should not be located closer to a school than a prescribed distance lest the school be contaminated and lest, to use the words of *The Christian Century,* we fail "to push and to keep church and state forever apart."[137] We would have to deprive all parochial schools and denominational colleges of local government services because the court-approved child benefit theory is a subterfuge. State authorizations to denominational colleges to grant degrees would have to be withdrawn; transfer credits from parochial schools to public schools would have to be denied; federal and state scholarships to students and research grants to faculty people in church-controlled universities would have to be discontinued lest any of these things imply an establishment of religion. It is true that nobody, not even the POAU, advocates going to such absurd lengths. Nevertheless, these extremes have the merit of highlighting the logic of radical separationism and awakening us to how far in that direction we have already gone.

Radical separationism is not neutral, in spite of what the UPUSA Report and the Supreme Court may say. To ignore religion can be more damaging than to attack it frontally. Everyone knows that the curricula of our public schools contain whatever the public authorities consider important. If these authorities consider a subject essential (e.g., English, mathematics, science), they make it a requirement. If they think a subject is not essential but merely worth while (e.g., Latin, music, speech), they offer it on an optional basis. If religion is not offered on an optional basis, as it is not supposed to be under the McCollum decision, the natural inference will be that the public authorities do not consider religion important. Emphatic denials and loud protestations that religion is important but should be regarded as the exclusive function of the church cannot blot out the inference, because even if the protestations are sincere, the fact remains that religion is the only instance where an important subject has been proscribed. Almost anything else is and can be taught in public schools nowadays. Furthermore, radical separationism does not merely result in the exclusion of religion from the curriculum but colors the way in which other subjects are taught. Teachers and textbooks can slant courses in the direction of humanism, positivism, pragmatism, Freudianism, geographic determinism, cultural determinism, or economic determinism. The only interpretation that may not be offered, even as a live option, is a theistic interpretation. Radical separationism is not freedom of religion but discrimination against religion.

The results of radical separationism are not hard to find, for they are all around us. Our public schools are turning out a nation of religious illiterates, thousands of whom could not name the Four Gospels, to whom biblical allusions are meaningless, for whom the works of literary giants like Milton and Dante are unintelligible, and for whom church history and Christian doctrine do not exist. They are unacquainted with the Christian answers to the basic problems of existence which every man must somehow or other face, such as evil, suffering, life, and death. When they have vague spiritual yearnings and look for something more substantial than religion-in-general, they cannot communicate with one another because they have no vocabulary with which to do so. If they were dealing with a subject like physics or law, they would take it for granted that a specialized vocabulary is indispensable, and no professor would let them get by without subjecting them to the iron discipline of learning the technical terms. There is no understanding the Christian faith without such words as revelation, sin, salvation, grace, atonement, sanctification, and justification. At no point in the education of our young people from elementary school through the graduate school of a state university have they been taught these indispensable tools of Christian thought. Moreover, a totally secular education does more than promote ignorance of the facts of religion and eliminate religious conceptual tools: it robs its victims of a sense of reverence for spiritual realities and Divine Providence.

Out of the ensuing religious vacuum come moral confusion and relativism, political corruption and duplicity, low and elastic standards of personal conduct, juvenile delinquency, broken homes, uncertainty in the face of the fanatic dedication of extreme rightist and leftist groups, gullibility toward spurious ephemeral panaceas, an agonizing dearth of purpose and direction, a feeling of lostness and alienation. Out of this religious vacuum come a conformity born of personal weakness, the pathetic unfulfilled yearning to belong, the utter unwillingness to be a hero or a saint or to excel in any other way, piety without faith, and faith without content. Surely Christians have no right to be complacent about an education which nourishes and sustains so appalling a situation.

Christians must admit, of course, that the situation is also a reflection on the churches. The reach of the churches should be extended in range and depth, but let us remember that more than half of the population of the United States have little or no contact with any church and that the vast majority of our children go to public schools and state universities. Are these young people to be abandoned to a completely secular education? Are the churches going to let unpaid amateur teachers try to achieve in one hour of one day per week what paid professional teachers achieve in five full school days per week? Will church leaders continue to soothe their conscience with the belief that, somehow or other, public schoolteachers who are Christians will fill the religious vacuum by the surreptitious teaching of Christian ethics and transmit their Christian faith to their classes by osmosis? Can church leaders really do this kind of thing in good conscience when they think that teaching religion in public schools is unconstitutional and when they know that teachers who witness to their faith, even indirectly, run the risk of being fired?

The only large body of Christians who have faced these questions honestly are the Roman Catholics. The Roman Catholics have recognized the enormous seriousness of the threat of a secularized education and have tried to counter it by erecting an entire school system of their own. For this they have been and still are much criticized. They are accused of setting up a rival system which is un-American and which threatens the unity of the nation. What is even more important, they have been discriminated against financially by being required to bear the heavy burden of paying for two school systems. To say, as many of us Protestants do, that the burden was not imposed by public authority but voluntarily assumed by Roman Catholics does not excuse an obvious injustice. Considering the secularized education being given in the public schools, the Roman Catholics felt compelled by their religious faith to provide a different kind of education. For them, the free exercise of religion, which is supposed to be protected by the First Amendment, demanded this step. By taking this step, Roman Catholics lightened the tax burden of Protestants and Jews who would otherwise have had to pay for the educational cost of accommodating Roman Catholic children in public schools. And yet one hears no Protestant or Jewish voices demanding that Roman Catholics be compensated. There is no way to get around the fact that religion is the reason, and the sole reason, why Roman Catholics are required to pay for the maintenance of two school systems. If they were atheists or agnostics, they would be paying only once. Furthermore, when parochial schools teach English, science, mathematics, history, and foreign languages, they are fulfilling a public function which deserves some public support—unless one adopts the radical separationist view that anything related in any way to religion is fatally tainted.

The threat of secularism does not necessarily mean that Protestants should follow the Roman Catholic lead by erecting a system of Protestant parochial schools. For a long time—indeed, until the twentieth century —Protestants did not have to be concerned with secularism, because public school teaching was Christian in content and spirit, with a strongly Protestant flavor. The influx of Roman Catholics and Jews, not to mention the growth in numbers of religiously indifferent people, meant that the old solution could no longer be retained in its existing form without doing an unconstitutional—and un-Christian—violence to these large minority groups.

The most feasible, if not the best, solution would seem to be the inclusion of religion in public schools on an optional basis, with each major religious group supplying the teachers, on the condition that the teachers meet the same professional standards as other teachers. In other words, we are recommending that Protestants support "released time," the very system which the Supreme Court found unconstitutional in the McCollum case. The Supreme Court's decision in this case was bad constitutional history and bad law, and ways must be found to persuade the Supreme Court to reverse its espousal of radical separationism. But the Supreme Court is hardly likely to reverse itself unless Protestants also reverse themselves and shake off their sinful apathy before the threat of secularism. In the meantime, we should undertake to compensate Roman Catholics to an extent equal to the contribution they make through their parochial schools to the education of the American people. On this point, too, we would probably encounter constitutional road blocks erected by radical separationists.

There is no doubt that released time raises problems in a religiously pluralist nation even though it is designed to meet the needs of just such a nation. Christians would be made conscious of their minority status in Jewish parts of New York City and in Buddhist parts of Hawaii; Protestants would feel the same way in certain parts of Louisiana; and so would Roman Catholics in North Carolina. But adults feel these differences anyway, and the schools did not create them. Why should children not learn to face the facts of life early in school and be taught to respect one another's faiths? For a minority, whether religious or irreligious, to deny the majority the opportunity of learning about their own faith or faiths would not be religious liberty but minority dictation. So long as religious instruction is optional, it violates the rights of no one. There may be those who look upon the expression or recognition of any belief different from their own as an affront. If so, it is important that they be taught as early in life as possible the meaning of tolerance and good citizenship. The peace and concord so necessary to a religiously pluralist society are not to be had by appeasement.

Other solutions such as "dismissed time" and "shared time" have been suggested, and the former was upheld by a divided Supreme Court in the case of Zorach v. Clauson. But these are variants of a single constitutional casuistry imposed by radical separationism. Radical separationism is the basic obstacle, hence the severity of our criticism of the UPUSA Report. In particular, all Christians should protest vigorously against the Supreme Court's adoption of Jefferson's phrase "wall of separation." The very phrase is odious, suggesting the monstrous evil of the Berlin Wall, the futility of the Chinese Great Wall, the crippling damage done by the Iron Curtain and the Bamboo Curtain. If we Christians want a relevant symbol, we should remember what happened when Christ died on the Cross: the curtain in the Temple was ripped from top to bottom, thereby announcing to the world that no human authority, ecclesiastical or temporal, has the right to interpose any curtain or wall between God and man.

CHRISTIAN STABILITY

Objectionable as the phrase "separation of church and state" is from a Christian standpoint, it is very unlikely that anyone can succeed in dislodging it. The phrase is too favorably entrenched in usage. The best that one can hope to accomplish is to strip it of its radicalism and invest it with a more moderate content, true to the real intent of the founding fathers and consistent with the Christian's duty to witness.

As it happens, we already have something of a model in another constitutional use of the word "separation." The reference is to the separation of powers between the legislative, executive, and judicial branches of government. In the case of the relations between the branches of government as in that of the relations between church and state, the word "separation" does not appear anywhere in the Constitution, nor was it ever inserted there by way of amendment. The word was an unofficial extraconstitutional incrustation, a kind of shorthand reference to a relationship which the founding fathers intended to establish. In both cases we are dealing with usage. The difference is that, in the case of the three branches of government, the word "separation" never acquired the radical meaning which is being thrust upon it in the area of church and state relations. No one argued that the separation of powers created three governments which it is our duty "to push and to keep forever apart." The development of another extraconstitutional phrase, checks and balances, prevented any such nonsense from getting a foothold. No one ever doubted that we had three branches of *one* government.

The problem was the one so familiar to Protestants of maintaining unity in diversity, separateness without alienation, liberty without anarchy, authority without subjugation. The separation of powers was the founding fathers' solution to the problem of creating a national government that is strong but not despotic. The parallel with the separation of church and state is unmistakable. The objective was the same: to secure liberty under God. The method was the same: to erect a measure of separateness to be determined in the light of changing conditions and the common sense of future generations. The attitude was the same: to eschew the kind of radicalism which makes an absolute out of either separateness or unity to the exclusion of the other. In all this the founding fathers demonstrated a distinctively Christian realism, and it is this kind of realism which we must reintroduce in the area of church and state relations.

The main significance of the constitutional provisions on religion, from a Christian point of view, is that the freedom of the church is guaranteed—as much as constitutional provisions can guarantee anything. Some support of churches on a nondiscriminatory basis is not precluded, except from an untenable doctrinaire radical separationist position, but such support must not reach a point where churches exchange dependence on their members for dependence on government. Dependence on government has the effects which Edmund Randolph so clearly saw in the establishment of the Episcopal Church in colonial Virginia: lethargy on the part of the clergy and irresponsibility on the part of the laity. Public money comes from all parts of the population, from the unbeliever and the believer. To the unbeliever an injustice is done because he is required to support beliefs to which he does not subscribe, and this naturally makes him resentful and cynical. To the believer an injustice is also done because he suffers the loss of his sense of stewardship, i.e., the free and grateful response of one who is conscious of his blessings. In theory, the believer could still give over and above what the government has provided. In practice, however, he is not likely to do so. Why should he? The need of the church for support is not apparent, and his own need to give is forgotten. The general effect on all, believer and unbeliever, is to dissociate financial support from religious faith.

Wider and deeper consequences follow. The realization that all property is a trust from God to be used for his glory in accordance with the parable of the talents is replaced by a feeling that property is an absolute right under natural law. Calvinistic capitalism degenerates into materialistic capitalism. Philanthropy cannot thrive in an atmosphere where people do by legal compulsion what they should and would like to do of their own volition. The damage done to the public weal is immense. Just how immense the damage is becomes apparent when we consider the educational, scientific, cultural, and charitable achievements of philanthropy in the United States. The financial support of churches by their own members has been the foundation of a strong sense of the social, moral, and spiritual responsibilities of ownership both for the property which is retained for private management and for the property which is given away for philanthropic purposes. The contribution of financially self-supporting churches to the establishment of a responsible conception of property and the responsible use of money is so taken for granted that we scarcely notice it.

We become keenly aware of this contribution, however, when we move to other parts of the world where it does not exist, e.g., in Latin America where the Roman Catholic Church is state-supported, or endowed, or accustomed to charge for its services. The Protestant churches in Latin America are having a hard struggle teaching their members what it means to support a minister and a church program. National pastors, even in large well-to-do congregations, often have to supplement their incomes by engaging in other paid activities such as teaching. For example, Dr. Benjamin Moraes, the pastor of an influential Presbyterian church in Rio de Janeiro, continued to be professor of criminal law at the University of Rio de Janeiro even during the years when he served as Moderator of the Brazilian Presbyterian Church. Protestant schools and hospitals have been financed and managed by mission boards in the United States, and even when these institutions are transferred gratis to a national church, there is some question whether the sense of stewardship of the members is strong enough to keep these institutions going. Stewardship education is an arduous uphill fight which demands a radical reconstruction of popular attitudes toward material possessions and money, and the connection between this reconstruction and the political, social, and economic stability of Latin American countries is undeniable.

When the radical separationists argue for disestablishment because it promotes stability, they are right for the wrong reason. As we have seen, the reason is not that stability is promoted by the systematic avoidance of controversy. The real reason is that financial disestablishment brings about a situation in which the churches become training schools for the kind of attitude toward money which promotes stability in the most fundamental sense. But let us not slip into secularism by making stability the justification for disestablishment, for there can be situations as in the days of the ancient Hebrew prophets when the church must espouse the cause of revolution and therefore, at least temporarily, of instability. It is important that we understand that stability is not the objective but the by-product of Christian stewardship, i.e., one of those things which are added unto those who seek first the kingdom of God and its righteousness.

Separation of church and state also means that government should not impose any particular theology by law. The prohibition applies as fully to what one might call Christianity-in-general as it does to any specific denomination or church. James H. Smylie has pointed out that when the First Amendment was being formulated in Congress, the Senate rejected three motions which were aimed at prohibiting denominational favoritism and which might have been construed as permitting the establishment of Christianity-in-general.[138] The Senate version, before it was modified by the Conference Committee to the text which was to be adopted, did not imply that the United States was not or should not be a Christian nation. It merely said that Congress should make no *law* that would establish "articles of faith or a mode of worship," [139] and this is what the final version of the First Amendment also says in slightly less specific language. The accent is on the word "law." This meant that one, but only one, avenue of witnessing on the part of government was shut off.

There are good reasons why this particular avenue was closed to public authority. A law is binding on all citizens regardless of religious faith. To require by law assent to a particular theology and conformity to a particular liturgy is to divorce theology from faith and liturgy from worship. There is nothing Christian about such a requirement. Conversion, not compulsion, is the objective of Christian evangelism. But conversion which is not based on intellectual conviction honestly arrived at and surrender of self freely given is no conversion at all. A grave injustice is done to non-Christians, for they are provoked into unhealthy though justified resentment, seduced into falsehood by being encouraged to profess what they do not believe, and robbed of the experience which a genuine conversion brings. Damage is also done to Christians who are tempted to an evangelistic laziness induced by reliance on legal compulsion to do their work for them, diluted by a great influx of pseudo Christians into the churches, misrepresented in the eyes of non-Christians, and robbed of the spiritual growth which comes from communicating the gospel to others. The impact of Christian theology itself is weakened by the implication that Christian truth cannot stand on its own but needs the support of legal compulsion.

The attempt to enact the Christian faith into law introduces an element of rigidity in church life. There is already more than enough rigidity now. Rigidity would be harmful even if the theology involved were absolutely free of error because truth will not save men unless it is believed freely and for its own sake. But no theology is absolutely free of error. The visible churches are never completely faithful to their Lord. Elements of corruption creep in, and sometimes they pour in. However, it is preposterous to entrust to the President, the Congress, the Supreme Court, or the state legislatures the task of eradicating corruption from the churches, for if church leaders are fallible in matters of religion, government officials are even more so. Moreover, government intervention is not necessary. The Holy Spirit intervenes. He safeguards the church invisible by supporting, shattering, merging, dividing, and reforming the visible churches. When public authority tries to freeze theology into law, therefore, it is making the work of the Holy Spirit harder on us because religious dissent becomes political sedition. Thus, the work of the Holy Spirit will be accomplished regardless of political opposition, but the cost to human beings is much greater. One of the by-products of this presumptuous attempt to limit the freedom of the Holy Spirit is political instability. The framers of the Constitution and the First Amendment were right on Christian grounds, therefore, in excluding the establishment of even Christian theology by law.

It is important that we remember what is the real ground for the constitutional restriction that government shall not enact theology into law. That ground is the compulsory character of law, which is presumptuous and unjust. But the constitutional restriction certainly does not mean that other avenues for witnessing by government officials, individually and collectively, are closed. There are many other avenues left open which can and should be used, notably in the field of policy-making. Even the Southern Baptists, who are radical separationists, unwittingly concede this point when they strive to influence government policy on gambling and drinking. So do Unitarians, who are also radical separationists, when they fight against racial segregation. The Southern Baptists, Unitarians, and other religious groups of the radical separationist persuasion support and oppose government policies for reasons which are religious in character, and when they do this, they breech their own version of the principle of separation of church and state. Besides the realm of policy, there is also that of moral leadership on the part of government officials. We recognize this factor in Abraham Lincoln, who threw the entire weight of his presidential office and personal prestige on the side of forgiveness and reconstruction against the vindictiveness of Thaddeus Stevens and Charles Sumner; in Woodrow Wilson, who did the same for collective security against the irresponsible isolationism of the Senate Republicans. There are also less personalized forms of witnessing. Presidential Thanksgiving proclamations, public prayers, public celebration or acknowledgment of religious holidays, religious mottos on coins ("In God We Trust"), religiously slanted pledges of allegiance (this nation "under God"), religious sentiments in national anthems, public support of chaplains, tax exemption of churches, the exemption from military service of clergymen and conscientious objectors, the favor shown by voters to candidates who have a religious background, the granting of scholarships and research grants to church-controlled educational institutions—these are all legitimate forms of public witnessing to the judgment that the religious vitality of the people is in the national interest. That these forms will reflect the Christian religion is to be expected in a predominantly Christian country and does not constitute a legitimate grievance on the part of non-Christians. Religious liberty requires respect for the expression, public and private, of religious faith on the part of all groups, minority groups no less than majority groups.

The stability of the nation is enhanced by the diffusion of the Christian faith. Secular-minded people who are concerned with political corruption, conflicts of interest among officeholders, influence peddling, the need for courage in making political decisions, the importance of loyalty, and other moral problems of public life should therefore recognize the Christian foundation of morality, including constitutional morality. Conservatives who are worried about increasing government intervention in private life should be among the first to appreciate the relevance of Christianity because a great deal of government intervention (e.g., corrupt practices legislation) is aimed at remedying moral deficiencies. Liberals who are concerned with the unimaginative conformism of our people should see in the Christian faith the secret of continued renewal and growth which they so ardently look for in the wrong places. The transforming power of the Christian faith as it relates to ideas, institutions, and men is the greatest possible factor in creating the kind of national stability we want. Government has a vital stake in the success of the Miltonian idea that the church should carry out its political mission of making the people fittest to choose and the chosen fittest to govern.

One of the greatest tributes ever paid to the Christian foundation of national stability came from no less a figure than Benjamin Franklin. This tribute, scriptural in content and even in language, was all the more remarkable because it was given by a man who had not been an evangelical Christian. Perhaps it was a return by an octogenarian to the early Christian training of his youth, a return induced by his advanced age and occasioned by the most serious crisis which the Constitutional

Convention at Philadelphia had to live through. Speaking to his colleagues in the convention, Franklin said: "We have been assured, Sir, in the sacred writings, that 'except the Lord Build the House they labour in vain that build it.' I firmly believe this; and I also believe that without his concurring aid we shall succeed in this political building no better than the builders of Babel: We shall be divided by our little partial local interests; our projects will be confounded, and we ourselves shall become a reproach and bye word down to future ages." [140]

Chapter VIII

FAITH AND FUTURE

W E have seen that the problems of national survival and world peace cannot be solved by either the natural or the social sciences. On any scientific basis, the prognosis is extremely bad. The most that can be expected from the sciences is an indeterminate but limited time. We have also seen that Christianity outpromises any and all human ideologies, and we have indicated some of the ways in which the Christian faith can transform the concepts and institutions of political life. The transformations we have analyzed are undoubtedly not free of error and must necessarily remain incomplete because one transformation leads to another, and man must be satisfied to advance step by step. Nevertheless, the transformations we have analyzed, despite their imperfection and incompleteness, are sufficiently specific to be meaningful, to give us a sense of direction, and to provide the incentive for further work. It is to be hoped that other political scientists who are Christians will be challenged to push further and deeper the work of intellectual reconstruction in their field. It is equally necessary that the same kind of intellectual reconstruction be undertaken by other specialists such as economists, psychologists, jurists, and sociologists in their respective fields.

Moreover, the required intellectual reconstruction cannot succeed on a national basis alone. We live in an interdependent world where the survival of one nation depends on that of other nations. What Jesus said about marriage also applies to nations: "What therefore God hath joined together, let not man put asunder." [1] Modern science has brought the world to the point where even the secularist can understand why the Great Commission directed the disciples to go unto all nations. We are therefore brought to the conclusion that the world's best hope lies with two related movements: the layman's movement and the ecumenical movement. The first is important because what one might call "applied Christianity" is a matter which lies primarily within the competence of laymen. The second is important because world survival is an international problem, and the ecumenical movement is international. Isolationism, whose latest and most malignant form is the Iron Curtain, must be overcome so that we may do together what cannot be done separately.

Someone is sure to point out, however, that intellectual reconstruction is not enough. There is a serious problem of dynamics involved here with which we must deal. We are beset by indifference, distrust, and ill will. Is there a power great enough to overcome these obstacles and to fulfill, even in part, the promises of the Christian religion? There is. That power is faith. It is faith which carried Washington and his army through Valley Forge and the vicissitudes of the American Revolution. Faith gave Abraham Lincoln the strength to save the Union in spite of military reverses, the threat of British intervention, contempt, disloyalty, insubordination, jealousy. It was faith that steeled him against the wavering support of the North that put his reelection in doubt, the hatred of the South which he loved and from which he came, and a lack of sympathetic understanding that chilled even his own home. It was faith that saved the British army at Dunkirk and stopped Rommel at the gates of Alexandria. It was faith that led General de Gaulle to London and prompted him to utter the magnificent words: "France has lost a battle, but she has not lost the war!" If anyone doubts that it was faith that saved us from the Axis, let him consider the testimony of Pierre Laval at the trial of Marshal Pétain for treason. What did Laval say on that occasion? Substantially this: "What reasonable man in his senses would have thought in 1940 that Germany would not win the war?" Exactly. No one relying on reason could have thought anything else. Laval's question revealed the enormous distance that separates faith from sight. General de Gaulle walked by faith, and Pierre Laval walked by sight.

DEFINITION OF FAITH

Well then, what is faith? Common usage often treats it as a synonym for such words as opinion, belief, theory, dogma, and judgment, but there is something wrong with every one of these approximations. The words just do not fit. Faith is too certain to be opinion, too firmly and deeply held to be belief, too vital to be theory, too dynamic to be dogma, and too forceful to be judgment. Fortunately, there is in the Epistle to the Hebrews an exceptionally adequate and illuminating definition of faith which reads thus: "Now faith is the substance of things hoped for, the evidence of things not seen." [2] This definition contains four inter-related ideas which we shall analyze in the following sequence: (1) the things not seen, (2) the things hoped for, (3) evidence, and (4) substance.

The first idea refers to those things which are not visible to our physical eyes. They are the realities of the spirit and of the intellect, which are perceived inwardly. They are the substratum of the material and human world and the meaningful content of innumerable familiar words. Patriotism, democracy, economy, justice, truth, peace, and money are all words which catch portions of great realities and refract them, albeit incompletely and flickeringly, into the consciousness of man. They are the basis of the work of parliaments, cabinets, courts, business establishments, and all kinds of human institutions. Not a single one of these realities is material in itself, and it is partly for that reason that they are the subject of unceasing debates about their existence, continuing differences of opinion about their meaning, endemic struggles about their applications. We are apt to lose sight of this truth about them when we live in a society in which there is general agreement on those points, but if we scrutinize these realities closely with the eye of pure intellect alone, their existence becomes uncertain, and their meaning is suddenly very much open to doubt.

The best way to clarify the relationship between things seen and unseen is to take an example and pick it to pieces. Money is an especially appropriate selection for this purpose because we ordinarily take money so completely for granted and because it is for many people the quintessence of reality. They believe this so much that the pursuit of money-making is often described as "materialistic," and some people go so far as to say that "money talks." What is money? A five-dollar bill is no more than a promise by the United States of America to pay the bearer on demand the sum of five dollars. It is just an I.O.U. Money, therefore, is nonmaterial—*one of the things not seen.*

The second idea in our scriptural definition of faith, the things hoped for, adds a modifying note by injecting the notion of time into the discussion. True, the realities involved are timeless in their essence. Man can perceive them directly, though dimly and imperfectly, but he cannot use them until they have been translated into the world of time and space. The words "hoped for" indicate that man believes that these realities are capable of being so translated to an extent sufficient to alter the material universe. They belong to the category of spiritual realities-to-be. The beginnings of this translation are shrouded in mystery and are unknowable, but later steps are more intelligible.

Thus, a great composer brings a new sonata to a famous pianist. The sonata is the composer's creation in the literal sense of the word. There was nothing like it before he conceived it, but after that there was. When he wrote it down on paper, it was sufficiently translated into material reality (material-ized) to be intelligible to the pianist. If the pianist is a great professional musician, he will not need to play it in order to know it. As his practiced eye moves over the little black symbols on the music paper, he will hear the sonata and respond to the power of its crescendos, the grace of its arpeggios, the beauty of its melodies, the architectonic perfection of its whole construction. But this is only the beginning. Less trained musicians and untrained music lovers will need to have that sonata further material-ized in recitals and concerts. The air will carry it to millions of listeners in auditoriums and symphony halls, over the radio and television, and from phonograph records. It will be distributed to thousands of people by copies of the printed score. This sonata will inspire other composers to creative activity, become a source of income to its composer, its publisher, and its performers. It will give rise to copyrights, bookings, concert tours, bank accounts, and library collections. From its nonmaterial beginning it will be translated into sound, paper, wax, metallic rolls. Out of the creative and unfathomable depths of the man who conceived it, this intangible reality was ejected like a projectile which strikes the great pool of material reality and starts a series of ever widening and seemingly endless eddies. These eddies are the things that were hoped for.

Lest anyone should suppose that this is a purely artistic phenomenon, let us take another kind of example. Here stands that colossus of German history, Otto von Bismarck. Around him are the two great states of Austria and Prussia, middle-sized states like Bavaria and Saxony, and a multitude of petty principalities and little sovereignties, which are like the spatterings of the German nation over the face of Europe. Beyond this Germanic world stand proud and mighty states: the British Empire, the Second French Empire, the Russian Empire, the Turkish Empire. This is the world of the things that are (to a "realist," anyway). But there is also the world of the things hoped for: the German Reich of 1871. But this is 1856: Bismarck has just become Prime Minister of Prussia, and he is about to begin his great career on the stage of European-wide politics reserved for high-ranking statesmen. The German Reich is one of the things not seen, except very dimly by a few Pan-Germans. It is still a thing hoped for, which is locked in the man Bismarck and has not yet emerged far enough to protrude into the realm of political facts and cast its lengthening shadow over the peoples of Europe. Fifteen years roll by, and behold, there stands the Bismarckian Reich no longer hoped for but a thing accomplished! It is still a thing not seen by physical eyes, but millions of mental eyes are dazzled by it, and all Europe looks upon it as one of the most real and pregnant facts of practical politics.

We now come to the third idea in the scriptural definition of faith: evidence. Faith is the evidence of things not seen. How strange! When so many people are engrossed in trying to find evidence for faith and arguing about it, the thought never crosses their minds that faith is itself evidence. Perhaps we ought to look at it *de novo* with a fresh mind swept clean of the cobwebs spun by centuries of argumentation and cleared of the stale air left behind by generations of dead religiosity. Is it really so surprising that faith should be evidence? If faith is not, what other evidence could things not seen have? The trouble is that we are led astray without realizing it by the unspoken assumption that logical demonstration and evidence are the same thing, whereas logical demonstration is only one of several forms of evidence. Even this correction does not go far enough, however, because logical demonstration is not strictly speaking evidence at all but a conclusion drawn from the evidence, a method by which evidence is brought to bear directly on the problem at hand. This is true even in the rigorous field of mathematics. When a proposition is proved, the evidence is already contained in the proposition itself, and what mathematical reasoning does is to extricate the evidence and put it on exhibit. Evidence is experiential, not a form of ratiocination. It is proof that something invisible or difficult to see really does exist, a proof sufficiently informative to enable one to reconstruct that something's main characteristics.

Now, proceeding on a perfectly common-sense basis, what is the best evidence of things not seen? what men do, using the verb broadly to include thinking, speaking, and writing. The foreign policy of a Secretary of State is a thing not seen. The best evidence of that policy is the action he takes. Sometimes his speeches may be enough, but since they can also be very misleading, the surest way to reconstruct the policy is from his acts. The difference between a high official's words and his deeds is the degree to which each engages his responsibility and reputation, and the one which goes furthest in this direction is the best evidence of the policy (i.e., the thing not seen) and a revelation of that official's real faith.

A foreign policy in the true sense of a meaningful succession of deeds is a commitment. It engages the responsibility and reputation of the official who directed it and willy-nilly identifies him with it. To write a book is a commitment which may advance or detract from professional success, bring money or no money at all, embroil the author in controversies, and cause the author to be "tagged" with certain ideas or movements. When men part with their valuable goods and services in exchange for money, it is evident to them that the money is certainly money. Moreover, their acceptance makes that fact evident to others who see their faith in the paper bills and thereby actually tends to make these bills money. These commitments are evidence of things not seen and a meaningful indication of what they are. Things not seen are credible; their existence is evident; and their nature is intelligible when men are committed to them. When those who endorsed the American Declaration of Independence affirmed the existence of certain self-evident truths, they committed themselves to the hilt by pledging their "lives," their "fortunes," and their "sacred honor," and proved it by years of war and revolution followed by decades of successful government dedicated to these truths. It is a commitment of this kind which refutes those who say that there are no such truths and that they will not work as a basis of government. Commitments are outward manifestations of an inward process. The former are directly traceable to the latter, like the sparks and flames that leap from a blazing fire.

The inward and outward aspects of commitment are one single phenomenon: faith. "Shew me thy faith without thy works," said the apostle James, "and I will shew thee my faith by my works." [3] Jesus demanded sacrifices of his disciples before recognizing their discipleship, rejected expressly those who merely said "Lord, Lord," and warned everyone that he who would follow him must bear his own cross. Jesus wanted faith, not admiration, cheers, sympathy, approval, or interest. And what did he say to those faithful disciples when he sent them out to evangelize the world? He told them, significantly, to be his *witnesses*. The greatest evidence of something that a man can submit to the Court of Common Sense is to pledge his faith to that something in the exacting sense of full commitment.

There is another aspect of the idea of evidence which must be considered. Faith must be considered from an individual as well as a social viewpoint. What if the things not seen are not visible to the individual who is committed to them? In this case he does not have the kind of evidence he would ordinarily require before committing himself, probably because it is not possible for him to do so for the time being. And therein, says Scripture, man is justified because there would be no merit in being committed to something he can see for himself.

The fourth and last idea in our scriptural definition of faith is substance. Faith is the *substance* of things hoped for. This is perhaps the most truly magnificent idea of the four. Not the things hoped for, not the things which were perhaps not hoped for at all or which one would be opposed to having, but the substance of one's hopes is what is at stake. The composer's faith was the substance of his sonata; Bismarck's faith was the substance of his German Reich; the faith of the signers of our Declaration of Independence was the substance of America. This significant truth may explain why so many creative men lose interest in their creation as soon as it is made—sometimes even before it is completed. What material-ization with all its inevitable imperfections could compare with the ideal conception upon which it is modeled and the faith whence came the conception? What need do really great creative spirits have of the applause and rewards of men? If they did need to see their creations and gather the rewards of men, they would not be great and creative. They would be like the public-praying and ostentatious alms-giving Pharisees.

Putting together the four basic ideas in our scriptural definition of faith, we get a full and usable concept of the great driving power on which we must rely. We know that faith means full commitment, being a witness, the evidence that proves the existence and outlines the character of the things not seen with physical eyes or the eyes of unaided reason, the substance of things hoped for. It would be better to say that faith has something of prophecy in it than to characterize it as a preview of the future. Faith is not a kind of running ahead of schedule to peep at the things that lie several jumps hence. It is more on the order of an X ray which pierces the opaqueness of the present and penetrates through time to apprehend directly the realities of the spirit. Even this analogy is somewhat faulty because it overlooks the important fact that faith also creates the reality which it grasps across the barriers of time and space. The faith of today is the substance of the realities of tomorrow. We have to wait for the material embodiments. We do not have to wait for the substance. Quite simply: our faith is our future.

POLITICAL POWER OF FAITH

We have thus far analyzed the nature of all faith, but our analysis is incomplete because no attention has been paid to content. We can speak of faith-in-general for purposes of analysis only, and it is one of the fashionable misconceptions of our time to believe that you can side-step the question of faith in what and in whom. There is no such thing as faith in faith, despite what some of our most prominent citizens appear to think. Faith-in-general, i.e., faith without content, is an intellectually neutral force. It is impossible to say that it is true and equally impossible to say that it is false. Faith-in-general is also morally neutral. To release the power generated by faith is as dangerous as to release atomic power. In both cases, the release of power is a blessing or a curse according to the ends it is made to serve. One of the greatest difficulties we have to face is the fact that there are always people who hope for things that are evil and who base themselves on conceptions that are untrue.

However much we may be opposed to Hitler and what he represented, we have to admit that he too was a man of faith. His career shows it, and so does his book *Mein Kampf*. The trouble with him was certainly not that he lacked faith. On the contrary, he had an uncommon amount of it. All one has to do to realize this is to imagine the situation from Hitler's personal viewpoint during the short time he stayed in jail. He had very few friends, if it is proper so to designate persons who were willing to support him for their own purposes but who would not publicly admit that support. He had low-grade army connections, but so did many other rabble-rousers and agitators during that period. He benefited from the leniency of disloyal magistrates, but this leniency was very shabby encouragement at best because it was based on an unflattering and mistaken estimate of his harmlessness and insignificance. It was the condescending kind that one accords to a fool whose ineffective pranks are meant well, a fanatic whose occasionally damaging acts can be forgiven or overlooked because he is on the "right" side. Various attempts by historians to straighten out the record may cause certain revisions of detail here and there. They will not alter the basic facts.

Here was a man who had been caught red-handed in an evil and silly plot against the state, a man who had no citizenship, no education, no money, no steady employment, no dependable friends, no social prestige whatsoever. The Weimar Republic, which he hated and which blocked his ambition, had survived its painful beginnings and showed signs of growing strength. Improving economic conditions threatened to do away with or seriously diminish the mass discontent on which he had been counting. Relations with France and the former Allied Powers were due for improvement, and the Stresemann era was at hand. Hitler's party was definitely on the downgrade, and his own position as leader was far from secure or beyond the challenge of ruthless and unprincipled rivals. Could any situation look more unpromising than that? And yet, in spite of it all, this physically weak little corporal, this unknown Austrian house painter, this queer upstart with a shady ancestry who spoke ungrammatical German with the thick accent of a South German peasant became the Chancellor and dictator of the Reich in ten years' time, and in a little less than ten years more he was the absolute master of nearly all Europe and came horribly near to achieving world dominion! His unwavering faith in himself and his cause carried him over all obstacles from the lowest depths to the dizziest heights. Faith, even in the wrong thing, generates stupendous power, but the power may be for destruction and self-destruction. So it was in Hitler's case because evil and error marred the content of his faith. In real life, therefore, we cannot dissociate faith from content. Faith-in-general is a delusion which is all the more dangerous because it is so fashionable.

The definition of faith given in the Epistle to the Hebrews grew out of Christian experience and refers to faith in Christ. For the Christian, Christ is the content of faith. When the definition speaks of the things not seen, it refers to the realities of the kingdom of God, including the whole of the Christian ethic contained in the Sermon on the Mount. The living faith of Christians in all times and places is the evidence of these realities. If it were not for this faith, the realities would still exist because they inhere in the will of God, but there would be no evidence for them that the natural man could see. When the definition speaks of the substance of things hoped for, it means that Christ is that substance. The man Jesus of Nazareth was God incarnate, the living embodiment of the will of God, the new Adam who lived a life of perfect obedience inwardly and outwardly, the man in whom there was not the slightest discrepancy between what he preached and what he was. After his ascension, the man Jesus of Nazareth ceased to live as a single physical being but continued to live in his church, because to have faith in him is to possess his substance, and to possess his substance means to possess his mind and spirit and to have access to his resources. The Incarnation grew with multiplication and was no longer confined to any one particular individual, time, and place. Through the Christian faith, therefore, lies the possibility of the intellectual, moral, spiritual—and political—reconstruction of the world. In the Christian faith lies the secret of perpetual renewal and growth which overcomes the aging process afflicting individuals, cultures, and movements. Because Christ is the substance of the Christian faith, the usual human limitations no longer need apply, and the worst of demonic forces can be overcome. The transformation of the world through Christ is possible.

Will this transformation take place? Most of our contemporaries would answer in the negative. They are obsessed with the minority status of Christianity in a religiously pluralist world and with the magnitude of the forces of evil all around us. They point to the very nominal nature of much Christian affiliation and the shallowness of much church life, to the pervasive secularization of the West, to the renewed vitality of the non-Christian faiths in the East, to the aggressive dedication and ominous spread of the communist faith. The result is that they dismiss the claims of the Christian faith as futile and look for some form of escapism. The most fashionable form of escapism nowadays is existentialism.

Existentialism as a contemporary force was born of disillusionment over political and constitutional reform, disenchantment not only with all political ideologies but with all philosophical systems and even with objective scientific knowledge, gnawing doubts about the viability of free private enterprise or any other economic system, utter pessimism about the feasibility of international peace, disbelief in the vitality and power of the church as an institution and of the Christian faith as a religion. When a whole universe has thus crumbled into a heap of ruins, is it any wonder that what is left is lostness, brokenness, alienation, and anxiety? And so men fall back on the one thing which they believe can be salvaged from the wreckage: mere existence. The past is all washed up—except that no one can abolish the past. So we get de-mythologizing, mythologizing, re-mythologizing of history on a pick-and-choose basis by a "self" which is arbitrary because it has no moorings. The future is blotted out in the name of "the moment of decision" except that no one can really blot out the future. So we get spurious "eschatologies," which are a travesty of the scriptural conception. The present is presumably left, but it is a lonely and forlorn present because of existentialist subjectivism, except that such subjectivism is impossible. So we get a partial reintroduction of nonsubjective elements in the form of "I-It," "I-Me," and "I-Thou" relationships. Still, however, there are no "I-They" and much less "We-They" relationships, and every relationship starts with "I."

One can find a similar pessimism among many sincere Christians. Their pessimism is not due to an unhealthy fascination with the enormity of the obstacles which stand in the way of the reconstruction of the world in the spirit of Christ. What concerns them is the fact that the Christian faith is not something which we can earn, or buy, or borrow, or inherit. It is a gift of God which comes to some people and does not come to other people. Both Scripture and experience testify to this fact. We do not understand why, but intellectual honesty demands that we acknowledge the fact and confess our inability to perceive the reason or reasons for it. We are faced here with the unfathomable mystery of divine election. On this theological ground, therefore, some sincere Christians take their place among the defeatists. We may know, they say, whether we as individuals are saved because we know whether or not we have faith in Christ, but we cannot know whether other people have faith in Christ, and therefore it is impossible for us to say that the world will be transformed in the spirit of Christ. The transformation of the world depends on the will of God and not on the work of man.

The pessimism emanating from these secular and Christian sources may seem to be well grounded in both cases, but it is unjustified nonetheless. To the secularist we must point out that minority status is no fatal handicap, and the religious pluralism we face today is much less monumental than it was in the days of the apostle Paul. Religious pluralism is nothing new, however much some of our contemporaries may think so. If it did not discourage first-century Christians, there is even less reason why it should discourage twentieth-century Christians. To allow ourselves to be overly impressed with the mere weight of numbers is to underestimate the power of determined minorities. History demonstrates that all the great revolutionary movements have been the work of minorities, often very small minorities. The frightening spread of communism since the Bolshevik revolution of 1917, less than fifty years ago, illustrates the point only too well. Contemporary life likewise demonstrates daily the superior strength of small groups, even single individuals, as against lukewarm and inert numerical majorities. One man with faith can dominate a whole multitude of men without faith. Actually, the struggle between the faithful and the faithless is an unequal one, which the latter are bound to lose regardless of their numbers. Far more equally matched and more dangerous is the struggle with rival faiths. But even in this case the struggle continues to be unequal, provided there is a like intensity of faith on both sides. Where two or more rival faiths are defended with equal dedication, it is the truth and not the intensity of the faith which will provide the margin of victory. There is and always will be strength in being right. The Christian faith must win because of the divine nature of its substance, which is Christ himself. As the apostle Paul said: "If God be for us, who can be against us?" [4]

To the pessimism which one finds in some Christian circles because of the doctrine of election, there is an answer too. The doctrine of election is true, but the pessimists misapply it. It is incorrect to say that we do not know whether it is the will of God that the world be transformed, for to say so is to deny the kingdom of God which Christ came to inaugurate and establish. Neither is it correct to say that we cannot know whether or not other people have faith in Christ, except that it is not up to us to pass sentence on other people in the sense of presuming to assign them to heaven or hell. But we do know where the Christian faith flourishes because we can see the evidence of its transforming power in individual and national life. Christ himself gave us the test: "Wherefore by their fruits ye shall know them." [5] To any Christian who is well grounded in the Gospels and the Epistles, there is no difficulty in recognizing the fruits. Finally, while it is quite true that the Christian faith is the gift of God, which is withheld from some and granted to others on grounds we do not understand, it is also true that Christ promised to give it to those who ask for it. No one who has sincerely turned to Christ for help ever failed to receive it, although the help is not always the kind expected or wanted, and the timing is not necessarily convenient or of our own choosing. The promise is explicit: "Ask, and it shall be given unto you; seek, and ye shall find; knock, and it shall be opened unto you: For every one that asketh receiveth; and he that seeketh findeth; and to him that knocketh it shall be opened." [6] And the reason which Christ gave for making this promise was not that we deserve it but that God is our Father who loves his children and looks after them infinitely more wisely than we look after our own. Before we start bemoaning the need for faith to ask for faith, let us remember the case of the father who sought help for his son from Jesus. "If thou canst believe," said Jesus, "all things are possible for him that believeth." [7] To this demand for faith, the father replied: "Lord, I believe; help thou mine unbelief." [8] And that minimal amount of faith, that petition for faith, was enough. The son was cured.

The problem of our present-day world is the same as that which confronted the people of Israel many centuries ago. It is the problem of choice: "I have set before you life and death, blessing and cursing: therefore choose life, that both thou and thy seed may live." [9] The problem is the same, only the number of people involved and the scope of the choice are different. Among the competing faiths which fight for the possession of the world, we must choose one and take the consequences. Our faith is our future.

NOTES

CHAPTER I

1   Reinhold Niebuhr, *The Nature and Destiny of Man; A Christian Interpretation* ("Gifford Lectures," 1939; 2 vols. [New York, 1941–43]).
2   Edward Crankshaw, *Khrushchev's Russia* (Baltimore, 1959), 137.
3   *Ibid.*, 136.
4   Glenn Tinder, "Human Estrangement and the Failure of Political Imagination," *The Review of Politics,* XXI (October, 1959), 611–30.
5   *Ibid.*, 625.
6   René de Visme Williamson, "The Challenge of Political Relativism," *The Journal of Politics,* IX (May, 1947), 147–77, esp. 166–73.
7   Paul Tillich, *The Protestant Era* (Chicago, 1948), 246.
8   Philip E. Jacob, *Changing Values in College: An Exploratory Study of the Impact of College Teaching* (New York, 1957), 9.
9   Will Herberg, *Protestant-Catholic-Jew: An Essay in American Religious Sociology* (New York, 1955), 53–54.
10 Sheldon S. Wolin, *Politics and Vision: Continuity and Innovation in Western Political Thought* (Boston and Toronto, 1960), 430.
11 *Ibid.*, 434.
12 Herberg, *Protestant-Catholic-Jew,* 284–85.
13 William H. Whyte, *The Organization Man* (New York, 1956), 404.
14 David Riesman, *The Lonely Crowd: A Study of the Changing American Character* (New York, 1956), 37.
15 Friedrich Nietzsche, *Beyond Good and Evil,* in *The Philosophy of Nietzsche* (New York, 1937), 125.
16 *Ibid.*, 129.

CHAPTER II

1   Matt. 18:13. All biblical quotations are from the King James Version unless otherwise stated.
2   John 1:4.
3   *Ibid.*, 10:10.
4   *Ibid.*, 3:16.
5   Luke 4:18.
6   John 8:31–32.
7   Augustine, *The City of God,* trans. Marcus Dods (New York, 1950), 112.
8   Matt. 6:19.
9   Phil. 4:11.
10 *The Nicomachean Ethics of Aristotle* (New York, 1911), 42.
11 Phil. 2:5.

12 Luke 23:43.
13 I Pet. 2:9–10.
14 John 3:17.
15 Matt. 16:18.
16 *Ibid.,* 5:45.
17 Luke 23:34.
18 I John 4:19.
19 Matt. 28:18.
20 John 16:33.
21 Matt. 6:48.
22 *Ibid.,* 10:8.
23 Jas. 4:1–3.
24 John 14:27.
25 Phil. 4:7.
26 *The Prose Works of John Milton: with a Biographical Introduction by Rufus Wilmot Griswold* (2 vols.; Philadelphia, 1847), II, 491.
27 Augustine, *The City of God,* 11.
28 Mark 10:42–44.
29 John Calvin, *Institutes of the Christian Religion,* trans. John Allen (2 vols.; Philadelphia, n.d.), II, 314.
30 Luke 4:29–30.
31 Matt. 10:16.
32 *Ibid.,* 11:5–6.
33 John 16:12.
34 Philippe Maury, *Politics and Evangelism* (New York, 1959).
35 *Ibid.,* 36.
36 *Ibid.,* 35, 36.
37 Paul Tillich, *The Dynamics of Faith* (New York, 1957), 18.
38 Tillich, *The New Being* (New York, 1955), 99–100.
39 Tillich, *The Protestant Era* (Chicago, 1948), 203.
40 Karl Barth, *Community, State, and Church,* (Garden City, N.Y., 1960), 151.
41 *Ibid.,* 160.
42 *Ibid.,* 156.
43 *Ibid.,* 181.
44 *Ibid.*
45 I John 4:18.
46 Rom. 14:23.
47 Matt. 28:30.
48 John 17:15.
49 Niebuhr, *The Nature and Destiny of Man,* II, 211.
50 Maury, *Politics and Evangelism,* 93, 94.
51 William Muehl, *Politics for Christians* (New York, 1956).
52 Alden D. Kelley, *Christianity and Political Responsibility* (Philadelphia, 1961).
53 *Ibid.,* 204.
54 Matt. 6:10. Emphasis supplied.
55 *Ibid.,* 6:33.
56 *Ibid.,* 7:7.
57 *Ibid.,* 10:19–20.

CHAPTER III

1 Wolin, *Politics and Vision,* 43.
2 II Cor. 3:17.
3 John 14:6.
4 Rom. 13:5.

5   *Ibid.*, 13:4.
6   John 9:11.
7   Calvin, *Institutes*, II, 772.
8   *Ibid.*, 774.
9   Rom. 14:23.
10 Stephen Cullen Carpenter, *Select American Speeches, Forensic and Parliamentary, with Prefatory Remarks: Being a Sequel to Dr. Chapman's 'Select Speeches'* (2 vols.; Philadelphia, 1815), I, 47.
11 Edmund Burke, *Thoughts on the Cause of the Present Discontents*, in *Masters of Political Thought*, ed. Edward McChesney Sait (4 vols.; New York, 1947), II, 341.
12 For an impressive and convincing, though somewhat overdrawn, case for a nationalist and centralist interpretation of the Constitution, see the monumental work of W. W. Crosskey, *Politics and the Constitution in the History of the United States* (2 vols.; Chicago, 1953).
13 John 11:50.
14 Luke 23:34.
15 John 3:4.
16 Rev. 21:5.
17 Rom. 12:2.
18 Edmund Burke, *Reflections on the French Revolution* in *The Harvard Classics* (50 vols.; New York, 1909–10), XXIV, 187–88.
19 Speech before the Italian Chamber of Deputies on May 26, 1927, quoted in Benito Mussolini, *Fascism; Doctrine and Institutions* (Rome, 1935), 40.
20 *The Desk Standard Dictionary of the English Language* (New York and London, 1944), 704.
21 See Chap. XXII, Pt. II, of Thomas Hobbes, *Leviathan* (New York, 1914).
22 *Ibid.*, 180.
23 Rom. 12:18.
24 Exod. 20:3.
25 Matt. 6:13.
26 John Milton, *A Defence of the People of England in Answer to Salmasius's Defence of the King*, in *The Prose Works of John Milton*, II, 41.
27 Martin Niemoeller, *God Is My Fuehrer* (New York, 1941).
28 Calvin, *Institutes*, II, 752.
29 Niemoeller, *God Is My Fuehrer*, 49.
30 Gen. 4:9.
31 Matt. 6:12.
32 Rom. 15:1.
33 *Ibid.*, 13:4.
34 John 3:19–20. Emphasis supplied.

CHAPTER IV

1   See Nicolás Perez Serrano, *La Constitución Española (9 Diciembre 1931): Antecedentes, Texto, Commentarios* (Madrid, 1932).
2   Augustine, *The City of God*, 112.
3   *Ibid.*, 699.
4   *Ibid.*
5   *Ibid.*, 706.
6   *Ibid.*, 163.
7   *Ibid.*, 166.
8   I Tim. 6:10.
9   Charles Louis de Montesquieu, *The Spirit of the Laws*, in *Masters of Political Thought*, ed. Sait, II, 228.
10 Fourteenth Amendment, Sec. 1.

11 Lawrence Dennis, *The Coming American Fascism* (New York and London, 1936), 152.
12 K. N. Llewellyn, *The Bramble Bush* (New York, 1930), 3.
13 *Ibid.*, 5.
14 Thurman Arnold, *The Symbols of Government* (New Haven, 1935), 56.
15 *Ibid.*, 173. Emphasis supplied.
16 Dennis, *The Coming American Fascism*, 13.
17 II Tim. 3:16–17.
18 Deut. 30:11–14.
19 Ps. 19:7–8.
20 Prov. 6:22–23.
21 Acts 17:11.
22 *The Confession of Faith of the Presbyterian Church in the United States*, Chap. I, Sec. IV.
23 Calvin, *Institutes*, I, 87.
24 *Ibid.*, 90.
25 Milton, *Of the Reformation in England*, in *The Prose Works of John Milton*, I, 14–15.
26 *The Confession of Faith*, Chap. I, Sec. IX.
27 For an excellent discussion of the futility of this idea, see Robert J. Steamer, "Statesmanship and Craftsmanship: Current Conflict over the Supreme Court," *Western Political Quarterly*, XI (June, 1958), 265–77.
28 Exod. 19:7–8.
29 John Winthrop, *'Little Speech' on Liberty* in *Free Government in the Making: Readings in American Political Thought*, ed. Alpheus Thomas Mason (New York, 1949), 61.
30 *Ibid.*
31 *Ibid.*
32 *Ibid.*
33 Carl J. Friedrich, *Constitutional Government and Politics: Nature and Development* (New York, 1937), 103.
34 Randolph G. Adams, *Selected Political Essays of James Wilson* (New York, 1930), 255–56.
35 *Ibid.*, 298.
36 *Ibid.*, 299.
37 *Ibid.*, 342.
38 Luke 2:14.
39 Adams, *Selected Political Essays of James Wilson*, 256.
40 *Collections of the New-York Historical Society, for the Year 1821* (3 vols.; New York, 1821), III, 34.
41 See Mason, *Readings in American Political Thought*, 537–38.
42 Carpenter, *Select American Speeches*, 471.
43 Rom. 7:24.
44 II Chron. 34:19.
45 *Ibid.*, 34:21.
46 *Ibid.*, 34:30.
47 II Cor. 3:6.
48 Deut. 30:19–20.
49 Eccles. 1:14.

CHAPTER V

1 For a discussion of the reasons why the framers of the Constitution did not include a full Bill of Rights in the original document, see René de Visme Williamson, "Political Process or Judicial Process: The Bill of Rights and the

Framers of the Constitution," *The Journal of Politics*, XXIII (May, 1961), 199–211.

2 Walter F. Berns, *Freedom, Virtue and the First Amendment* (Baton Rouge, 1957), 233.

3 John Locke, *Of Civil Government* (London, n.d.), 142, 143. Emphasis supplied.

4 Jean Jacques Rousseau, *The Social Contract* (London, 1927), 6. Emphasis supplied.

5 Note the like reasoning in Locke: "But though these are ties upon mankind which make the conjugal bond more firm and lasting in a man than the other species of animals, yet it would give one reason to inquire why this compact, where procreation and education are secured and inheritance taken care of, may not be made determinable, either by consent, or at a certain time, or upon certain conditions, as well as any other voluntary compacts, there being no necessity, in the nature of the thing, nor to the ends of it, that it should always be for life—I mean to such as are under no restraint of any positive law which ordains all such contracts to be perpetual." John Locke, *Of Civil Government*, 156.

6 Ralph Waldo Emerson, *Politics*, in *The Complete Writings of Ralph Waldo Emerson* (New York, 1929), 302–03.

7 Thomas Paine, *The Rights of Man* (London, 1935), 223.

8 Rousseau, *The Social Contract*, 18. Emphasis supplied.

9 *Ibid.*, 26.

10 Wolin, *Politics and Vision*, 348.

11 Rousseau, *The Social Contract*, 15.

12 Locke, *Of Civil Government*, 145. What a comfort it must be to know that reason and liberty are automatically guaranteed by the simple process of growing old!

13 Paine, *The Rights of Man*, 148.

14 Emerson, *The Over-Soul*, in *The Complete Writings of Ralph Waldo Emerson*, 207.

15 Paine, *The Rights of Man*, 282–83. Emphasis supplied.

16 John Stuart Mill, *Essay on Liberty*, in *Utilitarianism, Liberty, and Representative Government* (London, 1929), 117.

17 *Ibid.*, 124–25.

18 Emerson, *Self-Reliance*, in *The Complete Writings of Ralph Waldo Emerson*, 139.

19 "Justice Black and First Amendment 'Absolutes': A Public Interview," *New York University Law Review*, XXXVII (June, 1962), 549–63.

20 *Ibid.*, 562.

21 *Ibid.*, 553.

22 Hugo L. Black, "The Bill of Rights," *New York University Law Review*, XXXV (April, 1960), 865–81.

23 "Justice Black and First Amendment 'Absolutes': A Public Interview," 559.

24 *Ibid.*, 557.

25 *Ibid.*, 555.

26 *Ibid.*, 559.

27 *Ibid.*, 558–59.

28 *Ibid.*, 562. Emphasis supplied.

29 *Ibid.* Emphasis supplied.

30 *Ibid.*

31 Berns, *Freedom, Virtue and the First Amendment*, 72.

32 Thomas Hobbes, *Leviathan* (London, 1928).

33 *Ibid.*, 5.

34 *Ibid.*, 18.

35 *Ibid.*, 21.

36 *Ibid.*, 23.

37 *Ibid.,* 21.
38 *Ibid.,* 49.
39 *Ibid.*
40 *Ibid.,* 43.
41 *Ibid.,* 44.
42 *Ibid.,* 63.
43 *Ibid.,* 64.
44 *Ibid.,* 65.
45 *Ibid.,* 54.
46 *Ibid.,* 54–55.
47 *Ibid.,* 66.
48 *Ibid.,* 83.
49 *Ibid.,* 322.
50 *Ibid.,* 222.
51 *Ibid.,* 140.
52 *Ibid.,* 130.
53 *Ibid.,* 140.
54 *Ibid.,* 93.
55 *Ibid.,* 65.
56 *Ibid.,* 110.
57 *Ibid.,* 112.
58 *Ibid.,* 114.
59 Gen. 1:26–27.
60 *Ibid.,* 2:7.
61 *Ibid.,* 1:31.
62 John 1:4.
63 II Cor. 6:16.
64 Rom. 12:1.
65 I Cor. 15:14.
66 Ps. 8:5.
67 Milton, *A Defence of the People of England,* in *The Prose Works of John Milton,* II, 39–40.
68 Gen. 3:5.
69 *Ibid.,* 3:6.
70 *Ibid.,* 3:4.
71 *Ibid.,* 3:7.
72 *Ibid.,* 3:8.
73 *Ibid.,* 3:12.
74 *Ibid.,* 4:14.
75 Calvin, *Institutes,* I, 274.
76 Rom. 3:10.
77 I Cor. 2:14.
78 John 3:16.
79 Martin Luther, *Commentary on Galatians,* in *Martin Luther: Selections from his Writings and with an Introduction,* ed. John Dillenberger (Garden City, N.Y., 1961), 130–31.
80 Matt. 5:16.
81 John Courtney Murray, S. J., *We Hold These Truths: Catholic Reflections on the American Proposition* (New York, 1960), 298.
82 *Ibid.,* 109.
83 *Ibid.*
84 *Ibid.*
85 *Ibid.,* 110.
86 *Ibid.*
87 *Ibid.*
88 *Ibid.,* 111.
89 *Ibid.*

90 *Ibid.,* 335.
91 *Ibid.,* 297.
92 *Ibid.,* 328.
93 *Ibid.,* 330.
94 *Ibid.,* 296.
95 *Ibid.,* 296, 297.
96 *Ibid.,* 298.
97 *Ibid.,* 17.
98 Karl Barth, *The Epistle to the Romans,* trans. Edwyn C. Hoskins (London, 1933), 35.
99 Barth, *Community, State, and Church* (Garden City, N.Y., 1960), 163–64.
100 *Ibid.,* 165.
101 Rom. 2:14–15. John Bertram Phillips (trans.), *The New Testament in Modern English* (London, 1958).
102 Matt. 15:9.
103 Eph. 6:17.
104 Calvin, *Institutes,* I, 83.
105 *Ibid.,* 63.
106 *Ibid.,* 296.
107 *Ibid.,* 297.
108 *Ibid.,* 296.
109 Martin Luther, *Secular Authority: To What Extent It Should Be Obeyed,* in Dillenberger, *Martin Luther,* 401.
110 Luther, *An Appeal to the Ruling Class of German Nationality as to the Amelioration of the State of Christendom,* in Dillenberger, *Martin Luther,* 473.
111 Calvin, *Institutes,* II, 789.
112 Heinrich Emil Brunner, *Justice and the Social Order,* trans. Mary Hottinger (New York and London, 1945), 8.
113 John Courtney Murray, *We Hold These Truths,* 17.
114 H. Richard Niebuhr, *Christ and Culture* (New York, 1951), 14.
115 Brunner, *Christianity and Civilisation,* ("Gifford Lectures," 1947–48, 2 vols. [London, 1948–55]), I, 24.
116 Gen. 2:15.
117 *Ibid.,* 1:28.
118 *Ibid.,* 2:17.
119 Barth, *The Epistle to the Romans,* 167.
120 Calvin, *Institutes,* II, 789.
121 Montesquieu, *The Spirit of the Laws,* in Sait, *Masters of Political Thought,* II, 228.
122 Brunner, *Justice and the Social Order,* 39.
123 II Cor. 3:17.
124 Philemon 1:15 (J. B. Phillips trans.).
125 II Cor. 9:7.
126 Matt. 6:33.
127 See Calvin, *Institutes,* II, Book IV, Chap. XX.
128 Letter of April 28, 1786, of John Dickinson to George Read, in William Thompson Read, *Life and Correspondence of George Read, A Signer of the Declaration of Independence with Notices of Some of His Contemporaries* (Philadelphia, 1870), 412. Such a statement is all the more remarkable because John Dickinson was a Quaker, and the Quakers were one of the most persecuted sects in colonial times.
129 Brunner, *Justice and the Social Order,* 108. Emphasis supplied.
130 Paul Leicester Ford (ed.), *Essays on the Constitution of the United States Published During Its Discussion by the People, 1787–1788* (Brooklyn, N.Y., 1892), 149. Emphasis supplied.
131 Luther, *Secular Authority,* in Dillenberger, *Martin Luther,* 389.

132 Matt. 15:18.
133 John Stuart Mill, *Essay on Liberty,* in *Utilitarianism, Liberty, and Representative Government,* 138.
134 Phil. 4:13.

CHAPTER VI

1 Acts 16:37.
2 *Ibid.,* 25:11.
3 Matt. 4:17.
4 *Ibid.,* 6:9.
5 *Ibid.,* 6:33.
6 John 18:36.
7 Luke 17:21.
8 Walter Rauschenbusch, *A Theology for the Social Gospel* (New York and Nashville, 1917), 131.
9 *Ibid.,* 132.
10 *Ibid.,* 137.
11 I Pet. 2:9–10.
12 I Sam. 8:7. Emphasis supplied.
13 Calvin, *Institutes,* II, 778.
14 Mark 10:42–44.
15 *The Confession of Faith of the Presbyterian Church in the United States,* Chap. XXVII, par. vi.
16 Acts 2:47.
17 *Ibid.,* 2:7.
18 *Ibid.,* 2:13.
19 I Cor. 1:26–29.
20 John 20:29.
21 *The Westminster Larger Catechism,* Q. 45.
22 Eph. 2:19. Emphasis supplied.
23 John 3:3.
24 Augustine, *The City of God,* 166.
25 John 3:5.
26 Acts 2:38.
27 II Cor. 5:17.
28 Rom. 14:22.
29 I Cor. 9:22.
30 Eph. 4:14.
31 Phil. 4:12.
32 Matt. 5:42.
33 *Ibid.,* 5:23–24.
34 Gen. 2:18.
35 I Pet. 2:9.
36 Rev. 21:5.
37 Luther, *Freedom of the Christian,* in Dillenberger, *Martin Luther,* 80.
38 *Ibid.,* 76.
39 Calvin, *Institutes,* I, 758–59.
40 Augustine, *The City of God,* 696. Emphasis supplied.
41 Luther, *Freedom of the Christian,* in Dillenberger, *Martin Luther,* 53.
42 *Speeches at Mr. Burke's Arrival at Bristol, and at the Conclusion of the Poll, 1774,* in *The Works of the Right Honourable Edmund Burke* (8 vols.; London, 1855–64), I, 446–47. The italics are Burke's.
43 For a detailed analysis, see René de Visme Williamson, "The Fascist Concept of Representation," *The Journal of Politics,* III (February, 1941), 29–41.

44 Hobbes, *Leviathan,* 85.
45 Rom. 8:26.
46 *The Federalist* (New York, 1937), No. 27, p. 167.
47 Edmund Randolph, in Carpenter, *Select American Speeches,* I, 82.
48 James Wilson, *Of the Law of Nations,* in Adams, *Selected Political Essays of James Wilson,* 308.
49 *Ibid.,* 309.
50 Quoted in Roger Sherman Boardman, *Roger Sherman: Signer and Statesman* (Philadedphia, 1938), 296.
51 Quoted in Paul Leicester Ford (ed.), *Life and Writings of John Dickinson* (Philadelphia, 1895), II, 48–49. The italics are Dickinson's.
52 Rousseau, *The Social Contract,* 36.
53 Matt. 20:28.
54 Mark 10:44.
55 Matt. 7:21.
56 *Ibid.,* 25:40.
57 T. V. Smith, *The Legislative Way of Life* ("Green Foundation Lectures" [Chicago, 1940]), ix.
58 *Ibid.,* 54–55.
59 Luther, *Freedom of the Christian,* in Dillenberger, *Martin Luther,* 81.
60 Milton, *The Ready and Easy Way to Establish a Free Commonwealth,* in *The Prose Works of John Milton,* II, 183.

CHAPTER VII

1 Anson Phelps Stokes, *Church and State in the United States; Historical Development and Contemporary Problems of Religious Freedom under the Constitution* (3 vols.; New York, 1950).
2 Loren T. Beth, *The American Theory of Church and State* (Gainesville, 1958).
3 "Prayers, Bibles and Schools," *The Christian Century,* LXXIX (October 24, 1962), 1279.
4 This is also the opinion of Loren Beth: "The value of the separtion principle, however, is that it reduces the area of conflict between the political and the religious, and thus reduces also the number of conflicts. It cannot eliminate conflict, but it can minimize it. From the political viewpoint such conflicts *should* be minimized, because they may arouse passions which will threaten political stability." Beth, *The American Theory of Church and State,* 83.
5 "Prayers, Bibles and Schools," *The Christian Century,* LXXIX (October 24, 1962), 1280.
6 Quoted in Sanford H. Cobb, *The Rise of Religious Liberty in America: A History* (New York, 1902), 505.
7 Thomas Benton Hart (comp.), *Abridgment of the Debates of Congress, from 1789 to 1856* (16 vols.; New York, 1857–63), I, 137.
8 Gaillard Hunt and James Brown Scott (eds.), *The Debates in the Federal Convention of 1787 Which Framed the Constitution of the United States of America Reported by James Madison* (New York, 1920), 557.
9 *Abridgment of the Debates of Congress from 1789 to 1856,* I, 137.
10 *Ibid.,* 138. Emphasis supplied.
11 *Ibid.* Emphasis supplied.
12 "By brief grouping of them it appears, that in only two out of thirteen was full and perfect freedom conceded by law. These were Rhode Island and Virginia. Six of the states, viz., New Hampshire, Connecticut, New Jersey, the two Carolinas, and Georgia insisted on Protestantism. Two were content with the Christian religion, Delaware and Maryland. Four, Pennsylvania,

Delaware, and the Carolinas, required assent to the divine inspiration of the Bible. Two, Pennsylvania and South Carolina, demanded a belief in heaven and hell. Three, New York, Maryland, and South Carolina, excluded ministers from civil office. Two, Pennsylvania and South Carolina, emphasized belief in one eternal God. One, Delaware, required assent to the doctrine of the Trinity. And five, New Hampshire, Massachusetts, Connecticut, Maryland, and South Carolina, adhered to a religious establishment." Cobb, *The Rise of Religious Liberty in America: A History*, 507.

13 *Abridgment of the Debates of Congress from 1789 to 1856*, I, 138.
14 Stokes, *Church and State in the United States*, I, 544.
15 Mark DeWolfe Howe, *Problems of Religious Liberty*, in *Nomos IV: Liberty*, ed. C. J. Friedrich (New York, 1962), 270.
16 Stokes, *Church and State in the United States*, I, 516.
17 *Ibid.*, 517.
18 Murray, *We Hold These Truths*, 56–69.
19 Quoted in Stokes, *Church and State in the United States*, I, 497.
20 *Ibid.*, 498.
21 *Dictionary of American Biography*, ed. Allen Johnson (22 vols.; New York, 1928–58), XVIII, 145.
22 Charles R. King (ed.), *The Life and Correspondence of Rufus King Comprising His Letters, Private and Official, His Public Documents, and His Speeches* (6 vols.; New York, 1894–1900), VI, 681, 682.
23 *Ibid.*, 29.
24 *Dictionary of American Biography*, III, 2.
25 Theodore Sedgwick, Jr., *A Memoir of the Life of William Livingston* (New York, 1833), 86, 87.
26 Quoted in Harold Wesley Thatcher, *The Social Philosophy of William Livingston* (Private edition distributed by the University of Chicago Libraries; Chicago, 1938), 290.
27 Charles J. Stille, *The Life and Times of John Dickinson, 1732–1808* (Philadelphia, 1891), 239, 327, 329.
28 *Dictionary of American Biography*, VI, 445.
29 *Ibid.*, II, 40.
30 Letter of April 15, 1769, quoted in William Thompson Read, *Life and Correspondence of George Read, A Signer of the Declaration of Independence with Notices of Some of His Contemporaries* (Philadelphia, 1870), 36.
31 Letter of December 18, 1787, to Sarah Cantwell, in Read, *Life and Correspondence of George Read*, 460.
32 Moncure Daniel Conway, *Omitted Chapters of History in the Life and Papers of Edmund Randolph, Governor of Virginia, First Attorney-General, United States Secretary of State* (New York, 1888), 157.
33 *Ibid.*, 156.
34 *Ibid.*, 389.
35 David Hosack, *Biographical Memoir*, in *Collections of the New-York Historical Society for the Year 1821*, III, 135
36 *Ibid.*, 135.
37 *Dictionary of American Biography*, XIV, 616.
38 *Ibid.*, VI, 352.
39 Henry C. White, *Abraham Baldwin* (Athens, Ga., 1926), 19.
40 *Ibid.*
41 *Ibid.*, 31.
42 *Ibid.*, 35.
43 Read, *Life and Correspondence of George Read*, 187.
44 *Dictionary of American Biography*, XII, 334.
45 Quoted from the language of the bill by White, *Abraham Baldwin*, 89.
46 *Ibid.*, 89.
47 Ford, *Essays on the Constitution of the United States*, 21, 34.

48 Letter to George Read of April 28, 1786, in Read, *Life and Correspondence of George Read,* 412.
49 Letter of May 28, 1785, to Elbridge Gerry, in King, *The Life and Correspondence of Rufus King,* I, 95.
50 *Ibid.*
51 Letter of July 19, 1798, to Colonel Pickering, in King, *The Life and Correspondence of Rufus King,* II, 371.
52 Conway, *Omitted Chapters of History in the Life and Papers of Edmund Randolph,* 157.
53 Max Farrand (ed.), *The Records of the Federal Convention of 1787* (4 vols.; New Haven, 1911–37), III, 310.
54 Thatcher, *The Social Philosophy of William Livingston,* 2.
55 Sedgwick, *A Memoir of the Life of William Livingston,* 86.
56 Letter of May 29, 1778, to the Rev. Mr. John Mason, in Sedgwick, *A Memoir of the Life of William Livingston,* 289, 290.
57 Lawrence Shaw Mayo, *John Langdon of New Hampshire* (Concord, N.H., 1937), 285.
58 See Ralph Edward Bailey, *An American Colossus: The Singular Career of Alexander Hamilton* (Boston, 1933).
59 Letter of September 1825 of William Steele to Jonathan D. Steele which purports to be "as nearly as I can recollect, in the words of General Jonathan Dayton," in Max Farrand, *The Records of the Federal Convention of 1787,* III, 471, 472. In justice to Hamilton, it should be pointed out that Madison denied the authenticity of the story. On the other hand, Madison's denials were made late in life and do not harmonize with the account he gave earlier in his convention notes.
60 See Kate Mason Rowland, *The Life of George Mason, 1725–1792* (New York, 1892).
61 Oscar L. Shewmake, *The Honorable George Wythe, Teacher, Lawyer, Jurist, Statesman,* (Williamsburg, Va., 1921), 15
62 L. S. Herrink, "George Wythe," *The John P. Branch Historical Papers of Randolph-Macon College,* II, No. 4 (June, 1912), 285, 307, 308.
63 Blackwell P. Robinson, *William R. Davie* (Chapel Hill, 1957), 19.
64 J. G. de Roulhac Hamilton, "William Richardson Davie: A Memoir," *James Sprunt Historical Monograph No. 7* (Chapel Hill, 1907), 5.
65 Quoted in Robinson, *William R. Davie,* 260.
66 Letter of January 25, 1780, from Thomas Hart to William Blount, in Alice Barnwell Keith (ed.), *The John Gray Blount Papers* (Raleigh, 1952), I, 8–9.
67 Quoted in Henry P. Goddard, "Luther Martin: the 'Federal Bull-Dog,'" *Maryland Historical Society Fund Publication* (Baltimore, 1887), No. 24, p. 38.
68 *Ibid.*
69 *Ibid.*
70 "The Genuine Information," in Robert Yates, *Secret Proceedings of the Convention Assembled at Philadelphia in the Year 1787, for the Purpose of Forming the Constitution of the United States* (Albany, N.Y., 1821), 87.
71 Richard H. Barry, *Mr. Rutledge of South Carolina* (New York, 1942), 145, 368.
72 Hunt and Scott, *The Debates of the Federal Convention of 1787,* 442.
73 George C. Groce, Jr., *William Samuel Johnson: A Maker of the Constitution* (New York, 1937), 5.
74 *Ibid.,* 15.
75 *Ibid.,* 84.
76 Roger Sherman Boardman, *Roger Sherman: Signer and Statesman* (Philadelphia, 1938), 72.
77 *Ibid.,* 319.
78 *Ibid.,* 103.

79   Lewis Henry Boutell, *The Life of Roger Sherman* (Chicago, 1896), 217, 218.
80   Quoted in King, *The Life and Correspondence of Rufus King*, I, 420.
81   William Garrott Brown, *The Life of Oliver Ellsworth* (New York, 1905), 20, 21.
82   *Ibid.*, 328.
83   *Ibid.*, 330, 331.
84   "A Landholder, III," in Ford, *Essays on the Constitution of the United States*, 170, 171.
85   *Ibid.*, 169.
86   *Ibid.*, 171.
87   *Letters and Other Writings of James Madison. Published by Order of Congress* (4 vols.; Philadelphia, 1865), III, 503, 504.
88   Cobb, *The Rise of Religious Liberty in America: A History*, 494.
89   *Letters and Other Writings of James Madison, Fourth President of the United States*, I, 14.
90   *Ibid.*, 154.
91   *Ibid.*, III, 274.
92   *Ibid.*, 275.
93   *Ibid.*, 307.
94   Charles Page Smith, *James Wilson: Founding Father, 1742–1798* (Chapel Hill, 1956), 8, 24, 28.
95   *Of the General Principle of Law and Obligation*, in Adams, *Selected Political Essays of James Wilson*, 255, 256.
96   *Ibid.*, 270.
97   *Of the Law of Nature*, in Adams, *Selected Political Essays of James Wilson*, 298.
98   *Ibid.*, 286.
99   *Ibid.*, 286, 287.
100 *Of the Legislative Authority of the British Parliament*, in Adams, *Selected Political Essays of James Wilson*, 58, 186, 187, 188.
101 Daniel Walther, *Gouverneur Morris: Witness of Two Revolutions* (New York and London, 1934), 73.
102 Howard Swiggett, *The Extraordinary Mr. Morris* (New York, 1952), 13.
103 *Ibid.*, 5.
104 Quoted in Walther, *Gouverneur Morris: Witness to Two Revolutions*, 44.
105 Gouverneur Morris, from his inaugural address as president of the New York Historical Society, *Collections of the New-York Historical Society for the Year 1821*, III, 34.
106 *Ibid.*, 30.
107 *Ibid.*, 34. Emphasis supplied.
108 Charles de Montesquieu, *The Spirit of the Laws*, in Sait, *Masters of Political Thought*, II, 228.
109 Beth, *The American Theory of Church and State*, 87.
110 Howe, *Problems of Religious Liberty*, in *Nomos IV: Liberty*, 269.
111 *Ibid.*, 271.
112 *Relations Between Church and State: A Report to the 174th General Assembly of the United Presbyterian Church in the United States of America*, (Philadelphia, May, 1962). Hereafter we shall refer to this Report as the UPUSA Report (UPUSA is the accepted abbreviation for United Presbyterian Church in the United States of America).
113 UPUSA Report, 7.
114 *Ibid.*, 8.
115 *Ibid.*, 6.
116 *Ibid.*, 38.
117 *Ibid.*, 6.
118 Matt. 12:30.
119 Mark 9:40.

120 Matt. 10:32–33.
121 Rev. 3:15–16.
122 UPUSA Report, 20.
123 Howe, *Problems of Religious Liberty,* in *Nomos IV: Liberty,* 273.
124 UPUSA Report, 12.
125 *Ibid.,* 13.
126 Mark 9:40.
127 UPUSA Report, 12.
128 *Ibid.,* 21.
129 *Ibid.*
130 *Ibid.,* 22.
131 *Ibid.,* 10, 11.
132 *Ibid.,* 11.
133 *Ibid.*
134 *Ibid.,* 16.
135 *Ibid.,* 11.
136 "Prayers, Bibles and Schools," *The Christian Century,* LXXIX (October 24, 1962), 1280.
137 *Ibid.*
138 James H. Smylie, "The First Amendment and Bishop Pike," *The Christian Century,* LXXIX (October 31, 1962), 1316–18.
139 Quoted in *ibid.,* 1317.
140 Farrand, *The Records of the Federal Convention of 1787,* I, 451–52.

CHAPTER VIII

1 Matt. 19:6.
2 Heb. 11:1.
3 Jas. 2:18.
4 Rom. 8:31.
5 Matt. 7:20.
6 *Ibid.,* 7:7–8.
7 Mark 9:23.
8 *Ibid.,* 9:24.
9 Deut. 30:19.